The True Dharma Eye

Also by John Daido Loori

The True Dharma Eye

Zen Master Dōgen's

THREE HUNDRED KŌANS

WITH COMMENTARY AND VERSE BY

John Daido Loori

TRANSLATED BY

Kazuaki Tanahashi and John Daido Loori

Shambhala
BOSTON & LONDON
2009

Shambhala Publications, Inc.
Horticultural Hall
300 Massachusetts Avenue
Boston, Massachusetts 02115
www.shambhala.com

9 8 7 6 5 4 3 2 1

First Paperback Edition

Printed in Canada

⊛ This edition is printed on acid-free paper that meets the
American National Standards Institute z39.48 Standard.
♻ This book was printed on 100% postconsumer recycled paper.
For more information please visit www.shambhala.com.
Distributed in the United States by Random House, Inc.,
and in Canada by Random House of Canada Ltd

Interior design and composition: Greta D. Sibley & Associates

The Library of Congress catalogues the previous
edition of this book as follows:
Dōgen, 1200–1253.
[Shōbō genzō sanbyakusoku. English]
The true dharma eye: Zen Master Dogen's three hundred koans /
with commentary and verse by John Daido Loori;
translated by Kazuaki Tanahashi and John Daido Loori.
p. cm.
ISBN 978-1-59030-242-2 (hardcover: alk. paper)
ISBN 978-1-59030-465-5 (paperback)
1. Koan—Early works to 1800. I. Loori, John Daido. II.
Tanahashi, Kazuaki, 1933– III. Title.
BQ9449.D654.S5331715 2005
294.3´85—dc22
2005007961

*Dedicated with deep gratitude to our
dharma ancestors, and with deep confidence to
the new Western generations*

Contents

Acknowledgments

I would first like to acknowledge the contribution of Kazuaki Tanahashi. Translating with him the main cases collected by Dōgen was a pleasure. Kaz brought to the table not only his skills in the Chinese and Japanese languages but also a deep sense of appreciation for the spirit of Dōgen. I am deeply indebted to Vanessa Zuisei Goddard for her editing skills and continual assistance in bringing this book to fruition as well as for the research that produced the glossaries and cross-reference appendix. I am grateful to Andy Ferguson for creating a lineage chart specifically for this book; I am sure it will help readers to better understand the historical context that frames many of these cases.

I also owe a debt of gratitude to my successors, Bonnie Myotai Treace and Geoffrey Shugen Arnold, as well as dharma holder Konrad Ryushin Marchaj, for their meticulous proofreading of the manuscript; and to Ben Gleason and the Shambhala staff for their copyediting skills.

My deep appreciation goes to the countless unnamed Zen students who were present at Zen Mountain Monastery for the talks I gave on these kōans during the fifteen years that it took to develop this book.

Finally, nine bows to my teacher Kōun Taizan Maezumi, who encouraged me to create an American *Shōbōgenzō* and was always supportive of my work with Dōgen's three hundred kōans. Although *The True Dharma Eye* is not yet an American *Shōbōgenzō*, I hope that it will provide the first feeble steps in that direction.

—John Daido Loori Roshi

Translator's Note

The main cases for the three hundred kōans in this book were selected by Eihei Dōgen (1200–1253) from extensive volumes of Chinese Zen literature. As one of the first monastics transmitting the Zen teaching from China, Dōgen returned to Japan in 1228. During the earliest years of his teaching, he compiled this selection and called it *Shōbōgenzō* (Treasury of the True Dharma Eye).

This Chinese-language *Shōbōgenzō* served Dōgen as a lifetime notebook for writing his dharma essays. For another book of his with the same title, he used more than seventy stories from this selection. He would introduce a kōan story in Chinese and comment on it in a brilliantly poetic and philosophical style in the Japanese language, which was written in a combination of the Chinese characters called kanji and the Japanese phonetics called kana. He repeated this pattern in a number of his essays.

Of the two books by Dōgen titled *Shōbōgenzō*, the Chinese-language version (*Shinji*, or *Mana*, version), presented here, is less known than the Japanese-language version (*Kana*, or *Keji*, version). One of the standard versions of the *Kana Shōbōgenzō* consists of ninety-five fascicles. (A fascicle is a chapter-long text bound separately as a book.)

In 1767, Dōgen's original kōan collection with commentary by Shigetsu Ein was published by his disciple Honkō Katsudō after Ein's death. The text included Katsudō's preface, and was titled *Nempyō Sambyakusoku Funogo*. There was no other copy of the text available for study until the last century. But a hand-copied manuscript, dated 1287, containing seventy-nine cases, which had been kept in the Kanazawa Archive in Yokohama, Kanagawa Prefecture, was published by Tokujō Oya in 1934. Our translation is based on the annotated text in *Dōgen Zenji Zenshū* (Complete Work of Zen Master Dōgen), edited by Tokugen Sakai et al., Tokyo Shunjūsha, 1988–1993.

John Daido Loori Roshi has added his verses and commentaries to all three hundred cases of the *Shinji Shōbōgenzō*. I have had the pleasure of translating the main cases from Chinese into English with him. We worked together intensely at our occasional meetings at Zen Mountain Monastery from 1995 to 2002.

The addition of commentaries by a later Zen master to a collection of kōans is not unprecedented. For example, the *Blue Cliff Record*, one of the most revered Zen texts, was initiated by Xuedou Zhongxian (980–1052), who selected one hundred kōans and wrote capping verses to each case. Yuanwu Keqin (1063–1135) added pointers and commentaries after Xuedou's death.

Loori Roshi's addition of new commentaries, more than seven and a half centuries after the selection of these three hundred kōans, is extraordinary. In addition, the creation of a formal Zen text by a Western Zen teacher is unique. Loori Roshi has presented a number of these cases with commentaries in his weekly dharma discourses at Zen Mountain Monastery. I am honored to be part of the team creating the book that embodies the authenticity of Dōgen and the elucidation of the Zen teaching, made accessible to contemporary Western Zen practitioners.

—Kazuaki Tanahashi
Berkeley, California

Introduction by John Daido Loori

Dōgen and Kōans

Japanese master Eihei Dōgen was one of the most remarkable religious figures and teachers in the history of Zen. Although relatively unknown during his lifetime, he is now widely regarded as an outstanding philosopher, mystic, and poet. His works are having a tremendous impact, not only in Japan and within the Sōtō school of Zen Buddhism, but even more so in the West, where he's been discovered and studied extensively by philosophers, scholars, artists, and Buddhist practitioners. He is best known for his comprehensive and profound masterwork, the *Kana*, or Japanese, *Shōbōgenzō*. This monumental achievement, a collection of ninety-five discourses and essays composed in Japanese between the years 1231 and 1253, is a unique expression of the Buddhadharma based on Dōgen's profound religious experience.

A less-known work of Dōgen's is his *Mana Shōbōgenzō*, or *Shōbōgenzō Sambyakusoku* (Treasury of the True Dharma Eye: Three Hundred Cases), a collection of three hundred case kōans written in Chinese. This seminal work, which was to influence all of Dōgen's other teachings, remained in obscurity for many centuries. It wasn't until 1934 that it was rediscovered and made available to the general public by Professor Tokujū Oya, and only recently was its authenticity verified.

Mana Shōbōgenzō is a volume of three hundred kōans that Dōgen culled from Zen texts of the Song era during his travels in China between 1223 and 1227. And, unlike the classic collections of the period, these cases are not accompanied by either a title or a commentary. These traditional collections were the *Blue Cliff Record* (*Hekiganroku*) and the *Book of Serenity* (*Shōyōroku*). The *Blue Cliff Record* was a collection of one hundred kōans gathered by Master Xuedou, who appended his own verses and remarks as an aid to his students. Sixty years after Xuedou's death, Master Yuanwu Keqin gave a series of talks on this collection and added his own commentaries to each case. The *Blue Cliff Record* remains to this day an important text used for kōan introspection in the Rinzai school of Zen. Also a collection of a hundred kōans, the *Book of Serenity*, is held in high regard by the Sōtō school. It was created by Master Hongzhi, who also added a verse to each case. Later Master Wansong included his own commentaries.

Because in Dōgen's writings there are several examples of his criticism of kōan study, there are those who have insisted that he would never have collected or used kōans. Yet legend has it that before he departed from China to return to Japan, the young monastic stayed up all night and hand copied the *Blue Cliff Record*. And even before traveling to China and receiving dharma transmission from Tiantong Rujing, Dōgen was already familiar with kōan introspection as it was taught by his first teacher, Eisai, and his successor. In fact, Dōgen received Rinzai transmission in the Oryu line before leaving for China, and though that lineage died out in both China and Japan, it is preserved within the Sōtō school to this day. Years later, when Dōgen was establishing Kōshōhōrin Monastery, he gathered the three hundred kōans he was to use as seeds in his later writings, elaborating on them primarily in the *Kana Shōbōgenzō*. Here, 55 kōans were referred to in their entirety, and 281 were mentioned. In the *Eihei Kōroku*, 99 kōans were quoted entirely, and 109 were mentioned. Five more kōans were quoted in Dōgen's other works, and 21 were mentioned. Clearly then, Dōgen had more than just a casual interest in kōans.

My own interest in Dōgen and his use of kōans developed during the training I received from Maezumi Roshi at Zen Center of Los Angeles. Maezumi Roshi was a holder of both of the Yōgi Rinzai lineages: the Takujū and the Inzan lines. The Yōgi lineage comes to us through Hakuin, who revitalized it in the eighteenth century. Later it split into the Inzan and Takujū lines. Both of those lines have arrived in the West and are practiced here today. Miura Isshū of the First Zen Institute, Rukyō Sasaki, Harada Shōdō, Jōshū Sasaki, and Osaka Kōryū are all teachers of Western students in the Inzan line. Sōgaku Harada and Hakuun Yasutani transmitted the Takujū line, and their teachings have influenced Western Zen as well.

Maezumi Roshi received the Inzan line from Osaka Kōryū and the Takujū line from Hakuun Yasutani. The curriculum of kōans that he used in training his students includes 200 miscellaneous kōans, 48 kōans of the *Gateless Gate*, 100 kōans of the *Blue Cliff Record*, 100 kōans of the *Book of Serenity*, 53 kōans of the *Transmission of the Lamp*, the kōans on the Five Ranks of Master Dongshan, and 120 precept kōans. Toward the end of training, there are also the kirigami documents and oral teachings with kōans embedded in them. This represents roughly 700 cases.

In order to appreciate Dōgen's unique contributions to kōan literature, it is necessary to understand how traditional kōan study works. It is critical to differentiate between kōan study and formal kōan introspection in the context of a vital teacher-student relationship. Kōan study tends to rely on the intellect. It aims to shed light on the basic Buddhist teachings communicated in the kōan in a way similar to how a teacher will comment on a case in a teisho, or formal discourse, clarifying the kōan's key points. In kōan introspection, on the other hand, a student sits with the kōan in zazen, letting go of trying to solve or understand it, and works on the process of embodying it. The teacher then tests the student's direct insight into the kōan in dokusan, private face-to-face interviews.

Dokusan demands that one directly and dynamically present one's own understanding. Because of this, it can be said that there is no one answer to a kōan. Seeing into a kōan requires the embodiment of a certain state of consciousness rather than an abstraction of intellectual understanding. It is this direct "seeing into" that the teacher looks for and tests to determine the clarity of the student's understanding. And it is this direct understanding that is at the heart of realization—not the intellectualization of an idea.

Therefore we must keep in mind that when we say that the dharma is "transmitted" from teacher to student, it does not mean that the teacher gives the student important information about the enlightenment experience. In effect, nothing is transmitted. Many Western practitioners regard this as a tongue-in-cheek statement, but the fact is, the student must realize that which is already present—what is called the "wisdom that has no teacher." If it were not for this fact, every generation would simply be a clone of the previous one.

Historically, there are many examples of an authentic teacher-student relationship. One of them is the relationship between Yunyan Tansheng and Dongshan Liangjie. If we are to believe the records, Master Yunyan was generally not regarded as a particularly brilliant teacher. Indeed, his questions and dialogues with Master Dongshan could be understood any number of ways. One possibility is that he simply repeated the Zen one-liners of the time. However, his student Dongshan *was* brilliant, and what he must have realized from those dialogues and questions was an understanding of the dharma that seems to have far exceeded his teacher's.

In his writings, Dōgen also talks about the importance of the teacher-student relationship. But he comments on it—as he does of other aspects of the dharma—in a completely unique and fresh way, always offering new ways of understanding the traditional teachings.

Dōgen's Unique Commentary Style

My first encounter with Dōgen's singular way of dealing with kōans happened early in my training when I refused to follow my teacher's directions to work with the miscellaneous kōans I had already passed through with a previous teacher. Instead of arguing with me, Maezumi Roshi instructed me to sit shikantaza. Soon after, I came across Dōgen's *Genjokōan* and brought some questions about it into face-to-face teachings. Maezumi encouraged me to sit with Dōgen's lines in zazen, treating them as kōans. With time, reading other chapters of the *Kana Shōbōgenzō*, I began to develop a deepening appreciation of the way Dōgen presented kōans with an unprecedented degree of depth and breadth. Later still, as my traditional kōan training evolved, it became increasingly clear to me that Dōgen was a true master of the kōan form, offering an amazing vista of the Buddha-dharma through his kōan treatment.

As a Zen teacher, my chief interests in the two *Shōbōgenzō*s have to do with Dōgen's unique and creative way of commenting on kōans in the *Kana Shōbōgenzō*, as well as the choice of the kōans he collected in the *Mana Shōbōgenzō*, especially as they may affect modern practitioners.

Commentaries on many of the kōans that Dōgen deemed important and that were included in his *Mana Shōbōgenzō* can be found in the classic Song collections mentioned above. A careful comparison of these texts with Dōgen's elaboration in the *Kana Shōbōgenzō* shows no substantial differences in the expression of the truth of these kōans. I do not see discrepancies between the commentaries by Dōgen, the commentators in the classical collections, and the truth of these kōans as transmitted face-to-face in traditional kōan introspection practice. In other words, what these masters are saying—whether in the *Blue Cliff Record,* the *Book of Serenity,* or *Kana Shōbōgenzō*—is identical in principle but radically different in depth and style.

In addition, both the classic commentaries and Dōgen's writings are consistent with the traditional Mahāyāna teachings found in the sūtras. They accurately reflect the dharma of the historical Buddha, Śākyamuni. There is, however, a unique quality to Dōgen's expression of the Zen truth that sets his treatment of kōans in a class by itself.

Dōgen was a master of language. It is impossible to study his writings and not be moved by the poetry and creativity of his words. He brings to the kōans his literary sophistication, extensive familiarity with Buddhism, and what is perhaps an unparalleled appreciation of the dharma. In his teachings, he always communicates on multiple levels, with discursive language, poetic imagery, and "intimate words," *mitsugo.* Intimate words are a direct pointing to the truth, meant to be grasped in an instant and absorbed intuitively rather than in a linear, sequential way. Dōgen used all of these methods freely to transmit his understanding. His teachings had the "lips and mouth" quality that characterized the style of Chinese masters Zhaozhou Congshen and Yunmen Wenyan, teachers who used live, "turning words" to help practitioners see into their own nature.

Another aspect of Dōgen's unique treatment of kōans is his use of the Five Ranks of Master Dongshan to illuminate different perspectives available within a kōan. The Five Ranks—first delineated by Dongshan Liangjie and elaborated on by his successor Caoshan Benji—are a formulation of the coming together of dualities. The first rank is "the relative within the absolute." This is emptiness—no eye, ear, nose, tongue, body, or mind. The second rank is the realization of that emptiness and is referred to as "the absolute within the relative." This is where the enlightenment experience, or kensho, occurs. Yet absolute and relative are still dualistic. The third rank is "coming from within the absolute." No longer in the abstract, the whole universe becomes your very life itself, and, inevitably, compassion arises. Dongshan's fourth rank is "arriving at mutual integration"; the coming from both absolute and relative. At this stage, the absolute and relative are integrated, but they're still two things. In the fifth rank, "unity attained," there is no more duality. It is one thing—neither absolute nor relative, up nor down, profane nor holy, good nor bad, male nor female.

Dōgen never explicitly talked about the Five Ranks except to summarily dismiss them, yet he definitely engaged them in a way that reflects a singular understanding and appreciation of their method. In the fascicle *Sansuikyō*, for example, Dōgen writes:

> Since ancient times wise ones and sages have also lived by the water. When they live by the water they catch fish or they catch humans or they catch the Way. These are traditional water styles. Further, they must be catching the self, catching the hook, being caught by the hook, and being caught by the Way.

Then Dōgen introduces one of the kōans from the *Mana Shōbōgenzō*, case 90 (Jiashan Sees the Ferryman), and comments on it:

> In ancient times, when Chuanzi suddenly left Yaoshan and went to live on the river, he got the sage Jiashan of the flower-in-river. Isn't this catching fish, catching humans, catching water? Isn't this catching himself? The fact that Jiashan could see Chuanzi is because he is Chuanzi. Chuanzi teaching Jiashan is Chuanzi meeting himself.

This passage is presenting the first two of the Five Ranks. The line "The fact that Jiashan could see Chuanzi is because he is Chuanzi" is the relative within the absolute (or the absolute containing the relative), the first rank. The line "Chuanzi teaching Jiashan is Chuanzi meeting himself" (in other words, the teacher teaching the student is the teacher meeting him- or herself) is the absolute within the relative, the second rank.

Although Dōgen had some reservations about the Five Ranks, it was not because he did not find them true. He simply did not want them to become a formula—a mere intellectualization or abstraction. Dōgen did not use them in the way they were taught conventionally. He wanted them to be realized face-to-face in the kōan study between teacher and student.

"Catching the self," "catching the hook," "being caught by the hook," "being caught by the Way," are all expressions of the interplay of opposites—specifically about how that tension works within the teacher-student relationship. Again, in the fascicle *Kattō*, Dōgen writes about Bodhidharma's transmission of the marrow to Dazu Huike:

You should be aware of the phrases "You attain me, I attain you, attaining both me and you, and attaining both you and me." In personally viewing the ancestors' body/mind, if we speak of there being no oneness of internal and external or if we speak of the whole body not being completely penetrated, then we have not yet seen the realm of the ancestors' present.

For Dōgen, the relationship of a teacher and student is kattō, a spiritual entanglement, which from his perspective is a process of using complications to transmit complications. "Entanglements entwining entanglements is the buddhas and ancestors interpenetrating buddhas and ancestors." This is an expression of the merging of dualities. This is the relationship between Jiashan and Chuanzi. It is the relationship between Bodhidharma and Huike. And it is the relationship to which Dōgen directs himself whenever he expounds the nondual dharma in the kōans he is using. Case 105 of the *Mana Shōbōgenzō*, "The Hands and Eyes of Great Compassion," appears in two fascicles of the *Kana Shōbōgenzō*. Dōgen mentions this case in *Daishugyō* and devotes the entire chapter to it in *Kannon*. The same kōan appears as case 89 in the *Blue Cliff Record* and as case 54 in the *Book of Serenity*.

Because "The Hands and Eyes of Great Compassion" appears in all three collections, it is an interesting case to use in examining and comparing the commentaries by the three masters. In the kōan, a dialogue takes place between Daowu and Yunyan, who were dharma heirs of Master Yaoshan Weiyan. In addition to being dharma brothers—and possibly birth brothers—they were also close friends and traveling companions. Daowu was the more senior of the two in terms of understanding. Yunyan was later to become the teacher of Master Dongshan Liangjie, the founder of the Sōtō school of Zen. The main case of the kōan reads:

> Yunyan asked Daowu: "How does the Bodhisattva of Great Compassion [Kannon] use so many hands and eyes?"
> Daowu said: "It's just like a person in the middle of the night reaching back in search of a pillow."
> Yunyan said: "I understand."
> Daowu said: "How do you understand it?"
> Yunyan said: "All over the body are hands and eyes."

Daowu said: "What you said is all right, but it's only eighty percent of it."

Yunyan said: "I'm like this, senior brother. How do you understand it?"

Daowu said: "Throughout the body are hands and eyes."

In the *Blue Cliff Record* commentary, Yuanwu begins by extolling Yunyan's and Daowu's virtues, and he identifies Yunyan as Dongshan's teacher. He then refers to the eighty-four thousand arms of Kannon Bodhisattva as symbolic arms and says, "Great Compassion has this many hands and eyes. Do all of you?" With this question he challenges the reader to consider the statement from the point of view of intimacy. He then quotes Master Baizhang Huaihai as saying, "All sayings and writings return to one's self."

In the next paragraph he says, "Right at the start Daowu should have given him [Yunyan] a blow of the staff across his back to avoid so many complications appearing later." Here he emphasizes the need for Yunyan to be intimate with the thousand hands and eyes. The *whack* of the stick brings him home to the reality of the moment. Yuanwu then continues, "But Daowu was compassionate. He couldn't be like this [strike Yunyan]. Instead, he gives Yunyan an explanation of the reason, meaning to make him understand immediately." As we will see, Dōgen would never have called Daowu's response an explanation.

Yuanwu moves on to address "reaching back in search of a pillow" in the middle of the night. He asks the question, "[In this activity] tell me, where are the eyes?" Here the phrase "the night" is dealt with only briefly, in a single sentence, whereas Dōgen deals with it extensively, since it is a pivotal point of the kōan, necessary to appreciate Daowu's response to Yunyan. Yuanwu also deals with Yunyan's "All over the body are hands and eyes" and Daowu's "What you said is all right, but it's only 80 percent of it" and "Throughout the body are hands and eyes." He asks the question, "But say, is 'all over the body' right, or is 'throughout the body' right?" Then he himself indirectly answers this with the statement, "Although they seem covered with mud, nevertheless they are bright and clean," implying that although Daowu and Yunyan may appear to be having "a conversation in the weeds" (to be intellectualizing), in fact they are both expressing clearly the truth of the activity of Great Compassion.

Yuanwu continues by deriding practitioners who conclude that Yunyan's response must have been wrong, while Daowu's was right, explaining that these kinds of practitioner are people who get caught up in words and phrases and have not yet realized the truth. He then advises his students to cut off emotional defilements and conceptual thinking and to become naked, free, and unbounded, since this is the only way to understand the truth about Great Compassion.

Yuanwu concludes his commentary by further clarifying Daowu's statement, "What you said is all right, but it's only eighty percent of it." He quotes Master Caoshan who once asked a monastic, "How is it when the dharma body of reality is manifesting form in accordance with beings, like the moon reflected in the water?" The monastic answered, "It's like a donkey looking at a well." Caoshan said, "You have said quite a lot, but you have said only eighty percent of it." The monastic then asked, "What do you say, teacher?" Caoshan answered, "It's like the well looking at the donkey." Yuanwu says, "This is the same meaning as the main case." Although his example presents a similar situation, Yuanwu does not actually address the question of whether or not Yunyan's understanding is lacking. And although Dongshan's Five Ranks are implicit in Caoshan's response, Yuanwu does not refer to them to elaborate on Daowu's statement. On the other hand, Dōgen concentrates on this point with great detail, resolving the underlying question, yet leaving enough of its mystery to invite the reader to investigate and penetrate it further.

In the *Book of Serenity*, Wansong begins his commentary with a quote about this case: "Liao asked Ehu, 'What does the Great Compassionate One use a thousand hands and eyes for?' Ehu said, 'What does the emperor use public officials for?'" This exchange seems to imply that the thousand hands and eyes of Great Compassion are meant to facilitate the bodhisattva's functioning in the world. It is a reasonable and logical conclusion, but it entirely misses the truth of this kōan and clearly presents a much weaker understanding than that presented by Dōgen in his fascicle.

Wansong continues with the story of a mountain man who, after it rained, would wear pure white shoes on a muddy road to go to the market. "Someone asked, 'You're blind. How come the mud doesn't soil your shoes?' The mountain man raised his staff and said, 'There is an eye on this staff.'" Wansong says, "The mountain man is proof—when reaching for a pillow in the night, there is an eye in the hand; when eating there is an eye on the tongue; when recognizing people on hearing them speaking, there is an eye in the ears." He then introduces Su Zizhan (J., Soshisen), who, when conversing with a deaf man, just wrote. Zizhan laughed and said, "He and I are both strange people. I use my hand for a mouth, he uses his eyes for ears." Lastly, Wansong quotes the Buddha speaking of the interchanging function of the six senses. He then caps this paragraph with the statement, "It is true, without a doubt."

It seems that the various examples introduced by Wansong would help to explain the principles presented in the kōan, but they do not in any way clarify them for the reader. They just introduce more entanglements of words and ideas. Although the images of the eye on the staff, the eye on the hand, and the merging of the six senses are all grounded in solid dharma, Wansong does not use them to clarify the dialogue between Yunyan and Daowu. He speaks of the thousand eyes emanating light to illuminate the darkness, and he brings out the interdependency and mutual arising of compassion and suffering sentient beings. Indeed, were it not for the suffering of sentient beings, no need for compassion would arise. He then summarizes "All over the body, throughout the body" by saying, "to say 'What is the necessity?'—not necessarily. There seems to be shallow and deep, but really there is no loss or gain." With this statement he acknowledges the identity of the understanding of Yunyan and Daowu. He concludes his commentary by saying that arguing over these matters is like arguing about the shortness or length of turtle hair.

Dōgen begins his treatment of the kōan by extolling the virtues of both Yunyan and Daowu and immediately establishing their unity with each other. He then presents the identity of Kannon Bodhisattva and Yunyan, and the uniqueness of Yunyan's understanding of Kannon. He says: "Kannon is present in Yunyan, who has been experiencing it together with Daowu. And not only one or two Kannons but hundreds of thousands of Kannons are experiencing the same state as Yunyan."

Then, speaking of the eighty-four thousand hands and eyes of great compassion, Dōgen makes clear that they are not limited to any number. He introduces an infinite abundance of hands and eyes and then goes on to say, "They are indeed beyond the bounds of countlessness and limitlessness." He says, "Yunyan speaks and Daowu verifies." The limitlessly abundant hands and eyes are clearly the state of consciousness that Yunyan and

Daowu are experiencing together. With a unique twist Dōgen says, "Yunyan is asking Daowu, 'The use [of the hands and eyes] does what?'" He is inquiring here, "Is there any aim other than simply to function?" He is asking the reader to consider how Kannon uses her manifold hands and eyes and to ask, "Does what, moves what, expresses what?" Dōgen then uses Daowu's answer, "She is like a person in the night reaching back for a pillow," to launch into an exhaustive exploration of "in the night." He asks us to examine the difference between "nighttime as it is supposed in the light of day" and "the nighttime as it is in the night. In sum, we should examine it as that time which is not day or night."

Then he becomes even more specific. He says, "This nighttime is not necessarily only the nighttime of the day and night of human beings and gods." The night that Dōgen is speaking of is in the realm of the absolute, the nondual state of consciousness in which body and mind have fallen away. Extending this concept of night into the matter of searching for a pillow, he says, "You should understand that the expression used here by Daowu does not concern taking a pillow, pulling a pillow, or pushing a pillow. If you try to deeply understand what Daowu means when he speaks of 'reaching behind at night for a pillow,' you must examine it with night eyes. Look at it carefully."

He also asks, "Is the person in the words 'like a person' only a word in a metaphor? Or is this person, being a normal person, not an ordinary person? If studied as a normal person in Buddhism, [the person] is not just metaphorical, in which case there is something to be learned in groping for a pillow." He points out that Kannon's hands and eyes are not something attached to her body, which would make them separate entities, but rather the totality of her being.

The thrust that he begins to develop in this dialectic is essentially that all bodhisattvas—indeed all beings—manifesting infinite compassion with their limitless hands and eyes, and boundless bodies and minds, are a single indivisible thusness. Dōgen then brings up Yunyan's "I understand," making it clear that Yunyan is not saying that he understands the words of Daowu but rather that this is an understanding of the ineffable and that this understanding itself is causing the ineffable to express the truth.

When Daowu asks the question, "How do you understand?" Dōgen sees it as: "I understand. You understand. Could it be other than eyes understand, hands understand?" Dōgen then asks, "Is it understanding that has been realized or is it understanding that has not been realized yet? The understanding described by 'I understand' is the 'I' itself. At the same time, we should consider its existence as 'you,' and 'How do you understand?'" That is, Daowu's and Yunyan's statements should be appreciated nondualistically as the whole body itself, as hands and eyes limitlessly abundant.

Dōgen continues his commentary by taking up Daowu's statement, "What you said is all right, but it's only eighty percent of it." From Dōgen's point of view, this statement by Daowu means:

> Hitting the target by speaking. Clearly manifesting something by speaking and leaving nothing unexpressed. When what has hitherto been unexpressed is finally expressed so that nothing remains that words might express, the expression of the truth is just eighty or ninety percent of realization.

Dōgen is being very kind. He points to the truth of Daowu's statement in a way that Yuanwu's and Wansong's commentaries have not. He says, "An expression of the truth is eighty or ninety percent of realization." He is making clear that the words and ideas that describe a reality can never be equated with the direct experience that is the realization of that reality itself. Then, affirming the earlier commentaries, Dōgen too points out that people generally understand Daowu's statement as an indication that something is lacking in Yunyan's understanding. He says:

> People think that expressions of the truth can be one hundred percent of realization, and so an expression of the truth which does not reach that level is called eighty or ninety percent of realization. If the Buddhadharma were like that, it would never have reached the present day.

Next Dōgen takes up Yunyan's statement: "I am just like this, senior brother. How do you understand it?" He says, "Yunyan speaks about being just like this because he wants to make Daowu himself speak words that Daowu has called 'expression of eighty or ninety percent of realization.'" Dōgen points out that people interpret this as meaning that the words that Yunyan had just spoken are imperfect in expression. He says, "This is not the meaning of 'I am just like this.'" For Dōgen, this expression is an ex-pression of reality itself. He continues by saying that Yunyan's phrase "all over the body" and Daowu's "throughout the body" both express the truth as clearly as words can express them, and it's not that one is perfect in ex-pression and the other imperfect. Dōgen says, "Yunyan's 'all over the body' and Daowu's 'throughout the body' are both beyond relative comparisons, and rather it may simply be that in the limitlessly abundant hands and eyes of each respective master, such words are present."

Dōgen ends by saying that the Kannon spoken of by Śākyamuni Bud-dha is one of a thousand hands and eyes, and the Kannon spoken of by Yunyan and Daowu is one with limitlessly abundant hands and eyes. But, he reminds us, all of this is ultimately beyond a discussion of abundance and scarcity. When we understand Yunyan and Daowu's Kannon of limit-lessly abundant hands and eyes through our own direct experience, all bud-dhas realize Kannon samādhi as eighty or ninety percent realization.

Master Dōgen's exhaustive treatment of this kōan clearly functions within various levels of understanding and addresses subtleties that were not presented in the *Blue Cliff Record* and the *Book of Serenity*. This kōan is only one among the many examples of the unique style and profound in-sight that Dōgen brings to the understanding of classical kōans.

The Three Hundred Kōans and Their Relevance for Modern Practitioners

In addition to Dōgen's style and insight, the other interesting aspect of his treatment of kōans is how the particular cases he selected can assist practi-tioners to examine important aspects of spiritual practice in the twenty-first century. In writing the commentaries for these kōans, I have tried to embody Dōgen's unique perspective, applying it to situations that modern-day practitioners face. The three examples that follow highlight some of these areas. The first example is case 227, "Priest Xixian's 'I Am Watching'":

> Xixian Faan of Lushan was asked by a government officer, "When I took the city of Jinling with an army troop, I killed countless people. Am I at fault?"
> Xixian said, "I am watching closely."

A Japanese master commenting on this kōan says:

> As Buddhists we take a precept not to destroy life. The govern-
> ment officer was worried, since his position involved him in or-
> dering the killing of many people. That his actions were sinful, of
> course. If we judge his conduct, he committed many sins, but he
> was unable to avoid this in carrying out his duty. Master Xixian
> recognized the difficult circumstance of the officer's life, and so he
> wouldn't say that his actions were sins. He just said that he was
> always watching reality. In reality it is difficult at times to catego-
> rize the conduct of others as good or bad. Reality is very severe.
> Master Xixian recognized that the officer's life was in reality very
> severe, so that he himself was just watching the real situation. In
> reality, situations are usually complex. We must recognize the
> existence of such a fact. It is sometimes difficult to criticize or to
> affirm. If we see a snake crawling toward a baby and we are too con-
> cerned with following the precepts exactly, we may hesitate too
> long to save the baby. At the moment of the present, we must be
> free even from the precepts to act as the circumstances demand.

If I tried to give this kind of justification to my students, I would immediately be challenged. The commentary I added to this case in our translation of the three hundred kōans reads as follows:

> Priest Xixian's response, "I am watching closely," is at once fat-
> headed and misguided. He has missed an opportunity to cause an
> evil that has already arisen to be extinguished, and to cause good
> that has not arisen to arise. Both he and the general deserve thirty
> blows of my stick.
>   Governments and rulers are traditionally driven by power,
> politics, and money, and are usually not inclined toward clear
> moral commitments. However, for a Zen priest to avoid taking
> moral responsibility when asked is inexcusable.
>   Enlightenment without morality is not yet enlightenment.
> Morality without enlightenment is not yet morality. Enlighten-
> ment and morality are nondual in the Way. One does not exist
> without the other. The truth is not beyond good and evil as is

commonly believed. It is, rather, a way of living one's life with a definite moral commitment that is practiced, realized, and verified within the realm of good and evil itself, yet remains undefiled by them.

Setting aside impostor priests and phony followers, you tell me, how do you transform watching into doing, the three poisons into the three virtues? More important, what is it that you call yourself?

In working with this and other kōans that Dōgen included in the *Mana Shōbōgenzō*, I have attempted to address some of the areas of life and practice that were not explicitly covered by any of the Asian teachers or that, in some cases, were misconstrued because of political and social pressures. One Japanese Zen teacher who served in the Second World War wrote, "During the time I was a soldier, the killing of people was just to punish those who disturbed public order. Whether one kills or does not kill, the precept of forbidding killing is preserved." This is an unmitigated distortion of the dharma. He continued, "It is the precept forbidding killing that wields the sword. It is the precept forbidding killing that throws the bomb." When the teachings are used in order to protect and justify a self-centered view, there is something wrong.

Another kōan, "Sansheng's 'Golden Fish,'" case 52, reads:

Sansheng asked Xuefeng, "What does a golden-scale fish that goes through the net eat?"

Xuefeng said, "I will tell you after you come out of the net."

Sansheng said, "The teacher of fifteen thousand monastics—and you can't say a turning word."

Xuefeng said, "This old man is busy with abbot's matters."

My commentary reads:

The net is elusive. It appears and disappears. It creates edges that are nonexistent. The golden-scale fish is inherently free in every way when it knows it is in the net. Be that as it may, the golden fish that has passed through the net clearly does not eat ordinary food. What is its food?

Sansheng is a distinguished adept. Why does Xuefeng say, "I will tell you after you come out of the net"? Although Sansheng knows how to turn the spear around, old Xuefeng remains poisonous. Can it be said that these two have passed through the net, or are they just harmonizing in delusion?

This particular kōan can be seen in light of one of my current concerns—what we refer to in the West as "engaged Buddhism." Though there is no question that social action is indispensable, we need to ask ourselves whether it is based in the heart of the dharma, in realizing wisdom and compassion, or whether it is simply doing good. Doing good arises from a sense of self, while in compassion, there is no doer or anything that the doer does. There is not even a trace of separation between self and other. Given that fact, we should examine who is being served through our engaged Buddhism. Only through compassionate Buddhism can we arrive at truly engaged Buddhism—which, ultimately, must rest on the fundamental realization of wisdom.

When the dharma arrives in a new culture, it must respond to the relevant needs and conditions of that culture, but this does not give us license to distort the teachings according to our own self-centered views. "The net is elusive. It appears and disappears," says the commentary. What is the net in engaged Buddhism? How much do we justify where we stand? "It creates edges that are nonexistent." In actuality, the net does not exist. We manufacture it—consciously or unconsciously. But either way, it is our net. That is why we cannot afford to become satisfied with our goodness. Gary Snyder wrote, "Institutional Buddhism has been conspicuously ready to accept or ignore the inequalities and tyrannies of whatever political system it found itself under. This can be death to Buddhism because it is death to any meaningful function of compassion. Wisdom without compassion feels no pain." I would say that enlightenment without morality is not yet enlightenment. Morality without enlightenment is not yet morality.

The consequences of not engaging the wisdom of honest, raw practice are that real lives suffer, people die, our fragile and wondrous planet is treated poorly. We need to challenge and encourage one another to realize our clarity and compassion. That is our imperative.

Finally, case 211 is "Caoshan's 'Love between Parent and Child.'" The main case:

Caoshan was once asked by a monastic, "A child went back to her parent. Why didn't the parent pay attention to her?"

Caoshan said, "It is quite natural just like that."

The monastic said, "Then where is the love between parent and child?"

Caoshan said, "The love between parent and child."

The monastic said, "What is the love between parent and child?"

Caoshan said, "It cannot be split apart, even when hit with an ax."

The commentary takes this up as follows:

At the time of birth, parent and child become each other. This means that in the middle of the night, before the moon has appeared, do not be surprised that people meet without knowing each other. At this point, the empty sky has vanished and the iron mountain has crumbled. There is not an inch of ground to stand on. Be that as it may, mountains are high and valleys are low. Thus Caoshan says the love between parent and child neither arises nor vanishes. Then how can it be divided into fragments and segments?

All of this notwithstanding, how is it that parent and child can meet and yet not know each other?

In this kōan the reference to parent and child applies to the relationship between teacher and student as well as a biological kinship. The kōan could be reworded as follows:

Caoshan was once asked by a monastic, "A student went back to her teacher. Why didn't the teacher pay attention to her?"

Caoshan said, "It is quite natural just like that."

The monastic said, "Then where is the intimacy between teacher and student?"

Caoshan said, "The intimacy between teacher and student."

The monastic said, "What is the intimacy between teacher and student?"

Caoshan said, "It cannot be split apart, even when hit with an ax."

As parents and teachers, we are constantly communicating our understanding of who we are. And what is most indelibly transmitted to others is
what we do—not necessarily what we say. Master Dōgen called this kind of
teaching "teaching through the whole body and mind." Most of our lives
are filled with words and ideas, but that's just what they are: words and
ideas. This kōan—as any other kōan—is dealing with the actuality of our
lives. We need to be aware that every single one of our actions, our silence,
our movements, and even our thoughts, communicate. We can be thinking "I hate you" while smiling at someone, and what we'll communicate is
hate. That is why it is critical to look at the karma we create through body,
speech, and thought. What we do with our bodies, what we say, what we
think.

If we want our children, our students, our peers, to be wise and compassionate, *we* need to be wise and compassionate. We need to embody the
insights we gain through practice and realization, manifesting them in
everything that we do.

A Kōan Collection for the Twenty-first Century

This translation of the *Mana Shōbōgenzō* is an attempt to create a new
kōan text for kōan study and kōan introspection that may be of relevance
to modern Zen practitioners in the West. It is meant to be a kōan text that
presents Dōgen's dharma heart and addresses the imperative of this time,
this place, and these circumstances, while at the same time appreciating the
teachings of the ancient masters of the classical and literary periods of Zen.
Most important, it tries to address issues that were not dealt with in the past
for various political, social, or cultural reasons. As twenty-first-century
Western practitioners, we have a responsibility to use our religion, our
practice, to express the moral and ethical teachings implicit in Zen.

I also believe that in the process of working with these kōans, students
will be naturally drawn to access Dōgen's other works, such as the *Kana
Shōbōgenzō*, the *Eihei Kōroku*, the *Shōbōgenzō Zuimonki*, the *Eihei Shingi*, in
order to clarify some of the points made in the commentary to each kōan.
Every one of the elements of the commentary—the commentary itself, the
verse, and the notes—challenges the student to see the kōan broadly and
deeply, rather than just the main point, as in the wato style of kōan study.
They are also an invitation to reflect upon the kōan's relevance to everyday

life situations so the dharma can come down from the top of the mountain where enlightenment occurs and be manifested in the world.

The commentaries are short, in the style of the *Gateless Gate,* and they take up the different points—both primary and secondary—that need to be dealt with if the kōan is to be understood in its entirety. The capping verses, used extensively in Zen, are in effect dharma words. They are a poetic expression of the heart of the kōan. The notes act as "footnotes" to help clarify what is being said in each line of dialogue. And finally there is kyōgai, the way in which a kōan affects your consciousness—in other words, the effect that it has on your life. This is ultimately where it counts. Because no matter how many hundreds of kōans you pass through, if they do not change the way you relate to the rest of the world, then they are nothing but intellectual exercises. And as I said before, kōan introspection is not about gaining information; it is about transforming your life.

For me, the comparative use of the two *Shōbōgenzō*s and Dōgen's other writings, in conjunction with the traditional kōans in our kōan study and introspection, is of more than just theoretical interest. It is very practical. This kind of study has opened up new possibilities in the training of Western students of kōan study in a way that addresses their natural philosophical and psychological inclinations, without abandoning the heart of the dharma that was transmitted from Śākyamuni Buddha to the present. Seen within the context of Dōgen's outstanding body of work, the *Mana Shōbōgenzō* will, it is hoped, enable readers to appreciate the endless breadth and depth inherent in the teachings of this incomparable Zen master.

Prologue

Dropping Off Body and Mind

[From *Kōans of the Way of Reality*, compiled by Daido Roshi, Case 108: "Master Dōgen's Enlightenment." *Kōans of the Way of Reality* is a collection of kōans compiled at Zen Mountain Monastery over the last twenty-five years. It includes both kōans that appear in the traditional collections as well as pieces taken from other sources and treated as kōans because of their relevance for modern Western practitioners. "Master Dōgen's Enlightenment" is one of these cases, and it marks the pivotal moment of Dōgen's study under his teacher, the Chinese master Tiantong Rujing. Following the format of *The True Dharma Eye*, a commentary and capping verse were added to the main case. The dharma discourse given on this talk follows.]

Main Case

Dōgen studied with Master Rujing. One evening during the intensive summer training, in the first year of Baozhang, 1225, Rujing shouted at a disciple, "When you study under a master, you must drop the body and mind. What is the use of single-minded intense sleeping?"

Sitting right beside this monastic, Dōgen suddenly attained great enlightenment. Immediately, he went up to the abbot's room and burned incense. Rujing said, "Why are you burning incense?" Dōgen said, "Body and mind have been dropped off." Rujing said, "Body and mind dropped off. The dropped-off body and mind." Dōgen said, "This may only be a temporary ability. Please don't approve me arbitrarily." Rujing said, "I am not." Dōgen said, "What is that which isn't given arbitrary approval?" Rujing

xliii

said, "Body and mind dropped off." Dōgen bowed. Rujing said, "The dropping off is dropped."

Commentary

Beginning with his ordination at age fourteen, Dōgen's relentless search for the Way carried him from teacher to teacher throughout Japan. Yet the great doubt persisted. Finally, at age twenty-three, he crossed the ocean to China. When he arrived there, he immediately resumed his search for an authentic teacher. After visiting a number of monasteries, he discovered Rujing. The monastic environment at Rujing's monastery was marked by a severe and disciplined meditation. By this time, Dōgen was as far onto the edge of his practice as anyone can get. When the crack of Rujing's voice shattered the silence of the darkened meditation hall, the universe collapsed and the edge disintegrated for Dōgen.

"Body and mind fallen away" is a realm in which there are no doctrines or marvels, no certainties or mysteries. It's just "when you see, there is not a single thing." Having reached this place, Dōgen expressed it to his teacher. Rujing then approved and Dōgen bowed. Having passed through the forest of brambles, he then passed beyond the other side too. Rujing said, "The dropping off is dropped."

We should understand that this body and mind is not the bag of skin. So I ask you, what is it that is dropped off? Who is it that drops off? This is the place of inquiry that must be clarified. Haven't you heard the words of the teachers of old? When the ten thousand things have been extinguished, there is still something that is not extinguished. What is it?

Capping Verse

The thought-cluttered bucket's
   bottom broken,
Neither water nor moon
   remains.

When we read about the enlightenment experiences of the ancient teachers, we need to remember that they did not exist in a vacuum—that is, their realization emerged within a specific personal and cultural context. To fully appreciate the nature and significance of a person's enlightenment, we need to look beyond the time when he or she received approval and study the teachings that both preceded and followed the breakthrough. To understand Dōgen, we need to understand his enlightenment experience, the story of his life, the historical background of his spiritual search, and the evolution of his teachings.

When he was four years old, Dōgen learned to read Chinese poetry from his grandmother. At the age of seven, he presented his stepfather with a collection of poems that he had composed in Chinese. He was an extraordinary child, regarded as a prodigy by the local elders and Confucian scholars.

Dōgen lost his father when he was three and his mother when he was eight. His mother's death was especially devastating. It proved to be one of the pivotal events of his life, deeply impacting him and shaping his early religious and spiritual intentions. With his mother's death, Dōgen experienced a profound sense of grief and developed a determination to seek enlightenment.

In the spring of his ninth year, he read Vasubandhu's *Abhidharma-kosha* familiarizing himself with a wide spectrum of accessible Buddhist teachings. His uncle, the regent and chief advisor to the emperor of Japan, took in Dōgen as an adopted son, providing him with a thorough classical education and aristocratic connections. The uncle taught him the essentials of political affairs and, when Dōgen was thirteen, had him make his debut at the court with the intention of having him become a courtier.

Dōgen, however, had different plans. Soon thereafter, he secretly left his uncle's manor in the middle of the night and went to Mount Hiei to study Tiantai Buddhism. Another of Dōgen's uncles, his mother's brother, was a high priest and a master of the esoteric and exoteric schools at Mount Hiei. His name was Ryōkan. Dōgen asked to be ordained as a monastic. Ryōkan was very surprised and pleased, but queried Dōgen, "Won't your foster father be angry about this?" Dōgen explained, "When my mother was dying, she told me to leave home and study the Way. I also think I should do so. I don't want to be involved in the mundane world. I just want to leave home and be a monastic. I want to become a monastic to requite my debt to my mother and grandmothers." Ryōkan, weeping, took him up as a student.

At the age of fourteen, Dōgen had his head shaved by the high priest Kōun, and then received the universal precepts and became a monastic. He absorbed himself in the teachings of the Tiantai school and the meditation practices of "stopping and seeing," as well as the esoteric teachings from southern India. By the time he was eighteen, he had read all of the Buddhist canon that was available to him.

As Dōgen pursued his studies, he kept returning to an apparent paradox he encountered in his readings. The fundamental teachings of Buddhism proclaimed that the Way is perfect and complete and that all people and sentient beings are innately endowed with the buddha nature. If that is the case, Dōgen wanted to know, why do we have to practice? With time, this question became uppermost in Dōgen's mind and consumed him completely. At one point, he brought it to High Priest Kōyan, another uncle and a sage, and asked for clarification. Kōyan was unable to present a satisfactory answer but advised Dōgen to look for resolution to his dilemma within the new school of Buddhism that was arriving in Japan from China— Zen. Kōyan said that he had heard about a Japanese monastic, Eisai, who had gone to China and received the transmission of the Buddha seal that the great master Bodhidharma had brought to China from India. To find out about the Zen school, Kōyan directed Dōgen to go to Kenninji monastery in Kyoto or, better yet, to China.

By this time Eisai had passed away and Myōzen was his designated successor at Kenninji. Myōzen, like Dōgen's uncle Ryōkan, was an accomplished teacher in both the esoteric and exoteric schools of Buddhism. The annals of Kenninji stated: "The treasury of the teaching is entrusted to Myōzen alone; those who would seek such teachings of Eisai should ask Myōzen." So, in the fall of his eighteenth year (ca. 1218), Dōgen joined Myōzen's community at Kenninji. He was ordained as a Zen monastic, took the precepts again with Myōzen, and studied with him for a number of years. He was given the robe and bowl symbolic of the Zen tradition, obtained the secret teachings of esoteric rituals, studied the canon of monastic regulations, and began to learn about Rinzai Zen. After a couple of years, he received the transmission of Rinzai Zen as well as transmission in the esoteric and exoteric schools.

By the time Dōgen reached the age of twenty-four, his background in Buddhist academics and practice was very broad. He had taken up and passed kōans, mastered esoteric and exoteric teachings, gained fluency in tantric rituals, and delved into the mystical dimension of Buddhism. All of this was integrated into his persona. Still, he was not satisfied. The question that fueled his search remained unresolved, and his mind was not at ease.

After several years of study at Kenninji, he decided to head for China with Myōzen. There he met a number of teachers. He tested and was tested by them. He encountered Master Ruyan, who asked him, "When did you arrive here?" Dōgen responded, "Four months ago." Ruyan continued, "Did you come this way following a group?" Dōgen answered, "How is it when one comes thus not following a group?" Ruyan said, "This is still coming this way following a group." Dōgen said, "Since this is coming thus following a group, what's right?" Ruyan slapped him and exclaimed, "A talkative priest." Dōgen persisted, "Not that there is no talkative priest, but what's right?" Ruyan said, "Stay for some tea."

Later Dōgen visited Master Sizhuo. He asked him, "What is the Buddha?" Sizhuo answered, "The one in the shrine." Dōgen pressed on, "If it's the one in the shrine, how can it pervade the universe?" Sizhuo said, "Pervading the universe." Dōgen parried, "Fallen in words." These dialogues suggest that Dōgen was quite arrogant during his visits to the Chinese teachers. He clearly was not impressed with their appreciation of the dharma.

Just about the time when he was ready to give up his pilgrimage and head back to Japan, Dōgen met Master Rujing. He was immediately taken by Rujing's wisdom, integrity, and discipline of practice. Soon after arriving at Tiantong Monastery, he wrote a letter to Rujing, stating, "I have set my heart on enlightenment, and since my youth, I have sought the Way from various teachers in my own country and came to know something of the basis of cause and effect. I still didn't know the ultimate goal of Buddhism and lingered in the externals of names and forms. Later I entered the room of Zen master Eisai and first heard the way of Rinzai Zen. Now I have come to China with Master Myōzen and have gotten the opportunity to join your congregation. This is the luck of a past blessing. Now I pray that in your great compassion you will allow a foreigner, an insignificant man from a distant place, to freely come to your room and ask about the teaching, without the question of time or manner. So please be merciful and kind, and permit me this." And Rujing did let Dōgen come anytime, day or night, to do face-to-face interviews.

Dōgen had found the right teacher. An ancient master once said, "a teacher who, regardless of age or prestige, comprehends the right dharma clearly and receives the certification of a true teacher. He gives no precedence to words and letters or to intellectual understanding. With an unusual ability and extraordinary will power, he or she neither clings to selfishness nor indulges in sentimentality. He or she is the individual in whom living and understanding correspond to each other."

In one account of his practice with Rujing, Dōgen wrote, "After hearing the truth of the sole importance of zazen from the instruction of my teacher, I practiced zazen day and night. When the other monastics gave up zazen temporarily for fear that they might fall ill at times of extreme heat or cold, I thought to myself then, I should still devote myself to zazen, even to the point of death from the attack of disease. If I do not practice zazen, even without illness, what is the use of taking care of my body? I shall be quite satisfied to die from a disease. What good fortune it is to practice zazen under such a great teacher of the great country of Song, so to end my life and be disposed of by good monastics. Thinking thus continuously, I resolutely sat zazen day and night, and no illness came at all."

Then came the decisive moment. Dōgen was doing zazen in a dark and quiet zendo (meditation hall). It was early in the morning, about three o'clock according to most records. In the stillness of the zendo, Rujing bellowed at one of the monastics, "When you study under a master, you must drop body and mind. What's the use of single-minded intense sleeping?" Rujing's exclamation was not a profound statement, but Dōgen was poised; his whole body and mind were ripe. Sitting right next to the sleeping monastic, his doubts fell away and he attained great enlightenment.

There are many stories about Zen practitioners who, at the sound of a pebble hitting bamboo or seeing a falling blossom or hearing a single word from a teacher, are transformed by the event and realize themselves. When we try to understand how that happened, we study the moment and its immediate ingredients looking for clues. But that moment will not provide us with the full appreciation of the experience. Most stories of enlightenment don't tell us about the struggles that preceded realization. They don't tell us about the endless quest to resolve the question of life and death.

Dōgen had carried his doubts for more than twenty years, desperate to find the answers, studying completely at every juncture. He was intellectually brilliant and a very diligent practitioner. As he made the journey to China, he drew closer and closer to the edge of his practice, the spiritual tension of his quest primed. On that edge, a spring breeze or a floating feather could have knocked him off. In his case, what did it was Rujing's "You must drop body and mind."

Dōgen went to the abbot's room and offered incense. Rujing probed, and Dōgen said, "Body and mind have been dropped off." Rujing replied, "Body and mind dropped off. The dropped-off body and mind." Dōgen wasn't sure about this, so he said, "This may only be a temporary ability. Please don't approve me arbitrarily." Without hesitation, Rujing exclaimed, "I am not." What did he see? How did he know? Anybody can walk into a room, light incense, and say, "Body and mind have dropped off." How does a teacher know that something has actually transpired?

The fact of the matter is that realization transforms the entire body and mind. It's not something that is felt only internally; it manifests externally. It affects how you stand, walk, eat, dress, and relate to people. There are a hundred thousand ways of seeing it without a word's being uttered. If Dōgen had not gone up to the abbot's quarters and lit incense, Rujing would still have seen it. He probably wouldn't have approved Dōgen right off. He would have probed, poked at him, to get it to fully blossom in Dōgen's own consciousness.

As the exchange began, Dōgen was not aware of the full implications of what had transpired. He just knew something had happened. "Please don't approve me arbitrarily." Rujing said, "I am not." Dōgen said, "What is that which isn't given arbitrary approval?" Another way to say that is, "What do you see that makes you say it's not arbitrary?" Rujing answered, "Body and mind dropped off." He saw in Dōgen body and mind dropped off. What does that mean?

The commentary says, "'Body and mind fallen away' is a realm in which there are no doctrines or marvels, no certainties or mysteries. It's just 'when you see, there is not a single thing.'" Dōgen takes this up throughout his writings in the *Shōbōgenzō* (Treasury of the True Dharma Eye). In *Genjōkōan* he states, "To study the Buddha Way is to study the self. To study the self is to forget the self. To forget the self is to be enlightened by the ten thousand things. To be enlightened by the ten thousand things is to drop off body and mind of self and other. No trace of enlightenment remains, and this traceless enlightenment continues endlessly."

That last line is the key. "No trace of enlightenment remains, and this traceless enlightenment continues endlessly." Rujing said, "Body and mind dropped off." Dōgen bowed. Rujing responded, "The dropping off is dropped." That's "No trace of enlightenment remains, and this traceless enlightenment continues endlessly." "Having passed through the forest of brambles, he then passed beyond the other side too." How did he pass beyond the other side? What is the other side?

The commentary continues: "We should understand that this body and mind is not the bag of skin. So I ask you, what is it that is dropped off? Who is it that drops off? This is the place of inquiry that must be clarified. Haven't you heard the words of the teachers of old? When the ten thousand things have been extinguished, there is still something that is not extinguished. What is it?"

Later on Rujing said to Dōgen, "You have the discipline of the ancient buddhas. You will surely spread the way of Zen. My finding you is like Śākyamuni Buddha finding Kāśyapa." An echo of that exchange has found its way to our transmission ceremony. At one point during the ceremony, the disciple who's receiving the transmission kneels in shōkei and the teacher passes on the oral teachings. The student then takes several steps in shōkei toward the high seat, where the teacher is sitting, and the teacher rubs the crown of her head. In China, when a child was born, traditionally the parents would rub the crown of the baby's head. While rubbing the crown of the disciple's head, the teacher says, "The Buddha had Mahā-kāśyapa, and now I have you." This is one expression of a deep sense of bonding between a teacher and a student.

In 1225 Dōgen was formally recognized as a successor to Rujing. Rujing instructed him: "Return to your native country and spread the Zen way. Live in obscurity deep in the mountains and mature your enlightenment." Dōgen traveled back to Japan and immediately went to Kenninji. Myōzen had died while he and Dōgen were in China, and Dōgen brought his ashes to the monastery. Then, within a year, he expressed the sense of mission he was embarking on. He said, "In the first year of the Shaoding era [1228–1233] of the Song dynasty, I returned to my native place in Kyoto and vowed to propagate the dharma and save all beings in the world. I felt then that a heavy load was on my shoulders." In the fall of the same year, he wrote *Fukanzazengi,* a basic instructional text on zazen.

He stayed at Kenninji for three years. Slowly people became aware of the particular style of Zen that he was teaching. His name became famous, and he started to attract disciples. As his views were uncompromising and not in line with Kyoto orthodoxy, he started to get pressure from Mount Hiei. Eventually, to escape the political distractions, he moved to an abandoned temple in Fukakuza called Annuin. It was there that he wrote the fascicle *Bendōwa*.

In *Bendōwa* Dōgen stated, "In our country the principles and practice of zazen have not yet been transmitted. This is a sad situation for those who try to understand zazen. For this reason I have endeavored to organize what I learned in China, to transcribe some of the wise teachers' teachings, and thereby to impart them to those who wish to practice and understand zazen." We must recall that zazen, single-minded meditation, was not very prevalent in Japan at this time. This was the case even at Kenninji, where kōan tradition was being advanced. To Dōgen, zazen was the pivotal factor in coming to realization. For him, practice didn't have anything to do with the observance of rituals or enigmatic shouts. It had to do with what he was doing with his mind during periods of deep zazen.

In 1233 Dōgen moved again. He rebuilt and dedicated a temple, naming it Kōshōhōrinji. There he began to develop the monastic form of Zen, brand-new in Japan at that time. Based on the Chinese model, he constructed buildings to accommodate authentic practice of zazen and established monastic regulations and the way the monastics were to be trained. He was able to realize the vision of Baizhang Huaihai, who started the first Zen monastic communities in China. Very quickly, Kōshōhōrinji emerged as one of the most powerful centers of Buddhism in Japan.

Dōgen opened his monastic community to everyone, regardless of intelligence, social status, sex, or profession. His religion was, through and through, the religion of the people. Dōgen taught that everybody was capable of realization and encouraged everybody to practice. He abolished the separation between monastics and laypersons, declaring, "Those who regard the mundane life as an obstacle to the dharma only know that there's no dharma in secular activities. They do not yet know that no secular activities exist in the dharma." Monastics and laity are in essence one and the same. Enlightenment depends solely upon whether you have a sincere desire to seek it, not upon whether you live in a monastery or in the secular world.

It was around this time that Ejo became Dōgen's disciple. When he arrived, Ejo was already a mature practitioner. He became the first shuso (head monastic) of the temple. Soon other members of the Daruma school followed. These were monastics who had done kōan study based on the teachings of Dahui Zonggao. Responding to their background and inclinations, Dōgen wrote forty-four of the *Shōbōgenzō* fascicles. He seeded his talks with the three hundred kōans he had collected in China and began to present these kōans and the Buddhadharma in a radically fresh way.

As Dōgen's popularity continued to rise, his stubbornness and zealous sense of mission to bring Buddhism back onto an authentic track irritated the traditionally minded Buddhists, especially the Kyoto religious establishment. These were people of great power. Kōshōhōrinji became increasingly threatened by these traditionalists. Dōgen was given attractive invitations to relocate to Kamakura. He flatly refused, primarily because the offers were coming from within the ruling hierarchy. He did not want to sell out.

Finally he received an invitation from Hatano, one of his lay students and a member of the shogunate, to move to Echizen Province. Hatano offered Dōgen his own property for the site of a new monastery. Dōgen accepted. His original vision of the monastic ideal was difficult to carry out in urban surroundings and under political pressures. His dream was to disappear into the mountains and to maintain a traditional monastery there. He probably also remembered Rujing's instructions: "Don't stay in the center of cities or towns; do not be friendly with rulers and state ministers; dwell in the deep mountains and valleys to realize the true nature of humanity." And then there was Dōgen's unquenchable yearning for nature, reflected in his writings on mountains and rivers and the teachings of the insentient that emerge during this period.

In July of 1243 Dōgen moved again. With a small group of followers, he entered a desolate temple named Kippōji. In the fall of that year, he began teaching a handful of monastics, probably just three or four, given the references he made in his talks to teachers in antiquity who had only a few disciples. As winter arrived and the snow got deeper, the temperature dropped in his dilapidated and drafty monastery. The morale of his monastics must have faltered. Dōgen had to inspire them, convince them that what they were doing was the only genuine way to practice. In many of his talks during this period, he elevated monastic practice above lay practice, glorifying home-leaving.

While he was putting down lay practice, his main lay practitioner and supporter, Hatano, was building him the new temple, called Daibutsuji, the Great Buddha Temple. Dōgen moved into the new temple in 1244. The dharma hall and the monastics' hall were built in rapid succession. In April of 1245 Dōgen announced the opening of the monastery and changed its name from Daibutsuji to Eiheiji. "Eihei" means "eternal peace." At last Dōgen realized his long-cherished dream, the establishment of an ideal monastic community in the bosom of the mountains and rivers.

At Eiheiji, Dōgen wrote only eight chapters of the *Shōbōgenzō*. His efforts were directed primarily toward the formulation and guidance of the moral precepts and the disciplinary rules for the monastic community. He concentrated on the ritualization of every aspect of monastic life.

In 1253 he wrote the last fascicle of the *Kana Shōbōgenzō*, "The Eight Awarenesses of Great People." At the end of the chapter Ejo inserted the comment that Dōgen had hoped to compose a total of one hundred chapters for the *Shōbōgenzō* but could not accomplish it. "Unfortunately," Ejo wrote, "we cannot see the one-hundred-chapter version. This is a matter for deep regret." That was in January of the year 1253. In July of that same year, Dōgen appointed Ejo to be his successor as the head of Eiheiji monastery and, following Hatano's advice, left Echizen for Kyoto on August 5, accompanied by Ejo and several other disciples, in order to seek medical care. He was treated at the home of a lay disciple there, but his illness, aggravated by the journey, was already too advanced to be cured. On August 28 he bade farewell to his grieving disciples and died in the posture of zazen at age fifty-three.

> The thought-cluttered bucket's
>   bottom broken,
> Neither water nor moon
>   remains.

This is a capping verse that my teacher, Maezumi Roshi, wrote when we were working on one of the books at Zen Center of Los Angeles. I was collecting capping verses, and he looked through his notes and pulled this one out. I loved it, and I still love it. "The thought-cluttered bucket's bottom broken." The bucket is the container, the bag of skin, the illusion, the thing that we think we are. It's the thing that's in a constant state of becoming and change, the thing that we cling to, put our armor around, and try to protect so desperately. It's the illusion that separates us from everything else, from everything that we need and from everything that we love. When the thought-cluttered bucket's bottom is broken, body and mind fall away. The illusion falls away.

"Neither water nor moon remains." The water—mind. The moon—enlightenment. Both gone. What is it that remains? You should understand that when the ten thousand things have been extinguished, there is still something that is not extinguished. What is it?

If you don't know, you have an imperative to find out.

The True Dharma Eye

Eihei Dōgen's Preface

The treasury of the true dharma eye was held up by Great Master Śākyamuni. But has it been investigated thoroughly? Through direct transmission I have received it more than 2,180 years later. The Buddha's dharma children and dharma grandchildren in close and remote schools number myriad and myriad, three before and three after. Would you like to know the origin of this teaching?

Long ago in front of millions of beings on Vulture Peak, when the World-Honored One held up a flower and winked, Mahākāśyapa smiled. The World-Honored One approved it and said, "I have the treasury of the true dharma eye, wondrous mind of nirvāṇa. I entrust it to the great Mahākāśyapa."

Honorable Bodhidharma, the twenty-eighth-generation direct heir of Mahākāśyapa, went to Shaolin, China, and sat facing the wall for nine years. Pulling off weed and carrying wind, he got an excellent disciple to entrust his marrow to. This was the beginning of the dharma transmission in China. The Sixth Ancestor, Caoxi (Dajian Huineng), had Qingyuan and Nanyue. Transmitted from an excellent teacher to a strong student, heir to heir, the treasury of the true dharma eye is by itself evident.

Here are the three hundred cases clarified by these ancestors. On behalf of them I am presenting the cases to you for appreciation of the ancient splendor.

On the winter solstice, the first year of the Katei Era (1235). Dōgen, abbot of Kannondori Kōshōhōrin Monastery, monastic transmitting the dharma from China, writes this preface.

1 ∿

Qingyuan's Whisk

MAIN CASE

Zen master Qingyuan Xingsi [Hongji] of Jingju Monastery once asked Zen master Xiqian of Shitou [Wuji], "Where are you from?"[1]

Shitou said, "I am from Caoxi [where the Sixth Ancestor taught]."

Master Qingyuan held up a whisk and said, "Do they have this in Caoxi?"[2]

Shitou said, "Not in Caoxi, nor in India."[3]

The master said, "You haven't been to India, have you?"[4]

Shitou said, "If I had been there, it would have been there."[5]

The master said, "If you haven't been there, how can you say that?"

Shitou said, "Master, you should say something rather than letting me say it all."[6]

The master said, "It's not that I mind saying something, but I fear it would be misunderstood later."[7]

COMMENTARY

Master Qingyuan comes straight on like a flash of lightning, and although Shitou is able to respond, it turns out that when he is pressed by the old teacher, he has no space in which to turn. So he asks the teacher to say something.

Even though Qingyuan declines to elaborate, he clearly communicates the subtlety. You should vigorously investigate the question "Do they have this in Caoxi?" and reach that place where the whole body is naked and exposed. Then realize for yourself that neither Caoxi nor India is to be found in the raised whisk.

CAPPING VERSE

In holding up the fly whisk
    he revealed the entire Buddhist Canon.
Even though the whole essence is revealed,
    still, it is only half.

NOTES

1. He is not just being friendly.
2. Careful here, he is about to strike.
3. Pretty cocky for a rookie.
4. The old man is going to get him to expose himself completely.
5. Just as I thought; it's only a dragon mask.
6. He is just digging the pit deeper and deeper.
7. The master's patience is endless, but this monastic should be hit.

2 ∾
Baizhang Remains Seated

MAIN CASE

Zen master Xiyun of Mount Huangbo [Duanji] asked his teacher, Baizhang Huaihai, "How can we explain the teaching that has been handed down?"[1]
    Baizhang remained seated in silence.[2]
    Huangbo said, "If so, what will people in the future receive?"[3]
    Baizhang said, "They will say that you are a true person."[4] He then returned to the abbot's room.[5]

COMMENTARY

The true person is rankless and rootless and does not fall into the holy or mundane. Tell me, what is Baizhang pointing to? Is it that the teaching handed down cannot be explained, or did he indeed explain it by remaining silent?

Baizhang's response to Huangbo's question is neither here nor there. If you take it as not responding, remaining seated, or silently answering, you have missed Baizhang's teaching.

CAPPING VERSE

When the dharma wheel turns,
    it always goes in both directions.
Cutting through vines and entanglements,
    the old adept closes the gap with his body.

NOTES

1. Try to avoid this at all costs.
2. Lightning flashes, thunder rolls.
3. He seems intent on misleading future generations.
4. *Bah*! He was doing all right until he opened his stinking mouth.
5. He should have remained in the abbot's room to begin with, then all of this could have been avoided.

3 ∿
Nanquan's "Water Buffalo"

MAIN CASE

Zen master Congshen of Zhaozhou [Zhenji] asked his teacher, Nanquan, "Where will the one who knows go?"[1]

Nanquan said, "To a donor's house near the mountain, and become a water buffalo."[2]

Zhaozhou thanked him for his teaching.[3]

Nanquan said, "Late last night the moonlight came through the window."[4]

COMMENTARY

Questioned by Zhaozhou, Nanquan does not hesitate to bring it out, albeit still dripping with mud and water. Zhaozhou doesn't seem to mind the stench and thanks him for his teaching. But say, what teaching does Zhaozhou see? What is the meaning of Nanquan's "moonlight came through the window"?

If you examine it carefully, it's clear that they are both making a living in a ghost cave.

CAPPING VERSE

If you call it a water buffalo,
    it's really Nanquan.
If you call it Nanquan,
    it's really a water buffalo.

NOTES

1. Although it's an old question, still, everybody wants to know.
2. It makes you wonder how that can be.
3. People with the same illness tend to commiserate.
4. Each and every dewdrop reflects the moon.

4 ∾

Mazu's "*Heart Sūtra*"

MAIN CASE

Once, Lecturer Liang of Mount Xi studied with Mazu, who said, "Which sūtra do you teach?"[1]

Liang said, "The *Heart/Mind Sūtra*."

Mazu said, "How do you teach it?"

Liang said, "I teach it with the mind."[2]

Mazu said, "The mind is like an actor. The will is like a supporting actor. The objects of the six senses are like their company. How can they teach this sūtra?"[3]

Liang said, "If the mind can't teach it, can emptiness teach it?"[4]

Mazu said, "Yes, emptiness can teach it."[5]

Liang flipped his sleeves and walked away.[6]

Mazu called out, "Lecturer!"[7]

Liang turned his head.[8]

Mazu said, "From birth till death, it's just this."[9] At that moment Liang had realization.[10] He hid himself at Mount Xi [J., Sei] and was not heard from again.

COMMENTARY

In coming face-to-face with Mazu, Liang watches his notions crumble and his position disintegrate. Although he understands lecturing with the mind, he has not yet seen into lecturing with the body and mind of emptiness. Tell me, how do you lecture with the body and mind of emptiness?

In his attempt to sting his old master, Liang's plan backfires and in the end succeeds in cutting off his myriad streams of thought. Mazu's "From birth till death, it's just this" closes the illusory gap that Liang created between himself and the master. In realizing his own suchness, he at once realizes the suchness of the ten thousand dharmas.

CAPPING VERSE

Right within light there is darkness;
    right within darkness there is light.
Going to where life itself springs forth,
    the body of suchness is revealed.

NOTES

1. This is not a conversation; it's an examination.
2. Sorry to hear that.
3. Indeed.
4. It depends on what you are calling emptiness.
5. Oops! What is he saying? Mud is being slopped all over the place.
6. Indeed.
7. Mazu is being very kind.
8. Got him.
9. Indeed.
10. Say, what did he realize?

5 〜
Layman Pangyun's Awakening

MAIN CASE

Layman Pangyun asked Shitou upon his first meeting with the teacher, "Who is the one who does not accompany all things?"[1]

Shitou covered Pangyun's mouth with his hand.[2]

Pangyun had some understanding at this point.[3]

Later he repeated the same question to Mazu.[4]

Mazu said, "Wait till you swallow up the Xi River in a single gulp,[5] then I will tell you."[6]

Pangyun was immediately awakened.[7]

COMMENTARY

In transmitting the dharma, there is neither explanation nor teaching; there is neither hearing nor attainment. Since explanations never really explain anything, nor are they able to teach, why talk about it? Since listening isn't really hearing or attaining anything, then why listen? But say, since it cannot be explained nor heard, how can you enter the Way?

Put down the baggage, take off the blinders, and see for yourself that this very place is the valley of the endless spring, this very body is the body of the universe. At such a time, who is it who can accompany what?

CAPPING VERSE

When reasoning is exhausted,
    body and mind fall away.
When the defilement of things is eliminated,
    the light first appears.

NOTES

1. There is such a thing, you know. It just can't be discussed.
2. He wants him to shut up. But if he doesn't ask, how will he know?
3. What is it that he understood?

4. If he had an understanding, why is he still asking the same question?
5. There is such a thing, you know. It just can't be discussed.
6. There is no asking and no telling; what is he talking about?
7. Throughout the mountains and valleys the last speck of dust is extinguished.

6 ~

Master Langye's "Original Purity"

MAIN CASE

A monastic asked[1] Zen master Huijue of Langye [Guangzhao], "Purity is originally all embracing.[2] How is it that mountains, rivers, and the great earth suddenly appear?"[3]

Langye said,[4] "Purity is originally all embracing.[5] How is it that mountains, rivers, and the great earth suddenly appear?"[6]

COMMENTARY

It is formless, yet it spontaneously appears, filling the ten directions. Sight, hearing, discernment, and cognition are all the cause of birth and death; sight, hearing, discernment, and cognition are the gates of liberation.

All things exist because of causes and conditions. All things do not exist because of causes and conditions—two sides of the same coin. Mountains, rivers, the great earth, and the self—where are the distinctions to be found? Why is this all divided into twos and threes? How do the complications arise? Indeed, what is it you are calling your self?

CAPPING VERSE

See it with the ears
    and you will go blind.
Hear it with the eyes
    and you will go deaf.

NOTES

1. If you don't know, it's important to ask.
2. It covers heaven and embraces the earth.
3. If you separate yourself, everything is separate and distinct.
4. He's too kind.
5. It covers heaven and embraces the earth.
6. There is nothing outside of it.

7 ∾
Yangshan's "It's Not That There Is No Enlightenment"

MAIN CASE

Mihu of Jingzhao had a monastic ask Yangshan,[1] "Can people these days depend on enlightenment?"[2]

Yangshan said, "It's not that there is no enlightenment,[3] but how can we deal with falling into the secondary?"[4]

The monastic returned and reported this to Jingzhao, who then approved Yangshan.[5]

COMMENTARY

Enlightenment is not simply the absence of delusion, nor is it true that because there is enlightenment there is no delusion. Delusion does not become enlightenment. It is beginningless and endless. Enlightenment does not follow delusion. It is beginningless and endless. Thus, they are always manifesting in the present moment.

There is delusion within enlightenment, as there is enlightenment within delusion. Enlightenment can only be realized within delusion; delusion can only be realized within enlightenment.

With self and other forgotten, how can you even speak of them? Bringing them up in the first place makes them two. The nature of diamond wisdom is that it includes the whole universe.

CAPPING VERSE

Endless blue mountains,
    free of even a particle of dust.
Boundless rivers of tumbling torrents,
    ceaselessly flowing.

NOTES

1. Everyone in the whole world is the same. Still, it's important to investigate.
2. Practitioners inevitably get lost here, building nests and calling it the great matter.
3. He gingerly tiptoes barefoot through the dog shit.
4. Now he has dragged the monastic into it.
5. Although it's true, it's too bad he had to say so. Now people everywhere will carry this around for several decades.

8 ࿎

Nanyue Polishes a Brick

MAIN CASE

Zen master Mazu Daoyi was an attendant to Nanyue and personally received the mind seal from him, exceeding his peers. Before that, he lived in Kaiyuan Monastery and did zazen all day long. Knowing that Mazu was a dharma vessel, Nanyue went to him and asked, "Great monastic, what do you intend by doing zazen?"[1]

Mazu said, "I am intending to be a buddha."[2]

Nanyue picked up a brick and started polishing it.[3]

Mazu said, "What are you doing?"[4]

Nanyue said, "I am trying to make a mirror."[5]

Mazu said, "How can you make a mirror by polishing a brick?"[6]

Nanyue said, "How can you become a buddha by doing zazen?"[7]

Mazu said, "What do you mean by that?"[8]

Nanyue said, "Think about driving a cart. When it stops moving, do you whip the cart or the horse?"

Mazu said nothing.

Nanyue said, "Do you want to practice sitting Zen or sitting Buddha? If you understand sitting Zen, you will know that Zen is not about sitting or lying down.[9] If you want to learn sitting Buddha, know that sitting Buddha is without any fixed form.[10] Do not use discrimination in the nonabiding dharma. If you practice sitting as Buddha, you must kill Buddha.[11] If you are attached to the sitting form, you are not yet mastering the essential principle."[12]

Mazu heard this admonition and felt as if he had tasted sweet nectar.

COMMENTARY

You should understand that zazen is not meditation or contemplation; it is not about quieting the mind, focusing the mind, or studying the mind; it is not mindfulness or mindlessness. If you want to really understand zazen, then know that zazen is not about sitting or lying down. Zazen is zazen; it is undefiled.

With regard to "sitting Buddha," you should understand that the very moment of "sitting Buddha" is the killing of Buddha. Thus, sitting Buddha is beyond any set form and has no abode. Therefore, when the brick is a mirror, Mazu is Buddha. When Mazu is Buddha, Mazu is at once Mazu. When Mazu is Mazu, his zazen is immediately zazen. Each thing is not transformed into the other but is, in fact, originally the other. Practice is the unfoldment.

The reality of the universe fills your body and mind, yet it is not manifest without practice, nor is it realized without enlightenment. Unless you are prepared to move forward and take risks, the truth of your life and of the universe is never realized as this very life itself.

All of this notwithstanding, what is the truth of the universe that fills your body and mind? Don't tell me—show me.

CAPPING VERSE

On the tips of ten thousand grasses,
    each and every dewdrop contains the light of the moon.

Since the beginning of time,
 not a single droplet has been forgotten.
Although this is so,
 some may realize it, and some may not.

NOTES

1. Is this a real dragon or an imitation?
2. Can Buddha become Buddha?
3. What exists is not just what appears before our eyes.
4. He wants to understand.
5. What is he saying, really?
6. Indeed!
7. Indeed!
8. He understands polishing the brick, but does he understand the mirror?
9. Then what is it?
10. Nor any abode.
11. The virtue of realizing Buddha reveals killing Buddha.
12. It simply makes it two.

9 ∾

Minister Peixiu Sees a Portrait

MAIN CASE

Huangbo once left his assembly at Mount Huangbo and entered Daan Temple. There he joined the workers who cleaned the halls.[1] Once, Minister Peixiu visited the temple to offer incense and was greeted by the temple director. Peixiu looked at a mural on the wall and said, "What kind of painting is that?"[2]

The director said, "It is a portrait of a high monastic."[3]

Peixiu said, "Obviously it is a portrait. But where is the high monastic?"[4]

The director could not answer.

Peixiu said, "Is there a Zen person around here?"

The director said, "A monastic has been working in this temple. He seems to be a Zen person."

Peixiu said, "Could you ask him to come so I can ask him questions?"

Huangbo was quickly brought to the minister, who was happy to see him. The minister said, "I have a question, but all the masters I have asked this question of have been unable to answer it. Reverend, would you please respond to it?"

Huangbo said, "Please present your question, my lord."

Peixiu repeated the question he had asked the temple director.

Huangbo raised his voice, called out and said, "Minister!"[5]

Peixiu responded, "Yes?"[6]

Huangbo said, "Where are you?"[7]

Peixiu immediately understood.[8] It was just like finding a pearl in his own hair. He said to Huangbo, "You are a true master." Then he asked Huangbo to open the teaching hall and let him enter.

COMMENTARY

Mountains and rivers are not seen in a mirror. If you go to a mirror to see them, you make one reality into two things. Just let mountains be mountains and rivers be rivers. Each thing, perfect and complete, abides in its own dharma state.

Within the myriad sounds and forms of the ten thousand things, ultimately there is neither a single particle to be found nor the subtlest sound to be heard. You can only nod to yourself. To reach this realm, all mental activity and understanding must be cut off. But say, if mountains and rivers are not seen in a mirror, where can you see them?

CAPPING VERSE

Seeing forms and hearing sounds intimately
    is whole body and mind seeing and hearing.
It's not like reflections in a mirror or echoes in the valley—
    when you really see, you go blind,
    when you really hear, you go deaf.

NOTES

1. Wandering about, gouging healthy flesh.
2. This is not a casual question; the questioner is not a casual visitor.
3. He stumbles into a pit.
4. This one is not so easily satisfied.
5. It reaches heaven and covers the earth.
6. The calling was good but the answering was even better.
7. Indeed, who are you; what are you?
8. Tell me, what is it that he understood?

10 ॐ

Qingyuan's "Come Closer"

MAIN CASE

Once a monastic asked Qingyuan, "What is the meaning of Bodhidharma's coming from India?"[1]
Qingyuan said, "It's just like this!"[2]
The monastic asked further, "What do you have to teach these days?"[3]
Qingyuan said, "Come closer."[4]
The monastic moved closer.[5]
Qingyuan said, "Keep this in mind."[6]

COMMENTARY

The Great Way has no side roads. Those who walk it have all settled the true imperative. The truth is not in seeing or hearing, nor can it be found in words and ideas. When you have passed through the forest of brambles and have untied the chains of Buddha and dharma, only then will you have entered the peaceful dwelling.

In bringing it out for this monastic, Qingyuan is still dripping with water and covered in mud, but alas! the monastic could not get it—how awkward. Be that as it may, if you yourself can see into Qingyuan's truth, and see that the nature of coming and going is not a matter of understanding, then his compassionate effort will not have been in vain after all.

CAPPING VERSE

The bright shining sun
  lights up the sky.
The pure whispering wind
  covers the earth.

NOTES

1. This question has been batted about Zen monasteries for fifteen centuries; still, it remains fresh.
2. Each step follows the other.
3. This monastic is not very alert. Hello! Is there anyone at home?
4. He's so kind. A smack on the side of his head would do as well.
5. Can you beat that? He understood.
6. This instruction may be difficult for this monastic.

11 ☙

Zhaozhou's "Losing the Mind in Confusion"

MAIN CASE

Zhaozhou said to the assembly, "'If you have even a bit of discrimination, you lose your mind in confusion.'[1] Do you have anything to say about this?"[2]

A monastic hit Zhaozhou's attendant and said, "Why don't you answer the master?"[3]

Zhaozhou left and went back to the abbot's room.[4] Later the attendant asked Zhaozhou for guidance and said, "Did that monastic who struck me have understanding, or did he not?"[5]

Zhaozhou said, "The one who sits sees the one who stands; the one who stands sees the one who sits."[6]

COMMENTARY

Zhaozhou often uses the Third Ancestor's saying to test people, since there are many who misunderstand this phrase. They take his instructions as endorsement of blank consciousness. This is because they have not yet understood that in one there are many, and in two there is no duality.

Zhaozhou always deals with people from the perspective of the fundamental matter. Thus, he said, "The one who sits sees the one who stands; the one who stands sees the one who sits."

CAPPING VERSE

When thoughts disappear,
    the thinker disappears.
When the mind is at peace,
    the whole universe is at peace.

NOTES

1. It would seem that old master Jianzhi Sengcan (the Third Ancestor) is still prowling about.
2. What can possibly be said?
3. Although he acts like a good monastic, is he really?
4. Enough of this foolishness.
5. Although it may seem like a pitfall, it's not.
6. It just doesn't fall to this side or that side.

12 ∾

Dongshan's "Going Beyond Buddha"

MAIN CASE

Zen master Dongshan Liangjie [Wuben] of Mount Dong said to the assembly, "Experience going beyond Buddha[1] and say a word."[2]

A monastic asked him, "What is saying a word?"[3]

Dongshan said, "When you say a word, you don't hear it."[4]

The monastic said, "Do you hear it?"[5]

Dongshan said, "When I am not speaking, I hear it."[6]

COMMENTARY

The great matter of the experience of going beyond Buddha is not contained within practice nor attained after enlightenment. It is simply that when you speak about it, you cannot hear it. Manifesting outside of patterns and forms, it is not a matter of cause and effect. This is the wisdom that has no teacher. Therefore, it is not contained in either words or silence, hearing or not hearing.

CAPPING VERSE

It cannot be described;
   it cannot be pictured.
The beauty of this garden
   is invisible to even the great sages.
The magnitude of this dwelling is so vast,
   no teaching can stain it.

NOTES

1. There is such a thing, you know, but only a handful have experienced it.
2. With your throat, mouth, and lips shut, how will you speak?
3. From beginning to end, obscure and hard to understand.
4. When the tip of the tongue obstructs, you do not hear.
5. How can one get it by accepting another's interpretation?
6. The old master has snatched the monastic's ears and made off with his tongue.

13 ೲ

Touzi's Moon

MAIN CASE

Once a monastic asked Zen master Datong of Mount Touzi [Ciji], "How is it when the moon is not yet full?"[1]
   Touzi said, "It swallows up three or four."[2]
   The monastic said, "How is it after the moon is full?"[3]
   Touzi said, "It spits out seven or eight."[4]

COMMENTARY

Master Touzi is equally at ease killing or giving life. See how what he says is always spontaneously in accord with the principle and intertwines with the imperative. He never loses touch with the essential matter.

The monastic's question comes from within the realm of three or four, so old Touzi answers, "It swallows up three or four." These days when practitioners get here, they think that this is it and go about making a nest, not realizing that it does not impart strength for the road. It would have been awkward if the monastic had not asked, "How is it after the moon is full?" After all, people have been known to drown on dry land. Touzi's "It spits out seven or eight" almost settles the case, but still it must be said that this is only eighty percent of the truth. Furthermore, we should understand that the heart of Touzi's teaching is not to be found in the moon.

Be that as it may, you tell me, what is the heart of Touzi's teaching, and why is it still only eighty percent of the truth?

CAPPING VERSE

The light illuminates in accordance
　　with causes and circumstances, time and season.
In its fineness, it enters the spaceless,
　　in its boundlessness, it reaches everywhere.

NOTES

　1. Rattling his chains and dragging his net, he needs to know.
　2. Not a particle of dust can be found anywhere.
　3. You should not travel by night.
　4. He exposes or transforms according to the occasion.

14 ∾

Yangshan's "Dharma Positions"

MAIN CASE

Yangshan once asked his teacher, Zen master Guishan Lingyou [Dayuan] of Mount Gui, "How is it when millions of objects emerge all at once?"[1]

Guishan said, "Blue is not yellow. Long is not short.[2] All things abide in their own positions.[3] It does not concern me."[4]

Yangshan bowed.[5]

COMMENTARY

Each and all, the subjective and objective spheres are related, and at the same time independent. Related, yet working differently, though each keeps its own place. Two faces on a single die. Thus, no thing ever falls short of its own completeness; wherever it stands, it does not fail to cover the ground.

CAPPING VERSE

Though clouds may come
    and clouds may go.
The pure wind that carries them,
    only I can know.

NOTES

1. Pick up the whole great earth in your fingers and it's as big as a grain of rice.
2. The long one is a straight buddha, the bent one is a crooked buddha.
3. Perfect and complete, lacking nothing.
4. Don't mistake no concern for not caring.
5. What did he see that made him bow?

15 ∽
Xuansha's "One Bright Pearl"

MAIN CASE

Zen master Shibei of Xuansha [Zongyi] was once asked by a monastic, "You said that the entire world of the ten directions is one bright pearl.[1] How can I understand the meaning of this?"[2]

Xuansha said, "The entire world of the ten directions is one bright pearl. Why is it necessary to understand the meaning of this?"[3]

On the following day Xuansha said to the monastic,[4] "The entire world of the ten directions is one bright pearl. How do you understand the meaning of this?"[5]

The monastic replied, "The entire world of the ten directions is one bright pearl. Why is it necessary to understand the meaning of this?"[6]

Xuansha said, "Now I know that you are living inside the cave of demons on the black mountain."[7]

COMMENTARY

When your life is not free of fixed positions, you drown in a sea of poison. Following after another's words and mimicking others' actions is the practice of monkeys and parrots. As a Zen practitioner you should be able to show some fresh provisions of your own. Be that as it may, you should understand that even in the cave of demons on the black mountain, the one bright pearl's radiance is not diminished.

CAPPING VERSE

The question came from the cave of demons;
　　the master answered with a mud ball.
Beyond telling, absolutely beyond telling—
　　ultimately, we can only nod to ourselves.

NOTES

1. Tens of thousands know it, but how many have realized it?
2. What is the meaning of the meaning?
3. There is no place to take hold of this. It's sure to be misunderstood.
4. When he raises his head I can see horns. Be careful here!
5. *Gaa!* First he inflicts a flesh wound, now he goes for the monastic's throat.
6. This monastic is not very alert; he sees a pit and jumps into it.
7. Xuansha is a competent teacher of our school. Why doesn't he just drive him out?

16 ∾

Changsha's "Returning to Mountains, Rivers, and the Great Earth"

MAIN CASE

Zen master Jingcen of Changsha [Zhaoxian] was once asked by a monastic, "How do you turn the mountains, rivers, and great earth and return to the self?"[1]

Changsha said, "How do you turn the self and return to the mountains, rivers, and great earth?"[2]

COMMENTARY

Responding to the myriad things from the perspective of the self is delusion. Manifesting the self from the perspective of the myriad things is enlightenment. From ancient times to the present, people have regarded the myriad things as separate from themselves, not realizing that the universe is the body of the Buddha—this very body and mind itself.

What do you see when you behold the mountain? Can you see the real form of truth? What do you hear when you listen to the river sounds? Can you hear the subtle gāthās of rock and water? Or are you trapped in the superficiality of sound and form?

Mountains, rivers, and the great earth are ceaselessly manifesting the teachings, yet they are not heard with the ear or seen with the eye. They can only be perceived with the whole body and mind. Be that as it may, how do you turn the self and return to the mountains, rivers, and the great earth? What is it that you are calling mountains, rivers, and the great earth? Indeed, where do you find your self?

CAPPING VERSE

There is no place to hide
    the true self.
When the universe disintegrates,
    "it" remains indestructible.

This gigantic body
   ultimately has no abode.

NOTES

1. What is he talking about? It seems he has confused the horse with
   the cart.
2. Back in your own backyard, there is no place this does not reach.

17 ∾
Xiangyan's Great Enlightenment

MAIN CASE

Zen master Zhixian of Mount Xiangyan [Xideng] was bright in nature.
Being at the assembly of Guishan, he was well learned and had extensive
memory.[1]

Guishan one day said to Xiangyan, "Everything you say is what you've
memorized from commentaries. Now I am going to ask you a question.
When you were an infant—before you could even distinguish east from
west—at that time, how was it?"[2]

Xiangyan spoke and presented his understanding, explaining the principle, but could not get approval.[3] He went through the texts he had collected and studied, but he could not find an answer that would satisfy the
master.[4]

Deeply grieved and in tears,[5] he burned all his books and commentaries.[6] Then he said to himself, "I will never understand Zen in this lifetime. I will become a hermit monastic and enter a mountain and practice."[7]

Thus he entered Mount Wudang and built a hut near the grave site of
National Teacher Nanyang.[8] One day while he was sweeping the path, a
pebble struck a stalk of bamboo and made a cracking sound.[9] At that moment he suddenly had a great enlightenment experience.[10] He wrote a
poem expressing his understanding:

   One crack and all knowledge has dissolved.
   The struggle is over.

I follow the ancient Way, not lapsing into doubt.
Dignified bearing and conduct
    that is beyond sound and form;
    no trace remains of my passing.
Those who have mastered the Way
    call this the unsurpassable activity.[11]

He presented this poem to Guishan, who said, "This fellow has penetrated it completely."[12]

COMMENTARY

The buddhas and ancestors have not transmitted a single phrase. Guishan's dharma is transmitted face-to-face, mind to mind. It is not about pebbles, bamboo, seeing, hearing, or knowing.

Because the Way reaches everywhere, no communication whatsoever is possible. If you can penetrate through the forest of brambles and cut free from all clinging, you realize the peaceful dwelling wherever you are.

CAPPING VERSE

Hearing sounds with the whole body and mind,
    seeing forms with the whole body and mind,
    one understands them intimately.

NOTES

1. Brambles! A thousand feet high and a hundred miles deep.
2. The old man wants to kill this monastic. But then, that's the imperative of our school.
3. Explanations never do.
4. Even if he had found it, still it would not reach it.
5. It is Guishan who should be weeping.
6. It is like beating up your car because it won't start.
7. Good move. Time to shut up and sit!
8. The spirit of the National Teacher remains.

9. It's neither the pebble nor the bamboo that makes the sound. What is it?

10. Tell me, what did he see?

11. He's still as talkative as ever, yet there seems to be something to it.

12. Only a doting parent could muck it up like this.

18 ❧

Nanquan and the Land Deity

MAIN CASE

Zen master Puyuan of Mount Nanquan [family name Wang], once visited a village. For this occasion the village headsman had made arrangements to welcome him beforehand. Nanquan said, "Usually my coming and going is not known about by others, how is it that you knew of my coming and prepared for it like this?"[1]

The headsman said, "Last night the deity of this land told us that you were coming."[2]

Nanquan said, "Master Wang has not practiced hard enough and was seen by a spirit."[3]

His attendant said, "You are a master of great knowledge. Why is it that you were noticed by a spirit?"[4]

Nanquan said, "Offer a bowl of rice to the land deity."[5]

COMMENTARY

It seems that old Nanquan's transparency has failed. Deities and spirits follow his wake and know his every move.

Haven't you heard the saying "However many wise ones and sages have entered these mountains, no one has ever seen a single one of them. There is only the activity of the mountain?"

Adepts are tested using the three essential seals of sealing mud, sealing water, and sealing space. If you are noticed by deities and spirits who do not practice, it means that your own practice is still not strong enough.

But still, the question remains: what does the offering of rice have do to with alleviating Nanquan's problem, and indeed, what does Nanquan mean when he says, "Master Wang has not practiced hard enough?"

CAPPING VERSE

In whole body and mind seeing and hearing,
    there is intimacy.
In this continuum no trace of the self remains,
    and this tracelessness continues endlessly.

NOTES

1. If practice fills heaven and earth, how can there be coming and going?
2. How do the land deities get their news?
3. There must be tracks for the spirits to take notice.
4. Indeed!
5. Becoming aware of the gaps, he moves to close them.

19 ∾
"Ordinary Mind Is the Way"

MAIN CASE

Zhaozhou asked Nanquan, "What is the Way?"[1] Nanquan said, "Ordinary mind is the Way."[2]

    Zhaozhou said, "Shall I try to direct myself toward it?"[3]

    Nanquan said, "If you try to direct yourself toward it, you will move away from it."[4]

    Zhaozhou said, "If I don't try, how will I know it's the Way?"[5]

    Nanquan said, "The Way is not concerned with knowing or not knowing.[6] Knowing is illusion;[7] not knowing is blank consciousness.[8] If you truly arrive at the Great Way of no trying, it will be like great emptiness, vast and clear. How can we speak of it in terms of affirming or negating?"[9]

    Zhaozhou immediately realized the profound teaching.[10]

COMMENTARY

Ordinary mind is perfect and complete. It is self-contained and self-fulfilling and is its own accomplishment. Since it existed before the kalpa of emptiness, it cannot be attained. Since it transcends time and space, it is always in the eternal present. This ordinary mind is the dharma of each moment of existence—it has no before or after.

CAPPING VERSE

The enlightened and the deluded all live in its presence.
Move toward it, and the sickness is increased.
Describe it,
and you miss its reality.

NOTES

1. What is he saying? He seems to be asleep.
2. Only one on the path would be able to respond.
3. As it turns out, he misunderstands.
4. Why is he being so kind? Let Zhaozhou go chasing his tail for the rest of his life.
5. Now he is nostril deep in complications.
6. Without a bit of hesitation, he leaps into the mud pit.
7. What is he doing? He's trying to explain the dharma.
8. Where is all this leading?
9. *Bah*! The old monastic talks too much.
10. What is it that he realized?

20 ◌

Changsha's "Stop Illusory Thinking"

MAIN CASE

Changsha was once asked by Emperor's Secretary Du, "When you chop an earthworm into two pieces, both pieces keep moving. I wonder, in which piece is the buddha nature?"[1]

Changsha said, "Don't have illusory thoughts."[2]
Du said, "How are we to understand that they are both moving?"[3]
Changsha said, "Understand that air and fire are not yet scattered."[4]
Du said nothing.[5]
Changsha called Du,[6] and Du responded, "Yes?"[7]
Changsha said, "Isn't this your true self?"[8]
Du said, "Apart from my answering, is there another true self?"[9]
Changsha said, "I can't call you Emperor."
Du said, "If so, would my not answering also be my true self?"[10]
Changsha said, "It's not a matter of answering me or not. But since the beginningless kalpa, the question to answer or not has been the root of birth and death."[11] Then he recited a verse:

> Students of the Way don't know the truth.
> They only know their past consciousness.
> This is the basis of endless birth and death.
> The deluded call it the original self.

COMMENTARY

Inconceivably wondrous is the buddha nature. Exquisitely all-pervading is no buddha nature. It has nothing to do with cosmic consciousness or the divine self. Both buddha nature and no buddha nature exist in life and in death, as well as prior to life and death and after life and death.

Before there ever was scattering and no scattering, movement and stillness, being and nonbeing, there has always been buddha nature and no buddha nature. "It" is not metaphors, images, or thoughts. Indeed, it's not like anything. Don't be deluded. It is nothing other than what you do morning and night.

CAPPING VERSE

Bright day, blue sky—
    in a dream he tries to explain his dream.
See! The myriad forms arising and vanishing,
    all abiding in their own dharma place,
    constantly reveal the buddha nature.

NOTES

1. The buddha nature is chopped in two; which has the worm?

2. How nice! But will it awaken someone who is fast asleep?

3. See? Where is all of this leading?

4. When they scatter, where will the buddha nature be?

5. Did he get it, or is he just thinking about it?

6. Hey! Wake up! Come out of your hole.

7. *Ka*! Water in the bucket, rice in the bowl.

8. What is he doing? He is trying to explain it.

9. The more it's discussed, the more confusing it becomes.

10. Too much courtesy impairs one's virtue.

11. True enough, but did he get it?

21 ೲ

Panshan's "Cut a Fine Piece"

MAIN CASE

Once Zen master Baoji of Panshan [Ningji] went to the marketplace and overheard a customer speaking to the butcher.[1] The customer said to the butcher, "Cut a fine piece for me."

The butcher threw down his knife, folded his hands, and said, "Sir, is there any piece that is not fine?"[2]

Upon hearing these words, Panshan had an awakening.[3]

COMMENTARY

Panshan unexpectedly stumbles upon something extraordinary. Although the butcher does not look like a lion, he nevertheless roars like one. But tell me, what awakened Panshan? Haven't you heard the Diamond Sūtra's saying, "All things are equal: not some things high and other things low?" This being the case, why then are the Rocky Mountains high and the Catskill Mountains low?

You should understand that no thing ever falls short of its own completeness. Wherever it stands, it never fails to cover the ground. Since the totality of existence is contained in each and every thing, what is the origin of the scale that you use to evaluate? See into it here and you'll have seen into Panshan's awakening.

CAPPING VERSE

If you speak of gain and loss,
　　you are a person of gain and loss.
Don't you see? The tall one is a tall buddha,
　　the short one is a short buddha.

NOTES

1. What is he doing stumbling around the marketplace?
2. Clam guts open up, revealing pearls.
3. I wonder, what is it that he has awakened to?

22 ❧

Puhua's Bell Song

MAIN CASE

Puhua of Zhen Region would often go into town ringing a bell and chanting:

　　When brightness comes, hit the brightness.[1]
　　When darkness comes, hit the darkness.[2]

When four sides and eight directions come, give them a swirling hit.[3]
When emptiness comes, shuck it.[4]

Once, Linji sent a monastic to grab Puhua and say, "What will you do when no-brightness and no-darkness come?"[5]

Puhua pushed back the monastic and said, "In a few days there will be a meal offering at the Dabei Temple [Great Compassion Temple]."[6]

The monastic went back and reported this to Linji, who said, "I have always wondered about that fellow."[7]

COMMENTARY

Puhua does not discriminate brightness from darkness, nor enlightenment from delusion. Does this mean that he is just dull-witted, or perhaps asleep? At times his eyes are piercing and penetrating, but can it be said that he is wide awake? Is he a mindless fool or a mindful adept?

Even from a distance, Linji is able to see whether all of this is deep or shallow, alive or dead. If you too can see into it here, then I will grant that you can walk hand in hand with Master Linji. But say, what did Linji see?

CAPPING VERSE

Although his eyes see forms, it's as if he were blind;
    although his ears hear sounds, it's as if he were deaf.
Don't you know? Only the deaf, dumb, and blind
    know how to compound medicine and feed the hungry.

NOTES

1. Go away; too many complications.
2. Go away; as useless as an udder on a bull.
3. When it comes from all sides, get rid of it from all sides.
4. Nothing is still something. Get rid of it.
5. The sixteen-foot golden body appears in a pile of shit and garbage.
6. We must not miss such an auspicious occasion.
7. Seen through! Completely transparent.

23 ∾
Yangshan's "High and Low"

MAIN CASE

One day Zen master Huiji of Yangshan [Tongzhi] joined his teacher Gui-shan in plowing the rice field.[1] Yangshan said, "Master, this place is low. How can I level it with the higher place?"[2]

Guishan said, "Water is level, so why not use water and make the entire field level?"[3]

Yangshan said, "Water is not necessary. Master, high places are level as high and low places are level as low."[4]

Guishan approved.[5]

COMMENTARY

The house of Guiyang is like this, parent and child complementing each other's actions. Yangshan's question is just an excuse to interact with his teacher. How can he not know that high is perfect and complete just as it is, and low is perfect and complete just as it is? But say, is there some Zen truth here that is being revealed?

Although you may speak of the absolute and the relative as if they were two things, the truth is that they are in fact one reality. In one there are the ten thousand things, in the ten thousand things there is just one.

CAPPING VERSE

Each and every thing abiding in its own dharma state
        completely fulfills its virtues.
Each and every thing is related to everything else
        in function and position.

NOTES

1. Although this is a commonplace event, extraordinary things are sure to follow.
2. What is he saying? This dharma is equal—no high, no low.

3. The old master seems willing to go along and see what it will come down to.

4. Each thing has its own intrinsic value.

5. Say, is he approving?

24 ∾
Dasui's "Great Kalpa Fire"

MAIN CASE

Zen master Fazhen of Mount Dasui [Shenzhao] was once asked by a monastic, "It is said that the great kalpa fire will flash and annihilate the billion worlds.[1] Can you tell me if this very place will also be destroyed?"[2]

Dasui said, "It will."[3]

The monastic said, "If so, will I be part of it?"[4]

Dasui said, "Yes, you will."[5]

COMMENTARY

With his single question, it becomes clear that this monastic is drowning in the midst of the double barrier. Dasui, with great grandmotherly compassion, pushes his head underwater and holds it there. The monastic doesn't know how to roll over and emerge like a gourd, and so Dasui must act again. This time the arrow goes straight to the heart of the matter.

But say, what is the monastic's double barrier? What does it mean to roll over and emerge like a gourd? And indeed, what is the heart of the matter? Haven't you heard it said that "there is nowhere to hide the true self; when the world collapses, 'it' is indestructible"? This being the case, why does a renowned teacher of our school say it will be destroyed?

CAPPING VERSE

Dripping with mud and foul smelling,
    the old puppet dances to the jerks and pulls.
Like a bright mirror on its stand,
    the reflection is true to the form.

NOTES

1. Where did he get the news?
2. Concern is born.
3. What? How can it be?
4. This monastic is thoroughly exposed.
5. There is no place to hide. Now what will you do, monastic?

25 ℘

The Master's Portrait

MAIN CASE

Zen master Guichen of Dizang Monastery held a memorial service for his teacher Xuansha. He invited Baoen Xuanze and served him the evening meal.

When Baoen looked at the altar, there was no picture of Master Xuansha.[1] So he asked, "Do you have a portrait of your master?"[2]

Dizang folded his hands, bowed, and said, "Look!"[3]

Baoen said, "There is no picture."[4]

Dizang said, "It's clear that you don't see it, but it's here."[5]

COMMENTARY

Understanding it before a word is spoken is called silent discourse. Revealing it spontaneously without explanation is called hidden activity. Alas, although Baoen is served a lavish meal by Dizang, he still goes away hungry.

Aside from words and ideas, people don't seem to understand the truth of the Buddhadharma. Mind to mind, Xuansha and Dizang have sealed each other. Buddha to Buddha, the lamp passed from generation to generation. If you have not as yet seen clearly into this matter, then listen to the sound of the cold wind in the pine trees, look at the autumn mountains of green and gold. When you really see it, it is clearly not like something.

CAPPING VERSE

The transmission of the Way
     is not to be found in following after others.

If you want to know the truth of the universe,
>   see that the reality of ignorance is no other than buddha nature,
>   and the illusory form is itself the pure Dharmakāya.

NOTES

1. It's really there; it's just that he can't see it.
2. If you fill up on the hors d'oeuvres, you won't enjoy the meal.
3. Born in the same way, they die differently.
4. Wrong!
5. Why explain? Let him go on chasing apparitions.

26 ∽

The National Teacher's "Pure Dharma Body"

MAIN CASE

Zen master Huizhong of Nanyang [Dazheng] was asked by Emperor Suzong of the Tang dynasty, "What is the samādhi of no conflict [arana samādhi]?"[1]
>   Nanyang said, "Your Majesty, go trample on Vairocana's head."[2]
>   Emperor Su said, "I don't understand."[3]
>   Nanyang said, "Don't regard the self as the pure dharma body."[4]

COMMENTARY

See that which is immovable and silent and do not be deceived by sounds and forms. See sounds and forms and do not be deceived by that which is immovable and silent.

If you want to understand, you yourself must first walk upon Vairocana's head—only then will you realize the samādhi of no conflict. If you avoid all ideas about the pure dharma body, it becomes clear that in the whole universe nothing is hidden. There are no barriers.

CAPPING VERSE

In our frantic search for the "gold,"
>   discriminating mind dominates and we miss the truth.

This is the cause of the endless cycle of birth and death,
   yet the deluded take it for the body of reality.

NOTES

1. There is such a thing, you know.

2. He wants the emperor to see both sides of the mountain.

3. He can't give you the whole thing; you must fill in the details
   yourself.

4. No nesting will be permitted anywhere.

27 ∾
Linji's Enlightenment

MAIN CASE

Zen master Yixuan of Linji Monastery [Huizhao] had been at the assembly
of Huangbo practicing single-mindedly for three years.[1]

The head monastic admired him, saying, "He is young, but there is
something special about him." He sent Linji to the abbot (Huangbo) and
had him ask, "What, exactly, is the essential meaning of the Buddhadharma?"[2]

Linji went to the master as instructed. Before he had finished speaking,
Huangbo hit him. Linji asked the question three times, and Huangbo hit
him three times.[3]

Linji went back to the head monastic and said, "You compassionately
advised me to ask a question of the master. I asked three times and was hit
three times. I regret that something keeps me from understanding his profound teaching. I am leaving here today."[4]

The head monastic said, "If you are leaving, you should bid farewell to
the master."

The head monastic went first to the master and said, "The young man
who asked you a question fits the dharma. If he comes to bid farewell to

you, please guide him with skillful means. Later he will manifest as a huge tree and provide shade for the world."[5]

Linji went up to the abbot's room to bid him farewell. Huangbo said, "Don't go anywhere other than Gao'an Dayu's place."

Linji visited Gao'an, who asked him where he was from. Linji said, "Huangbo's."

Gao'an said, "What did Huangbo have to say?"

Linji said, "I asked him a question three times and was hit three times. I don't know if I was wrong or not."

Gao'an said, "Huangbo had such a grandmotherly heart. He exhausted himself for you. Why do you ask if you were wrong or not?"[6]

Linji immediately had an awakening and said, "Huangbo's Buddha-dharma is not so extraordinary."[7]

Gao'an pushed him down and said, "You devil in the toilet! A few moments ago you were wondering if you had been wrong or not. Now you are saying that Huangbo's dharma is not extraordinary. What principle do you see? Say it. Say it!"[8]

Linji punched Gao'an's ribs three times.

Gao'an pushed him back and said, "Your teacher is Huangbo. I have nothing to do with you."

Linji left Gao'an and returned to Huangbo, who said, "You come and go. When is it going to stop?"[9]

Linji said, "Just because your old grandmotherly heart is profound." He made a bow and stood next to the master.

Huangbo said, "Where did you go?"

Linji said, "Following your direction, I went to see Gao'an."

Huangbo said, "What did he say?" Linji told the story.

Huangbo said, "If that guy comes to me, I will give him a set of severe blows."

Linji said, "Why do you talk about waiting? Do it now." Then he hit the master.[10]

Huangbo said, "You crazy monastic, coming here and grabbing the tiger's whiskers!"

Linji shouted.[11]

Huangbo said to his attendant monastic, "Take this crazy monastic and show him to the monastics' hall."[12]

COMMENTARY

Linji practiced at Huangbo's monastery for three years and never asked a single question until he was forced to by the head monastic. Can this be called ceaseless practice? Three times the old master answered, but Linji couldn't get it.

In the end, it took the old hermit Gao'an to bring him to realization.

Be that as it may, tell me, what is the meaning of Huangbo's hitting Linji three times? What is the meaning of Linji's hitting Gao'an three times? Since Linji enters the Way by virtue of Gao'an's turning word, is he a successor of Gao'an or Huangbo?

The only saving grace about the whole farce is that, in the end, it all perished with the blind donkey.

CAPPING VERSE

Huangbo's kindness was excessive;
　　Gao'an's mouth was too extravagant.
Still, the mist opened and revealed in a cloudless sky
　　the autumn moon, alone.

NOTES

1. Is this a dead tree stump, or ceaseless practice?
2. Since he avoids the furnace, the head monastic must create one.
3. Even though his kindness was boundless, it was not articulate enough.
4. Don't let him off so easily.
5. In spite of all the shouting and hitting, this monastery seems filled with kind old grandmothers.
6. The old hermit talks too much.
7. A tiger is about to come to life.
8. Gao'an had to bring it to completion or it might have been misunderstood.
9. It needs to be examined.
10. It will take several generations for this to exhaust itself.
11. This too must ultimately pass.
12. Another twenty or thirty years of training are still needed.

28 ⌒

"Dragon Howling in a Withered Tree"

MAIN CASE

Xiangyan was once asked by a monastic, "What is the Way?"[1]

Xiangyan said, "A dragon howling in a withered tree."[2]

The monastic said, "What does it mean?"[3]

Xiangyan said, "Eyeballs in a skull."[4]

Later, another monastic asked Shishuang Chuyuan, "What is a dragon howling in a dead tree?"[5]

Shishuang said, "It still has joy."[6]

The monastic said, "What are the eyeballs in a skull?"[7]

Shishuang said, "They still have senses."[8]

Later, another monastic asked Zen master Benji of Caoshan [Yuanzheng], "What is the dragon's howling in a dead tree?"[9]

Caoshan said, "Bloodstream has not stopped."[10]

The monastic said, "What are the eyeballs in a skull?"[11]

Caoshan said, "Dry all the way."[12]

The monastic said, "I wonder, can anyone hear it?"[13]

Caoshan said, "Throughout the entire earth, there is no one who does not hear it."[14]

The monastic said, "Which verse does the dragon sing?"[15]

Caoshan said, "I don't know which verse it is, but all those who hear it are lost."[16]

COMMENTARY

Do not mistake a withered tree for a dead tree; it abounds with life and celebrates each and every spring with new foliage. It's just that few have realized this. As for the dragon's roar, actually, everyone is able to hear it, because it exists everywhere. And yet, there can be no dragon's roar unless there is a withered tree.

If you can see through to the point of this kōan and make it your own, then your own voice will be the dragon's roar and you will be able to make use of it among the ten thousand things. If, however, you are unable to perceive it, then the worldly truth will prevail and everything will appear to be an impenetrable barrier.

You should understand that illumination and function are a single truth, principle and phenomena are not two realities. These old masters know how to simultaneously roll out and gather in. Letting go of the primary, they open the gate of the secondary.

When the great function manifests, it does not hold to any fixed standards. Sometimes a blade of grass can be used as the sixteen-foot golden body of the Buddha; sometimes the sixteen-foot golden body of the Buddha can be used as a blade of grass. All of this notwithstanding, tell me, how do you understand the great function?

CAPPING VERSE

Letting out the hook,
　　just to fish out the dragons.
The mysterious devices outside of convention
　　are only for those who wish to know the self.

NOTES

1. An old question, but still it deserves an answer.
2. I wonder if the monastic will get it.
3. I think he has missed it.
4. Stop trying to mystify him; just hit him and let him go.
5. The word has spread fast.
6. Thank you for your answer.
7. If he had understood the answer, this question would be unnecessary.
8. This old teacher is wasting his time with this monastic—drive him out!
9. These questions are beginning to be sickening.
10. These answers are beginning to be sickening.
11. These monastics should all form a group and, together, shut up and sit.
12. Yet the bottom cannot be seen.
13. Everyone but you, monastic—because you must first shut up to hear it.
14. Except for our questioner.

15. Go away frog, this is about dragons.
16. Body and mind fallen away, nothing remains.

29 ∾
Daowu Won't Say

MAIN CASE

Jianyuan Zhongxing once accompanied his teacher Daowu on a condolence call to a family funeral. When they arrived, Jianyuan tapped the coffin and said, "Is this life or is it death?"[1]

Daowu said, "I won't say life. I won't say death."[2]

Jianyuan said, "Why won't you say?"[3]

Daowu said, "I won't say. I won't say."[4]

On their way back, Jianyuan said, "You should quickly say it for me, or I will hit you."[5]

Daowu said, "Hit me if you will, but I will not say."[6]

Jianyuan hit him.[7]

After returning to the monastery, Daowu said to Jianyuan, "You should leave for a while. I am afraid if the head monastic finds out about this he will make trouble for you."

After Daowu passed away,[8] Jianyuan went to see Daowu's successor, Shishuang Qingzhu, told him the story, and asked for guidance.[9]

Shishuang said, "I won't say life. I won't say death."[10]

Jianyuan said, "Why won't you say it?"[11]

Shishuang said, "I won't say it. I won't say it."[12]

Jianyuan immediately realized it.[13]

COMMENTARY

Grappling within the forest of brambles, Zen practitioners the world over probe the question of life and death. Before it is realized, it is like a ten-mile-high wall or a bottomless gorge. After it is seen, it is realized that, from the beginning, the obstructions have always been nothing but the self.

Lost in the double barrier of life and death, the monastic has to know. Because of intimacy, the old master won't say. From the time of the Buddha down to the present, this is how it has been. However, if you think this old kōan is about the corpse being alive or dead, then you too have missed the old master's teaching.

There is no place to put this gigantic body. When the universe collapses, "it" is indestructible.

CAPPING VERSE

In arriving, not an atom is added—
    thus life is called the unborn.
In departing, not a particle is lost,
    thus death is called the unextinguished.

NOTES

1. Caught between two iron mountains, he wants to drag his old teacher into it.
2. Seeing the imperative, he compassionately points it out for him.
3. He doesn't understand—the iron mountains prevail.
4. Hearing his anguished cry for help, the old adept kindly shows him again.
5. Separation always breeds confrontation.
6. Relentless in his kindness, he exposes his heart and viscera, holding back nothing.
7. *Bah*! Let him go on deceiving himself for the rest of his life.
8. Tell me, where did he go?
9. His dullness is exceeded only by his persistence.
10. How new, how fresh!
11. How dull, how numb!
12. The waves of Caoxi continue generation after generation, but they don't resemble each other.
13. Within death he has found life. But say, what is it that he realized?

30 ∾
Caoshan's "No Change"

MAIN CASE

Caoshan bid farewell to his teacher Dongshan Liangjie.[1] Dongshan said, "Where are you going?"[2] Caoshan said, "I am going to the place of no changing."[3]

Dongshan said, "Can you leave from the place of no changing?"[4]

Caoshan said, "Leaving is not change."[5]

COMMENTARY

The place of no changing is neither permanent nor impermanent. When the universe is destroyed, "it" remains indestructible. Where is the place of no changing?

See the apple blossoms
     still wet with morning dew.
Know that they bloom
     no place but here.

As for Caoshan's "Leaving is not change," you should understand that when it is cold, throughout heaven and earth it is cold; when it is warm, throughout heaven and earth it is warm.

CAPPING VERSE

In arriving, nothing is added—
     in departing, nothing is lost.
Ultimately, how is it?
Coming and going is always right here.

NOTES

1. He won't get off so easily.
2. The old man is not through with him after all.

3. What is he talking about? Sounds like a board-carrying monastic to me.

4. Dongshan presses against the edges.

5. He redeems himself. Since they are from the same household, they know the pantry well.

31 ∾
Deshan's Thirty Blows

MAIN CASE

Zen master Xuanjian of Deshan [Jianxing] said to the assembly during an informal talk, "I am not going to give an answer tonight. Anyone who asks a question will get thirty blows."[1]

A monastic came up and bowed.[2] Deshan hit him.[3]

The monastic said, "I haven't asked a question. Why did you hit me?"[4]

Deshan said, "Where are you from?"[5]

The monastic said, "I came from Silla [in Korea]."[6]

Deshan said, "Before you even got on board the ship, you deserved thirty blows."[7]

COMMENTARY

It is said of old Deshan that he gives thirty blows for answering and thirty blows for not answering. What is his point? Tell me, is there a Buddhist principle being revealed here or not? Should the monastic receive thirty blows or not? If you say he should be hit, then mountains, rivers, and the great earth itself should all be hit. If you say that he should not have been hit, then Deshan is just using his power to mystify the monastic. If you can see into it here, you will understand that the monastic came looking for iron and was given gold. It's a pity he can't see it. Say a word on behalf of this monastic, and leap free of old Deshan's pitfall. If you're still unable to do so, then look to your own practice. Where do you find yourself, and what is it that you seek?

CAPPING VERSE

Your coming and going
    always take place right where you are.
Your laughing and crying
    are always the voice of the dharma body.

NOTES

1. Thank you for your teaching.
2. Wrong! He deserves thirty blows.
3. He wants the monastic to see past his agenda.
4. I'm afraid he's missed the old man's kindness completely.
5. His kindness is excessive. He's going to try to explain it to him.
6. Wrong! It's easy to see what this monastic's provisions are.
7. Why explain? Hit him again—drive him back to Silla!

32 ❧
Taiyuan Fans Himself

MAIN CASE

Senior Monastic Fu of Taiyuan asked his student Gushan, "Where are the nostrils you had before your parents were born?"[1]
    Gushan said, "Born right now."[2]
    Taiyuan did not approve[3] and said, "You ask me and I will tell you."[4]
    Gushan said, "Where are the nostrils you had before your parents were born?"[5] Taiyuan just fanned himself.[6]

COMMENTARY

Taiyuan seems to create problems where there are none. However, this is the imperative for teachers of our school. Only those who can find their way through the vines and entanglements can be called true practitioners. Taiyuan wants to know if Gushan is such a true person.
    Since Gushan has a sharp and active edge to his practice, he is able to

bring the ten thousand kalpas home. This, however, does not satisfy Tai-yuan. Seeing the crack caused by the flow of the myriad impulses, the old teacher is able to fill the gap without uttering a single phrase.

CAPPING VERSE

Autumn's wind blows
    and falling leaves fill the air.
When they fall, they always come to rest
    no place but here.

NOTES

1. You may describe it, but words won't reach it; picture it, but to no avail. What realm is this?
2. Good words; nevertheless, they miss it.
3. The old man wants to see him have the full meal.
4. If there is no question, there can be no answer.
5. How new, how fresh! Where did he hear of this?
6. With each action, the pure wind arises.

33 ∾
Caoshan's "Falling and Rising"

MAIN CASE

Caoshan was once asked by a monastic, "It has been said since ancient times that no one has fallen on the ground who has not risen without using the ground.[1] What is falling?"[2]
    Caoshan said, "If you are in accord with this, falling is just as it is."[3]
    The monastic said, "What is rising?"[4]
    Caoshan said, "Rising!"[5]

COMMENTARY

Falling down exists thus; it has no before or after. Rising exists thus; it too has no before or after.

Just as falling down is dependent on the ground, rising is also dependent on the ground. The principle of enlightenment of all the buddhas of the three times is said to be like someone fallen on the ground who rises by using the ground. This is so because falling and rising are nondual—an absolute event. Free of before and after, it fills the universe and exists thus.

CAPPING VERSE

Do not be distressed by wrong;
> do not delight in right.
For the ancient buddhas, all things are like
> flowers and blossoms.
Peony flowers are red,
> plum blossoms are white.

NOTES

1. Medicine and sickness always heal each other.
2. Knock him off his feet!
3. What is it when you are not in accord with it?
4. He knows, yet he deliberately offends.
5. The tall one is a tall buddha; the short one is a short buddha.

34 ∾

The World-Honored One's "Intimate Speech"

MAIN CASE

Zen master Daoying of Mount Yunju [Hongjue] was once asked by a government official who had brought an offering, "It is said that the World-Honored One had intimate speech[1] and Mahākāśyapa did not hide it.[2] What is the World-Honored One's intimate speech?"[3]

Yunju said, "Officer."[4] The officer said, "Yes!"[5]

Yunju said, "Do you understand?"[6]

The officer said, "No, I don't."[7]

Yunju said, "If you don't understand it, that is the World-Honored One's intimate speech.[8] If you do understand it, that is Mahākāśyapa's not hiding it."[9]

COMMENTARY

The intimate speech of the Buddha is the original face of all buddhas and ancestors. It cannot be given, nor can it be received. It is not inherent, nor is it newly acquired.

If you think that Master Yunju's calling and the official's answering is the Buddha's intimate speech, you have missed it.

In intimacy, the ten thousand things have merged and thus cannot be spoken of. In understanding, heaven and earth are separated and nothing is hidden.

CAPPING VERSE

One had intimate speech,
  the other did not conceal it.
The World-Honored One held up a flower,
  Mahākāśyapa smiled.
No gaps.

NOTES

1. No communication whatsoever is possible.
2. Indeed, there is no place to hide it.
3. What will he say? It simply cannot be explained.
4. Can this be called intimate speech?
5. Can this be called not hiding it?
6. What is he saying? Where is this going?
7. His honesty is admirable.
8. I don't understand either.
9. He pushes down the cow's head to make it eat grass. It just doesn't work.

35 ∾
Touzi's "Harmonizing the Ten Bodies"

MAIN CASE

Touzi Datong was once asked by a monastic, "What is the harmonizing of the ten bodies of the Buddha?"[1]
Touzi got down from the sitting platform and stood with folded hands.[2]
On another occasion a monastic asked, "What distance is there between ordinary ones and sacred ones?"[3]
Touzi got down from the sitting platform and stood with folded hands.[4]

COMMENTARY

If you want to experience for yourself the harmonizing bodies, you must first leap clear of your habitual active consciousness and see that from the beginning there has never been anything that can be apprehended. Just see into that which is silent and still. Touzi stumbles and falls for the monastic, but the monastic doesn't get it.

If you want to gauge the distance between ordinary and sacred, you need to know that ordinary is each and every thing south of the north pole; whereas the sacred is all that is north of the south pole. Haven't you heard it said: "Within the ordinary there is no sacredness. Within the sacred nothing is ordinary?" Again Touzi stumbles and falls for the monastic, and again the monastic misses it.

CAPPING VERSE

Each and every one—all real,
    each and every thing—all complete.
Where there is no affirmation and no negation,
    there it stands alone, revealed.

NOTES

1. Where did he get this question? Where did he hear the news?
2. The old master does the best he can, given the question. What could he have said?

3. Ignoring his own provisions, he wastes his time sniffing around his neighbor's cupboard.

4. Touzi is a little lame, but he gets there all the same.

36 ⌘

Deshan's "Assembly on Vulture Peak"

MAIN CASE

Deshan Dehai was once asked by a monastic, "Who was able to hear Śākyamuni Buddha at the assembly on Vulture Peak?"[1]

Deshan said, "The ācārya heard it."[2]

The monastic said, "I wonder what was spoken at the assembly on Vulture Peak?"[3]

Deshan said, "The ācārya understands it."[4]

COMMENTARY

The meeting at Vulture Peak still resounds throughout the whole universe. Yet, this monastic is stumbling about trying to understand it. Deshan doesn't hold back and reveals the family secret without hesitation. Still, the monastic is unable to see it. Do you see it?

If you wish to understand the truth of this dialogue, then you must first see into the word "ācārya." Is this Kāśyapa [Mahākāśyapa, the Buddha's successor], Deshan, the monastic, or is it you? The treasury of the eye of truth is always given and received by oneself. There has never been anything given to another; there has never been anything received from another. This is called the truth of the Buddhadharma. This being the case, how can the meeting on Vulture Peak be anywhere but here? But say, what is the family secret revealed by Deshan?

CAPPING VERSE

The spiritual potential of the thousand sages
    is not easily attained.

Dragon daughters and sons, do not be irresolute—
  ten thousand miles of pure wind,
  only you can know it.

NOTES

1. This old case is dragged out again into the light of day.
2. The question is, who is the ācārya?
3. It's not so much what was spoken, but what was not spoken that matters.
4. When it's cold, heaven and earth are cold; when it's warm, heaven and earth are warm.

37 ∾
Yuezhou's "Path to Nirvāṇa"

MAIN CASE

Yuezhou Qianfeng was once asked by a monastic, "Bhagavāns in the ten directions have one path to the gate of nirvāṇa.[1] I wonder, what is the path?"[2]
  Yuezhou drew a line with his staff[3] and said, "It's right here."[4]

COMMENTARY

Here is not in opposition to there. Here is complete in every respect. It contains there, not there, not here, both here and there, and neither here nor there.

The staff fills the entire universe; the one path contains the entire universe; "It's right here" is the entire universe. Do not lose the staff in meanings and concepts, and do not mistake "It's right here" as being like something.

If you are not intimate with it, when it's revealed, you'll end up thinking about it for the rest of your life. When words and ideas are finally obliterated, the light first appears. Light or no light, wet with the morning dew, the truth appears on the tips of the thousand grasses.

CAPPING VERSE

Vast and boundless, nothing is hidden,
    and all the way to heaven is heaven itself.
The rains have passed,
    and the summer river runs deep and fast.
Looking to the left, looking to the right—
    there are no seams, no flaws.

NOTES

1. True; it's always been like this.
2. It's right in your face, right on your head. The question really is, where are you?
3. Thank you for your teaching.
4. This old monastic is much too talkative.

38 ൦

Xuefeng's "Turning the Dharma Wheel"

MAIN CASE

Zen master Yicun of Mount Xuefeng [Zhenjue] pointed with his finger at a furnace and said to Xuansha, "All buddhas in the three worlds are in here, turning the great dharma wheel."[1]
    Xuansha said, "The king's regulations are rather strict."[2]
    Xuefeng said, "How so?"[3]
    Xuansha said, "Stealing is not permitted."[4]

COMMENTARY

These ancient buddhas had a family style—their words clearly show their abilities. Rolling out and rolling in, both sides are exposed. Right off, we should understand that the place of wisdom and compassion is where all the buddhas in the three worlds turn the great dharma wheel in the fire. So why did Xuefeng feel it necessary to point it out? Xuansha let out the other side of the matter, saying, "Stealing is not permitted." What is the stealing? What is Xuansha's meaning?

CAPPING VERSE

Xuefeng is clearly a thief who steals in broad daylight,
    but Xuansha steals the thief's horse and pursues him.
It finally just comes down to two monastics playing with mud balls.
After all, sweet is just sweet, bitter is just bitter.

NOTES

1. He ought to have been hit before he finished talking.
2. Those who know the law worry about it. Where is he going with this?
3. He wants to hear about it.
4. An accomplished thief doesn't strike a poor household.

39 ∾
Jingqing's "Buddhadharma at the New Year"

MAIN CASE

Jingqing Daofu of Longce Monastery was asked by a monastic, "Is there Buddhadharma at the beginning of the New Year?"[1]
    Jingqing said, "Yes."[2]
    The monastic said, "What is the Buddhadharma at the beginning of the New Year?"[3]
    Jingqing said, "The beginning of the year is auspicious. The myriad things are all new."[4]
    The monastic said, "Thank you for your answer."[5]
    Jingqing said, "I lost virtue today."[6]
    Later, another monastic asked Zen master Shuangquan Shikuan [Mingjiao], "Is there Buddhadharma at the beginning of the New Year?"[7] Mingjiao said, "No."[8]

The monastic said, "Every year is a good year. Every day is a good day. How is it not in the New Year?"[9]

Mingjiao said, "When old man Zhang drinks wine, old man Li gets drunk."[10]

The monastic said, "Old, old, big, big. A dragon head, a snake tail."[11]

Mingjiao said, "I lost virtue today."[12]

COMMENTARY

Since both monastics ask, "Is there Buddhadharma at the beginning of the New Year?" why does Jingqing say "yes" and Mingjiao say "no?" If you go to words and phrases to see into this, you will never get it. If, however, you are free of mind and objects and have attained complete liberation, you certainly have a life apart from "yes" and "no." Tell me, what is life apart from "yes" and "no"?

Before the New Year, the cold moon illuminates the endless mountain. After the New Year, the sweet fragrance of apple blossoms fills the valley. On New Year's Day itself, there is no before or after, just the vast and boundless sky, free of all hindrance. It is from here that both masters answer.

If I had been there when the monastic said "Thank you for your answer," I would have hit him with my stick and said, "Now I have gained virtue." When the other monastic said "A dragon head, a snake tail," I would have driven him out with a shout and said, "Now I have gained virtue."

CAPPING VERSE

One raises it up,
    the other pushes it down.
In their loss of virtue,
    both are completely free.

NOTES

1. What New Year?
2. He goes out of his way to extend kindness to this monastic.
3. If he doesn't ask, he will never know.
4. Moment to moment, the whole universe is refreshed.
5. What did he see that made him thank the master?

6. Indeed, what a pity.
7. Where did he get the question?
8. Not at the beginning of the New Year, before the New Year, or after the New Year.
9. This monastic arrived with an agenda.
10. When the mind is empty, all things are empty.
11. I fear he has misunderstood the old man.
12. Indeed, what a pity.

40 ∽

Sansheng's Blindness

MAIN CASE

The second-generation abbot of Baoshou Monastery took the high seat. Zen master Huiran of Sansheng Monastery pushed a monastic forward. Baoshou Yanzhao hit the monastic.[1]

Sansheng said, "This guidance of yours does not only blind this monastic, but it also blinds everyone in the entire city."[2]

Baoshou threw down the staff and went back to the abbot's room.[3]

COMMENTARY

The second-generation abbot of Baoshou Monastery is about to address the assembly during his installation ceremony. Sansheng, wanting to see how deep the waters are, pushes a monastic forward. Baoshou immediately hits the monastic. Forceful or subtle, family styles may differ, but the message is always the same. Tell me, what is the message? Sansheng says, "This guidance of yours does not only blind this monastic, but it also blinds everyone in the entire city."

Since Sansheng is Linji's "blind ass," it can be said that he knows a thing or two about the five kinds of blindness. Tell me, what kind of blindness is he talking about? As for Baoshou, what is the meaning of his throwing down the staff and returning to the abbot's room? Can this too be called blindness?

CAPPING VERSE

The staff transforms into a dragon
    and swallows the universe.
When the host is reverent, the guest becomes pompous.
The underlying meaning—what is it?

NOTES

1. After all, the imperative must be carried out.
2. It's because of his own blindness that he sees like this.
3. After all is said and done, it still only comes down to half.

41 〜

Shitou's "Ask the Pillar"

MAIN CASE

Shitou was once asked by a monastic, "What is the significance of Bodhidharma's coming from India?"[1]
    Shitou said, "Ask the pillar."[2]
    The monastic said, "I don't understand it."[3]
    Shitou said, "I don't understand it either."[4]

COMMENTARY

This question has been rattling around Zen monasteries since ancient times, and hundreds of various answers given by different masters are recorded in Zen literature, which makes it impossible to come to any logical conclusion regarding the meaning of Bodhidharma's coming from India. If the truth of this kōan is not to be found in logic or rationalizations, then where is it to be found?

    What does it mean to "ask the pillar"? Haven't you heard Master Dōgen's saying "You should put your questions to a pillar and practice intensively with a wall"? If you wish to penetrate this barrier, you must first see that mind and objects are a single reality. Then all dualities merge into a single thusness. At just such a time, self and other, is and is not, good and bad, are no longer seen in the realm of yin and yang.

The monastic does not understand; the master does not understand. Are the master's and the disciple's not understanding the same, or different? If you say the same, you have missed it; if you say different, you have missed it; if you say neither or both, you are ten thousand miles from the truth. What do you say?

CAPPING VERSE

There is no place to search for the truth—
   though it's right beneath your feet, it can't be found.
Look at springtime—when the snow has melted,
   the scars of the landscape are no longer hidden.

NOTES

1. Why don't you ask the blue-eyed monastic?
2. An iron hammerhead with no hole.
3. This is understandable.
4. This too is understandable.

42 ∾
Jingqing's Thirty Blows

MAIN CASE

Jingqing asked a monastic, "Where have you been?"[1]
   The monastic said, "Three Peaks."[2]
   Jingqing said, "Where were you during the summer?"[3]
   The monastic said, "Five Peaks."[4]
   Jingqing said, "I give you thirty blows."[5]
   The monastic said, "What is my fault?"[6]
   Jingqing said, "The problem is that you go in and out of monasteries."[7]

COMMENTARY

The point of this questioning is to get to know this monastic intimately before he even opens his mouth. This conversation in the weeds takes place for the sake of compassion. If the monastic had a spark of life in him, he would have immediately seen where the old teacher was heading.

Don't you see? If you persist in prowling about from mountain to mountain, where will you have today? This monastic deserves thirty blows even before he begins his pilgrimage. Anything that can enter through the gate cannot possibly be the family treasure.

CAPPING VERSE

When reason is exhausted
    and all considerations are forgotten,
    it becomes clear that wherever you may go
    there is always the frosty night's moon.

NOTES

1. He wants to get to know him. Still, this is not a casual question.
2. Although he is truthful, it seems that he misunderstands.
3. The old man presses to see where he will come down.
4. Go away. You don't understand.
5. Indeed!
6. How could you have missed it? It's not your fault; it's the old teacher's fault.
7. Don't explain it. Let him go on chasing rainbows for the rest of his life.

43 ∞
Guizong Cuts a Snake

MAIN CASE

Zen master Zhichang of Guizong Monastery was cutting grass when a lecturer came by to study with him. It so happened that they saw a snake passing by. Guizong cut the snake in two with his spade.[1]

The lecturer said, "I have heard of your fame for a long time. But now I see, after all, that you are just a śramaṇa of coarse practice."[2]

Guizong said, "Am I coarse, or is it you that is coarse?"[3]

The lecturer said, "What is coarse?"[4]

Guizong held up the spade.[5]

The lecturer said, "What is fine?"[6]

Guizong made a gesture of cutting a snake.[7]

The lecturer said, "If this is so, then I will practice accordingly."[8]

Guizong said, "Aside from practicing accordingly, where did you see me cut the snake?"[9]

The lecturer was silent.[10]

COMMENTARY

Both are trapped between two iron mountains. The lecturer has tied himself to the precepts and sees only coarseness. Guizong acts freely and unrestrainedly and sees only refinement.

The truth of the matter is not about dividing it all into coarse and fine, or cutting and not cutting. If you wish to leap free of the dichotomy, then understand that the act of cutting the snake is at once an evil act and a buddha act.

Be that as it may, the snake is dead. So, tell me, how could all of this have been avoided in the first place? Haven't you heard it said, "When at an impasse, change; when you change, then you can pass through"?

CAPPING VERSE

Coarse, fine—
    heads and tails are on one coin.
The sword that kills is none other
    than the sword that gives life.

NOTES

1. Wrong!
2. So it would seem, but is he really?
3. He wants his nostrils.
4. A fine parry indeed.

5. There is always this.

6. He persists. But say, where is all of this going?

7. *Bah*! He is hopping around looking for a way out.

8. Wrong!

9. Good question. If he can see into it here, the snake's death will not have been in vain.

10. What a waste of a fine snake.

44 ❧

Guishan's "I Have Already Exhausted Myself for You"

MAIN CASE

Guishan sat on the teaching seat. A monastic came up and said, "Master, please expound the dharma for the assembly."[1]

Guishan said, "I have already exhausted myself for you."[2]

The monastic bowed.[3]

COMMENTARY

This monastic asks Guishan to expound the dharma. Guishan says, "I have already exhausted myself for you." What is his meaning?

If you wish to understand Guishan, you first of all need to realize that expounding the dharma is not necessarily limited to expression in words, nor does wordlessness imply the lack of expression. Haven't you heard Master Zhaozhou saying, "If you spend a lifetime not leaving the monastery, sitting in stillness without speaking for ten years or for five years, no one can call you mute. You might be beyond even the Buddha"? Therefore, a lifetime without leaving the monastery is a lifetime of expounding the dharma. Sitting in stillness without speaking for five or ten years is expounding the dharma for five or ten years. Tell me then, what is the dharma that Guishan has expounded for the monastic?

What Guishan is imparting does not enter through the gate. It is a truth that does not reside in words, sounds, gestures, or silence. It does not spring from the realm of intent. In intent the mind moves and there is communication. In the teaching of the essential matter no communication whatsoever takes place.

When I examine this matter closely, it seems that it's not so much that Guishan has used up all his provisions as it is that he never had any to begin with. The monastic bows. Does he get it? Do you get it? If so, say a word.

CAPPING VERSE

Deaf, mute, and blind—
    already illuminating before it is said.
Manifesting the body as preaching,
    saving all sentient beings.

NOTES

1. Don't be greedy. He has already given him everything he has to give.
2. Poor old teacher. There is nothing left of him.
3. It's easy to bow, but what does he really mean by doing so?

45 ∿
Xuansha's "The Three Vehicles and the Twelve Divisions of Sūtras"

MAIN CASE

Xuansha was once asked by a monastic, "The Three Vehicles and the Twelve Divisions of Sūtras are unnecessary.[1] What is the meaning of Bodhidharma's coming from India?"[2]

Xuansha said, "The Three Vehicles and the Twelve Divisions of Sūtras are totally unnecessary."[3]

COMMENTARY

If you think Xuansha is saying that the Three Vehicles and the Twelve Divisions of Sūtras are totally unnecessary, you have totally missed this old master's teaching. On the other hand, if you have concluded that the Three Vehicles and the Twelve Divisions of Sūtras is the meaning of the Ancestor's

[Bodhidharma's] coming from India, that too is a hundred miles from the truth. Finally, if you consider the Three Vehicles and the Twelve Divisions of Sūtras as necessary, you are simply placing a head on top of the one you have.

Haven't you heard it said that the answer is always contained in the question? Since Zen teaching is carried on in accord with the conditions and in harmony with the situation, Xuansha fans the fire and says, "The Three Vehicles and the Twelve Divisions of Sūtras are totally unnecessary." Do you understand? This is known in the teachings as creating illness and dispensing medicine according to circumstances.

CAPPING VERSE

When the words and ideas that describe reality fall away,
    all that remains
    is reality itself.

NOTES

    1. Where did he hear about this? What does he think it means?
    2. Generations of Zen practitioners have all stumbled here.
    3. All the ancestors suffer from this same illness.

46 ∾
Zhaozhou's Four Gates

MAIN CASE

Zhaozhou was once asked by a monastic, "What is Zhaozhou?"[1]
    Zhaozhou said, "East gate, south gate, west gate, north gate."[2]
    The monastic said, "I did not ask about this."[3]
    Zhaozhou said, "You asked about Zhaozhou, didn't you?"[4]

COMMENTARY

This monastic is undeniably extraordinary, coming to examine the tiger in his lair like this. Zhaozhou, however, is up to the task and directly shows him the whole thing. The monastic misunderstands, and turning his back on Zhaozhou, looks to the city. He does not understand that the gates all face each other and are always open. Nothing is excluded.

CAPPING VERSE

North of the capital,
    south of the capital.
The peaceful dwelling is not
    a place of yin and yang.

NOTES

1. It's really difficult to pin it down; still, it's also difficult to miss it.
2. There is not much more that can be said without being misleading.
3. What else is there?
4. His tongue has fallen to the ground. Why is he being so kind to this monastic?

47 ∾
Guishan's "Do Not Betray Others"

MAIN CASE

One day after sitting Guishan pointed at the straw sandals and said to Yangshan, "All hours of the day, we receive people's support. Don't betray them."[1]

    Yangshan said, "Long ago in Sudatta's garden, the Buddha expounded just this."[2]

    Guishan said, "That's not enough. Say more."[3]

    Yangshan said, "When it is cold, to wear socks for others is not prohibited."[4]

COMMENTARY

Old masters throughout time have always tended to the guiding and aiding of all living beings. They set up their shops according to their capacities and in response to the imperative of time, place, position, and degree. Appearing and disappearing in harmony with the occasion, they create countless kinds of expedient means to alleviate suffering.

Guishan wants everyone to know, so he stirs things up by saying, "All hours of the day, we receive people's support. Don't betray them." Yangshan is an adept and cannot help but respond. Guishan's intention, however, is unfathomable—he wants more. Without hesitation Yangshan again rises to meet the old man's challenge. But say, what is Yangshan's meaning?

We should understand that "to wear socks for others" is a very personal matter. It is the seamless dharma activity that is the ten thousand hands and eyes of great compassion itself. It is the spiritual light of the four virtues of a bodhisattva manifesting in the ten directions. But tell me, right now, how do you manifest it in your life?

CAPPING VERSE

Pure jeweled eyes, virtuous arms—
    formless and selfless, they enter the fray.
The great function works in all ways—
    these hands and eyes are the whole thing.

NOTES

1. This is pertinent. He wants the whole world to know about it.
2. When the wind blows, the grasses bend.
3. What can he say? It simply can't be explained.
4. Very intimate, but what does it mean?

48 ∿
Xuansha's Blank Letter

MAIN CASE

Xuansha one day sent a monastic to deliver a letter to Xuefeng. Xuefeng received the monastic while he was teaching, opened the letter, and found a blank piece of paper. He showed it to the assembly and said, "Do you understand this?"[1]

After a while he said, "Can't you see what he says? Virtuous persons have the same understanding, even though they are one thousand li apart."[2]

The monastic went back and reported this to Xuansha.

Xuansha said, "The old man on the mountain passed by me without knowing it."[3]

COMMENTARY

Only the clear-eyed can recognize the fishing line when they see it. Only adepts can handle devices outside of patterns. Xuansha's relationship with Xuefeng was like that of older and younger brothers. They where always testing and polishing each other.

When Xuefeng holds up the blank piece of paper and says "Do you understand this?" he is creating a forest of brambles to see who will have the skill to pass through it. Teachers of our school have always used the forest of brambles to test people. If they just relied on ordinary words and phrases to test, they would not be able to see where people are sticking.

What do you see in the blank paper? A piece of paper, blank paper, no message, empty, inexpressible, wordless? These are all concepts. Is there something beyond concepts that Xuefeng is trying to communicate? And if so, what is it? He says, "Virtuous persons have the same understanding, even though they are one thousand li apart." Understanding of what?

Xuansha says, "The old man on the mountain passed by me without knowing it." Is he agreeing or disagreeing with his old teacher?

CAPPING VERSE

If you can see reality outside of patterns
    and embody the truth that cannot be taught,
    you enter the valley of the endless spring
    riding the ox backward.

NOTES

1. The hook is baited, the line is in the water.
2. Since they are both from the same household, they know the contents of the pantry well.
3. One thousand li away the bait is taken.

49 ∾
Dongshan's "Top of the Mountain"

MAIN CASE

Dongshan Liangjie asked a visiting monastic, "Where have you been?"[1]

The monastic said, "I have visited a mountain."[2]

Dongshan said, "Did you get to the top of the mountain?"[3]

The monastic said, "Yes, I did."[4]

Dongshan said, "Was there anyone on top of the mountain?"[5]

The monastic said, "There was no one there."[6]

Dongshan said, "You did not get to the top of the mountain."[7]

The monastic said, "If I hadn't, how would I know that there was no one there?"[8]

Dongshan said, "Reverend, why don't you stay here for a while?"[9]

The monastic said, "It's not that I mind staying. It's just that there is someone in India who may not approve it."[10]

Dongshan said, "I have my suspicions about this fellow."[11]

COMMENTARY

The monastic had personally come from the mountain. Why then did Dongshan say, "You have not been to the mountain?"

When reason is exhausted and all permutations and considerations are set aside, there is only the cold autumn moon illuminating the valley below. What can this possibly be compared to?

CAPPING VERSE

The Cold Mountain hermit
    forgot the way he had come.
Deaf, dumb, and blind,
    he found his resting place.

NOTES

1. He wants to know this monastic's state of mind.
2. Honesty is always the best policy.

3. Dongshan digs deeper.
4. What is he saying?
5. This conversation in the weeds needs to come to a conclusion.
6. Is he being truthful or is he blind?
7. The old master is like a hammerhead shark—he just won't let him go.
8. This makes sense, but does it reveal insight?
9. Dongshan is being very talkative. He should be careful of his eyebrows.
10. What is he saying?
11. I have my suspicions too.

50 ⁖

Shilou's Shortcomings

MAIN CASE

Shilou was once asked by a monastic, "I don't know the original nature yet.[1] Master, please show me by skillful means."[2]

Shilou said, "I don't have earlobes [I have no ear to hear you]."[3]
The monastic said, "I know I have shortcomings."[4]
Shilou said, "This old monastic has faults too."[5]
The monastic said, "What are your faults?"
Shilou said, "My fault lies in your shortcomings."[6]
The monastic bowed.[7]
Shilou hit him.[8]

COMMENTARY

Fundamentally there is no difference between buddhas and sentient beings. The ten thousand things and your self—how could there be any distinction? Why are there so many complications?

It has always been the tradition in our school that when a question is asked, the answer is immediately manifest. Why doesn't the monastic get it?

Old Shilou's compassion is boundless: he cooks the meal, serves the meal, spoons the food into the monastic's mouth, and even washes the bowls and clears the table. Yet the monastic has no idea that he has been to a fine dharma banquet. Why then does he bow? Why does Shilou hit him?

CAPPING VERSE

Where can we put this gigantic body?
There is no place to put it.
Ultimately, how is it?
When clouds gather on the mountain,
     thunder fills the valley.

NOTES

  1. He will never know it.
  2. Sitting in the pantry, he is dying of starvation.
  3. Not only is he deaf, but he is blind as well.
  4. This monastic is deaf too, but it is a different kind of deafness.
  5. Why is he being so kind? This monastic is sure to misunderstand.
  6. Having swallowed the whole universe, he can't evade the responsibility.
  7. He misunderstood.
  8. He was forced to act in accord with the imperative.

51 ॐ

Niutou and the Fourth Ancestor

MAIN CASE

Nanquan [Wang] was once asked by a monastic, "Before Niutou Farong met the Fourth Ancestor, why did hundreds of birds hold flowers in their beaks and offer them to him?"[1]
    Nanquan said, "With each step, Niutou climbed the buddha ladder."[2]
    The monastic said, "Why didn't the birds offer flowers after Niutou met the Fourth Ancestor?"[3]
    Nanquan said, "Even if he had not climbed the buddha ladder, he's still on Master Wang's single road."[4]

COMMENTARY

When Niutou sat in meditation in a rock grotto on Mount Niutou, hundreds of birds with flowers in their beaks came to pay homage to him.

Although he was following the Buddha Way step by step, he had not as yet eliminated constructional thought and discrimination.

Haven't you heard that when the goddess of the house of Vimalakīrti showered the great disciples and bodhisattvas of the Buddha with heavenly flowers, the flowers fell off the bodies of the bodhisattvas but stuck to the bodies of the great disciples?

There are no three worlds to cast off. There is no bodhi that can be attained, no need to practice cleansing austerities. Simply live a life free of desire, with a mind that is without anger, or anxiety—a mind completely at ease and without hindrance.

CAPPING VERSE

Realization of the source
   is realization of the tributaries.
Realization of the tributaries
   is realization of the source.
Seeing the connecting link
   is seeing the Way.

NOTES

1. With each step the pure wind arises.
2. Though hidden on a solitary mountain, he radiates celestial signs.
3. He is somewhere on this mountain, but his exact whereabouts are unknown.
4. Wang's road is vast and boundless, not a particle of dust is excluded.

52 ∽
Sansheng's "Golden Fish"

MAIN CASE

Sansheng asked[1] Xuefeng, "What does a golden-scaled fish that goes through the net eat?"[2]

Xuefeng said, "I will tell you after you come out of the net."[3]

Sansheng said, "The teacher of fifteen thousand monastics—and you can't say a turning word."[4]

Xuefeng said, "This old man is busy with abbot's matters."[5]

COMMENTARY

The net is elusive. It appears and disappears. It creates edges that are non-existent. The golden-scaled fish is inherently free in every way when it knows it is in the net. Be that as it may, the golden fish that has passed through the net clearly does not eat ordinary food. What is its food?

Sansheng is a distinguished adept. Why does Xuefeng say, "I will tell you after you come out of the net?" Although Sansheng knows how to turn the spear around, old Xuefeng remains poisonous. Can it be said that these two have passed through the net, or are they just harmonizing in delusion?

CAPPING VERSE

The old mountain pond,
    crystal clear through and through.
The solitary carp swimming by
    flourishes its tail and stirs up the bottom.

NOTES

1. This is not a casual Zen pilgrim; he is an adept to be reckoned with.
2. Neither the questioner nor the question should be taken lightly. There is something going on here.
3. The old man is not impressed; he doesn't hesitate to diminish his reputation.
4. The dragon's roar has an echo to it.
5. Lightning flashes, the pure wind blows, and when the dust finally settles, it's clear that this has been a meeting of adepts.

53 ∾
Shitou's "Great and Small Canon"

MAIN CASE

Qingyuan said to Shitou, "Everyone is saying that there is something happening in Caoxi."[1]

Shitou said, "There is someone who doesn't say something is happening in Caoxi."[2]

Qingyuan said, "How did you get the Great Canon and the Small Canon?"[3]

Shitou said, "It all comes from here and nothing is lacking."[4]

COMMENTARY

The Great Canon and Small Canon are written in the typefaces of holding up the flower and taking down the banner. They are expounded by the sound of rock and water. They are manifested by the six realms—by the long and the short, the high and the low, the sentient and the insentient. Each in its own language and expression manifests the timeless truth of the universe.

If you can see into this kōan, you will realize that the truth of Caoxi has never been transmitted nor received; it is not in the realm of understanding nor believing, for it is the wisdom that has no teacher. Therefore, you should avoid running around in the midst of sound and form, and searching in seeing and hearing. Take the backward step and simply see that the truth of Caoxi has always been inherent in one's self.

CAPPING VERSE

Breathing in, the whole universe is swallowed.
Breathing out, the ten thousand dharmas are manifested.
A hundred thousand scriptures
    ceaselessly proclaiming the truth.

NOTES

1. How did he get the news? It's a hundred thousand miles away and there is no relationship whatsoever between them.
2. Now, here is a live one. It's difficult to impress a member of the household.
3. It's easy to talk about it, but has he seen something? Shitou needs to find out.
4. The waves of Caoxi always correspond to the weather conditions.

54 ∾
Baizhang's Second Visit to Mazu

MAIN CASE

Zen master Huaihai of Baizhang went back to study with Mazu.[1] Mazu held up a whisk.[2]

Baizhang said, "Does it stay with its function, or does it go beyond its function?"[3]

Mazu hung the whisk back where it had been.[4] Baizhang stood there for a while.[5]

Mazu said, "How can you guide people by flapping the lips?"[6]

Baizhang took the whisk and held it up.[7]

Mazu said, "Does it stay with its function or does it go beyond its function?"[8]

Baizhang hung the whisk back where it had been.[9]

Mazu shouted.[10]

Baizhang told Huangbo later, "Some time ago I was yelled at by Mazu. It made me deaf for three days."[11]

COMMENTARY

For twenty years Baizhang served as Mazu's attendant, and although he was pierced by Mazu's arrow in their encounter with the wild geese, it was not until this second visit to the great master Mazu that the arrow finally killed him.

Baizhang not only went deaf for three days but was deaf, dumb, and blind for the remainder of his life. When the great function appears, it does not keep to any fixed standards. Sometimes a phrase cuts off the tongues of everyone on earth, and sometimes it simply follows the waves and the current.

CAPPING VERSE

The earthshaking thunderclap
    still resounds in these mountains and valleys.
Baizhang's impairment has nourished countless generations
    of Zen practitioners throughout the world.

NOTES

1. I wonder what it was that brought him back?
2. It covers the sun, the moon, and the great earth itself.
3. What is he saying?
4. Do you understand?
5. He seems to have lost his tongue.
6. Mud and water is streaming off him. Why doesn't he just drive him out?
7. He really wants to show some life.
8. Using the same pitfall, he draws Baizhang in.
9. Careful here. After all, if all the waves of Caoxi were the same, people would drown on dry land.
10. Lightning flashes, thunder crashes, and the sun vanishes from the sky.
11. But say, what does all of this mean?

55 ❧
Dongshan's "Dharma Bodies"

MAIN CASE

Dongshan Liangjie was once asked by a monastic, "Among the three buddha bodies, which one expounds the dharma?"[1]
    Dongshan said, "I am always intimate with this."[2]

Later a monastic asked Caoshan, "Dongshan said, 'I am always intimate with this.' What does it mean?"[3]

Caoshan said, "If you need a head, chop my head off and take it with you."[4]

Also, a monastic asked Xuefeng about this. Xuefeng suddenly hit the monastic with his staff[5] and said, "I have also been to Dongshan."[6]

COMMENTARY

This monastic questioning Dongshan wants to break up the truth of the universe into fragments and segments. The old master holds up intimacy for him to see. Later this became a sticking point for Zen monastics all over China. Caoshan offers his head to make the same point, but it does not seem to settle the matter. Another monastic, bringing it up with Xuefeng, feels the sting of his staff.

Dongshan plays a tune that few can hear; Caoshan hearing it knows how to dance to it, and Xuefeng, seeing it all come down, claps out the beat. Can you hear them? Although it's in three-part harmony, it is in reality just one thing. See into it here and you too will be able to join in and make it a quartet.

CAPPING VERSE

The old master's intimacy is indeed touching.
But until you know the skin of your own face,
    you will never know it,
    and yet, you cannot avoid it.

NOTES

1. Show me one of the three bodies and I will tell you.
2. What is *this*? Is it one, two, or three?
3. You have come to the wrong place to find a meaning.
4. Which part expounds the dharma, the head or the body?
5. Finally, all the extra is stripped away. You can always count on Xuefeng to get to the heart of the matter.
6. In the heat of the kitchen he obtained Dongshan's dharma.

56 ∾
Guishan's Gift

MAIN CASE

Guishan said to Yangshan, "I have a lay student who gave me three rolls of silk to buy a temple bell in order to bestow happiness upon the people of the world."[1]

Yangshan said, "When the lay student brought you the silk for the temple bell, what did you give him in return?"[2]

Guishan hit the sitting platform three times and said, "This was my offering."[3]

Yangshan said, "If you offered him that, how will it benefit him?"[4]

Guishan again hit the platform three times and said, "Why is it that you dislike this?"[5]

Yangshan said, "It's not that I dislike it. It's just that the gift belongs to everyone."[6]

Guishan said, "Since you know that it belongs to everyone, why did you want me to repay him?"[7]

Yangshan said, "I just wondered how you understood that since it belonged to everyone, you could still make it a gift."[8]

Guishan said, "Don't you see? The great master Bodhidharma, who came to this land from India, also brought a gift.[9] We are always receiving gifts from others."[10]

COMMENTARY

Giving and receiving are nondual. Self and other are nondual. When the Way is surrendered to the Way, you enter the Way. In enlightenment, the Way invariably comes through itself. The self gives itself for the sake of giving the self; it is purposeless. Other gives the other for the sake of giving the other; there is no intention. Spiritual teachings and material wealth are also nondual.

The practices of giving as well as receiving should always be in accord with need and the imperative of time, place, position, and degree. To build a bridge, cook a meal, or make an offering is the practice of giving. Loving a mountain, eating a meal, or receiving an offering is the practice of receiving.

When such actions are without design, both giver and receiver are united in a single indivisible thusness.

CAPPING VERSE

The great earth innocently
    nurtures the flowers of spring.
Birds trust freely
    the strength of the wind.
All of this derives from the power of giving,
    as does the self, coming into being.

NOTES

1. He wants to benefit all sentient beings.
2. This is not a casual question; he is testing his old master.
3. The sound is still resounding centuries later.
4. This one has no intention of settling easily. If you want to know the forest path, you must walk the forest path.
5. They drag each other into the fire pit.
6. Indeed! How will the old master leap clear of this?
7. When he is pushed, he immediately turns the spear around and comes back with it.
8. Only an adept could stand his ground like this. He is a lion cub after all.
9. Yes, but wasn't it always there?
10. Heaven is filled by it; earth is covered by it. The hand that gives is also the hand that receives.

57 ॐ

Where Wisdom Cannot Reach

MAIN CASE

Zen master Zongzhi [Yuanzhi] of Mount Daowu left Yaoshan and went to visit Nanquan. Nanquan said, "Reverend, what is your name?"[1]

Daowu said, "Zongzhi [source wisdom]."²

Nanquan said, "Where wisdom does not reach, what do you make of the source?"

Daowu said, "I would rather not speak."³

Nanquan said, "Bright and clear; but if you speak of it, horns will emerge."⁴

Three days later, Daowu was in the washroom, sewing with Yunyan. Passing by, Nanquan saw him and said, "The other day you said that you would rather not say it. And I said, 'If you say it, horns will emerge.' How then do you practice?"⁵

Daowu left and entered the monastics' hall.⁶ Then Nanquan went away. Daowu came back and sat down.

Yunyan said, "Senior brother, why didn't you answer the master?"⁷

Daowu said, "How come you are so brilliant?"⁸

Yunyan did not press further. He went to [see] Nanquan and said, "[About the question of the other day], why did Ascetic Zhi [Daowu] not answer you?"⁹

Nanquan said, "He practices among other types of beings."¹⁰

Yunyan said, "What is practicing among other types of beings?"¹¹

Nanquan said, "Don't you see what was said? 'Where wisdom does not reach.' 'I prefer not to say it.' 'If you say it, then horns will emerge.' Thus you go toward different types of beings."¹²

Yunyan did not understand it. Seeing that Yunyan did not accept it, Nanquan said, "This person does not have a reason to stay here."¹³

Both [Daowu and Yunyan] went back to Yaoshan. Yaoshan saw them return and asked Yunyan, "Where have you been?"

Yunyan said, "I have been with Nanquan."

Yaoshan said, "What did Nanquan say?" Yunyan told him the story.

Yaoshan said, "How did you understand his teaching at that time?"

Yunyan said nothing, and Yaoshan laughed hard.¹⁴ Yunyan said, "What is practicing among other types of beings?"¹⁵

Yaoshan said, "I am tired today. Come back some other time."¹⁶

Yunyan said, "I have come back specifically for this matter."¹⁷

Yaoshan said, "Go away for now."¹⁸ Yunyan left.

Outside the abbot's room, Daowu, overhearing Yaoshan's not confirming Yunyan's understanding, bit his finger to bleeding without noticing. He went back to Yunyan and said, "Junior brother, what did you say to the master [Yaoshan]? How was it?"

Yunyan said, "The master did not answer me."[19] Daowu bowed.[20]

Later, when Daowu and Yunyan were with Yaoshan, Yaoshan said, "Where wisdom does not reach, you prefer not to say. If you say it, horns will emerge."[21]

Daowu thanked him and went away.[22]

Yunyan finally asked Yaoshan, "Why did [my] senior brother Zhi [Daowu] not answer you?"[23]

Yaoshan said, "I have a backache today.[24] Daowu understands this matter. Go and ask him."[25]

Yunyan went [to Daowu] and said, "Senior brother, why did you not answer the master?"[26]

Daowu said, "I have a headache. Go and ask the master."[27]

Later, before passing away, Yunyan sent his last words to Daowu.[28] Daowu read them and said, "I did not know that Yunyan had it.[29] I regret that I did not say it to him at that time. Even so, he was still an heir of Yaoshan."[30]

COMMENTARY

Although Yunyan studied with Daowu for twenty years and then visited many other eminent Zen masters, it was not until he studied with Yaoshan that circumstances ripened and he attained clarity. At this point, however, he seems to continually fall short of seeing it. Daowu seems clear enough to avoid falling into explanations. Yunyan seems not to know what is going on. Is it that Yunyan is deluded, or is he clever enough to be clumsy? Putting aside Yunyan, and without going to Daowu's words, where wisdom does not reach, how do you understand the source? Furthermore, what is the meaning of "horns emerge" and "practicing among other types of being"? If you wish to see the wisdom that has never been spoken, you must first move beyond the permutations of assertion and denial, and let your tongue fall to the ground.

CAPPING VERSE

Before the kalpa of emptiness,
    one complete circle.
Even the yellow-faced old master never understood it.
How then, can we speak of transmitting it?

NOTES

1. Although he asks about his name, this is not what he's really after.
2. Ungraspable, truly ungraspable.
3. This is no ordinary monastic; he knows better.
4. Three feet long on either side of the head.
5. Since he couldn't get him the first time, he's trying a second time.
6. After all, this seems reasonable.
7. What? What is he saying?
8. There's a knife in his words.
9. He makes up for his dullness with persistence.
10. He seems to be using his power to mystify this poor monastic.
11. This one is not easily satisfied.
12. I think I see horns sprouting right now.
13. Let him chew on it for a few more years.
14. What is the meaning of Yunyan's silence and Yaoshan's laugh?
15. He really wants to know.
16. Thank you for your teaching.
17. He has missed it again.
18. When the bell is rung, it is not necessarily dismissive; it is just an opportunity to reflect.
19. You should be grateful.
20. He is grateful.
21. How fresh! How new!
22. What else could he do?
23. Is he a divine fool, or is he just dull?
24. The teacher is as persistent as the student.
25. Thank you for your answer.
26. The entire lineage seems to suffer from the same sickness.
27. Say, how long can this go on? It seems like a different tack is called for.
28. Right down to his last moments he has something to say.
29. Had what? What did the note say that made him speak like this?
30. Tell me, what is it that made him an heir of Yaoshan?

58 ⌒

Shishuang's "Nothing Is Concealed"

MAIN CASE

Zen master Qingzhu of Mount Shishuang [Puhui] was once asked by a monastic, "It is heard three thousand li away that Shishuang has 'this not turning back to look.'"[1]

Shishuang said, "Right."[2]

The monastic said, "Myriad things are evident.[3] Do you reflect or not reflect on this?"[4]

Shishuang said, "If I answer, it won't startle the assembly."[5]

The monastic said, "Not startling the assembly does not accommodate the myriad things.[6] How is it when there is no reflection?"[7]

Shishuang said, "Nothing is concealed in the entire universe."[8]

COMMENTARY

Nothing hidden in the entire universe means that all things exist thus; it means that the ten thousand entities are self-evident. Therefore, all reflection always takes place here and now. Because of this, true reflection is not connected with the subject that reflects or with the object of reflection; it is rather the unity of the subject-object duality in an instant of time. It is simply reflection, here and now. Do you see?

The monastic's question, "Do you reflect or not reflect?" is a tiger trap, so Shishuang says, "If I answer, it won't startle the assembly." When the monastic's question finally becomes pointed, Shishuang says, "Nothing is concealed in the entire universe."

CAPPING VERSE

When views and comparisons are at last set aside,
    the forest of patterns is no longer hidden
    and the myriad forms are clearly evident.

NOTES

1. There is such a thing, you know.
2. An honest person is hard to find.
3. Where did he get the news?
4. What would he have the master reflect on?
5. Even your not answering is not so startling.
6. True.
7. Ah! So here is the question.
8. Sweet fragrance fills the air.

59 ∾
Huineng Doesn't Understand

MAIN CASE

Zen master Dajian Huineng of Mount Caoxi was once asked by a monastic, "Who has grasped the significance of Huangmei [the Fifth Ancestor, Daman Hongren]?"[1]
    Huineng said, "Those who understand the Buddhadharma have it."[2]
    The monastic said, "Do you have it, Master?"[3]
    Huineng said, "No, I do not have it."[4]
    The monastic said, "How come you don't have it?"[5]
    Huineng said, "Because I don't understand the Buddhadharma."[6]

COMMENTARY

In understanding, just understand clearly without settling down in understanding. In not understanding, just don't know without attaching to not knowing.
    The Buddhadharma is beyond knowing and not knowing. Knowing is being caught up in the words and ideas that describe reality; not knowing is blank consciousness. The reality of things cannot be found in either extreme.

CAPPING VERSE

The illiterate woodcutter from the south
    still doesn't understand.
It's not that there is no such thing;
    it's just that it cannot be grasped.

NOTES

1. This fellow is playing with shadows. Once you grasp it, what do you have?
2. What is he saying? Planting grass seeds doesn't produce cabbages.
3. Suddenly they are both up to their nostrils in foul water.
4. He pleads his innocence, but it's embarrassing that it's come this far.
5. He wants to know. He hasn't realized yet that the ground beneath his feet is about to disappear.
6. Even the yellow-faced old barbarian didn't understand.

60 ॐ
Xuansha's Seamless Stūpa

MAIN CASE

When Xuansha traveled with Xuefeng, Xuefeng pointed at the ground in front of him and said, "This piece of field may be suited for building a seamless stūpa."[1]

Xuansha said, "How high should it be?"[2]

Xuefeng looked up and down.[3]

Xuansha said, "It's not that you don't have a good influence on humans and devas. It's just that you have not even dreamed of the Buddha's affirmation of the attainment of Buddhahood on Vulture Peak."[4]

Xuefeng said, "How would you say it?"[5]

Xuansha said, "Seven or eight feet."[6]

COMMENTARY

The point of this encounter is not whether Xuefeng's answer is wrong or Xuansha's answer is right. Rather, it is about the affirmation of Mahā-kāśyapa by the Buddha. In the affirmation of Mahākāśyapa, all sentient beings are affirmed in their suchness. Thus dragons and snakes, sages and fools, you and I, are all affirmed at once.

Xuefeng's looking at the height of the stūpa is not what is affirmed by the Buddha. What is affirmed is not merely symbolic but, rather, an expression of the truth of suchness. Xuansha's "seven or eight feet" is an affirmation of and by this very moment.

CAPPING VERSE

The seamless stūpa fills all of space—
    nothing is hidden.
Vast and boundless, without edges—
    the truth is affirmed, generation after generation.

NOTES

1. Without a seam or all seams—either way is OK.
2. He wants to test his teacher.
3. How big is up and down?
4. After all, Xuefeng never really got the last word of Zen.
5. He wants the child to take up the parent's work.
6. This seems pretty specific; what does he have in mind?

61 ∾

Guishan's "Exploring Spiritual Powers"

MAIN CASE

One day Guishan was lying down[1] when his student Yangshan Huiji came in.[2] Guishan turned over and lay facing the wall.[3]

Yangshan said, "I am your student. You don't need to be formal."[4]
Guishan sat up[5] and Yangshan started to leave.[6]
Guishan called Yangshan, "Huiji."[7]
Yangshan turned his head.[8]
Guishan said, "Listen to this old monastic's dream."[9]
Yangshan lowered his head and was ready to listen.[10]
Guishan just said, "Interpret my dream for me. Let me see how you do it."[11] Yangshan brought a basin of water and a towel.[12] Guishan washed his face and became seated.[13]

Then Xiangyan came in.[14]

Guishan said, "I have been having a mystical communication with Huiji. It's no small thing."[15]
Xiangyan said, "I overheard you."[16]
Guishan said, "Now you try it and I will see."[17]
Xiangyan made a bowl of tea and brought it to him.[18]

Guishan sighed and praised them, saying, "You two students surpass even Śāriputra and Maudgalyāyana!"[19]

COMMENTARY

Cooking a meal and washing the dishes are none other than the activity of the marvelous mind of nirvāṇa. Stacking cordwood and building a spring-house are in themselves the exquisite teachings of formless form. This very body is the all-pervading true dharma body.

Since these are the activities of everyone on this great earth, why is it that there is so much pain and suffering, so much greed, anger, and igno-rance? Why can't everyone emanate light and move heaven and earth?

If we can see, hear, and realize the spiritual power in these activities, we have realized the truth of the Tathāgata.

CAPPING VERSE

Unifying the myriad reflections,
    one's own light is without hindrance.
Opened up, the ground of being
    ceaselessly meets itself.
Realizing wisdom, manifesting compassion—
    how many have this kind of spiritual power?

NOTES

1. Like a lioness with a cave full of cubs.
2. He takes off his slippers and marches right up to the old man.
3. *Grrrr.* A deep-throated growl is not to be mistaken as a purr.
4. Lip pulled back, nose curled, still he pulls the lioness's whiskers.
5. It doesn't pay to let him go.
6. After all, he's from the same pride of golden-haired ones.
7. What good is a patched-robed monastic who is pushed here and there by circumstances?
8. Free to ride the clouds and follow the wind.
9. A lioness hunts this way. She circles her prey, pretends to walk away, then strikes like a bolt of lightning.
10. Being well-trained himself, he stalks stiff-legged, neck extended, eyes like slits.
11. Fang and claw unsheathed. Who can deal with this? Still, mud pies are mud pies.
12. Ten thousand foaming billows wash the heavens.
13. There must be more mischief afoot. A hungry lioness is not easily satiated.
14. A crowd begins to gather.
15. He wants to drag the whole saṃgha into the mud pit with him.
16. An adept should know. The three of them eat the same bread, drink the same water. Guishan stubs his toe, Yangshan yells in pain, and Xiangyan rubs his foot.
17. He can't let him go. He might have misunderstood.
18. Ten thousand foaming billows wash the heavens.
19. I've given you all I have, yet you haven't received anything.

62 ∾

Dongshan's "Disclosing Mind, Disclosing Nature"

MAIN CASE

Zen master Sengmi of Shenshan was traveling with his dharma brother Dongshan Liangjie.

Dongshan pointed to a temple on the roadside and said, "In that temple is a person who discloses the mind and discloses the buddha nature."[1]

Shenshan said, "Who is it?"[2]

Dongshan said, "Someone who has just achieved complete death as you asked."[3]

Shenshan said, "Who discloses the mind and discloses the [buddha] nature?"[4]

Dongshan said, "Someone who has achieved life in death."[5]

COMMENTARY

The teaching of eliminating the mind and eliminating the nature has been transmitted generation to generation from Śākyamuni Buddha down to the present time. It is the holding up of the flower on Vulture Peak and Mahā-kāśyapa's smile. It is the Sixth Ancestor's shaking the sieve and Dōgen's falling away of body and mind. The mountain's form and the river's sound are none other than disclosing the mind, disclosing the buddha nature.

When mind appears, the whole universe appears. When mind disappears, the whole universe disappears. The truth of this teaching is not to be found in mind, no-mind, buddha nature, or in things. If you can see into it here, you will understand that even the buddhas and the ancestors have not attained it.

CAPPING VERSE

Though we may speak of it, it cannot be conveyed;
    try to picture it, yet it cannot be seen.
When the universe collapses, "it" is indestructible.

NOTES

1. Although this is common enough, it is rarely understood.
2. Having asked, it turns out there is only one exit.
3. The blind man wants to drag his companion into it.
4. He obliges, how nice. But say, where is all of this leading?
5. This fellow likes to create complications. But tell me, what does he really mean?

63 ᖰ
Baofu's "Point of Attainment"

MAIN CASE

Zen master Qinghuo of Baofu Monastery was studying with Shuilong. One day Master Shuilong asked him, "Which teachers have you seen? And did you experience enlightenment?"[1]

Baofu said, "I once visited Dazhang Qiru and attained certainty."[2]

Shuilong then went up to the dharma hall, called the assembly together, and said, "Reverend Baofu, come out, face the assembly, burn incense, and speak about your point of attainment. This old monastic will verify it for you."[3]

Baofu took up the incense and said, "The incense has already been offered.[4] Enlightenment is no other than no-enlightenment."[5]

Shuilong was delighted and approved him.[6]

COMMENTARY

Zen practitioners these days inevitably misunderstand this kōan and as a result, end up making a nest in the secondary. Haven't you heard Yangshan's saying, "It's not that there is no enlightenment, but how can we deal with falling into the secondary?"

Although Shuilong rejoices and approves Baofu, what is he approving? You should understand that when the ten thousand things fully come home to the self, the last vestige of enlightenment vanishes. It is this traceless enlightenment that ceaselessly unfolds. But before you can step off the top of a hundred-foot pole, you must first ascend the pole.

CAPPING VERSE

The truth of the universe is intimately perfect
    and inconceivably subtle.
How can it be spoken of in terms
    of delusion and enlightenment?

NOTES

1. This is sure to raise a stink of Zen that even the spring's fragrance will not be able to cover.
2. Although he has climbed out of the cesspool, he doesn't seem to notice that he is still covered with shit.
3. It would be impossible for a master of our school not to act on this.
4. What is he saying?
5. Although this is so, it is nonetheless misleading. He seems to know too much. Too bad.
6. *Bah!* They are both covered in mud, and now the whole assembly has been dragged into it.

64 ∽

Nanquan's "Content and Container"

MAIN CASE

One day Nanquan saw Deng Yinfeng of Mount Wutai coming. Nanquan pointed to a water jar and said to Yinfeng, "The jar is the container. There is water in the jar.[1] Bring the water to this old monastic without moving the container."[2]

Yinfeng took the jar and poured the water in front of Nanquan.[3]

Nanquan shut up.[4]

COMMENTARY

Since they are from the same household, Nanquan, seeing Yinfeng coming, wants to see if the waters are deep or shallow. He says, "Bring the water without moving [disturbing] the container [circumstances]." Knowing fully the nondual nature of content and container, Yinfeng takes up the jar and pours the water in front of Nanquan.

We should understand that in the reality of circumstances (container) there is water, and in the reality of water there are circumstances (container). Since they are not two, neither water nor circumstances are disturbed.

Individual and community, entity and surroundings, practitioner and saṃgha, organism and environment, subject and object, watershed and inhabitants, are likewise a single interdependent reality. What transpires for the least significant member transpires at once for the whole.

CAPPING VERSE

It has been spoken for us—
　　the time of light and dark, hand in hand.
North, south, east, west;
　　let us return to the deep river
　　in its journey to the great ocean.

NOTES

1. He seems to be weaving a tight net to catch a big fish.
2. What is he saying? He's just calling daddy "poppa."
3. But of course. Since it's all dirt from the same hole, what else did you expect?
4. He got it. But the question is, do you get it?

65 ∾
Guizong's "One-Flavor Zen"

MAIN CASE

A monastic bid farewell to Guizong Zhichang.
　　Guizong said to him, "Where are you going?"[1]
　　The monastic said, "I am going to many places to study the five-flavor Zen."[2]
　　Guizong said, "There is one-flavor Zen in my place."[3]
　　The monastic said, "What is your one-flavor Zen?"[4]
　　Guizong hit him.[5]

COMMENTARY

Guizong is being much too kind to this monastic. Dazzled by the promise of something new or esoteric, the monastic is prepared to go off searching for a head to place on top of his own. There are times when even the teachings can be misleading. Each and every one must directly realize the source outside the teachings. The principle cannot be grasped within words and ideas.

Guizong wants to show this directly—he lowers a hook to fish out a question. The monastic, greedy for the bait, climbs onto the hook, saying, "What is your one-flavor Zen?" Guizong follows the imperative and hits him. Clearly, there is no other truth. Can you see it?

CAPPING VERSE

The Great Way is vast and all-pervading—
    if you direct yourself toward it, you move away from it.
For the mind unified with the Way,
    all striving ceases.

NOTES

1. Teachers have always been concerned with students' coming and going.
2. He will just wear out his sandals searching for something that does not exist.
3. The old master sees a cage, so he builds a cage.
4. The monastic walks right into it and closes the door behind him.
5. This is as it should be. The monastic should be grateful.

66 ∾

Yaoshan's "Birth of a Calf"

MAIN CASE

One night at the monastics' hall of Zen master Weiyan of Yaoshan [Hongdao] there was no lamp.[1] The master said to the assembly, "I have a single phrase.[2] When the iron ox gives birth to a calf, then I'll tell you."[3]

A monastic in the assembly came forth and said, "An iron ox has just given birth to a calf.[4] Still, you haven't said it."[5]

Yaoshan said, "Light the lamp."[6]

The monastic returned to his seat.[7]

COMMENTARY

It is said that Master Yaoshan's saṃgha was small and so poor that at times they didn't have oil for the lamps. In the darkness of the hall, the old master offers to give a turning phrase to anyone with an eye to see it. The monastic who comes forward is indeed unusual, but why does he show himself? Yaoshan has no choice but to carry out the imperative, so he says, "Light the lamp." Tell me, what is the meaning of the monastic's returning to his seat? Does he understand the old master? If you can see into it clearly, then tell me, how do you light the lamp?

CAPPING VERSE

The light illuminates the whole universe—
    nothing is hidden.
Following the winding road,
    you ride the iron ox home.

NOTES

1. In the middle of the night it is hard to distinguish this from that.
2. He's already dripping with mud and now he wants to drag the whole saṃgha into it.
3. Extraordinary, inconceivable! How can it be expressed?
4. He appears to have awakened in the dark.
5. Would you hear it if it were said?
6. After all, if you're going to make your way, you will need some light.
7. Did he get it?

67 ∾
Zhaozhou's "Wash Your Bowls"

MAIN CASE

Zhaozhou was once asked by a monastic, "I have just entered the monastery for the first time.[1] Please teach me, Master."[2]
    Zhaozhou said, "Have you eaten the morning meal?"[3]

The monastic said, "Yes, I have."[4]
Zhaozhou said, "Then wash your bowls."[5]
The monastic immediately had realization.[6]

COMMENTARY

If your potential does not leave its fixed position, you will sink on dry land. The moment there is affirmation and denial, the mind is lost in confusion and you fall into grades and stages.

Old Zhaozhou knows how to see through this patch-robed monastic. In one word, one phrase, one encounter, one response, he can see whether the monastic is deep or shallow. Then, with a single phrase, he snatches it all away.

But say, what is it that Zhaozhou snatched away? Moreover, what is it that the monastic realized?

CAPPING VERSE

When the dharma has not yet filled our body and mind,
    we think we've had enough.
When the dharma fills our body and mind,
    we realize something is missing.

NOTES

1. Stop looking and searching. It's not out there.
2. Just shut up and sit!
3. Are you really hungry, or are you just curious about the menu?
4. Curious about the menu, this one thinks he has a bellyful.
5. Step by step, each one follows the other.
6. Each action emits its own light. Then throw it away!

68 ∾
Yangshan Plants His Hoe

MAIN CASE

Yangshan was asked by Guishan, "Where have you been?"[1]
  Yangshan said, "In the midst of the rice fields."[2]
  Guishan said, "How many people were there in the rice fields?"[3]
  Yangshan held his hoe in folded hands and kept standing.[4]
  Guishan said, "Nowadays there are many people weeding here in South Mountain."[5]
  Yangshan walked away, dragging the hoe.[6]

COMMENTARY

Parent and child perform a dharma dance to blaze the trail for later generations. But how many will understand, and how many will make a nest here? It is said that the family style for the Guiyang school has set a standard for many generations of practitioners. How can we not be grateful? Bringing up the real and the conventional together, they complement each other's actions. Gathering up and rolling out, they settle the matter. But say, what is the meaning of Yangshan's walking away, dragging his hoe?

CAPPING VERSE

Beyond stages, transcending expedient means,
    mind to mind in accord.
When the mile-high weeds wither,
    the boundless horizon appears.

NOTES

1. His disciple is carrying a hoe. Can it be that he doesn't know where he's coming from?
2. He doesn't avoid dealing with the old man.

3. Acres and acres of rice.
4. Why doesn't he say something?
5. Following the winding road, they ultimately end up face-to-face.
6. This is the most difficult point of all to handle. Look! It has horns, so it's not a snake. Look! It has no feet, so it's not a dragon. What is it?

69 ∾
Families Use It Daily

MAIN CASE

Venerable Chen of Longxing Monastery asked a scholar, "What scripture do you specialize in?"[1] The scholar said, "*Yijing* [*I Ching*]."[2]

Chen said, "In the *Yijing* it is said, 'Families use it daily and yet do not understand it.'[3] What is it that they do not understand?"[4]

The scholar said, "They do not understand the Way."[5]

Chen said, "How do you understand the Way?"[6]

The scholar couldn't respond.[7]

Chen said, "Indeed, just as I suspected—no understanding."[8]

COMMENTARY

If you understand the principle, go by the principle. If you have not as yet realized the principle, go by the example. What is the example?

In silence and stillness, you forget all words. Clearly and vividly, the truth appears before you.

When you realize it, the ten thousand things have no boundaries. When you actualize it, the ten thousand things come to life.

CAPPING VERSE

If the eye does not sleep,
    all dreams cease of themselves.
If the mind does not discriminate,
    all things are of one suchness.

NOTES

1. What? What? Go away and I'll pretend I didn't hear you.
2. Wrong!
3. The imperative is set; he must follow through.
4. Throughout heaven and earth there is just this.
5. Wrong!
6. Indeed, how will you jump out of your jar, frog?
7. Is this dullness or is it understanding?
8. With the tender concern of an old grandmother, he takes him out.

70 ∾
Caoshan's "Raising Livestock"

MAIN CASE

Zen master Wenyan of Mount Yunmen [Kuangzhen] asked Caoshan, "What is the practice of a śramaṇa?"[1]
   Caoshan said, "Savoring the seedlings from the temple grounds."[2]
   Yunmen said, "How is it when the seedlings are gone?"[3]
   Caoshan said, "Do you raise livestock?"[4]
   Yunmen said, "Yes, I do."[5]
   Caoshan said, "How do you raise your livestock?"[6]
   Yunmen said, "Wearing a robe and eating a meal. There is nothing difficult about it."[7]
   Caoshan said, "Why didn't you say wearing fur and having horns?"[8]
   Yunmen made a bow.[9]

COMMENTARY

"Wearing a robe, eating a meal." How can this compare to horns three feet long and fur an inch thick all over the body? Yunmen is still polishing the mirror, so old Caoshan brings out Vairocana's seal within a single phrase for him to see.
   These two adepts examine how to raise an ox. Although Yunmen is close, it is not yet intimate. Although Caoshan is intimate, it is still only

eighty percent. From Mahākāśyapa down through the successive generations to the present time, Zen teachers all over the world have always just been naming and describing. That is why it's said that you can only nod to yourself.

CAPPING VERSE

A white buffalo on open ground
    is truly hard to come by.
If you can immediately understand,
    you see it doesn't come from outside.
If you cannot immediately understand,
    you certainly will never recognize it.

NOTES

1. The pilgrim sees the master; the master sees the pilgrim.
2. Where the grass is thick, the grazing is good.
3. I am afraid he has misunderstood.
4. He is willing to clarify the matter.
5. Yunmen is willing to investigate the matter.
6. He sees an opportunity and acts.
7. I am afraid he misunderstands.
8. His kindness is extraordinary; he exposes or transforms in accord with the circumstances.
9. What did he see that made him bow?

71 ॰

Cuiwei's "Meaning"

MAIN CASE

Zen master Lingzun of Mount Qingping [Faxi] asked his teacher, Cuiwei, "What is the exact meaning of the Bodhidharma's coming from India?"[1]
    Cuiwei said, "I will tell you when no one is around."[2]

After a while Qingping said, "There is no one now. Please tell me, Master."[3]

Cuiwei got down from the meditation platform and took Qingping into a bamboo yard.

Qingping said again, "There is no one here. Please tell me."[4]

Pointing to bamboo, Cuiwei said, "This bamboo is tall just as it is.[5] That bamboo is short just as it is."[6]

COMMENTARY

Looking into the great mirror of samādhi, form and reflection see each other. At once you are not it, yet it is clearly you. Such is the dharma of thusness. If you can see that a tall bamboo stalk is tall and a short bamboo stalk is short, then understand that the truth of the universe is just this and nothing more.

Just this and nothing more is the direct mind-to-mind transmission of the buddhas and ancestors as realized in each and every generation for the past twenty-five hundred years. Indeed, both gods and demons are constantly living this truth, although some may realize it and some may not.

CAPPING VERSE

The hazy moon's light
    barely illuminates the valley.
The warm spring breeze
    greens the frozen riverbanks.
Evening's frost
    becomes the morning dew.

NOTES

1. An age-old question; yet each time it is raised, it must be answered.
2. Cottonwood seeds know how to ride the wind.
3. Sunflowers turn toward the sun.
4. Clearly, he really wants to know.
5. Vertically extending through past, present, and future.
6. Horizontally spreading, covering the ten directions.

72 ⌘

Dongshan's "Not-Buddha"

MAIN CASE

Dongshan Liangjie said, "You should understand buddha going beyond buddha."[1]

A monastic said, "What is buddha going beyond buddha?"[2]

Dongshan said, "Not-buddha."[3]

Yunmen later said, "It is unnameable and unshapeable. So it is called 'not.'"[4]

Fayan later said, "Through skillful means, it is called buddha."[5]

COMMENTARY

"Buddha going beyond buddha" is the state of being without buddha, which is called not-buddha. This is a state that should not be understood as existing before or after being buddha, nor is it a state that surpasses or is inferior to buddha. It is simply the state of having dropped off the body and mind of buddha. No trace of buddha can be found.

Not-buddha is a ceaseless development that cannot be named, attained, transmitted, or received. Yet do not think that there should be no resolve or that practice and enlightenment are nonexistent; it's just that it cannot be named nor attained. Therefore Yunmen says, "It is called 'not.'"

CAPPING VERSE

Although the highest peak of the sacred mountain
    has been ascended,
        you should realize that there are still
        endless heavens beyond.

NOTES

1. Although rare, there is such a thing.
2. Odd that he should ask.
3. If not, then what? Why didn't the monastic persist?
4. He really doesn't know either.
5. They all seem to get their food from the same cupboard.

73 ∾
Mimoyan's Pitchfork

MAIN CASE

Priest Mimoyan of Mount Wutai always held a two-pronged pitchfork.[1]
When he saw a monastic coming, he would hold up the pitchfork and say,
"What kind of demon has made you leave the household?[2] What kind of
demon has caused you to wander?[3] If you can say it, you will be killed with
this pitchfork.[4] If you can't say it, you will be killed with this pitchfork.[5] Say
it now, quickly!"[6]

COMMENTARY

Leaving home and entering the Way is not for the sake of yourself or for
others. It is beyond coming or going, holy or mundane, active or inactive.
Indeed, it can be said that it is beyond any relationship whatsoever.

Even if you are a person of great learning and can eloquently expound
the teachings, this is of little value in passing through Mimoyan's barrier.
Only those who can cast aside the discriminating mind are truly free of the
demons. If there is even a trace of this and that, all will be lost in confusion.
How then, will you, Zen practitioners of today, avoid Mimoyan's pitchfork?

CAPPING VERSE

Holding up the pitchfork,
> he carries out the imperative.
Where committing and negating merge,
> even the tongues of sages fall to the ground.

NOTES

1. A long time ago, on Mount Gridhrakūta, it was a flower.
2. The deluded demon of duality. Haven't you heard? There is no
   payoff.
3. What is it that you are seeking?
4. It seems as though this would not be a good time for explanations.

5. It seems as though this would not be a good time for silence.

6. How will you turn the pitchfork around?

74 ~

Zhaozhou Rotates the Canon

MAIN CASE

Zhaozhou was once given a donation by an elderly woman who requested that he rotate the Great Canon.[1] Zhaozhou got down from his seat on the meditation platform, circumambulated the platform once, and said to the woman's messenger, "I have finished rotating the Great Canon."[2]

The messenger told the woman about this. She said, "I asked him to rotate the entire canon.[3] How come the master rotated only half of the canon?"[4]

COMMENTARY

If you understand how it is that Zhaozhou rotates the canon in the first place, you will see why the old woman complains that he only rotated half of it. Is it Zhaozhou or the old woman who is at fault?

You should understand that although Zhaozhou circumambulates the meditation platform in response to the woman's request to rotate the canon, rotation of the canon is not limited to this. Rotation of the canon should not be seen as being confined to any particular activity or thing. Reading, rotating, chanting, copying, giving, receiving, and possessing the canon cover heaven and earth with their virtue. This is the practice and enlightenment of all buddhas of the three times.

The black characters written on white paper that we call the Great Canon are also written in the sky and sea, on mountains and rivers, in the wind and the clouds, as well as within one's self. Yet, in spite of its all-pervading nature, it is rare to encounter the canon directly. Only the buddha mind can rotate the canon; only the buddha eye can read the canon.

CAPPING VERSE

When you see the Great Canon,
 you go blind.

When you hear the Great Canon,
  you go deaf.
Eighty-six generations—
  yet no one knows the Great Canon.

NOTES

1. There are 108 billion characters in the oceanic storehouse. Does she want them all?
2. Why did he give her so much more than she asked for?
3. Does this woman have an eye or not?
4. The other half is up to you, old woman. Actually, she deserves a refund for keeping her active edge sharp.

75 ☙
Yantou's "Sit Still"

MAIN CASE

Zen master Quanhuo of Yantou [Qingyan] was once asked by a monastic, "What can I do when the three worlds all arise together?"[1]
  Yantou said, "Sit still."[2]
  The monastic said, "I don't understand what you mean, Master."[3]
  Yantou said, "Bring Mount Lu here and I will tell you."[4]

COMMENTARY

When the mind moves, images appear. Even if the mind does not move, this is not yet true freedom. You must first take off the blinders and set down the pack if you are to bring forth Mount Lu. When you are finally able to let go and be totally alive to the suchness of this very moment, then you will see, at once, that it is beyond telling, absolutely beyond telling.

CAPPING VERSE

If your mind does not stop chasing thoughts,
  how will you ever free yourself?

Morning mist hovering in the mouth of the valley
     causes many people to miss the source.

NOTES

  1. How do you understand the three worlds?
  2. Don't mistake this as an instruction to engage in inactivity.
  3. This is really not a matter of understanding.
  4. It can be done, you know.

76 ❧
"No-Mind Is the Way"

MAIN CASE

[Guishan] Dagui was once asked by a monastic, "What is the Way?"[1]
     Dagui said, "No-mind is the Way."[2]
     The monastic said, "I don't understand it."[3]
     Dagui said, "It's good to understand not-understanding."[4]
     The monastic said, "What is not-understanding?"[5]
     Dagui said, "It's just that you are not anyone else."[6]

COMMENTARY

The Way is beyond understanding and not-understanding. Understanding is grasping at words and phrases; not-understanding is blank consciousness.
     When Zen practitioners hear, "It's good to understand not-understanding," they make a nest here, saying, "Just this is it!" They have not yet realized the intimacy that old Dagui is pointing to. What is Dagui's intimacy? It's not mind; it's not no-mind. It's not like something.

CAPPING VERSE

The Great Way is not difficult;
     just avoid picking and choosing.
In one there are many;
     in two there is no duality.

NOTES

1. It is long and broad—the ten directions cannot contain it. This monastic sure isn't alert.
2. *Bah!* He is just building a pile of bones on level ground.
3. Indeed, it's hard to swallow. There are many people who have doubts about this.
4. What is he talking about? In understanding not-understanding, doesn't the mind still move?
5. He presses the old man. This monastic really wants to know. What a pity.
6. It covers heaven and contains the earth. This kindness is hard to requite. But tell me, what does it really mean?

77 ∾
Disclosing Is Not as Good as Practice

MAIN CASE

Zen master Huanzhong of Mount Daci [Xingkong] said to the assembly, "To speak about ten feet is not as good as to practice one foot. To speak about one foot is not as good as to practice one inch."[1]

Dongshan Liangjie said, "Speak what cannot be practiced.[2] Practice what cannot be spoken."[3]

COMMENTARY

You should clearly realize that it is not wrong to speak of ten feet; it's just that to practice one foot is far more important than speaking about ten feet. But do not think that either is lacking in virtue—in each the totality of ceaseless practice is present.

Therefore, the true meaning of Master Dongshan's "Speak what cannot be practiced. Practice what cannot be spoken" is that practice and speech thoroughly interpenetrate. Activity and expression are interdependent. Thus, a full day of speaking is none other than a full day of practice, and a full day of practice is none other than a full day of speaking.

CAPPING VERSE

Practice without understanding
    is like eyes opened in the darkness.
Understanding without practice
    is like eyes closed in the daylight.
When practice and understanding have merged
    eyes are open in the bright light of day.

NOTES

1. Where did he get the news?
2. I fear my tongue will fall to the ground.
3. As it turns out, he talks too much.

78 ∾

Dongshan's "Where Is the Fault?"

MAIN CASE

Dongshan Liangjie once invited Head Monastic Tai to have fruit with him and asked, "There is something that holds the sky above and the ground beneath.[1] It is as black as lacquer.[2] It is always in activity but cannot be received within activity.[3] Tell me, where is the fault?"[4]

The head monastic said, "The fault is activity."[5]

Dongshan shouted and then had the attendant take the fruit away.[6]

COMMENTARY

Before Dongshan even finishes speaking, he deserves to have his meditation seat overturned. He seems to be using his power to mystify the monastic. Can all of you see his trap? In responding the way he did, this monastic's failure is no small thing.

Though Dongshan's statement is correct, nonetheless it is biased, and although it is biased, it is complete. Seeing that the monastic missed this altogether, he makes one last feeble attempt to wake him.

CAPPING VERSE

Looking into the ancient mirror,
    form and reflection see each other.
In an instant, it is seen that you are not it,
    but it is clearly you.

NOTES

    1. Although this is true, no one has ever been able to find it.
    2. It is not a thing.
    3. Just don't reject your head by grasping at its shadow.
    4. He digs a pit and then invites the monastic to jump in.
    5. He jumps in; too bad.
    6. Why does he keep repeating himself?

79 ∾

Yaoshan's Discourse

MAIN CASE

Yaoshan had not given a discourse in the dharma hall for some time. The monastery director said, "The assembly has long been wanting to receive teaching from you.[1] Please give a discourse to the assembly, Master."[2]

    Yaoshan asked him to sound the han.[3] The monastics came together. Yaoshan took the high seat, sat there for a while, got down, and went back to the abbot's room.[4]

    The monastery director followed him and asked, "Master, you agreed to give a discourse to the assembly. Why didn't you say a word?"[5]

    Yaoshan said, "Scriptural teachers are for scriptures. Commentary teachers are for commentaries. What do you expect from this old monastic?"[6]

COMMENTARY

Since the dharma of suchness is not about kōans, scriptures, or commentaries, is this what has left Yaoshan speechless, or is it that he just has nothing to say? Or is it possible that he did say something after all? If so, what did he say? If you go to speech to express it, you have missed it. If you resort to silence to express it, you are still a thousand miles from the truth. If you think it's neither speech nor silence, or both speech and silence, you are practicing the self-styled Zen of the dilettante. What did Yaoshan say?

CAPPING VERSE

The dharma of suchness,
     infinitely profound and minutely subtle.
In twenty-five hundred years of transmission,
     it has never passed from mouth to ear.

NOTES

1. It seems that although the monastery director has eyes to see and ears to hear, he has missed it.
2. Haven't you heard that in forty-seven years of teaching, the Buddha never uttered a single word?
3. What can he say? It simply can't be explained.
4. Clouds gather, and thunder and lightning fill the valley.
5. Missed it again.
6. Now he's getting talkative.

80 ॰

Zhaozhou's Buddha

MAIN CASE

Once a monastic bid farewell to Zhaozhou. Zhaozhou said, "Where are you going?"[1]

The monastic said, "I will visit various places to study the Buddha-dharma."[2]

Zhaozhou picked up his whisk and said, "Do not abide in a place where there is a buddha.[3] Pass by quickly a place where there is no buddha.[4] Upon meeting someone, do not misguide that person."[5]

The monastic said, "That being the case, I will stay here."[6]

Zhaozhou said, "Pick up the willow blossoms. Pick up the willow blossoms."[7]

COMMENTARY

Zhaozhou, seeing this monastic teetering on the edge, loses no time in precipitating the situation. Finding no place to abide, the monastic is stopped dead in his tracks. Again, the old bodhisattva pulls the rug out from under him. Do you understand? There are no side roads along the Great Way, yet there is no place it does not reach. The truth of the Way is not in seeing or hearing, nor is it in words and ideas. If you can cut through the entanglements and untie the bonds of the buddhas and ancestors, you have discovered the land of clarity and peace where even heaven and hell cannot reach. If you seek it from others, you go astray. If you seek it within, you are far removed from it. What will you do?

CAPPING VERSE

This old buddha has a way of teaching:
       thirty blows of the stick without raising a hand.
Directing yourself toward it, you move away from it.
What person's life is lacking?

NOTES

1. In coming and going, Zen practitioners reveal much about their practice.
2. From California to the New York highlands, looking for his head.
3. It only creates complications.
4. A forest of brambles.
5. Do not deceive yourself; do not deceive others.
6. Look! He wants to create a nest.
7. Don't just sit there. Do something!

81 ❧

Yunmen's "Everyone's Light"

MAIN CASE

Yunmen said to the assembly, "All people are in the midst of illumination.[1] When you look at it, you don't see it; everything seems dark and dim.[2] How is it being in the midst of illumination?"[3]

No one in the assembly responded.[4]

Yunmen answered for them,[5] "Monastics' hall, buddha hall, kitchen, monastery gate."[6] He also said, "A good thing does not compare with no thing."[7]

COMMENTARY

The pure light encompasses the whole universe, existing right here now. Why is it then that you cannot see it? Being in the midst of illumination means the light is not shining on anything, nor do things exist for the light to shine upon. The light contains everyone, as everyone contains the light. See! There are no shadows to be found anywhere.

Since no one in the assembly can respond, Yunmen rolls it out for them, and before anyone can create a nest, in a flash, he snatches it away. He wants it to be clear that it is because Avalokiteśvara Bodhisattva is deaf, dumb, and blind that she can wield the ten thousand hands and eyes of great compassion.

CAPPING VERSE

When you point to the light,
    she shows you the dark.
When you point to the dark,
    she shows you the light.
When light and dark are both forgotten,
    the ten thousand hands and eyes spontaneously appear.

NOTES

1. This is something that cannot be seen with the eye nor found in the environment.
2. Although it is light, when you are asked about it, you don't know. Isn't this dark and dim?
3. When the wind blows from the east, the grasses all bend toward the west.
4. Is the whole assembly asleep, or has the old man mystified them with his slick tongue?
5. Thank you for your kindness, but when will they learn to tie their own shoelaces?
6. If you have a particle of life in you, this should get your engine revved up.
7. He gives with one hand and takes away with the other.

82 ～

Dongshan's "No Grass"

MAIN CASE

Dongshan Liangjie told the assembly at the end of the summer training period,[1] "When summer ends and autumn begins, go straight to a place where there is not an inch of grass for ten thousand miles."[2]

No one in the assembly could respond.[3]

Later, a monastic told Shishuang about it.[4]

Shishuang Chuyuan said, "Why didn't you say, 'There is grass all over one step outside the gate'?"[5]

COMMENTARY

Going to a place where there is not an inch of grass for ten thousand miles is truly auspicious, but if there is no grass, how can there be coming and going to begin with?

If you are to enter the endless spring of real activity, you must first be free of both sides and then let go of even the middle.

CAPPING VERSE

Passing through the forest of brambles,
    we enter clear ground.
Then, like the spring breeze,
    we must enter the scars of the burned-out fields.

NOTES

1. It isn't over till it's over.
2. He wants to bury the whole assembly in the same pit.
3. With tongues hanging to the ground, they are all waiting to exhale.
4. If he doesn't ask how will he know? He wants to know.
5. Before you even go out the gate, there is grass all over.

83 ～

Yunyan Sweeps the Ground

MAIN CASE

One day Zen master Tansheng of Mount Yunyan [Wuzhu] was sweeping the ground.[1] His dharma brother Daowu said, "Working hard?"[2]
    Yunyan said, "What is not working hard?"[3]
    Daowu said, "Then is there a second moon?"[4]
    Yunyan held up the broom and said, "Which moon is this?"[5]
    Daowu walked away without a word.[6]

COMMENTARY

Yaoshan teaches his cubs well. In playing together, they learn to clarify the business of the mountain lion. Yunyan's "What is not working hard?" is a phrase that contains the merging of the sacred and the profane. Can you see it? Daowu is not impressed, so he presses further to see if Yunyan will try to set up a reality body apart from the physical body. Yunyan responds to the imperative without falling into intellectual explanations. With a single stroke of the broom, he sweeps up heaven and earth. But say, has Daowu exposed Yunyan, or is it Yunyan who has exposed Daowu?

CAPPING VERSE

Working hard or not working hard—
    this is not a matter of yin and yang.
How could the first moon be anything other
    than the second moon?

NOTES

1. There is no one else who can do it.
2. In Dongshan's school, mutual polishing is a specialty of the house.
3. How many realities do you live in, brother?
4. What kind of a question is this for a Zen monastic to ask?
5. He should have just whacked him with the broom.
6. Actually, neither of these two knows good from bad.

84 ⌘

Yunyan's "Not a Single Word"

MAIN CASE

One day Yunyan said to the assembly, "There is a child in this household. If you ask a question, there is nothing he can't answer."[1]
    Dongshan Liangjie then asked, "How large a library does he have?"[2]
    Yunyan said, "Not a single word."[3]
    Dongshan said, "Then how come he is so learned?"[4]
    Yunyan said, "He does not sleep day or night."[5]
    Dongshan said, "If we ask him about the single matter, can we get a response?"[6]
    Yunyan said, "Although he can speak, he won't answer."[7]

COMMENTARY

The truth of the universe cannot be found in words, letters, or technology; it is a knowledge that has no teacher, a wisdom that cannot be communicated. It can only be realized through the backward step of zazen. The diligent practice of zazen is the dharma gate to the inconceivable; it is the undefiled practice and verification of all buddhas of the three times.

Spring is in the frozen branches, buried beneath three feet of snow. Without falling into intellection, and without getting caught up in gain and loss, how can this be expressed? Don't you see? To be in the mountains is a flower opening in the world.

CAPPING VERSE

Those who have realized the truth cannot say it—
  they can only nod to themselves.
Those who say it have not yet realized it—
  the truth cannot be communicated.

NOTES

1. The land is broad and boundless, and the people who can see it are few.
2. It's not about that.
3. Even if the cupboards were full, they still would not satisfy hunger.
4. Actually, he is deaf, dumb, and blind. Still, it can be discussed.
5. Whether sitting, standing, or lying down, the true dragon is always puffing smoke and breathing fire.
6. Each and every action, each and every dharma, is always eloquently expressing it.
7. It's not that he can't; he just won't.

85 ॐ
Shishuang's "A Single Hair Pierces Innumerable Holes"

MAIN CASE

Shishuang Chuyuan was once asked by Senior Monastic Quanming, "When does a single hair pierce innumerable holes?"[1]
  Shishuang said, "Ten thousand years later."
  Quanming said, "What will happen ten thousand years later?"[2]

Shishuang said, "It is you who will pass the examination and excel among people."

Later Quanming asked the same question of Zen master Hongyin of Jingshan [Faji].

Jingshan said, "You personally will have to shine your sandals and harvest the fruit."[3]

COMMENTARY

A single hair piercing innumerable holes is a formidable task requiring diligent effort and relentless perfection. Raising the bodhi mind, practice, and realization—whether in sacred or secular realms—require the same single-minded dedication. Quanming's question is: when is the goal reached? Shishuang says, "Ten thousand years later." What is his meaning?

If you wish to appreciate Shishuang's teaching, you must first realize that the process and the goal are a single reality, and then you must understand that to attain one dharma is to penetrate one dharma, and to encounter one activity is to practice one activity. This is called one-practice samādhi. In it there is no past, present, or future. There is just this single moment that transcends all space and time.

Ultimately, this is not the doing of self or other but, rather, the myriad dharmas advancing and realizing the self. But say, what does Jingshan mean when he says, "You personally will have to shine your sandals and harvest the fruit?" I ask, what are you calling your self?

CAPPING VERSE

Difficult to express, even for an adept—
     how many know how to beat the ancient drum?
Mountains and rivers are not seen in a mirror—
     where one side is illuminated, the other side is dark.

NOTES

1. Difficult, difficult.
2. See how difficult it is to understand?
3. Examine for yourself what this is!

86 ∾

Yaoshan's "This Buddha, That Buddha"

MAIN CASE

Monastic Zun was at the assembly of Yaoshan and was the head altar attendant.[1] While he was bathing buddha images, Yaoshan asked him, "Have you bathed this one[2] or have you bathed that one?"[3]

Zun said, "Please hand that one to me."[4]

Yaoshan stopped.[5]

COMMENTARY

Yaoshan creates an awkward scene. He tries to weave a web of this and that, all to no avail. Zun is nimble, Zun is quick, there is no place where Zun will stick. If you know on your own how to ride an ox backward, you will not be stuck following after people all your life.

In the mundane truth, there are many who have become enlightened. In the sacred truth, there are many who have become deluded. When the sacred and the mundane have unified, who can speak of enlightenment or delusion? Having shed enlightenment and delusion, there are not so many complications. The tall one is a tall buddha; the short one is a short buddha.

CAPPING VERSE

There are ten thousand dharmas
    in the valley of the dry bones.
If you don't see it, you shrivel up and die;
    when you do see it, the dead trees come to life.

NOTES

1. Attending the altars, offering incense—everyday activities. Only those who have investigated it fully would know.
2. Although he tries to be subtle, the pattern is already evident.
3. He makes it sound like there are two.
4. A fine horse gets up and goes at the shadow of the whip.

5. Look! Zun has chased him up a tree, yet there is no color of shame on his face.

87 ～
Nanquan's "Nothing Special"

MAIN CASE

Zen master Baoyun of Mount Luzu would sit facing the wall whenever monastics went to see him.[1] One day, Nanquan Puyuan went to see him, and Luzu sat facing the wall.[2] Nanquan finally patted him on the back.[3]

Luzu said, "Who is it?"[4]

Nanquan said, "It's Puyuan."[5]

Luzu said, "What are you doing?"[6]

Nanquan said, "Nothing special."[7]

COMMENTARY

Luzu seems to be practicing a bit of ostrich Zen. There may be something to this, but still, it makes it difficult to distinguish the long from the short. Nanquan, seeing his exposed end, checks to see if there is any life.

Zen practitioners inevitably fall to one side or the other because they have not yet seen that principle and phenomena are not two, illumination and function are simultaneous. Because nothing is missing, it can be said that it's nothing special.

CAPPING VERSE

Rotating the heavens,
     revolving the sun and moon.
Each and every action
     contains the universe.

NOTES

1. Before the encounter begins, it's over.
2. At least it can be said that he is consistent.

3. Wake up! Come out of your hole.
4. He seems to have some life.
5. An honest person is hard to find. It's not so complicated.
6. Because it's so simple, sometimes it's easy to miss.
7. It's just because it leaves out nothing.

88 ∽
Lingzhao's "Bright and Clear"

MAIN CASE

While sitting, Layman Pangyun asked his daughter Lingzhao, "A teacher of old said, 'Bright and clear are the one hundred grasses;[1] bright and clear is the meaning of the ancestral teaching.'[2] How about yourself?"[3]

Lingzhao said, "How could someone who is mature and great say such a thing?"[4]

Pangyun said, "How would you say it?"[5]

Lingzhao said, "Bright and clear are the one hundred grasses; bright and clear is the meaning of the ancestral teaching."[6]

Pangyun laughed.[7]

COMMENTARY

Saṃsāra is nirvāṇa, nirvāṇa is saṃsāra. There is fundamentally no difference between them. Mountains, rivers, the great earth, and one's own self—where is the distinction to be found? This being the case, why is everything divided into two sides?

Where dragons and snakes are intermingled, even the sages cannot see into it. When going against and in accord with it, vertically and horizontally, even the buddhas cannot speak of it.

CAPPING VERSE

The ten thousand things are the true dharma,
     the ten directions are one reality.

Don't you know?
The Dharmakāya is not like anything.

NOTES

1. Exiting the gate, there is grass all over. Entering the gate, there is grass all over. There is no place where it does not reach.
2. Although it's so, it's a shame to have said it.
3. It would seem that he wants to drag her into the pit with him.
4. She will have none of that.
5. He won't let her go.
6. They know how to switch heads without batting an eye.
7. This is a thief recognizing a thief. Since they are from the same household, they know well the contents of the cupboard.

89 ∾

Shishuang's "This Side and That Side"

MAIN CASE

One day, Shishuang Chuyuan said to his attendant monastic,[1] "Daowu once said to a monastic, 'Do not discard that side to get to this side.'[2] How do you understand this?"[3]

The attendant monastic said, "It's the same as your understanding, Master."[4]

Shishuang said, "What is my understanding?"[5]

The attendant monastic walked from west to east and stood there.[6]

Shishuang said, "You have just discarded that side to get to this side."[7]

COMMENTARY

Under clear skies in the bright light of day, there is no need to point out this and that anymore. Still, the imperative of time and place requires the dispensing of medicine in accord with the sickness. But tell me, is it better to hold fast or to let go?

CAPPING VERSE

This side, that side—
    heads and tails are two parts of the same coin.
A single moment of yes and no,
    and heaven and earth are separated.

NOTES

1. This old fellow wants to shake things up and see what falls out.
2. His statement makes them two; still, it's OK to separate them.
3. Clouds gather, lightning flashes, and thunder fills the valley.
4. He just walks up and places his nostrils in the old man's hands—as if the truth belonged to someone else.
5. Indeed, he'll have none of that. Show me your own provisions!
6. Right there, he should have been driven out with a stick.
7. Why explain? Let him go on like this for the rest of his life. But say, how do you not discard that side in moving to this side?

90 ☞

Jiashan Sees the Ferryman

MAIN CASE

Chuanzi Decheng was practicing together with Daowu and Yunyan at Yaoshan's community. Chuanzi left Yaoshan and lived on a small boat on a river in Huating Prefecture. Before he left, he had said to Daowu, "If you meet a promising teacher, please send him to me."

Zen master Shanhui of Jiashan [Chuanming] was abbot of Zhulin Monastery. Daowu happened to visit the monastery and attended one of Jiashan's lectures. A monastic asked, "What is the dharma body?"[1]

Jiashan said, "The dharma body has no form."[2]

The monastic asked again, "What is the dharma eye?"[3]

Jiashan said, "The dharma eye has no scratch."[4]

Daowu could not help laughing.[5] Jiashan noticed it. After getting down from the teaching seat, he invited Daowu, made a formal bow, and said,

"Did you laugh because I gave a wrong answer to that monastic?[6] Please be kind enough to explain."[7]

Daowu said, "Although you have become the abbot of this fine monastery, you have not yet met a true master."

Jiashan said, "Please tell me where my fault lies."

Daowu said, "I cannot explain it to you, but I have a peer who gives teachings on a boat in Huating. Let me suggest that you go and meet him. I am sure you will attain something."

Jiashan said, "Who is this person?"

Daowu said, "There is not half a slate above him. There is not an inch of ground beneath him. But when you go, you had better not wear your robe."

Jiashan soon dissolved his assembly, changed his clothes, and went straight to Huating.

Seeing Jiashan, Chuanzi said to him, "Of which monastery are you the abbot?"

Jiashan said, "I am not abbot of a monastery, or I wouldn't look like this."

Chuanzi said, "What do you mean by 'not like this'?"[8]

Jiashan said, "It's not like something right in front of you."[9]

Chuanzi said, "Where did you study?"

Jiashan said, "No place that ears or eyes can reach."[10]

Chuanzi said, "The phrase you understand can still tether the donkey for a myriad kalpas." Then he said, "I hang a line one thousand feet deep, but the heart is three inches off the hook. Why don't you say something?"[11]

Jiashan was about to open his mouth. Chuanzi knocked him into the water with the boat pole.[12] Jiashan surfaced and climbed onto the boat. Chuanzi said, "Say something. Say something!"

Jiashan was about to open his mouth when Chuanzi hit him again.[13] Jiashan was suddenly awakened and bowed three times.[14]

Chuanzi said, "You are welcome to the fishing pole. However, the meaning of 'It ripples no quiet water' is naturally profound."[15]

Jiashan said, "Why do you give away the fishing pole?"

Chuanzi said, "It is to see whether a fish of golden scales is or is not. If you have realized it, speak quickly; words are wondrous and unspeakable."

While Chuanzi was speaking, Jiashan covered his ears and began to walk away.[16] Chuanzi said, "Quite so, quite so." Then the master instructed Jiashan, saying, "From now on, erase all traces, but do not hide your body. I was at Yaoshan's for thirty years and clarified just this. Now you have this. Do not live in a city or a village. Just be in a deep mountain or on a farm and guide one or half a person. Succeed in my teaching and don't let it be cut off."

Jiashan accepted Chuanzi's entrustment and bid him farewell. He went ashore and started to walk away, looking back again and again.

Chuanzi called out, "Reverend, reverend!" Jiashan turned around.

Chuanzi held up the oar and said, "There is something more."[17]

Upon uttering these words, he jumped out of the boat and disappeared into the mist and waves.

COMMENTARY

In order to master the teachings of our school, you must know how to take charge of the situation; know how to advance and retreat and understand right and wrong, capture and release, killing and giving life.

Be that as it may, what is it that Jiashan realized that made Chuanzi pass over the fishing pole? If you say that the dharma can be transmitted, then who would receive what? If you say that the dharma cannot be transmitted, then why was Jiashan approved? Most important, what is the meaning of Chuanzi's "There is something more"?

CAPPING VERSE

Clouds vanish and the sun appears—
    the endless spring is revealed.
This is not a time of yin and yang.
Thus, no communication whatsoever is possible.
The truth is not like something.

NOTES

1. There are many practitioners who have doubts about this.
2. True enough. Nonetheless, wrong!
3. This monastic is pressing the old abbot.
4. True enough. Nonetheless, wrong!
5. This is serious. Why does he laugh?
6. After all of this, he still wants explanations.
7. Even a hundred thousand buddhas stacked one on top of the other could not explain.

8. Like a crouching lion, without a second's hesitation, he moves in for the kill.
9. *Bah!* He still carries the same baggage. As before, true—but wrong.
10. On the surface, it seems hopeless. What does Chuanzi see that makes him persist?
11. Sooner or later, this will lead to further dharma pontifications.
12. *Ka!* It's about time to shut up and see it!
13. The first hit was light; this one goes deeper.
14. Tell me, what did he see that made him bow?
15. Go to the ear and the eyes go blind; go to the eyes and the ears go deaf. How will you discern it?
16. That's it, that's it!
17. The old pond, shallow or deep—its bottom can never be seen.

91 ∾
Huangbo's Single Staff

MAIN CASE

Huangbo told a monastic, "All the venerable ones in various places all over the country are on top of my staff."[1]
The monastic bowed.
Later the monastic went to see Dashu and told him the story.
Dashu said, "Huangbo said so, but has he seen various places?"[2]
The monastic went back to Huangbo and told him about it.
Huangbo said, "My words have already reached all over the country."[3]
Langye commented on this, "Dashu's response was like someone who seemed to have eyes but was really blind. Huangbo's single staff cannot be bitten and chewed by anyone in this country."[4]

COMMENTARY

If you are to understand Huangbo's teaching, you must first understand Huangbo's single staff. This single staff—what is it? It can't be seen with the eyes, it can't be held in the hands, it cannot be perceived with the ears, it can't be grasped by the mind. It is not to be found within the realm of form, nor is it formless. It is not a metaphor, it is not a thing. Yet here it is, thus!

When the monastic questions Dashu about this matter, Dashu, groping in the dark, stumbles and falls. Langye says he is like someone who seems to have eyes but is really blind. I say it is really Huangbo who is blind. But tell me, how do you understand the blindness of Huangbo and that of Dashu? Are they the same or different?

If you can see into it here, then I would agree that you and Huangbo are knocking and resounding together. If not, you must go beyond the words to the single staff itself and make it your own. Although we use words to reveal the Way, the path itself is fundamentally without words. Therefore, it is said that when you receive words, you must discern the source.

CAPPING VERSE

It supports you crossing the river on a moonless night,
   it eases your burden in ascending a mountain.
This single staff, seven feet long—
   once it's understood, you can swallow the universe.

NOTES

   1. What is he saying? He is trying to be host and guest at the same time.
   2. Alas, he misunderstands.
   3. You should know, teacher, you said it.
   4. Only someone on the same path could know this.

92 ❧

Teaching and Not Teaching

MAIN CASE

Sansheng said, "When I meet someone, I go away. When I go away, I don't guide him."[1]

His dharma brother Cunjiang of Xinghua Monastery said, "When I meet someone, I don't go away. When I go away, I guide him."[2]

COMMENTARY

In forty-seven years of dharma work, the World-Honored One never taught a single phrase. The buddha of supremely penetrating wisdom sat on the bodhi seat for ten kalpas, and yet the Buddhadharma was not manifested, nor did he attain Buddhahood. Yet, Zen practitioners the world over continually search and grasp, looking for the truth.

Haven't you heard old master Huangbo's saying: "In all of China there are no Zen teachers and nothing to teach?" Then why are there so many Zen centers and monasteries with teachers expounding the dharma? Indeed, since there is nothing to teach, what is a Zen teacher?

We should understand that there is a wisdom that has no teacher. It is called silent discourse or knowing before speech. If you want to see into it, you must first take the backward step. Then, when the myriad impulses cease, the eyes spontaneously open.

CAPPING VERSE

It's not that the truth is not there,
    but when you look for it, you go blind.
Clever talk—how can it compare to
    the sounds of the river valley,
    the form of the mountain?

NOTES

1. There is an echo in these words. Do you hear it?
2. Though born in the same way, one rolls it in, the other rolls it out.

93 ဏ
Dongshan's "Each Stitch"

MAIN CASE

Shenshan was sewing[1] when Dongshan Liangjie said, "What are you doing?"[2]

Shenshan said, "I am sewing."[3]

Dongshan said, "What is sewing?"[4]

Shenshan said, "Each stitch follows the other."[5]

Dongshan said, "If my companion of twenty years says so, I guess there is a point."[6]

Shenshan said, "What would you say, Elder?"[7]

Dongshan said, "Each stitch is like the earth exploding."[8]

COMMENTARY

In cooking, eating, sewing, and sweeping, you should realize the meeting points of enlightened reality and mundane reality. In the Caodong lineage, this is known as simultaneous inclusion. Dongshan sees an open seam and moves to close it for Uncle Mi (Shenshan).

But say, where is Shenshan's shortcoming? Indeed, is there anything lacking in his response? If you can see into Dongshan's point, you will understand clearly the dharma dance of the sacred and the mundane.

CAPPING VERSE

When a sage realizes it,
    she becomes an ordinary person.
When an ordinary person realizes it
    she is a sage.
Sage or ordinary, stitch after stitch,
    the gap is closed.

NOTES

1. This is no ordinary activity; the clothes need mending.
2. This is no ordinary conversation; he wants to see if he understands.
3. His straightforwardness is admirable, but how does he see it?
4. It is not easy to satisfy old Dongshan.
5. It's not wrong; it's just dull.
6. Let him drown in his dullness.
7. It would seem there is a sign of life after all.
8. It reaches heaven and encompasses the earth.

94 ॐ

Yunju's "Place That Cannot Be Contained"

MAIN CASE

Yunju was once asked by a monastic, "When you are born, why don't you know you exist?"[1]
    Yunju said, "Existence is not the same as being born."[2]
    The monastic said, "How about the time when you are not yet born?"[3]
    Yunju said, "You never die."[4]
    The monastic said, "When you are not yet born, where are you?"[5]
    Yunju said, "Such a place cannot be contained."[6]

COMMENTARY

Because the dharma of suchness is unborn and unextinguished, it cannot be contained anywhere. Reach for it and you miss it, for it is ungraspable. Ignore it and you miss it, for it must be engaged.

    When the mind stops moving and you have stepped outside patterns, then mountain after mountain, and river after river, you will meet the truth of the unborn at every turn. It is because this marvelously bright illuminative wisdom has no teacher that it can only be seen in this way. Not a single sage of antiquity has ever been able to address this truth. Ultimately, you can only nod to yourself.

CAPPING VERSE

Seeing that which is creating and that which is destroying,
    one understands them intimately.
If you wish to understand this for yourself, then look!
    The river flows in tumbling torrents into the great ocean.

NOTES

    1. Great doubt makes for a fine cutting edge.
    2. One is real, the other apparent.

3. He misunderstands the old teacher.
4. That which has not arisen cannot perish.
5. What are you calling yourself, monastic?
6. *Bah*! The old teacher should know by now that explanations just create further complications.

95 ∾
Buddha's "Teachings of a Lifetime"

MAIN CASE

Yunmen was once asked by a monastic, "What is the Buddha's teaching of a lifetime?"[1]

Yunmen said, "He teaches facing one."[2]

The monastic said, "What happens if he has no listener or nothing to talk about?"[3]

Yunmen said, "He teaches upside down."[4]

COMMENTARY

Since the teachings are always manifested in accord with the times and seasons, causes and conditions, Yunmen says, "He teaches facing one." Forty-seven years of the Buddha's teaching comes down to just this. But say, what does teaching facing one mean?

The monastic is an adept, so he presses the old master and asks for more instruction. This time, Yunmen says, "He teaches upside down." His whole intent is to knock out the wedges and pull out the nails for the monastic. But say, what does teaching upside down mean?

If you are able to say a word of Zen on this matter, I will grant that you are able to walk hand in hand not only with Yunmen but with old yellow-faced Gautama as well.

CAPPING VERSE

Facing one, upside down—
    the differences between them are night and day.

Dividing the river,
    half is above the falls and half is below the falls.

NOTES

    1. This question has been reverberating for twenty-five hundred years.
    2. When the ancients got here, they did not stay.
    3. You can't drive a stake into empty space.
    4. Food in the bowl, water in the bucket.

96 ∾
Puhua Knocks Over a Table

MAIN CASE

Puhua received a meal offering with Linji at a donor's house. Linji asked
Puhua, "A strand of hair swallows the ocean. A poppy seed contains Mount
Sumeru.[1] Is it a miracle or a natural matter?"[2]
    Puhua knocked over the table.[3]
    Linji said, "Crude."[4]
    Puhua said, "How can you speak of this in terms of crude and fine?"[5]
    Linji became silent and went away.[6]
    The next day, both of them went to another house and received a meal
offering.[7]
    Linji said, "How does today's meal compare with yesterday's?"[8]
    Puhua knocked over the table again.[9]
    Linji said, "Crude."[10]
    Puhua said, "Blind man, where is crude or fine in the Buddhadharma?"[11]
    Linji stuck out his tongue in awe.[12]

COMMENTARY

Linji comes to dinner with Vimalakīrti's poppy seed stuck in his throat. In
the process of having it extricated, complications begin to develop. Before

the matter is finally settled, mud is splattered all over the place. Do you understand how the matter was finally settled?

The great mystical powers of the buddhas and ancestors are neither a miracle nor a natural matter, neither existent nor nonexistent. Mystical power produces mystical power. Taking a meal, rowing a boat, maintaining a business, living and dying, are all the miraculous activities of the six mystical powers. Indeed, it is within the ten thousand actions of daily existence that the mystical powers and wondrous activities of the buddhas and ancestors are realized and actualized.

Putting aside explanations, how do you understand Puhua's knocking over the table? If you can see this far into it, then you'll be able to say a word of Zen and free Linji from the iron mountains of crude and fine. What do you say?

CAPPING VERSE

Let others search for the miraculous
    or judge crudeness or fineness.
I only know plum blossoms are white,
    azalea flowers are red.

NOTES

1. Thousands of years later, Vimalakīrti's poppy seed still afflicts Zen monastics.
2. Is there a difference?
3. Is this a miracle or is it a natural matter?
4. Not crude, not fine.
5. Stop explaining; let him go on deluding himself.
6. Tell me, did he get it? Do you?
7. History has a way of repeating itself.
8. Linji has this quality about him: he likes to pull on the tiger's whiskers.
9. How new, how fresh!
10. Undeniably, this one is stuck.
11. The first arrow grazed him, this one went deep.
12. Got it!

97 ∾

Shushan and the Stone Workers

MAIN CASE

A monastic told Zen master Kuangren of Shushan that he had built a stūpa for a long life.¹

· Shushan said, "How much are you going to pay the stoneworkers?"²

The monastic said, "It's up to you, Master."³

Shushan said, "Are you going to give them three pennies, two pennies, or one penny? If you can say a word, you will build a stūpa for me, too."⁴

The monastic could not answer.⁵

At that time, Luoshan was living in a hut on Mount Dayu. The monastic went to see Luoshan and told him the story.

Luoshan said, "Is there anyone who could say such a thing?"

The monastic said, "Not yet."

Luoshan said, "You should return to Shushan and say, 'If you give the stoneworkers three pennies, the stūpa will never be built.⁶ If you give them two pennies, you and the stone workers will hold out your hands together.⁷ If you give them one penny, it will bind them and their eyebrows and beards will fall off.'"⁸

Upon hearing these words, Shushan dressed formally and bowed in the direction of Mount Dayu, saying, "Although I didn't think there was a genuine person, an authentic buddha is at Mount Dayu, radiating light even here."⁹ Then he said to the monastic, "Go to Mount Dayu and tell Luoshan that 'this is like a lotus in winter.'"¹⁰

The monastic returned this message. Luoshan said, "Let me tell you this: tortoise hair is already three feet long."¹¹

COMMENTARY

Although Shushan's questioning this monastic may appear like playing with mud balls, you should understand that there are thorns in the mud. The monastic does not understand, so Shushan clarifies it. Three, two, one— what will you do with this? The monastic cannot answer, and so concern is born. He travels to Mount Dayu only to encounter more complications.

Shushan however, seems impressed with Luoshan's answer. To understand what caused him to bow in the direction of Mount Dayu and to call it a lotus in winter is easy. But to understand Luoshan's "Tortoise hair is already three feet long" is a matter that only adepts know how to grapple with. How do you understand Luoshan?

CAPPING VERSE

Picking up what comes to hand,
> he knows how to use it skillfully.
Everywhere life is sufficient in its way,
> no matter if one is not as clever as others.

NOTES

1. This casual statement is sure to lead to complications for this monastic.
2. Although it may not sound like it, this question is not about money.
3. He knows how to dodge a bullet, but does he understand the essential matter?
4. Only an adept would know how to handle this.
5. Clearly, not an adept.
6. True, but why?
7. I ask you, who is giving and who is receiving?
8. Too much generosity impairs your virtue.
9. What does he see that impresses him so?
10. *Bah!*
11. Pure fiction.

98 ❧
Dongshan's Illness

MAIN CASE

When Dongshan Liangjie was not feeling well,[1] a monastic said, "Master, you are not feeling well.[2] Is there anyone who doesn't get sick?"[3]
Dongshan said, "Yes, there is."[4]

The monastic said, "Does the person who doesn't get sick take care of you?"[5]

Dongshan said, "I have the opportunity to take care of the person."[6]

The monastic said, "What happens when you take care of that person?"[7]

Dongshan said, "At that time, I don't see the sickness."[8]

COMMENTARY

Because of the illness of all sentient beings, Vimalakīrti is sick.

Daowu's attending the sick, Mazu's "sun-faced buddha, moon-faced buddha," and Yunmen's medicine and sickness are the activities of adepts of our school acting in accord with the imperative.

Sometimes they compound medicine to heal the sickness. At other times they manifest illness to heal the medicine. You should understand that the ten thousand hands and eyes of great compassion are deaf, dumb, and blind.

This great earth and all of its multiplicity of forms, up to and including you and me, are at once medicine. At such a time, where do you find your self?

CAPPING VERSE

Rather than heal the body,
  heal the mind.
When the mind is at peace,
  the body is at ease.
When body and mind are both free,
  the dragon roars in the withered tree.

NOTES

1. He will inevitably drag everyone into it.
2. There is an echo in this monastic's words. He wants to test the old man.
3. How will he explain this away?
4. Without a second's hesitation, he walks into the monastic's belly.
5. This seems like a reasonable proposition, but the monastic confuses reason with reality.
6. When the dharma wheel turns, it always goes in both directions.
7. This monastic still has not seen Dongshan.

8. This is where everyday practice empowers in time of need. But say, where did the sick self go?

99 ᘐ
Layman Pangyun's Stringless Lute

MAIN CASE

Layman Pangyun asked Mazu, "Master, please look up at the clear, original person."[1]

Mazu looked right down.[2]

Pangyun then said, "How splendid is this stringless lute. Only you can play it!"[3]

Mazu looked straight up.[4]

Pangyun bowed.

Mazu went back to the abbot's room.[5]

Pangyun followed him into the room and said, "You were skillful enough to do something clumsy."[6]

COMMENTARY

The layman was an adept who had studied with Shitou and Mazu and eventually became Mazu's successor. He comes carrying the clear, original person, and Mazu turns it upside down for him. Don't you see that a non-doing, unconcerned person is still oppressed by golden chains in the deep pit of liberation? Tell me, when Mazu looks down, why does Pangyun call it playing the stringless lute? What is the clear, original person and where is she to be found?

Pangyun's bow only drives Mazu back into the abbot's room. Pangyun follows and says, "You were skillful enough to do something clumsy." What is his meaning? If you can say a turning word here, I'll acknowledge that you have seen through this old kōan.

CAPPING VERSE

The moon above the pines is full
    this cold spring night.

Music of the iron flute fills the air—
    if you know its sound, we can listen together.

NOTES

1. What is he talking about?
2. The old man knows how to pull the rug out.
3. But can you hear it?
4. Do you hear it now?
5. Enough!
6. Inept questions require clumsy answers.

100 ❧

Yunmen's "Dharma Body"

MAIN CASE

Yunmen was once asked by a monastic, "What does it mean to go beyond the dharma body?"[1]
    Yunmen said, "It is not difficult to tell you about going beyond it.[2] But how do you understand the dharma body itself?"[3]
    The monastic said, "Master, please show me an example."[4]
    Yunmen said, "I will give you an example.[5] But first, how do you understand the dharma body itself?"[6]
    The monastic said, "It's just as it is."[7]
    Yunmen said, "This is what you have learned in the monastics' hall.[8] Let me ask you, does the dharma body eat rice?"[9]
    The monastic could not respond.[10]

COMMENTARY

As to what exists before a single thought arises, not a phrase has been transmitted. Stepping forward from the top of a hundred-foot pole, Yunmen wields the sword of Mañjuśrī.
    This was the custom of the ancient masters, and it's still the pivotal upāya to this day. Tens of thousands preserve the self. Only a handful have entered the tiger's cave. Ultimately, the only one who can know is you.

CAPPING VERSE

Without a word,
    the four seasons manifest freely.
Without a voice,
    the ten thousand things reveal
    the true body of the Buddha.

NOTES

1. Asking like this, he splits one into two.
2. Thank you for your answer.
3. Why indulge this monastic? Still, he must respond.
4. He really wants to know.
5. We've already attended to that.
6. Even the ten thousand sages can't leap out of this.
7. He hesitates. Hit him, or else he'll be a zombie for the rest of his life.
8. In the land of dreams, there are only dreamers.
9. Robots don't take food. The man's dead.
10. Fatheaded and dull. After all the effort, he still didn't get it.

101 ∾

Nanyue's "It's Not Like Something"

MAIN CASE

Zen master Huairang of Nanyue [Dahui] went to study with the Sixth Ancestor, Dajian Huineng [Caoxi]. The Sixth Ancestor said, "Where are you from?"[1]
    Nanyue said, "I came from National Teacher Huian of Songshan."[2]
    The Sixth Ancestor said, "What is it that has come like this?"[3]
    Nanyue could not answer.[4] He attended on the master for eight years
and worked on the question. One day he said to the Sixth Ancestor, "Now I
understand it.[5] When I first came to study with you, you asked me, 'What is
it that has come like this?'"
    The Sixth Ancestor said, "How do you understand it?"[6]
    Nanyue said, "To say it's like something misses it."[7]

The Sixth Ancestor said, "Does it depend upon practice and enlightenment?"[8]

Nanyue said, "It's not that there is no practice and enlightenment. It's just that they cannot be defiled."[9]

The Sixth Ancestor said, "Just this nondefilement is what buddhas have maintained and transmitted. You are like this. I am like this. Ancestors in India were like this."[10]

COMMENTARY

To set up monasteries and establish the teachings is like adding flowers to brocade. The wisdom that has no teacher pervades the whole universe, reaching everywhere. When it is truly seen, you go deaf, dumb, and blind. What is there to compare this to? How can it be expressed? Indeed, how can it be understood? Take off the blinders, set down the backpack. This is the peaceful dwelling. This is why it is said, "The ten thousand sages have not transmitted a single particle of the truth. Yet students throughout the world labor over appearances and grasp at reflections."

Tell me, since it is not transmitted, then why are there so many complicated kōans and teachings?

CAPPING VERSE

Blue sky, bright sun—
    there is no distinguishing east from west.
Yet acting in accord with the imperative
    still requires dispensing medicine when the sickness appears.

NOTES

1. This is by no means a casual question.
2. An honest person is hard to find. But is this what the old teacher asked?
3. The rumbling sound of sudden thunder. The dragon uncoils.
4. Mouth agape, tongue hanging out, he doesn't know what to say.
5. Careful here. He may have been better off just not knowing.
6. The old man walks right into his belly.
7. It covers heaven and earth. If the waves of Caoxi were the same, people would get bogged down.

8. It may seem extra, but still, he must be sure.
9. Dragon sons and daughters are always born of dragon parents.
10. In his delight, he runs off at the mouth and adds error to error.

102 ～

Baizhang and the Fox

MAIN CASE

When Master Baizhang Huaihai taught, an old man would always come to hear his dharma talk. He always left when the assembly did, but one day he didn't leave. Baizhang asked, "Who is it that stands there?"[1]

The old man said, "I am not a human being. I was abbot of this monastery at the time of Kāśyapa Buddha. A student asked me, 'Does an enlightened person fall into cause and effect?' I said to him, 'No, such a person does not.'[2] Because I said this, I became a wild fox for five hundred lifetimes. Reverend master, please say a turning word for me. Free me of this wild fox body."

Then he asked Baizhang, "Does an enlightened person fall into cause and effect?"

Baizhang said, "Don't ignore cause and effect."[3]

Immediately the old man was greatly enlightened. He bowed and said, "I am now liberated from the body of the wild fox. My fox body will be found on the other side of the mountain. Master, please do me a favor and bury it as you would a deceased monastic."

Baizhang asked the head of the monastics' hall to announce to the assembly that they were going to have a funeral for a deceased monastic after their meal. The monastics said to one another, "Everyone here is well and no one in the nirvāṇa hall is sick. What's going on?"

After the meal, Baizhang led the assembly to the base of a rock behind the mountain. With his stick he poked out a dead wild fox. Respecting proper procedure, they cremated the body.

In the evening Baizhang gave a dharma talk and told the story of the old man. Then Huangbo asked, "The teacher of old gave a wrong answer and became a wild fox for five hundred lifetimes. What would have happened if he hadn't given a wrong answer?"[4] Baizhang said, "Come closer and I will tell you."[5] Huangbo went closer and slapped Baizhang's face.[6] Baizhang clapped his hands in laughter and said, "I've heard of barbarians whose beards were red. Here is a red-bearded barbarian."[7]

COMMENTARY

If you say "falling into causation," you go straight to hell as quick as an arrow. If you say "not falling into causation," you are a fox through and through. How will you leap clear of Baizhang's trap?

Only Huangbo is able to see through Baizhang's clumsy ghost story. If you fall into the words and ideas or try to imitate Baizhang or Huangbo, you too will be a fox spirit. Say a word that goes beyond dualistic discriminations and free yourself of the fox body.

CAPPING VERSE

Self and other are two parts of the same reality.
When the activity of the mind ceases,
    the ten thousand things return to the self,
    where they have always been.

NOTES

1. He wants to test the stranger.
2. Wrong!
3. Wrong!
4. Tread carefully here; this is a lion stalking its prey.
5. The old man has a strategy of his own.
6. The lion cub is a few steps ahead of him.
7. Ultimately, it's all dirt from the same hole.

103 ∾

Yangshan's Succession

MAIN CASE

When Guishan was meditating, Yangshan Huiji attended on him.[1] The master said, "Yangshan, you recently became a successor of the Zen school.[2]

How is that?[3] Many monastics are wondering about this."[4] Then he said, "Huiji, how do you understand it?"[5]

Yangshan said, "When I'm sleepy, I close my eyes and rest. When I'm feeling fine, I meditate. Therefore, I haven't ever said anything."[6]

The master replied, "To achieve this level of understanding is no easy matter."[7]

Yangshan then said, "According to my understanding, even being attached to this phrase is a mistake."[8]

The master said, "Is it that you are the only one who cannot speak of it?"[9]

Yangshan said, "From ancient times until now, all the sages were just like this."[10]

The master replied, "There are some who would laugh at your answering in this way."[11]

Yangshan said, "The ones who would laugh at me are my colleagues."[12]

The master asked, "How do you understand succession?"[13]

Yangshan walked in a circle around the master, who was sitting on the high seat.[14]

The master said, "The lineage transmitted uninterruptedly from ancient times until now has been broken."[15]

COMMENTARY

Setting up monasteries, establishing the teachings, is like gilding the lily. When you take off the blinders and let go of the baggage, you discover that you have always been in the time and season of great peace.

If you can discern a phrase outside the patterns, the sword of Mañjuśrī is in your hands. The buddhas have not transmitted a single thing. The ancestors have not attained anything. Yet, Zen students everywhere grasp at appearances and struggle over reflections. But say, since it's not transmitted, why so many questions and answers? Furthermore, what have all the successors succeeded to?

CAPPING VERSE

Buddhas have not appeared in the world,
      nor is there anything to be given to the people.
There is just seeing into one's own heart and mind.
It is here that the eternal spring is manifest.

NOTES

1. A single mouth, no tongue.
2. It has never been transmitted, nor has it ever been received.
3. Indeed, how is that? What succession are we speaking about?
4. All of the buddhas and ancestors since time immemorial wonder about it.
5. Diamond-thorn steel brambles. No ordinary monastic can leap clear of this.
6. He holds up the sky and supports the earth. He's found his way amid the brambles. Still, it's difficult not to leave tracks.
7. Neither difficult nor easy. The ancient teachings are found on the tips of a thousand grasses.
8. Good trackers will cover their own tracks.
9. When the fish swims, the water is muddied. When the bird flies, a feather falls.
10. Like what? He wants to drag everybody into it.
11. It takes a fool to recognize a fool.
12. It's all dirt from the same hole. What's the use of so much talk?
13. Again he comes on directly. He wants everybody to know.
14. Deaf, dumb, and blind, he acts according to the imperative.
15. This is as it should be. What end will there ever be to it all?

104 ∾

Deshan's Enlightenment

MAIN CASE

Deshan Xuanjian was a scholar of the *Diamond Sūtra*.[1] He heard that the Zen school was widely spreading in the south and wanted to know why. He dissolved his study group, let his students go, and went south, carrying books of commentaries on the sūtra. He first visited the monastery of Longtan. Entering the monastery gate, he said, "For a long time I heard about the Dragon Pool [Longtan]. But now that I have arrived, I see neither the dragon nor the pool."[2]

Longtan said, "You have arrived personally at the Dragon Pool."[3]

Deshan bowed and walked away. Later that evening he was invited to enter the abbot's room. Deshan stayed with Longtan until the night was deep.

Longtan said, "Why don't you take your leave?"

Deshan then said good night, raised the screen, and walked out. Seeing that it was dark, he turned around and said, "It's dark outside."

Longtan lit a paper lamp and offered it to him. When Deshan was about to take the lamp, Longtan blew out the light.[4]

Deshan suddenly experienced great enlightenment and made a full bow.[5]

Longtan said, "What did you see that made you bow?"[6]

Deshan said, "From now on I will not doubt your words."[7]

On the following day, Longtan gave a talk in the dharma hall and said, "There is a person here. His fangs are like swords. His mouth is like a tray of blood. When I give him a blow, he does not turn his head. Someday he will get to the top of a solitary peak, stand on my path, and advance."[8]

Deshan then took out the books of commentaries he was carrying, held up a torch in front of the dharma hall, and said, "Investigating commentaries is like placing a hair in the vast emptiness. It is like adding a drop of water to an ocean of essential matters in the world."

Then he burned his books and bowed.[9]

COMMENTARY

Deshan made the long journey to southern China in order to discredit the "special transmission outside the scriptures" only to be defeated by an old woman selling rice cakes who buried him in his own rhetoric. Since Deshan did not ask for clarification, the old woman did not give any.

Deshan finally found his way to Longtan, where, although his eyes went blind, he nonetheless ultimately lost his nostrils. Yet even in his blindness, he was able to find his way to Guishan, who tried to get him to step off the hundred-foot pole, but the time was not yet ripe. In the end, however, he was finally able to untie that which was bound and see the last word of Zen. Then, carrying his bowls, he followed the clouds and was freely blown by the wind. Now tell me, what is Deshan's blindness and how did he lose his nostrils?

CAPPING VERSE

Within darkness there is light;
    within light there is darkness.
If you really see it,
    you will go blind.

NOTES

1. Although he is like an overburdened mule, still, there's a fragrant air about him.
2. There is little doubt that he is blind. The question is, what kind of blindness is it?
3. This is too intimate a statement for him. He doesn't get it.
4. Teacher, student, temple, discussion—all taken by the sheer darkness. Nothing remains.
5. What did he see?
6. Easy to say, but what is it really?
7. *Bah*! He should be driven out. First it was the sūtra hanging from his nostrils, now it's a teacher. Where are your own provisions?
8. Like an overly meddling grandparent, he spoils the child.
9. Blind! The baby gets tossed out with the bathwater.

105 ∾

The Hands and Eyes of Great Compassion

MAIN CASE

Yunyan asked Daowu, "How does the Bodhisattva of Great Compassion [Avalokiteśvara] use so many hands and eyes?"[1]

Daowu said, "It's just like a person in the middle of the night reaching back in search of a pillow."[2]

Yunyan said, "I understand."[3]

Daowu said, "How do you understand it?"[4]

Yunyan said, "All over the body are hands and eyes."[5]

Daowu said, "What you said is roughly all right. But it's only eighty percent of it."[6]

Yunyan said, "Senior brother, how do you understand it?"[7]
Daowu said, "Throughout the body are hands and eyes."[8]

COMMENTARY

If your whole body were an eye, you still wouldn't be able to see it. If your whole body were an ear, you still wouldn't be able to hear it. If your whole body were a mouth, you still wouldn't be able to speak of it. If your whole body were mind, you still wouldn't be able to perceive it.

Because the activity of the Bodhisattva of Great Compassion is her whole body and mind itself, it is not limited to any notions or ideas of self or other. Asking the question in the first place is a thousand miles from the truth. Answering only serves to compound the error. Don't you see? Avalokiteśvara Bodhisattva has never understood compassion.

CAPPING VERSE

All over the body, throughout the body—
    it just can't be rationalized.
Deaf, dumb, and blind,
    virtuous arms and penetrating eyes
    have always been right here.

NOTES

1. Why does he ask? Is it out of curiosity or is it an imperative?
2. Miraculous activity is not to be taken lightly.
3. That's exactly the problem that you had in the first place. Stop understanding.
4. It won't do to let him get away with it.
5. Many Zen practitioners fall into this pit.
6. It's because he understands it that he only got eighty percent of it.
7. Make it your own. Don't rely on another's provisions to support your life.
8. No gaps! But say, did he really say it all? If you say he did—wrong! If you say he didn't, you have missed it. What do you say?

106 ❧

Tianhuang's "Essential Dharma Gate"

MAIN CASE

Chongxin of Mount Longtan was making rice cakes[1] for a living. When he met Tianhuang, he bowed and left his household.

Tianhuang said, "Be my attendant. From now on I will teach you the essential dharma gate."[2]

After one year passed Longtan said, "When I arrived, you said that you would teach me the essential dharma gate. I haven't received any of your instruction yet."[3]

Tianhuang said, "I have been teaching you for a long time."[4]

Longtan said, "What have you been teaching me?"[5]

Tianhuang said, "When you greet me, I join my palms. When I sit, you stand beside me. When you bring tea, I receive it from you."[6]

Longtan was silent for a while.[7]

Tianhuang said, "When you see it, you just see it.[8] When you think about it, you miss it."[9] Longtan then had great enlightenment.[10]

COMMENTARY

Longtan comes looking for iron and finds gold. Blinded by expectation, he cannot see the master's grandmotherly kindness in following him around and pointing out that which is high and that which is low.

But say, is Tianhuang's teaching the same or different than Longtan's making rice cakes before he was ordained? If you say the same, you have not seen what Longtan realized. If you say different, you don't understand Tianhuang's teaching. Since the truth is not to be found in these two places, in the end, where do you go to find it?

CAPPING VERSE

Within darkness there is light,
    but don't look for that light.
Within light there is darkness,
    but do not try to understand that darkness.

NOTES

1. A noble profession. Even the great sages cannot praise it fully.
2. Don't deceive the poor man; it can't be done.
3. The gap is enormous; he can't even see the other side.
4. *Gaa!* Now he's going to try to explain it.
5. If he doesn't ask, how will he know?
6. Great foamy waves reaching to the sky.
7. Uh-oh! He's gone. The permutations and combinations can be endless.
8. Body and mind filling the universe.
9. Like leaves scattered in the ten directions.
10. No gaps!

107 ∾

Yunmen's "Two Types of Sickness"

MAIN CASE

Yunmen said, "When light does not penetrate fully, there are two types of sickness.[1] One is that in facing objects it is still not clear if there is something before you.[2] The other is that even having understood the emptiness of all things, in a subtle way there is still something that seems like an object;[3] this is also a case where light has not fully penetrated.[4]

"There are also two types of sickness regarding the dharma body.[5] One is that even having reached the dharma body, one abides at the margins of the dharma body because attachments to self-view still persist.[6] The other is that even having penetrated it, one cannot let go of having penetrated it.[7] You should examine this state carefully and see what kind of freedom you are really breathing,[8] as this kind of freedom is also a sickness."

COMMENTARY

When the thought-cluttered bucket's bottom is not yet broken through, even a single weed in a parched field will in time multiply and create a forest of weeds one hundred feet high. We must be diligent in our practice, realization, and actualization. Thus it is said, "If you have a staff, I will give you a staff. If you don't have a staff, I will take it away."

Yunmen's first illness is about not really having arrived yet. His second illness is having arrived, but not being sure that you have. His third affliction is knowing that you have arrived, and the fourth affliction is having arrived and not being able to leave. Therefore, when moving outwardly, do not pursue ramifications. When moving inwardly, do not abide in a trance. In this way you will naturally pass through Yunmen's sicknesses.

Teachers of our school compound medicine in accordance with the sickness, always employing the appropriate technique for the particular time, place, and condition. You tell me, what is your prescription for the healing of these illnesses?

CAPPING VERSE

My unmoored canoe drifts freely,
  carried by the current.
With each bend of the river,
  finding wonder with the flow.

NOTES

1. Only two?
2. Apparitions dogging each step.
3. Stumbling about in darkness, you keep bumping into yourself thinking it's someone else.
4. Funny, yesterday it all seemed so clear.
5. Only two?
6. I hear you knocking but you can't come in.
7. A good thing is not as good as no thing.
8. Panting is not the same as breathing.

108 ❧

Mazu's "Meaning of the Ancestor's Coming from India"

MAIN CASE

A monastic asked Mazu, "Aside from the four propositions and a hundred negations,[1] please tell me the meaning of the Ancestor's [Bodhidharma's] from India."[2]

Mazu said, "I am tired today. I cannot answer your question.[3] Go and ask Citang Zhizang."[4]

The monastic asked the same question of Citang.[5]

Citang said, "Why don't you ask the master?"[6]

The monastic said, "The master has sent me to you."[7]

Citang said, "I have a headache today, I cannot answer your question.[8] Go and ask Senior Hai [Baizhang Huaihai]."[9]

The monastic asked the same question of Hai.[10]

Hai said, "Having gotten to this point, I don't understand it."[11]

The monastic went back to Mazu and told him the story.[12]

Mazu said, "Citang's head is white. Hai's head is black."[13]

COMMENTARY

This monastic is sad indeed; his questions only succeed in driving these adepts nostril deep in muck and water trying to help him, yet in the end he doesn't get it.

Be that as it may, do you get it? Mazu is tired and sends the monastic to Citang. Citang tries to send him back to Mazu, and when that fails, he says he has a headache and sends him to Baizhang, who in turn says he doesn't understand it. These adepts are accomplished dharma masters; why do they avoid such a challenge? Is it just that it is inexpressible, given the context of the monastic's question, or do they indeed address the matter?

If you can see clearly into this, you will understand that from the outset, the whole scenario was a redundant disaster up to and including Mazu's "Citang's head is white. Hai's head is black." At the same time, it all went beyond the four propositions and a hundred negations.

CAPPING VERSE

The sky is clear, the sun is bright—
    still, he flounders in darkness.
Pines are straight, brambles crooked—
    all things abide in their own dharma place.

NOTES

1. He wants to cut off the old man's tongue before he even asks his question.

2. This is an old question, but still it deserves an answer.
3. This kind of straightforwardness is truly admirable.
4. Can it be that he's trying to duck the question?
5. His questions are fine. It's just that his hearing is a little impaired.
6. What's going on here?
7. There doesn't seem to be a glimmer of life in this monastic.
8. It would seem that Mazu's whole lineage suffers from the same disease.
9. Why does this monastic let himself be shuffled about? Wake up and come out of your cocoon, butterfly!
10. He makes up for his dullness with his persistence.
11. Neither does the poor monastic.
12. This monastic has the tenacity of a hammerhead shark.
13. Nothing in this universe is hidden.

109 ☙

Xuefeng's "Size of the World"

MAIN CASE

Xuansha was once told by Xuefeng, "The size of the world is ten feet. The size of the ancient mirror is ten feet."[1]

Xuansha pointed to the fireplace and said, "What is the size of the fireplace?"[2]

Xuefeng said, "It is as large as the ancient mirror."[3]

Xuansha said, "The tips of your feet have not yet touched the ground."[4]

COMMENTARY

The ancient mirror is not square or round, bright or dull, large or small. It is the eyeball of the buddhas and ancestors. It is completely devoid of borders or edges. Xuefeng brings this up, not only for Xuansha, but for all beings. He wants us to know how to accommodate that which appears in the clear mind of equanimity. But say, since it is boundless, why does Xuansha speak of it in terms of feet and why did Xuefeng avoid saying that the fireplace was ten feet wide?

Xuefeng's "It is as large as the ancient mirror" is the gateway of this kōan. See into it here and you too will lack a square inch of earth upon which to stand.

CAPPING VERSE

Gazing into the ancient mirror,
    form and reflection see each other.
You are clearly it,
    but it is not you.

NOTES

    1. He wants everyone to know; the ten directions cannot contain it.
    2. Is it that he does not understand, or can this be called a confrontation?
    3. Obviously, but nevertheless it is difficult to understand.
    4. There is no place to put this gigantic body.

110 ॰

Guishan Tests His Students

MAIN CASE

One day Guishan asked his students to present their views, saying, "I will see you outside sound and form."[1]

Senior Monastic Jianhong said, "I am willing to come forward; I have no eyes."[2]

Guishan did not approve it.[3]

Yangshan addressed Guishan four times. First he said, "I see what is not seen."[4]

Guishan said, "It is as fine as the tip of a hair and as cold as snow and frost."[5]

The second time Yangshan said, "Who wants to see you outside sound and form?"[6]

Guishan said, "You are holding on to the fan of renunciation."[7]

The third time Yangshan said, "Two mirrors reflect each other with no image in between."[8]

Guishan said, "What you are saying is correct. However, I am right and you are wrong. You have already created an image."[9]

Finally Yangshan said, "As my mind is vague, my answers are clumsy. When you were studying with Master Baizhang Huaihai, what view did you present?"[10]

Guishan said, "I said to Master Baizhang, 'It's like hundreds and thousands of bright mirrors reflecting an image. Although lights and shadows illuminate one another, they are not dependent on one another.'"[11]

Yangshan bowed in gratitude.[12]

COMMENTARY

Distinguishing pebbles from pearls, understanding the difference between profound and naïve, is the work of teachers of our school. Cutting off the myriad streams of thought, dying together and being born together, is the practice of disciples of our school. Guishan and Yangshan are respected in Zen circles as examples of a perfect teacher-disciple merging. When Guishan tests his saṃgha's understanding, it is always Yangshan who relentlessly pursues the truth.

One day Guishan challenges the assembly to meet him outside of sound and form. Senior Monastic Jianhong goes first. Unfortunately his tongue is so long that he steps on it, stumbles, and falls. Yangshan is next. His first try is promising, but not enough to satisfy the old master. His second attempt moves further away from the truth, as he buries his head in the sand. His third attempt is correct in principle, but it fails in expression. But say, how does it fail in expression? How would you say it?

Finally Yangshan admits defeat and asks for instruction. Guishan without hesitation drags out the net of jewels for him to see. Although Guishan's kindness is admirable, he is still trailing mud and dripping water. Haven't you heard the old Zen saying, "Communion by speech without communion with the source is like the sun hidden by clouds. Communion with the source without communion by speech is like a snake in a bamboo tube. Communion with the source and communion by speech together is like the bright sun in the open sky. Communion neither with the source nor by speech is like a dog howling at the moon"? Without separating source and speech, how do you meet Guishan beyond sound and form?

CAPPING VERSE

Dying away, coming to life,
    one should arrive in the bright light of day.
When has the buddha principle ever been a principle?
Don't you know? Real emptiness is not empty.

NOTES

1. When things get quiet you can count on old Guishan to stir things up.
2. *Bah!* This is not even worth discussing.
3. It must have been embarrassing for the old man.
4. He sees the source, but can't seem to express it.
5. Guishan is being kind. He clearly favors this one.
6. What kind of talk is that for a Zen monastic?
7. Again, too kind. Yangshan should not have gotten off so easily.
8. Is he guessing, or does he know what he is saying?
9. Guessing. But say, what image did he create?
10. An honest person is hard to find. He really needs to know.
11. Each and all, the subjective and objective spheres are related, and at the same time independent. Related, yet working differently, though each keeps its own place.
12. Did he get it? Do you get it?

111 ⚭

Fayan's "Eye of the Way"

MAIN CASE

Once Zen master Fayan Wenyi had the well uncovered. The outlet was clogged up with sand. He said to a monastic,[1] "When the eye of the spring is obstructed, sand is in the way.[2] When the eye of the Way is obstructed, what is in the way?"[3]

The monastic could not answer.[4]

Fayan answered for the monastic, "The eye is in the way."[5]

COMMENTARY

When the true eye is clear, it sweeps away all discriminating thoughts and allows us to see absolute intimacy. When the dharma eye is clear, it allows us to see that nothing is hidden in the universe. All things are complete in their suchness.

The true eye is the eye of wisdom which, like the diamond sword of Mañjuśrī Bodhisattva, cuts away all illusions and delusions. The dharma eye is the eye of compassion, whose unconditioned love is the boundless mercy of Avalokiteśvara Bodhisattva, responding to the pain and suffering of all beings.

Everyone has these two eyes, as does the Buddha. When we understand the opening of both eyes, we have obstructed the eye of the Way. When the eyes are opened by the Way itself, there is only blindness. It is thus that the eye of the Way is opened.

CAPPING VERSE

Ten thousand kinds of clever talk and understanding;
    how can they compare with directly seeing the great reality?
Piercing the clouds, penetrating rock,
    never declining the real work.
How can the mountain torrent be held back?
It always finds its way to the great ocean.

NOTES

1. This won't be a casual question.
2. A truthful person is hard to find.
3. What way is he talking about?
4. It seems as though this monastic would prefer to avoid the edge.
5. What eye is he talking about?

112 ∾

The Three Worlds Are Mind

MAIN CASE

Dizang was once asked by his teacher, Xuansha, "How do you understand that the three worlds are just one mind?"[1]

Dizang pointed at a chair and said, "Master, what do you call this?"[2]

Xuansha said, "A chair."[3]

Dizang said, "You don't understand that the three worlds are just one mind."[4]

Picking up a stick, Xuansha said, "I call this a bamboo stick.[5] What do you call it?"

Dizang said, "I also call it a bamboo stick."[6]

Xuansha said, "It's impossible to find a single person in the entire world who understands the Buddhadharma."[7]

COMMENTARY

The Buddha taught that "the triple world is only mind; there is nothing else outside of mind." We should not think that this means that the whole universe is produced by our mind. The reality of the Buddha's statement is that not only is the mind the triple world, but the triple world itself is the mind. They are not one or two, but rather perfect in nonduality.

Be that as it may, tell me, why does Dizang not approve Xuansha? Moreover, why does Xuansha say, "It's impossible to find a single person in the entire world who understands the Buddhadharma?" We should also clarify both "understand" and "you don't understand," as well as the meaning of "I call this a bamboo stick."

CAPPING VERSE

On the summit of the great mystic peak
    the teaching of equanimity is realized.
Each thing perfect and complete,
    lacking nothing.

The three worlds, mind, and things
    are without separation.
Therefore, how can it be spoken of or understood?

NOTES

1. His question makes it sound as if they were two things.
2. He turns the spear around and sends it back.
3. Thank you for your teaching.
4. He too errs. But say, is this a challenge or a compliment?
5. This is all dirt from the same hole. Still, it takes a clear eye to examine it thoroughly.
6. Two fellows playing with mud balls. It's a dirty job, but somebody has to do it. They seem to agree, but what does it really mean?
7. Does either of them really understand "The three worlds are nothing but mind"?

113 ❧

Baofu's Blocking of the Eyes, Ears, and Mind

MAIN CASE

Dizang asked a monastic from Baofu Monastery, "How does your master teach the Buddhadharma?"[1]

The monastic said, "Once Master Baofu Congzhan told the assembly, 'I cover your eyes to let you see what is not seen.[2] I cover your ears to let you hear what is not heard.[3] I restrain your mind to let you give up thinking.'"[4]

Dizang said to the monastic, "Let me ask you, when I don't cover your eyes, what do you see?[5] When I don't cover your ears, what do you hear?[6] When I don't restrain your mind, what do you discern?"[7]

Upon hearing these words the monastic had realization.[8]

COMMENTARY

Baofu covers the monastic's eyes, ears, and mind in order to reveal that which cannot be seen, heard, or perceived. What is revealed that cannot be seen, heard, or perceived? Dizang asks, when eyes, ear, and mind are not covered, what is perceived?

One pushes down; the other lifts up. One stands on the summit of the great mountain and raises waves that encompass heaven and earth. The other descends to the depths of the great ocean and raises mud and sand. Do these two adepts speak of the same thing, or is what they point to different? Is Baofu's covering the same as or different from Dizang's not covering?

Haven't you heard? "If you intend to make a living on the road, you will have to travel by day, not by night." How do you travel by day?

CAPPING VERSE

If they have an eye, I cover it up;
     if they don't have an eye, I uncover it.
The jet black darkness emits light—incredible!
     The whole universe is illuminated.

NOTES

1. Is he testing the monastic or his master?
2. Truly blind. Now, what is in front of your eyes?
3. Truly deaf. Can you hear it?
4. Truly dumb. If it's not a thing, then what is it?
5. His eyes pop out of his head.
6. The 108,000 hymns fill the valley.
7. Beats me! How about you?
8. Like finding a candle in the darkness. But say, what did he realize?

114 ∾
Zhaozhou's Dog

MAIN CASE

A monastic asked Zhaozhou, "Does a dog have buddha nature?"[1]
     Zhaozhou said, "Yes."[2]
     The monastic said, "If so, how does it get into its skin bag?"[3]

Zhaozhou said, "It intentionally offends."[4]
Another monastic asked, "Does a dog have buddha nature?"[5]
Zhaozhou said, "No."[6]
The monastic said, "All sentient beings have buddha nature. How come a dog doesn't have buddha nature?"[7]
Zhaozhou said, "Because it has karmic consciousness."[8]

COMMENTARY

This teaching of Zhaozhou's has created a forest of brambles for countless generations of Zen practitioners. They all seem to confuse the buddha nature with the notion of a separate self rather than the totality of existence. This view exists because they have not yet encountered themselves, encountered others, encountered a teacher, encountered encountering. We should realize that buddha nature is not about enlightenment, knowing, or understanding.

As for the dog and buddha nature, Zhaozhou is not just saying that a dog does or does not have buddha nature. In reality, he is compounding medicine to heal the sickness and compounding sickness to heal the medicine. The question is, what is the sickness? If you wish to understand why Zhaozhou answers the way he does, you must first examine carefully what these two monastics have to say.

CAPPING VERSE

Caught in the sea of affirmation and denial—
    difficult, difficult.
"No" contains the many,
    "yes" has no duality.

NOTES

1. What causes him to doubt?
2. Yes! But it cannot be attained.
3. He seems annoyed with this. How did you manage to create your skin bag?
4. Don't you feel offended?
5. What caused him to doubt?

6. No! Yet it cannot be extinguished.

7. Indeed! This monastic seems sad.

8. Does it make you wonder about yourself?

115 ๏

Dagui's "No Buddha Nature"

MAIN CASE

[Guishan] Dagui once said to the assembly,[1] "Sentient beings have no buddha nature."[2]

At another time, Yanguan said to his assembly, "Sentient beings have buddha nature."[3]

Two monastics from Yanguan's community were visiting Dagui to check on his teaching. They heard Dagui's dharma discourse but could not understand the depth of his teaching. They grew arrogant.[4] When they were sitting in the garden, they saw Yangshan coming. They advised him, saying, "Senior brother, it's not easy; you should study Buddhadharma diligently."[5]

Yangshan drew a circle in the air, showed it to them, and threw it over his back.[6] Then he stretched out his arms and asked them to return the circle.[7] The two monastics were dumbfounded and did not know what to do.

Yangshan advised them saying, "It's not easy; you should study the Buddhadharma diligently."[8] He paid his respects and left.

While the two monastics were on their way back to Yanguan, after traveling thirty miles, one of them had realization and said in admiration, "Dagui's words 'Sentient beings have no buddha nature' are not mistaken."[9] He went back to Dagui.[10] The other monastic had realization when he was crossing a river. He said in admiration, "Regarding Dagui's words, 'Sentient beings have no buddha nature,'[11] there must be a reason for saying that."[12] He also returned to Dagui.

COMMENTARY

The floating gourd, when pressed down, turns and pops to the surface. A multifaceted jewel in a sunbeam changes its shape as the light changes.

Sometimes Yangshan points south and he calls it north. Is this mindful or is it mindless? When you call it existence, he points to nonexistence. If you say it's nonexistence, he points to existence. If you say it is neither existence nor nonexistence, he is able to manifest the sixteen-foot golden body of the Buddha in a heap of dust.

Be that as it may, tell me, what is Yangshan's intention? Furthermore, since Dagui's teaching and Yanguan's teaching do not accord, whose is the correct view? If you say Dagui's, you have missed it. If you say Yanguan's, you have also missed it. To say both or neither is a hundred thousand miles from the truth. What will you say?

CAPPING VERSE

Buddha nature, no buddha nature—
    trapped between two iron mountains.
All over the world explanations and excuses.
Seeing the flaw he hides the jewel—
    people everywhere search for it.

NOTES

1. Unavoidably, complications are sure to follow.
2. A competent teacher of our school is naturally independent.
3. This has always been a nest for Buddhist practitioners.
4. Ungraspable. It's right in your face, right on your head. Where are you?
5. Physician, heal thyself. Not easy, not hard.
6. He hides his body but reveals his shadow.
7. They don't know they have it. Indeed, this is an occasion to be sad.
8. Not easy, not hard. There's an echo in these words.
9. Where did he get the news? *Bah!* He's on his way to a ghost cave.
10. Mistake!
11. Where did he get the news? He comes following along adding error to error.
12. Fundamentally, it's not a matter of interpretation or understanding.

116 ∽

Nanyue's "Mirror Cast as a Buddha Image"

MAIN CASE

Nanyue was once asked by a monastic, "When a mirror is cast as a buddha image, where does the reflection go?"[1]

Nanyue said, "The face you had before you left home, where did it go?"[2]

The monastic said, "How come the mirror does not reflect after becoming a buddha image?"[3]

Nanyue said, "Even with no reflection, it does not deceive you even a bit."[4]

COMMENTARY

The mirror is like reality itself. It reflects what is before it without prejudice. When a foreigner appears before it, a foreigner is reflected. When a native appears, a native is reflected. However, we should understand that what is being spoken of here is not polished copper, reflections, or images but, rather, the matter of the mirror's ability to be cast into a buddha image. This is the point we should study.

In answer to the monastic's question, Nanyue produces a mirror to reflect the monastic's face, saying, "The face you had before you left home, where did it go?" Indeed, I ask you, what is your own true face, the face you had before your parents were born?

The monastic persists, "How come the mirror does not reflect after becoming a buddha image?" Nanyue then says, "Even with no reflection, it does not deceive you even a bit." Do you understand his meaning? The before and after of mirror and image contains the whole universe, thus! Therefore, how can it deceive?

Further, we should investigate taking up an image and casting a mirror, as well as taking up a mirror and casting an image. When the great wheel of the teachings turns, it always moves in both directions.

CAPPING VERSE

Few have really understood the monastic's questions,
    fewer still are able to grasp the master's answer.

The mirror faces form without subjectivity,
    the image devoid of reflections enlightens.

NOTES

1. Look to the place where the image came from.
2. After all, coming and going is always right here.
3. A mirror is a mirror; a buddha image is a buddha image. Is this the same or different?
4. Mind ground meets itself.

117 ∾

Jinhua's Ancient Mirror

MAIN CASE

A monastic asked Jinhua Hongtao, "How is it when the ancient mirror is not yet polished?"[1]
    Jinhua said, "An ancient mirror."[2]
    The monastic said, "How is it after it is polished?"[3]
    Jinhua said, "An ancient mirror."[4]

COMMENTARY

There is a time when the ancient mirror is polished; there is a time before it is polished, and there is a time when it is being polished, but it is always the ancient mirror through and through. Further, as Master Dōgen said, "There are times when we polish without making anything; there are times when it would be possible to make something, but we are unable to polish. All are equally the traditional practice of the buddhas and ancestors."

    There is a bit of fragrant air about this monastic. We should therefore consider his question carefully. Is the ancient mirror the same or different before and after it is polished? If you say the same, you cloud its true thusness and miss it. If you say different, you are bogged down in mind and environment, and are lost on the road of interpretation. At a time such as this, what do you say?

CAPPING VERSE

The great primordial mirror
    has no flaws, gaps, or impurities.
There is not a single speck of dust in the universe
    that is not the ancient mirror itself.

NOTES

1. This question is too lofty. You will just have to see for yourself.
2. The old master easily explains, but what is his meaning?
3. Take a look for yourself, monastic.
4. Is there any difference between the two?

118 ❧

Yangshan Can't Say It

MAIN CASE

[Guishan] Dagui asked Yangshan, "I hear that you gave ten answers to one question when you were studying with Baizhang Huaihai.[1] Is it true?"[2]

Yangshan said, "Not at all."[3]

Dagui said, "How do you say one phrase about going beyond Buddhadharma?"[4]

Just as Yangshan was about to speak,[5] Dagui shouted.[6] Dagui asked Yangshan this question three times,[7] and three times he shouted before Yangshan could speak.[8]

Yangshan hung his head and said with tears rolling down his cheeks,[9] "My late master said, 'When you meet a genuine person, you will get it.'[10] Today I have met a genuine person."[11] Then he decided to go off and take care of the buffalo for three years.

One day when Dagui went to the mountains,[12] he saw Yangshan doing zazen under a tree.[13] Dagui tapped Yangshan on the back once with his staff.[14] Yangshan turned his head.[15] Dagui asked, "Huiji, can you say it?"[16]

Yangshan replied, "Although I cannot say it,[17] I will not depend upon someone else's mouth."[18]

Dagui said, "Huiji, you've got it!"[19]

COMMENTARY

The sky is mute, yet the four seasons in all their beauty and diversity take place there. The earth is deaf, dumb, and blind, yet the ten thousand things are born here. How can you tolerate creating patterns? What sense is there in describing reality when it can be experienced directly?

These days, where can we find an adept who has abandoned words and speech? When you have cut off emotional defilements and conceptual thinking, only then will you become clean and naked, free and unhindered. Otherwise, how will you impart strength to others?

CAPPING VERSE

The buffalo's head sprouts horns
    as he emerges from the weeds.
In a dream, he tries to speak
    of the valley of the timeless spring.
Although he has bathed in the fragrant waters,
    I hit, saying, "Not good enough.
    How will you impart strength to others?"

NOTES

1. This is no casual conversation.
2. The hook is baited. The fisherman is old and skilled.
3. He's undeniably truthful. It's good news too.
4. Dagui is used to getting his own way. The hook doesn't work, so he employs a net and hauls the monastic in. He knows his own abilities.
5. Strike! Got him!
6. This is as it should be. This kind of imperative can't be ignored.
7. It pays not to be misunderstood.
8. Perhaps if he'd used his stick instead, all of this wouldn't have taken so long.
9. Are these tears of remorse or joy?
10. It takes an adept to be like this. If Dagui hadn't recognized him, he would probably have let him go.
11. Yangshan meets himself, but he hasn't realized it yet.
12. Following the wind, pursuing the fragrant grasses.

13. Even though this is nothing special, still it amounts to something.
14. Is he awake or asleep?
15. Alive and well, tending the buffalo.
16. He already opened his guts a while ago. It's important that he finish it.
17. Hard to respond, even for an adept. Thank you for your answer.
18. *Bah*! He just can't say it. Still, an honest man is hard to find.
19. Singing and clapping, they accompany each other. Those who know the tune are few indeed. They add error to error.

119 ∾
Zhaozhou's Cypress Tree

MAIN CASE

A monastic asked Zhaozhou, "What is the meaning of the Ancestor's [Bodhidharma's] coming from India?"[1]

Zhaozhou said, "The cypress tree in the garden."[2]

The monastic said, "Master, please don't teach using an object."[3]

Zhaozhou said, "I am not showing an object to you."[4]

The monastic said, "What is the meaning of the Ancestor's coming from India?"[5]

Zhaozhou said, "The cypress tree in the garden."[6]

COMMENTARY

Zhaozhou's Zen cuts off the myriad streams and stuns the mind. There is just no place to take hold of it. This cypress tree is not to be found in the world of phenomena, nor can it be found in the realm of emptiness. Then where shall we search for it?

Putting aside the cypress tree, I ask you, what is the meaning of the Ancestor's coming from India? If you can clearly see into the monastic's question, you will see through Zhaozhou's response.

If you think there's any meaning whatsoever, then you won't be able to save even yourself. If you say there is no meaning, you are still a hundred miles from the truth. What will you say?

CAPPING VERSE

Nothing whatsoever to say.
The pine trees singing
    in spring's warm breeze.
The ten thousand hymns of forest and wind
    fill the river valley.

NOTES

1. Again?
2. Open your eyes.
3. What is he talking about?
4. The old man tries to set it straight.
5. Again?
6. Why even bother? Let him go on deceiving himself.

120 ♋

Priest Jin Asks About the Nature of Life

MAIN CASE

Head Priest Jin asked Head Priest Longji Shaoxiu, "Even if we understand
the unborn nature of life, why are we confined by life?"[1]
    Xiu said, "A bamboo shoot will be a bamboo ladle in the future. But can
we use it as a bamboo ladle now?"[2]
    Jin said, "You will understand it some day."[3]
    Xiu said, "I am like this now. How about you?"[4]
    Jin said, "This is the monastery office. That is the monastery kitchen."[5]
    Xiu made a full bow.[6]

COMMENTARY

These two priests are from the same household, so they know the kitchen
pantry well. Jin's question, though it seems like a simple inquiry, in reality

conceals the hook and line that determine power and assess level. Xiu too has an undeniable command of the teachings, so he says, "A bamboo shoot will be a bamboo ladle in the future. But can we use it as bamboo ladle now?" This is known as sitting still on a level plain. Haven't you heard Master Baizhang Huaihai's saying, "Understanding the meaning according to the sūtras is the adversary of all buddhas of the three times?"

Jin spins the dharma wheel in the other direction for Xiu, laying out a trail free of traces or tracks. Seeing the opening of living potential, Xiu gets it and bows. But tell me, what is the road of living potential that is realized?

CAPPING VERSE

Ranks and stages create subdivisions
    where there are none.
Spontaneously empty and at ease,
    who lacks the ability to eat and dress?

NOTES

1. Careful here! Hidden beneath the silky soft mud lies a bed of thorns.
2. If you are going to wade the river, you should first know where the ford is.
3. Suddenly a wolf appears from beneath the sheepskin.
4. Not only is he willing to stand his ground, but he paws the turf.
5. Suddenly it's a different ball game in a different place.
6. He is with it in an instant. But what did he see that made him bow?

121 ❧

Mayu Locks the Gate

MAIN CASE

Lecturer Liangsui went to study with Mayu Baoche for the first time. Mayu saw him coming, picked up a spade, and plowed under some weeds.[1] When Liangsui got to where Mayu was working, Mayu turned and went back to the abbot's hut and locked the gate without paying attention to him.[2]

The following day Liangsui went to the hut and knocked on the gate. Mayu said, "Who is it?"[3]

Liangsui said, "My name is Liangsui," then suddenly had an awakening by saying his own name.[4] Then he said, "Master, please don't shut me out. If I hadn't come to pay respect to you, I would have been entangled by sūtras and commentaries all my life."[5]

Liangsui went back to his study group and announced: "What everyone knows, I know.[6] What I know, I alone know."[7] He then dissolved the study group.[8]

COMMENTARY

Mayu's kindness is unsurpassed. He is like a doting parent spoiling a child with overindulgence. If one is not careful, this could all end up in what the ancients called the deep pit of liberation. Under a clear sky and in the bright light of day, there is no longer a need to point out this and that. Still, the causality of time, place, conditions, and degree requires the ability to dispense medicine in accordance with the sickness.

Can you see Liangsui's sickness? Haven't you heard it said that "what comes in through the front gate isn't the family treasure"? Do you understand Mayu's medicine? It's not that he doesn't know who is knocking; it's just that he wants to know "Who is it?"

In a single phrase there is killing, and there is giving life. In a single action there is holding fast and there is letting go. Do you understand?

CAPPING VERSE

Asking without knowing,
    answering without understanding.
The moon is cold, the wind is high—
    perched on a cliff's edge, a frozen pine.

NOTES

1. Better to have removed them altogether.
2. Mayu is not taking him lightly; only an adept can truly appreciate what is going on.

3. The depth of his kindness is unfathomable.
4. Tell me, what was he awakened to?
5. He wants to sweep away his tracks.
6. His everyday affairs are no different from anyone else's.
7. It's just that he himself knows how to naturally harmonize.
8. Good one.

122 ∾
Fayan's Fire God

MAIN CASE

Baoen was once studying in the community of Fayan.[1] One day Fayan said, "How long have you been with us?"[2]

Baoen said, "I've been in your community for three years."[3]

Fayan said, "You are a junior person in the monastery. How come you never ask questions?"[4]

Baoen said, "I don't want to mislead you. I must confess. When I was with Master Yuezhou, I attained the peaceful bliss."[5]

Fayan said, "By what words did you enter that place?"[6]

Baoen replied, "When I asked Master Yuezhou, 'What is the self of the practitioner?' he said, 'The fire god seeks fire.'"[7]

Fayan said, "Good words, but I'm afraid you didn't understand them."[8]

Baoen said, "The fire god belongs to fire, fire seeking fire is just like the self seeking self."[9]

Fayan said, "Indeed, you didn't understand. If the Buddhadharma were like that, it wouldn't have come down to this day."[10]

Fayan said, "Why don't you ask me?"

Baoen then said, "What is the self of the practitioner?"[12]

Fayan said, "The fire god seeks fire."[13]

At that, Baoen experienced a great awakening.[14]

COMMENTARY

If you have seen it clearly, you have the freedom to manifest it in the marketplace or on the road. Like a hawk in the sky or the salmon sporting the rapids, there is no hindrance. If you're still not clear, you're tossed about by circumstances, positions, and expectations. It's like a rabbit in a snare: the more it struggles, the tighter the snare gets.

When a person of clarity meets another of equal clarity, there is no doubt about what is correct or incorrect, and each further illuminates the other. However, when a clear-eyed one meets a person of knowledge, regardless of rank or position, then teacher meets disciple and the great function is brought out. Tell me, what is the great function?

CAPPING VERSE

If you are not intimate with it, when it's revealed,
    you'll think about it for the rest of your life.
That which gains entry through the gate
    is not the family treasure.

NOTES

1. Why does he hang around Zen monasteries like this? What is he seeking?
2. After all, he must ask. If he didn't, this could go on endlessly.
3. All that he values most is about to be stolen. Even worse, he draws a map for the thief.
4. Like a falcon taking a pigeon, he sweeps down, talons extended.
5. What a pity. Still, it's possible to show some life.
6. Strike one! It wouldn't do to let him go.
7. He digs a deep pit and hurls himself into it. Clearly, he's dull-witted.
8. Strike two! The true imperative must be carried out.
9. Strike three! He's out.
10. What a pity. If there's even a spark of life, there's still life.
11. Good move. Three times knocked down, four times get up.
12. How new! How fresh!
13. If you understand it, all things are separate and different. If you don't understand it, all things are one.
14. The task of study is now completed.

123 ᴄᴠ

Mayu's "Nature of the Wind"

MAIN CASE

Master Baoche of Mount Mayu was fanning himself.[1] A monastic approached and said, "Master, the nature of wind is permanent and there is no place it does not reach.[2] Why then must you still fan yourself?"[3]

"Although you understand that the nature of the wind is permanent," the master replied, "you do not understand the meaning of its reaching everywhere."[4]

"What is the meaning of its reaching everywhere?"[5] asked the monastic. The master just fanned himself.[6] The monastic bowed with deep respect.[7]

COMMENTARY

If you have realized the truth of this kōan, you will know that to encounter one activity is to practice one activity, to attain one dharma is to penetrate one dharma.

If, however, this is not yet clear, then take the backward step and see for yourself how Mayu's fanning himself is not only the wind reaching everywhere but the fan, Mayu, the monastic, and you yourself reaching everywhere.

CAPPING VERSE

Words cannot convey the action,
    letters cannot embody the truth.
How can they compare
    with old Mayu just fanning himself?

NOTES

1. Fragrant air fills the ten directions.
2. Where did he hear about this?
3. It's not that the light doesn't shine everywhere, it's just that this monastic can't see it.

4. Lowering a hook, the old master responds to the imperative.
5. Seeing the bait, the monastic climbs onto the hook.
6. Throughout the heavens and encompassing the earth, there is no place it does not reach.
7. Tell me, what did the monastic see that made him bow?

124 ∾
Monastic Shen's Fish and Net

MAIN CASE

One day Senior Monastic Shen and Senior Monastic Ming visited the river Huai. They saw a fisherman pulling in a net from which a carp escaped.[1] Shen said, "Brother Ming, look how splendid the fish is! It is just like a skilled practitioner."[2]

Ming said, "It is indeed. But how come the fish did not avoid being trapped by the net in the first place?[3] It would have been much better."[4]

Shen said, "Brother Ming, there is something keeping you from being enlightened."[5]

At midnight Ming understood the meaning of the conversation with Shen.[6]

COMMENTARY

If you know the music the moment the violin strings begin to vibrate, then you know how to navigate through the forest of brambles and entanglements with freedom and ease. If, on the other hand, you think that with practice the forest of brambles and entanglements will altogether disappear, then right from the beginning you are hopelessly entangled and won't find your way.

Monastic Ming cannot see the freedom of the golden-scaled fish as it leaps free of the net. He is lost in the hope of a future in which there will be no barriers and a present that is free of all difficulties. Senior Shen compassionately points this out to Ming, who then realizes it for himself in the middle of the night. If you wish to realize this teaching as your own, then when one dharma is encountered, one dharma is practiced. At such a time, the forest of brambles and entanglements is itself realized as the marvelous mind of nirvāṇa.

CAPPING VERSE

When a fish swims, water is muddied;
 when a deer passes, its tracks remain.
No one falling on the ground can rise
 without using the ground.

NOTES

1. Leaping over the three-tiered gate, a dragon is born.
2. Magnificent! Can you see the workings of the great function?
3. Why didn't you avoid the quicksand that you are sinking into?
4. *Aye!* Now there's the rub—better and worse.
5. Ideas, notions, attachments, joys, regrets, accomplishments, goals— *bede bam, beda boom.*
6. In the middle of the night is not like anything.

125 ∾

Caoshan's Dharmakāya

MAIN CASE

Caoshan asked Senior Monastic De,[1] "Buddha's true dharma body is like empty sky.[2] It reflects forms just like water.[3] How do you express this principle?"[4]

De said, "It's like a donkey looking at a well."[5]

Caoshan said, "You have got the point,[6] but you have said only eighty or ninety percent of it."[7]

De said, "Master, how would you say it?"[8]

Caoshan said, "It's just like a well looking at the donkey."[9]

COMMENTARY

Sacred and secular intermingled, dragons and snakes living together. Even the wise ones and sages cannot distinguish between them.

Look at the great net of Indra. Whose face is it that's revealed in each diamond? Walking the razor's edge, the lotus blooms in the fire. Those who can see into it here not only save all sentient beings but are saved by all sentient beings.

CAPPING VERSE

When the teacher sees the student,
  the student sees the teacher.
For the student to meet the teacher,
  he must be the teacher.
Isn't this the teacher meeting herself?
Isn't this the student meeting himself?

NOTES

1. In creating complications, filial piety is requited.
2. This old monastic talks too much. He should shut his mouth.
3. How else would you have it?
4. What will he say? How can it be explained?
5. Although it's just so, it fouls the air to say it.
6. It won't do to let him get away with it.
7. There's an echo in these words. Is he deceiving this monastic?
8. The monastic comes back at him. After all, he's a lion cub.
9. We may call it this and that, but still, it's all dirt from the same hole.

126 ✲

Dadian Remains Silent

MAIN CASE

One day Lord Hanyu Wengong said to his teacher Dadian Baotong, "I have many state affairs to oversee. Let me ask you as your student, what is the essential point for my work?"[1]

Dadian was silent for a while.[2] Wen was confused about this.[3]

At that time Sanping Yizhong was Dadian's attendant monastic. Sanping struck the meditation platform three times.[4]

Dadian said, "What is it?"[5]

Sanping said, "Lord, you should first push with samādhi, then pull with prajñā."[6]

Wen thanked Sanping and said to Dadian, "Your teaching standard is so high that your attendant has made a place for me to enter."[7]

COMMENTARY

If you can transcend discriminations, you will enter unity and discover your true form. Master Dadian awkwardly tried to reveal this by trying to cut off the myriad streams of thought for the official, but before the dust had time to settle, the attendant, still unripened and eager, meddled in the encounter and carried the official off with him into the forest of brambles.

Although the attendant had an eye, he had not yet clarified how to impart strength to others. Buddhist texts and universities are filled with this kind of Zen, but of what use is it on the road? Haven't you heard that in explaining the dharma there is neither explanation nor teaching; in listening to the dharma there is neither hearing nor attainment? This being the case, what is the meaning of Dadian's silence?

CAPPING VERSE

If your words do not leave the old clichés,
> how will you free yourself from the vines and entanglements?
The mist-covered mouth of the valley
> causes many to miss the source.

NOTES

1. Tens of thousands of Zen practitioners get stuck here every day.
2. Although his great compassion is extraordinary, I'm afraid the official will not understand.
3. He does not understand.
4. Although he stands on neutral ground, he sees through it and acts accordingly.
5. Again he does not understand.
6. Unfortunately the whole encounter has degenerated into words and explanations. The attendant should be hit on his fat mouth.
7. *Bah!* What did he enter?

127 ∾
Mañjuśrī's "Three Three"

MAIN CASE

Mañjuśrī asked Longquan Wenxi [Wuzuo], "Where are you from?"[1]

Longquan said, "From the south."[2]

Mañjuśrī said, "How is Buddhadharma being maintained in the south?"[3]

Longquan said, "Monastics in the declining age seldom follow the precepts."[4]

Mañjuśrī said, "How large are the assemblies?"[5]

Longquan said, "Some three hundred—others five hundred."[6] Then Longquan asked, "How is Buddhadharma maintained here?"[7]

Mañjuśrī said, "Ordinary people and sages are living together, dragons and snakes are intermingled."[8]

Longquan said, "How large are the assemblies?"[9]

Mañjuśrī said, "In front, three by three; in back, three by three."[10]

COMMENTARY

Longquan carried on a dialogue with an apparition, and though it was the Bodhisattva of Wisdom himself, somehow he still could only see half. At that time, when Mañjuśrī first asked, "How is Buddhadharma being maintained in the south?" Longquan should have showed him with his traveling staff. Then further complications would have been avoided.

Mañjuśrī, seeing past the dragon mask, compassionately tried to settle the uncertainty. Wielding the diamond sword of wisdom, in a single phrase there is killing, there is giving life; in one action there is letting go, there is holding fast. Tell me, did Longquan get it? If so, then what is it? If not, do you get it?

CAPPING VERSE

Holding up the adamantine sword,
    freely killing and giving life.
Where positive and negative interfuse,
    every day is a good day.

NOTES

1. Never mind where he came from. Where did you come from?
2. When in doubt, honesty is always the best policy.
3. This is not a casual question. Please don't take it lightly.
4. Too bad. He took it lightly.
5. Mañjuśrī's heart is huge. He won't give up easily.
6. Today we have encountered a person who is fast asleep.
7. It seems as though he is pushing back, but not really.
8. Isn't it nice? He doesn't omit anyone.
9. What else could he say, since he has no idea about what is happening?
10. For more than a thousand years, monastics the world over have been trying to bite into this.

128 ⚬

Baizhang's "Gate of Essential Nature"

MAIN CASE

During a work period at his monastery, Baizhang Huaihai was plowing the ground.[1] A monastic heard the sound of the drum ending the work period.[2] At that moment he held up his hoe, burst into laughter, and went back to the monastery.[3]

Baizhang said, "Wonderful. This is Avalokiteśvara entering the gate of essential nature."[4]

After Baizhang returned to the monastery, he sent for the monastic and asked, "What did you see to make you laugh like that?"[5]

The monastic said, "I was hungry. As soon as I heard the drum, I returned to have the noon meal."[6]

Baizhang laughed.[7]

COMMENTARY

In the practice of the Zen school, it is important to avoid chasing after sounds and clinging to forms. In spite of the fact that it is possible to clarify the mind upon hearing a sound, one should still transcend discriminating consciousness and avoid attaching to phenomena. How do you transcend discriminating consciousness and avoid attaching to phenomena?

Among the myriad sounds, there is perceiving and there is understanding. In reality, there's only whole body and mind intimacy. Hearing intimately is not like ordinary hearing. Ordinary hearing is done with the ear. In intimacy there is hearing with the eye and seeing with the ear. How do you hear with the eye and see with the ear? Let go of the ear, and the whole body and mind is nothing but the ear. Let go of the eye, and the whole universe is nothing but the eye.

CAPPING VERSE

Seeing forms and hearing sounds intimately
    is the whole body and mind seeing and hearing.
It's not like reflections in a mirror
    or echoes in the valley.

NOTES

    1. A day of no work is a day of no food.
    2. Does the sound come to the ear, or does the ear go to the sound?
    3. Like reaching back for a pillow in the middle of the night.
    4. When lightning strikes the mountain, thunder rolls through the valley.
    5. It's important to know if this is apparent or real.
    6. When the wind comes from the east, the leaves gather in the west.
    7. Among the three kinds of laughs, what kind of laugh is this?

129 ❧
Yaoshan's "Nonthinking"

MAIN CASE

When Yaoshan was sitting in meditation,[1] a monastic asked,[2] "What do you think about as you sit in steadfast composure?"[3]

Yaoshan said, "I think not-thinking."[4]
The monastic said, "How do you think not-thinking?"[5]
Yaoshan said, "Nonthinking."[6]

COMMENTARY

Abide in neither thinking nor not-thinking. Thinking is linear and sequential—a separation from the reality that is the subject of thought, and thus is an abstraction rather than the reality itself.

Not-thinking is suppressive—it cuts away thoughts the moment they arise, making the mind into a great impenetrable mountain: dead and unresponsive. Nonthinking has no such edges. It is the boundless mind of samādhi that neither holds on nor lets go of thoughts. It is the manifestation of the buddha mind in which the dualism of self and other, thinking and not-thinking, dissolves. This is the dharma of thusness that is the "right thought" of all the buddhas of the ten directions.

CAPPING VERSE

When the dharma wheel turns,
    it always goes in both directions.
The still point is its hub, and from here,
    all of our myriad activities emerge.
Rather than give solace to the body,
    give solace to the mind.
When both body and mind are at peace,
    all things appear as they are:
    perfect, complete, and lacking nothing.

NOTES

1. What is he doing? Even Kashō Buddha didn't attain it with hundreds of kalpas of zazen.
2. Why doesn't he leave the old man alone?
3. Eh? What are you thinking in asking such a question, venerable monastic?
4. He is much too kind. It really can't be explained. He's just setting the monastic to thinking.

5. Now they are both in the same hole. Just shut up and sit!

6. How kind. But say, what does it mean?

130 ∽

Yangshan's Karmic Consciousness

MAIN CASE

Guishan asked Yangshan, "If someone says that all sentient beings have only karmic consciousness, which is vast and there is nothing to depend upon, how would you prove it?"[1]

Yangshan said, "I have a way to prove it."[2]

Then, as a monastic passed by, Yangshan called out to him, "Reverend!" The monastic turned his head.[3]

Yangshan said, "Master, this is karmic consciousness, which is vast and there is nothing to depend upon."[4]

Guishan said, "This is a drop of lion's milk that splatters away six gallons of donkey's milk."[5]

COMMENTARY

Karmic consciousness is a result of past actions conditioned by delusion. Delusion exists as a result of consciousness, consciousness results from ignorance, and ignorance is dependent on mind. Yet mind is originally pure. It has no origination or cessation. It is without doing or effort, without karmic retribution, without superiority or inferiority. It is still, serene, and intelligent.

We should understand that one's original, unchanging self-nature is neither holy nor profane, neither deluded nor enlightened. The delusions of ordinary beings and the enlightenment of the buddhas are one reality, which has nothing to do with the senses or its objects nor mind or its environment.

This being the case, tell me, what is it that Yangshan uncovered when he examined the monastic that caused Guishan to say, "This is a drop of lion's milk that splatters away six gallons of donkey's milk"? Haven't you heard of the ancient who hung a signboard at the gate that said, "Beware of dog. On top he takes people's heads, in the middle he takes people's midsection, at the bottom he takes people's legs. Hesitate and you are lost." As soon as he saw a newcomer, he would shout, "Look out for the dog!" The moment the visitor turned his head, the master would return to the abbot's room. This kōan too is like that.

CAPPING VERSE

Vast and boundless, open and free—
    there are no gaps.
Who are the sentient beings?
Who are the buddhas?

NOTES

1. These two were in the habit of exchanging faces several times each day.
2. Hesitancy was not one of Yangshan's disadvantages.
3. How come he turned his head?
4. Is there something lacking here?
5. The old man overindulges him. It's still just a drop.

131 ও
Anguo's "The Master's Flesh Is Still Warm"

MAIN CASE

Master Huiqiu of Anguo, who was also called Lying Dragon, asked Monastery Director Liao, "My late master said that the entire universe of the ten directions is the true human body.[1] Do you still see the monastics' hall?"[2]

Liao said, "Master, I don't have illusory visions."[3]

Anguo said, "Although my master has passed away, his flesh is still warm."[4]

COMMENTARY

The meaning of "the entire universe of the ten directions is the true human body" is that the eye, ear, nose, tongue, skin, flesh, bones, and marrow of each one of us is at once the liberated manifestation of the ten directions. It is not limited to the superficial notions that we use to define the skin bag.

This entire universe of the ten directions is the self before our parents were born, and it is actualized as our present existence. Furthermore, it does not move from place to place. It simply exists thus.

Anguo wants to see if the temple director is clear about this. He says, "Do you still see the monastics' hall?" Liao shows he is free from two or three, saying, "Master, I don't have illusory visions." He clearly must be blind. But say, what kind of blindness does he suffer from? If you can say a turning word, then Xuansha's warm flesh has reached the twenty-first century. If not, you should investigate this question thoroughly.

CAPPING VERSE

Parent and child become each other,
      they become each other.
Before spring has arrived,
      the fragrance of blossoms fills the valley.

NOTES

1. It is so big that there is no place it can abide.
2. He wants to see if his vision is impaired.
3. There are no ghosts in front of this skull.
4. *Nieee!* I snap my fingers three times.

132 ∿

Boshui's "Sound Itself Is No Sound"

MAIN CASE

Boshui Benren said to the assembly, "Normally we don't want to confuse descendants by talking about what is before sound and after a phrase. Why is this so? Sound is not sound. Form is not form."[1]

A monastic said, "What is sound that is not sound?"[2]
Boshui said, "Can you call it form?"[3]
The monastic said, "What is form that is not form?"[4]
Boshui said, "Can you call it sound?"[5]
The monastic could not say another word.[6]
Boshui said, "Let me say that if you understand this, I will approve that you have entered the place."

COMMENTARY

In the teachings of the Way, the phrase "a transmission outside of words and letters" is commonly misunderstood as a negation of the expression of sounds in communicating the dharma. Here Master Boshui points to the truth that precedes sound, and to the intuitive perception that follows a phrase. In the Buddhadharma this is called intimate talk—expression that can be recognized and understood even though it has no sound. However, we should appreciate that although there is no sound, it cannot be called silent, for this is not a matter that exists in the realm of yin and yang.

Master Yunju, when asked by a government official, "What is the World-Honored One's intimate speech?" said, "Minister!" The official said, "Yes!" Yunju said, "Do you understand?" The officer said, "No, I don't." Yunju said, "If you don't understand it, that's the World-Honored One's intimate speech. If you *do* understand it, it's Mahākāśyapa's not hiding it." Do not mistake the calling and answering as intimate talk, because in intimate talk no communication whatsoever can take place. The great master Dōgen says, "'If you don't understand it' is to sanction a course of quietly learning in practice. 'If you *do* understand it' does not mean to grasp it as intellectual understanding."

Just as sound contains not-sound, so too, form contains not-form. Each is unified in a single ineffable reality existing right here now. Spirit and matter are the same reality. There is not a special spiritual force that exists separate from the phrases we utter or the forms we perceive. If you can understand this, you have entered the "place" Boshui speaks of. If you don't understand it, you must then study the place that is before sound and after a phrase.

CAPPING VERSE

The Buddha gave an intimate discourse,
   Mahākāśyapa did not conceal it.
Flowers open in a night of falling rain,
   valley streams at dawn fill with spring fragrance.

NOTES

1. This matter simply cannot be discussed, so why bring it up in the first place?
2. When a bell is struck, its resounding is sure to follow.
3. If you say so, but so what?
4. This monastic is now in it up to his nostrils.
5. Where is this all leading to?
6. The monastic is now in a pit six feet deep with no way out.

133 ∾
The Woman of Daishan

MAIN CASE

There was an old woman on Mount Dai path. A monastic asked her, "Where is the path to Mount Dai?"[1]
   The old woman said, "Go straight ahead."[2]
   The monastic went on.[3]
   The woman said, "My dear Reverend, you too go off like that."[4] Monastics came one after another to ask the same question and received the same answer.[5]
   Later, one of the monastics told Zhaozhou about it. Zhaozhou said, "Wait here for a while. Let me check her out."[6]
   He went to the woman and said, "Where is the path to Mount Dai?"
   The woman said, "Go straight ahead."[7]
   Zhaozhou went on.[8]
   The woman said, "My dear Reverend, you too go off like that."[9]

Zhaozhou came back and said to the assembly, "I have checked out that woman for you."[10]

COMMENTARY

If the old woman's eye was really open, why did she say, "Go straight ahead"? Then again, if she did not have an eye, why did she say, "My dear Reverend, you too go off like that"?

If you are able to clearly see how Zhaozhou saw through the old woman, then you will see that the old woman saw through Zhaozhou as well. But say, what did Zhaozhou see? If you can take a bite out of this point, then I will concede that you have eaten the full meal.

CAPPING VERSE

Before the question is asked,
      you have already arrived.
Before taking a step,
      you are already home.

NOTES

1. South of the north pole, north of the south pole, you can't miss it.
2. She is being helpful but not in the way one might think.
3. He doesn't know how deep the mud is right under his feet.
4. She hits him with a mud ball right in back of the head.
5. It must be said she is dependable.
6. He needs to check the eye of the source.
7. Got it! But say, what did Zhaozhou see?
8. When the wind blows the reeds bend.
9. He doesn't seem to mind the mud on his sandals.
10. Now the whole assembly has grown horns.

134 ∾

Guishan's "Is It the Weather or the Person That Is Cold?"

MAIN CASE

Guishan asked Yangshan, "Is the weather cold, or is a person cold?"[1]
    Yangshan said, "The great house is right here."[2]
    Guishan said, "Why don't you talk straight?"[3]
    Yangshan said, "So far I have not gone around. How about yourself?"[4]
    Guishan said, "It flows straight away."[5]

COMMENTARY

It is the family style of the members of the Guiyang school to polish their understanding through probing and encounter. Guishan wants to see if Yangshan's understanding has developed any edges. He asks, "Is the weather cold, or is the person cold?" Yangshan skillfully avoids the pitfall by saying, "The great house is right here." Although this is a transcendent statement, it still has the echo of a voice from the top of a one-hundred-foot pole.

Guishan tries to open it up by pressing the matter further, but Yangshan holds fast and turns the spear around. Seeing that the river is frozen solid, the old master acts according to the imperative. He says, "It flows straight away." But what does this mean?

We should understand that to uphold the treasury of the true dharma eye, we must move beyond transcendence and be able to respond equally in all ten directions. Right now, how do you respond equally in all ten directions?

CAPPING VERSE

Rain and thunder, with news of the world,
    thaw the frozen river.
The path to the great ocean
    is naturally opened.

NOTES

1. This is not about the weather; it's about where are you now?
2. When it's cold, heaven and earth are cold; when it's hot, heaven and earth are hot.
3. It's not so much that it's crooked; it's just not straight.
4. He is certain enough to be willing to grapple with the old man.
5. Rolling it out, he leaves nothing concealed.

135 ∾
Zhaozhou's Brick and Jewel

MAIN CASE

Zhaozhou said, "I will take your questions. If you have a question, bring it to me."[1]

A monastic came out and bowed.[2]

Zhaozhou said, "Recently I cast a brick and caught a jewel. Today here is another brick." Saying so, Zhaozhou got off his seat.[3]

Later Fayan asked Guangxiao (Iron Beak) Huijue about the meaning of this story.

Huijue said, "Let me give you an example. When the Imperial Court wanted to commission a commander, they asked 'Who has the qualifications to accept the position?' Whenever a person answered 'I have got it' their reply was, 'You haven't got it.'"[4]

Fayan said, "I understand it now."

COMMENTARY

Zhaozhou doesn't need the shout of Linji or the blows of Deshan to kill a monastic. His "lips and mouth Zen" has a killing as well as a life-giving edge. When Zhaozhou invites questions, this monastic brings out a bellyful of Zen. Zhaozhou responds to the imperative and snatches it away. He knows how to take away what you don't have and give you what you do have. Haven't you heard Master Dōgen's saying, "When the truth does not fill our body and mind we think that we have enough. When the truth fills our body and mind, we realize that something is missing"? But say, what does Zhaozhou see that prompts his response?

Hearing of this, Fayan asks Zhaozhou's successor, Guangxiao Huijue, for some clarification. Iron Beak only succeeds in dumping another bucket of muddy water on the whole thing. If you want to attain the truth of the matter, you must go right to the source yourself and not depend on hearsay. Tell me, what is the truth of the matter?

CAPPING VERSE

Don't be fatheaded!
　　The limits of the knowable are unknowable.
How much rain does it take
　　before the great ocean is full?

NOTES

1. Although he appears like a kindly old man, he conceals the fangs and claws of a lion.
2. Alas, he has fished out a dead one. It's best not to try to fool people.
3. The old man wastes no time in exposing the hoax.
4. Although it may have been helpful, fortunately it has nothing to do with the matter.

136 ∿

Zhaozhou Asks about the Great Death

MAIN CASE

Zhaozhou asked Touzi Datong, "How is it when a person who has died the great death comes to life?"[1]

　　Touzi said, "They should not go by night.[2] They must arrive in daylight."[3]

COMMENTARY

It seems as though Zhaozhou is going out of his way to torment this old hermit. When the ancient masters traveled around like this visiting adepts, they wanted to see if their eyes were open. If there is even the slightest attempt to understand this encounter in terms of Buddhist doctrine or theory, this is not yet having died the great death. On the other hand, if you turn to blank consciousness to perceive it, you will only see the darkness of a ghost cave.

It can be said that this is truly a case where the answer is in the question and the question is in the answer. Haven't you heard? Spring is always in the frozen branches, buried beneath six feet of snow. However, unless you first realize the truth you cannot engage it. So cut off both light and darkness and say a word.

CAPPING VERSE

A frozen tree blossoms
    in the dead of winter.
Rising autumn mist reveals
    a collage of red and gold.

NOTES

1. Although he is alive, he is deliberately offensive with his dead question.
2. Otherwise, you will just stumble around and never find your way.
3. Bread on the table, water in the pitcher.

137 ❧
Xuefeng's "Not a Snowflake Remains"

MAIN CASE

Yunju asked Xuefeng, "Has the snow outside the monastery gate gone away?"[1]

Xuefeng said, "Not even a flake is left. What else is there to go away?"[2]
Yunju said, "Gone."[3]

COMMENTARY

These two adepts both studied with Dongshan and knew the dharma ter-
rain well. Yunju's question, though seemingly casual, is a trap to fell a tiger.
Xuefeng, too, has reached the point where he knows how to shift and turn
in accord with circumstances. He says, "Not even a flake is left. What else is
there to go away?" Haven't you heard Master Dōgen's saying, "For every
flake of falling snow, where could it fall or land?" Again, he said, "Ten tril-
lion people open the wondrous gates." Do you understand?

Existence and nonexistence, buddhas and ordinary beings—fundamentally, where are the differences? Mountains and rivers and one's own self—
how could there be any distinctions? Why then, is it all divided into two
sides? Take off the blinders and see, nothing is hidden. Set down the pack
and let it go, and you will find that the gate of great liberation is right here
now, and that boundless freedom of action is within your own body and
mind.

CAPPING VERSE

Buddhahood is not a principle;
    the absolute is not empty.
Ultimate reality exists right here,
    in the midst of chaos.

NOTES

1. He is not just inquiring about the weather. Can you see where he is
   going?
2. All-pervading throughout heaven and earth, yet it cannot be found.
3. He just added frost on top of snow.

138 ⌁
Zhaozhou's Brightness and Darkness

MAIN CASE

Zhaozhou asked Nanquan, "Does brightness accord, or does darkness accord?"[1]

Nanquan got off his seat and went back to the abbot's room.[2]

Zhaozhou said, "That old priest is always talking, and yet he couldn't say a word when I asked a question today."[3]

The head monastic said, "Don't say the abbot could not say a word. It's only that you didn't get it."[4]

Zhaozhou slapped him and said, "This slap is for the abbot."[5]

The head monastic was silenced.[6]

COMMENTARY

Zhaozhou asks his old teacher, Is it the mind of differentiation that is in accord with realization or is it the mind of equality that is in accord with realization? To accord with differentiation misses the unity of the ten thousand things. To accord with unity ignores the variety of the myriad things. How are these diverse views to be reckoned with? Nanquan is just too old and experienced a teacher to be bamboozled by his student, so he just walks away without a word.

Zhaozhou's harsh response in reality conceals a deep admiration for the old man. However, the head monastic missed the point of the dharma dance of teacher and student and scolded Zhaozhou. Now I ask you, was the head monastic correct? Did Nanquan say a word that Zhaozhou missed? Without a moment's hesitation, Zhaozhou changed faces with his teacher and hit the monastic. See how host and guest merge and transform in accord with circumstances?

If you can see into Zhaozhou's question, you will understand Nanquan's action. If you understand Nanquan's action, you will appreciate Zhaozhou's comment. If you can appreciate Zhaozhou's comment, you will recognize the imperative created by the head monastic and the necessity for Zhaozhou's mandate.

CAPPING VERSE

The forest of patterns is clearly apparent;
    the myriad forms are evident.
Too much talking can impair virtue;
    silence is certainly effective.

NOTES

1. There are thorns in the soft mud.
2. Not a growl or a whimper from the old lion. He just walks away.
3. He is really impressed with the old man, though he doesn't act it.
4. Although this sounds very confident, he is just scratching before it itches.
5. As it turns out, the child must take up the parent's work.
6. It's fortunate that he doesn't get it. If he had pressed further it would have been embarrassing for everyone.

139 ॰

Yangshan's "Entering Nirvāṇa"

MAIN CASE

Yangshan asked Commander Lu, "I hear that you achieved enlightenment by reading a sūtra? Is this true?"[1]

Lu said, "Yes, Master. When I read the *Nirvāṇa Sūtra*, it said, 'Without cutting off desire enter nirvāṇa.'"[2]

Yangshan held up a whisk and said, "How can this enter nirvāṇa?"[3]

Lu said, "There is no need for even the word 'enter.'"[4]

Yangshan said, "'Enter' is not for you."[5]

Lu stood up and left.[6]

COMMENTARY

Commander Lu is a government official reputed to have attained enlightenment by reading a sūtra. When he is questioned by Yangshan, it becomes apparent that he is talking about a dream and has not yet realized the reality the *Nirvāṇa Sūtra* is pointing to.

The Sixth Ancestor came to realization upon hearing the words of the *Diamond Sūtra*. Master Shitou experienced great enlightenment upon reading the *Zhao Lun* treatises. To be awakened to the Way by words is not uncommon, but when it occurs, it is revealed in one's words and actions. It's not just a matter of believing or understanding.

When Yangshan asks how his fly whisk can enter nirvāṇa, Lu mimics the sūtra, saying, "There is no need for even the word 'enter.'" Yangshan has no choice but to act on the imperative and say, "'Enter' is not for you." Do you understand? If you do, then say a word for Lu and tell me, without cutting off desire, how do you enter nirvāṇa?

CAPPING VERSE

"Thus I have heard" through "I believe"
    are words that describe reality.
Stop chasing after thoughts and ideas,
    and see into the adamantine wisdom directly.

NOTES

1. Such things have been known to happen.
2. Indeed, so it says, but where are you?
3. He has his suspicions, so he must be tested.
4. His logic is flawless—but.
5. The distance between the ideas that describe reality and reality itself is equal to the distance between heaven and earth.
6. Confirmed, he does not want to play anymore.

140 ∾
Dayi's "No Mind"

MAIN CASE

Dayi Daoxin asked his teacher Jianzhi Sengcan, the Third Ancestor, "What is the mind of the ancient buddhas?"[1]

Sengcan said, "What kind of mind do you have now?"[2]

Dayi said, "I have no mind."[3]

Sengcan said, "Since you have no mind, why would you think buddhas have mind?"[4]

Dayi immediately ceased to have doubt.[5]

COMMENTARY

It is clear that Dayi is an adept and has investigated the Way. He has to a certain degree eliminated conceptual thought and intellectual defilement. But still, there is this "What is the mind of the ancient buddha?" Indeed, what is the mind—any mind, *your* mind? How big is it? Where does it reside? Does it really exist or not? The answers to these questions require that each one of us plummet the depths of our own mind.

When pressed by his teacher, Dayi, like his dharma grandfather Huike before him, has to admit that mind is ultimately ungraspable. Do you understand? Because the mind has no form, it pervades the whole universe, existing right here now. This truth comes from the direct experience of plunging into another dimension of consciousness. It is not a matter of understanding or knowing.

Sengcan presses again, saying, "Since you have no mind, why would you think buddhas have mind?" The ice begins to melt, the waters begin to flow, and no further communication is possible.

But say, since Dayi has no mind, where was he holding the doubt that he ceased to have?

CAPPING VERSE

When thoughts disappear, the thinker disappears,
    and all things manifest as they are.
In this reality, all intentional efforts vanish.
In this world of suchness, nothing is excluded.

NOTES

1. What can he say? This is something that simply cannot be explained.
2. Answering the question with a question, Sengcan wants his student to discover his own provisions.

3. The three worlds are nothing but mind. Where will you seek for the mind?
4. A cosmic enema cleans out everything.
5. Boiling water always melts the ice.

141 ∾

The World-Honored One Ascends the Teaching Seat

MAIN CASE

One day the World-Honored One ascended the teaching seat and the assembly came together.[1]

Mahākāśyapa struck the mallet and announced: "The World-Honored One has just expounded the dharma."[2]

The World-Honored One descended from the teaching seat.[3]

COMMENTARY

While the World-Honored One is still settling in his seat, Mahākāśyapa steps in and precipitates the whole matter, so the World-Honored One descends from his seat. If at that time there had been a live one among the assembly, the hoax would have been revealed.

There are some that think the meaning of this case lies in the World-Honored One's silence or his taking the high seat in the first place. Nothing can be further from the truth. There are others that look to the striking of the mallet to understand. This too misses it completely. The dharma is not to be found in ascending the seat, striking the mallet, Mahākāśyapa's speech, or the World-Honored One's silence. If you can see into it here, you have seen into the hoax.

CAPPING VERSE

A single path of spiritual light—
    from the beginning nothing is hidden.
Subtly communicated without effort—
    at once, the spring breeze opens a thousand blossoms.

NOTES

1. What for? Is there something to be imparted?
2. Before a word is spoken, he understands.
3. Ascending and descending in a thousand assemblies. Still, there is only one who got it.

142 ∽

Yangshan's Discourse

MAIN CASE

Yangshan Huiji was once asked by a monastic, "Does the dharma body understand a dharma discourse?"[1]

Yangshan said, "I can't speak about it,[2] but someone else can."[3]

The monastic said, "Where is the person who can?"[4]

Yangshan pushed forward a pillow.[5]

Guishan heard about it and said, "Huiji used the blade of a sword."[6]

COMMENTARY

Because the dharma body is deaf, dumb, and blind, old Yangshan has to resort to extraordinary measures. This monastic's potential is bound up in thought, and Yangshan wants to set it free. If you want to see the point of Yangshan's answer, you must first see the point of the monastic's question. When a tree is pruned properly, it will ultimately grow stronger, and the fruit will be sweeter.

Yangshan's pushing forward of a pillow should not be taken as zazen. However, zazen should not be ignored. Just avoid all intellectual interpretations, see into the matter directly, and say a word of Zen.

CAPPING VERSE

No thing ever falls short
    of its own completeness.
It always manages to cover the ground
    upon which it stands.

NOTES

1. What are you calling the dharma body?
2. Somewhere along the way he has lost his tongue.
3. He wants to drag the monastic into the pit with him.
4. The monastic seems willing to go along with it.
5. Why doesn't he just hit him in the head with it?
6. Although it was a bit excessive, still, the point was made. But say, what's the point?

143 ও

Touzi's Clarification of the Ancestors' Intention

MAIN CASE

Furong Daokai said to his teacher Touzi Yiqing, "'The intentions and phrases of the buddhas and ancestors are like everyday meals.' Besides this, are there any other words for guiding people?"[1]

Touzi said, "When the emperor of the nation issues a decree, does he need to confirm this with the ancient emperors Yu, Tang, Yao, or Shun?"[2]

Furong was about to open his mouth to speak, when Yiqing covered his mouth with his fly whisk[3] and said, "As soon as your mind arises, you deserve twenty blows of the stick."[4]

Furong had realization, made a bow, and began to leave.

Touzi called out, "Reverend!"

Furong didn't even turn his head.[5]

Touzi said, "Have you reached the place of no doubt?"[6]

Furong covered his ears and left.[7]

COMMENTARY

Although Furong knows how to say, "The intentions and phrases of the buddhas and ancestors are like everyday meals," it is clear that he has not yet experienced the miracle of this truth. The eating and drinking of everyday meals is the essential truth of all dharmas. To eat and to drink is to experience any activity, and at the very moment of fully experiencing an activity, we merge with its ultimate reality. Thus, dharma is eating and eating is dharma. This truth can only be realized by oneself, can only be verified by oneself.

Just as Furong is about to fall into a thicket of word brambles, Touzi snatches away his tongue. Having broken the rhinoceros horn of doubt, there is no calling him back. Tell me, what is this place of no doubt that Touzi asks about?

If you can show it, then whether you dwell in the canyons of a city or the stillness of the wilderness, I will grant that you are free, unhindered, and complete wherever you stand. If not, you must study this matter of every-day meals carefully.

CAPPING VERSE

Winding river, endless mountains—
    the dark forest breathing mist.
There is no road into the sacred place.
It's just that, the deeper you go,
    the more wondrous it becomes.

NOTES

1. Although he can talk the talk, he cannot yet walk the walk.
2. Little toad, come out of your hole and see for yourself.
3. Endless conversation always leads to distraction.
4. When the mind arises, brambles appear. Even if the mind does not arise, this is not yet it.
5. When its stomach is full, you can't push down a cow's head to eat grass.
6. The old master will create complications if he can.
7. Enough. Enough!

144 ∿

Xuansha's "Twenty Blows of the Stick"

MAIN CASE

Xuansha was one day attending Xuefeng, when two monastics passed near the steps. Xuefeng said, "Those two seem like promising grass that can produce seeds for planting."[1]

Xuansha said, "I would not say that."[2]

Xuefeng said, "What would you say then?"

Xuansha said, "I would give them twenty blows of the stick."[3]

COMMENTARY

The ability to distinguish dragons from snakes, discern diamonds from stones, differentiate the profound from the naive, and settle all lingering doubt is the occupation of teachers of the Zen school. Although Xuefeng and Xuansha seem to differ in their opinion of the two monastics, both see their potential. One wants to harvest, the other wants to cultivate.

If you want to enter the mind ground of equanimity, investigate Xuefeng's words and realize your own promise. If you want to penetrate the truth, go directly to Xuansha's phrase and practice your own potential. But say, is what they are saying different or the same?

All of this notwithstanding, we should realize that chick and hen must be of one mind, tapping and pecking must accord, or else the moment of opportunity will be missed.

CAPPING VERSE

Born of the same lineage, they share the knowledge;
    dying of different lineages, they are separate and distinct.
If the waves of Caoxi were all the same,
    ordinary people would get mired in the mud.

NOTES

1. What does he see that makes him speak in this way?
2. Only an adept would act this way.
3. Xuefeng should have given him a taste of his own medicine.

145 ∾

Deshan's "Neither Asking nor Not Asking"

MAIN CASE

Deshan Xuanjian said to the assembly,[1] "If you ask,[2] you have missed it.[3] If you don't ask,[4] you have also missed it."[5]

Then a monastic stepped forward[6] and made a bow.[7] Deshan hit him.[8]

The monastic said,[9] "I haven't even asked yet. Why did you hit me?"[10]

Deshan said, "What difference would it make if I had waited till you spoke?"[11]

COMMENTARY

As soon as we create one side, the other side arises spontaneously. Caught in this and that, our freedom is lost in confusion. But say, is it more effective to hold fast or to let go? At this point, if you approach it with ideas and concepts, you will miss it by a hundred thousand miles. How is this to be addressed then? We should bring our attention to the place that is beyond thought. We must see into that which is beyond words and ideas. What is the place that is beyond words, ideas, and thought? It's just this! Be that as it may, tell me, how do you avoid Deshan's blows?

CAPPING VERSE

Fundamentally it's not a matter
    of interpretation or knowledge.
Summed up, it's not worth a single word.
When the myriad mental activities cease,
    truth is miraculously manifested.

NOTES

1. He gathers the clouds and brings on the rain.
2. If we don't ask, how will we know?
3. The eye of humans and gods has been blinded.
4. If we ask, how will we know?

5. Who is it who can deviate, and from what?
6. Among the dead, here is a live one.
7. Why bow? Knock the old geezer out of his seat.
8. Obviously! He has no choice but to act in accord with the imperative.
9. Hit him again! Otherwise he'll go on like this forever.
10. He wants to know but the old monastic can't explain.
11. *Bah*! Now that foolish monastic has the old man explaining. Thirty blows.

146 ॐ
The Sixth Ancestor's "Your Mind Is Moving"

MAIN CASE

The Sixth Ancestor, Dajian Huineng, went to Faxing Monastery,[1] where the temple flag was waving in the wind. Two monastics were arguing about whether it was the wind or the temple flag that was moving.[2] They discussed this back and forth but could not agree on the truth of the matter.[3] The Sixth Ancestor, seeing this, said, "It's neither the wind nor the flag that is moving. It's your mind that is moving."[4] The two monastics were immediately awestruck.[5]

COMMENTARY

It's not the wind or the flag that moves, nor is it both the wind and the flag that move, nor can it be said that it is neither the wind nor the flag that moves. Seeing that the monastics are mired in duality, the Sixth Ancestor says, "It's your mind that is moving."

Although the ancestor is compassionate, he nevertheless creates an awkward scene. Haven't you heard Nun Miaoxin's saying "It's neither the wind nor the flag nor the mind that is moving?" This being the case, can it be said that the Sixth Ancestor is mistaken, or is it Miaoxin who is mistaken? If you can see what this all comes down to, you will be able to open up a road for others. Say a word of Zen and leap clear of dualistic thinking.

CAPPING VERSE

Wind, flag, mind—
      bah, humbug!
If you wish to attain intimacy,
      just close the gap.

NOTES

1. After fifteen years hidden in the mountains, the tiger again prowls the monasteries.
2. Why?
3. Endless dialogue rarely leads to truth.
4. What is the mind that moves?
5. It's easy to impress others, but what did they see?

147 ∾
Linji's "True Person of No Rank"

MAIN CASE

Linji said to the assembly,[1] "There is a true person of no rank.[2] This person goes in and out of your senses.[3] Those who are beginners and have not had realization, look, look!"[4]

COMMENTARY

The true person of no rank is the real form of truth as it appears throughout the universe. It is fluid and in a constant state of becoming. The true person of rank is the real form of truth as it appears throughout the universe. It, too, is fluid and in a constant state of becoming. Rank and no rank are nondual. Therefore, each and every thing up to and including each one of us exists thus!

The essence of all phenomena is thusness; the real nature of body and mind is thusness. Therefore, it cannot be attained by any personal effort. Realized or not, it has always been manifesting as our very life itself.

CAPPING VERSE

It is at once you,
    yet you are not it.
It must be understood in this way,
    if you are to merge with suchness.

NOTES

1. This old mountain monastic reveals or transforms according to the occasion.
2. When you really see it, you go blind.
3. Everywhere the light shines. Of what use is employing coming and going?
4. Why is it necessary to look for it? It's never been lost.

148 ∾

Dongshan's "Teachings of the Insentient"

MAIN CASE

Dongshan studied with Yunyan. Dongshan asked Yunyan, "Who can hear the teaching of the insentient?"[1]

Yunyan said, "It can be heard by the insentient."[2]

Dongshan asked, "Do you hear it, master?"[3]

Yunyan said, "If I heard it, then you would not hear my teaching."[4]

Dongshan responded, "That being the case, then I don't hear your teaching."[5]

Yunyan replied, "You don't even hear my teaching. How could you hear the teaching of the insentient?"[6]

Dongshan was enlightened on hearing this[7] and responded in verse:

Wondrous, marvelous!
The teachings of the insentient are inconceivable.

If you listen with the ears, you won't understand.
When you hear with the eyes, then you will know.[8]

COMMENTARY

The ten thousand things are neither sentient nor insentient; the self is neither sentient nor insentient. Therefore, the teaching of the insentient cannot be perceived by the senses.

This teaching is heard before there is a body and after mind is forgotten. It was heard before our parents were born and before the Buddha appeared. It is not a matter of ordinary consciousness.

How then, can it be heard? When body and mind have fallen away, in the stillness that follows, the teaching is intimately manifested in great profusion. Whether we are aware of it or not, it is always taking place.

CAPPING VERSE

The teaching of the insentient:
 if you try to grasp it, you will miss it—
  it has no form.
If you try to let it go, you cannot separate from it—
  it is not formless.
Subtle and wondrously inconceivable,
 the muse constantly reveals the mysterious teachings
  of the ten thousand things.

NOTES

1. Fences, walls, tiles, pebbles, the Brooklyn Bridge.
2. This is not the province of either existence or nonexistence.
3. He presses the old master; he really wants to understand.
4. When sentient beings hear it, they are no longer sentient beings.
5. This monastic is becoming slippery.
6. The old man leaps into his belly.
7. If you try to grasp this, you cannot get it. It has no form, so it's non-existent. If you try to get rid of this, you cannot let it go, for it is you yourself. It is not nonexistent. What did Dongshan see?
8. This is not cognition or thought. It has no relationship to any physical or psychological object. Indeed, it's not like something.

149 ∾
Xuefeng's Rice Field

MAIN CASE

One day Xuefeng said to the assembly, "What we are talking about is like a rice field.[1] It is dependent upon the people plowing the fields and planting the seeds.[2] Do not miss receiving this gift."[3]

Xuansha said, "Then what is the rice field itself?"[4]

Xuefeng said, "Look!"[5]

Xuansha said, "Although what you say is correct, I wouldn't say it that way."[6]

Xuefeng said, "Then how would you say it?"[7]

Xuansha said, "One by one, each and every person."[8]

COMMENTARY

Those lost in the mundane seek solace in the sacred. This is because they have not as yet understood the sacred matter of ordinary household activity. The wholehearted practice of the Way simply has no edges.

It is because the truth of life is beyond existence and nonexistence that there is plowing the fields, planting the seeds, and thus a rice field. Indeed, it is because of this gift of activity that one's own self has come into being.

CAPPING VERSE

The buildings and the grounds
    protect the dharma and bring peace to all.
The saṃgha in the ten directions
    grows in wisdom and compassion.
How this comes to us,
    is a gift we should not miss.

NOTES

1. Actually, it's ultimately not like anything.
2. Blinking the eyes, raising a hand, covers the heavens and encompasses the earth.

3. Thus we bow to each other.
4. Did he miss the point, or is he testing his old master?
5. He has taken in everything.
6. This one is not easily satisfied. But say, where can he go with it?
7. He wants to know if this is an impostor or an adept.
8. Living in the same household, they both know the cupboard well.

150 ∾

Mazu's "Raising the Eyebrows and Blinking the Eyes"

MAIN CASE

Mazu said to Yaoshan, "Sometimes I have him raise his eyebrows and blink.[1] Sometimes I do not have him raise his eyebrows and blink.[2] Sometimes having him raise his eyebrows and blink is right.[3] Sometimes having him raise his eyebrows and blink is not right."[4]

COMMENTARY

If the great function were to remain within fixed patterns, the full human potential would never be realized. Therefore, teachers of our school have always devised methods outside of patterns and in accord with the imperative of time, place, position, and degree.

Mazu wants Yaoshan to know that the single vehicle of incomparable liberation can be seen from different perspectives. On the one hand, the ten thousand things are one reality; on the other hand, the one reality is the ten thousand things. They are at once different and equal, interdependent—and yet, neither one of them is the absolute basis of reality.

Be that as it may, tell me, what is the meaning of raising the eyebrows and blinking the eyes, and why is it that sometimes this is right and sometimes it is not right?

CAPPING VERSE

Among the myriad forms,
   a single body is revealed.

In the single body,
    the myriad forms are contained.

NOTES

1. Now is not like the past; the future will not be like now.
2. Past, present, and future are this very moment.
3. The ass looks at the well.
4. The well looks at the ass.

151 ❧

Yaoshan's "Precious Treasure of the Way"

MAIN CASE

A monastic asked Yaoshan, "What is the most precious treasure of the Way?"[1]

Yaoshan said, "Don't flatter others for your own benefit."[2]

The monastic said, "How is it when one does not flatter others?"[3]

Yaoshan said, "Even if an entire nation were offered, it would not be accepted."[4]

COMMENTARY

If one always acts as a guest flattering the host, then by virtue of this action the countless treasures belong to others. Each and every being in itself is perfect and complete, lacking nothing. What need is there to seek anything outside ourselves? When we search for a reality outside the self, we obscure our own true nature and thus will never realize it.

The monastic wants to know how it is when one does not flatter others. Yaoshan says, "Even if an entire nation were offered, it would not be accepted." What is his meaning? Can you see that secular power has no sway over someone who has realized her own spiritual power and wondrous functioning? But say, what is spiritual power and wondrous functioning? There are questions and there are answers. There is guest and there is host. Tell me, how is it when there is no guest and host?

CAPPING VERSE

The monastic had the precious treasure but didn't know it.
Yaoshan lifted it up for him to see.
The forest of brambles clearly revealed,
    the ten thousand forms, self-evident.

NOTES

1. Why create waves where there is no wind?
2. Is it OK to flatter others for their benefit?
3. He first wants to know what the payoff is going to be.
4. This one just can't be bought.

152 ॰ঌ

The National Teacher's Stone Lion

MAIN CASE

Nanyang arrived at the front of the palace with Emperor Suzong.[1] Nanyang pointed at a figure of a stone lion[2] and said to the emperor, "Your Majesty, this lion is extraordinary.[3] Please say a turning word."[4]

Emperor Su said, "I cannot say anything.[5] Will you please say something?"[6]

Nanyang said, "It is my fault."[7]

Later Danyuan Yingzhen asked Nanyang,[8] "Did the emperor understand it?"[9]

Nanyang said, "Let's put aside whether the emperor understood it.[10] How do you understand it?"[11]

COMMENTARY

The teacher of three emperors has an obligation to fulfill. How else will there be peace in the land? The emperor thinks the old master is talking about an object and cannot find a way in. The National Teacher answers for him, going in every direction at once. Do you see it?

Range upon range of endless mountains, rocks, and bluestone cliffs—all deliver their profound sermon. Murmuring streams and roaring rivers expound the teachings of formless form day and night. The insentient all hear it. Can you? If you stop to think, as the emperor did, you will surely miss it. When you have not as yet seen it, it's all like an impenetrable forest of brambles. When you do see it, you will discover that you are the impenetrable forest of brambles. The time and season of great peace is simply not a matter of this and that.

Danyuan's later question is superficial, so the National Teacher makes it real. To make it real for you, I ask again, how do you understand the National Teacher's "It is my fault?"

CAPPING VERSE

The mountain monastic's fault—
    inexhaustible, truly inexhaustible.
I think of Annie Oakley:
    two silver dollars from the hip,
    with a single bullet.

NOTES

1. Traveling with this old troublemaker is bound to result in complications.
2. He rattles his sword.
3. There's only this in the whole universe. That's how rare it is.
4. *Gaaah!* He squeezes the emperor's head.
5. An honest man is hard to find these days.
6. He lets the cook taste it first.
7. The stone lion bites the royal ass. Very intimate, very intimate indeed!
8. Why is he asking? What's unresolved?
9. That was yesterday's breakfast. What about now?
10. Seeing the opportunity, the thief strikes again.
11. Spent arrows are not wasted by this old campaigner. Did the monastic understand? Do you?

153 ⌇

Layman Pangyun's "Power-Attaining Phrase"

MAIN CASE

Bailing once saw Layman Pangyun on a street. He asked Pangyun, "Some time ago you had a power-attaining phrase at Nanyue. Have you used it for guiding others?"[1]

Pangyun said, "Yes, I have been speaking it."[2]

Bailing said, "To whom have you been speaking?"[3]

Pangyun pointed at himself and said, "To Mr. Pangyun."[4]

Bailing said, "This is more than Mañjuśrī and Subhūti can praise."[5]

Pangyun in turn asked Bailing, "Who knows the power-attaining phrase?"[6]

Bailing put on his straw hat and walked away.[7]

Pangyun called out, "Have a good journey!"[8]

Bailing kept walking without turning back.[9]

COMMENTARY

The old layman calls out, and he himself answers. Alone throughout heaven and earth, he can ultimately only nod to himself. But say, what about the matter of guiding others that Bailing asks about? Although he may praise the layman, the fact is, no matter how you cut it, you can't drive stakes into empty space.

In the end, Bailing's own power-attaining phrase carries him off, staff across his shoulders, into the myriad peaks. Does the layman understand? Indeed, do you understand?

CAPPING VERSE

When you see it, it's not that it's not there,
      but if you dawdle too long, you'll go blind.
Stepping off the hundred-foot pole,
      there is work to do,
      songs to sing, dances to be danced.
Linger, and you miss the opportunity.
Act too soon, and you'll break your neck.

NOTES

1. Poking with his staff, he wants to know how deep the pond is.
2. He is making dragon sounds, but does he have both horns?
3. The old adept pokes around a little more.
4. He must be lonely.
5. Why is he being so kind?
6. The layman too has a probing pole.
7. Seeing the imperative, he acts.
8. I don't think he can hear him.
9. He doesn't hear him.

154 ∾

Nanquan's Sickle

MAIN CASE

Nanquan was once on the mountain, working.[1] A monastic came by and asked him, "Which is the Way that leads to Nanquan?"[2]

Nanquan raised his sickle and said, "I bought this sickle for thirty cents."[3]

The monastic said, "I am not asking about the sickle you bought for thirty cents. Which is the Way that leads to Nanquan?"[4]

Nanquan said, "It feels good when I use it."[5]

COMMENTARY

This monastic is clearly in search of a head to put on top of his own. Nanquan kindly reveals the truth for him. Lost in a dream, the monastic cannot see past his expectations. However, it should be clearly understood that if you go to the sickle to understand Nanquan, you are already ten thousand miles from the truth. The monastic persists. Nanquan, like a doting old grandfather, shows him again. If he had chased the monastic away with the sickle right at the start, all of this could have been avoided.

Now you tell me, what is the meaning of Nanquan's holding up the sickle that he bought for thirty cents and his saying, "It feels good when I use it?" If you can give a turning word on these points, Nanquan's effort will, after all, not have been in vain.

CAPPING VERSE

Don't be deluded by the words
   "the Great Way."
Realize that it is nothing other
   than what you do from morning till night.

NOTES

1. Everyone should know that there is one that is not working.
2. The sky is above, the earth is below. What are you looking for?
3. Thank you for your answer.
4. How sad. Today he has encountered a monastic who is fast asleep.
5. Thank you for your answer.

155 ∿
Lingyun's Peach Blossoms

MAIN CASE

Once Zen master Lingyun Zhiqin had realization upon seeing peach blossoms.[1] He then wrote a poem:

For thirty years I have looked for a sword.
Many times leaves fell, new ones sprouted.
One glimpse of peach blossoms,
now no more doubts—just this.[2]

He presented his understanding to Guishan. Guishan said, "One who enters the Way with ripened causes will never leave. You should maintain it well."[3]

Later Xuansha heard about it and commented, "You've got it right, senior brother, but you have not as yet achieved maintaining it."[4]

COMMENTARY

A simple glimpse of peach blossoms and Lingyun enters the valley of the endless spring. Life, death, buddhas, demons, enlightenment, and delusion have all vanished with the falling away of body and mind.

But say, flowers bloom and abound each and every spring. Why doesn't everyone who sees them attain the Way? What does Lingyun see that helps him to realize the Way? Furthermore, why is it that Xuansha still expresses doubts in spite of Guishan's approval?

CAPPING VERSE

The mountain form is the body of truth;
    only the ear can see it.
The valley sounds are the voice of the teachings;
    only the eye can hear them.

NOTES

1. Seeing forms with the whole body and mind, one understands them intimately.
2. "Just this" is not like anything.
3. It has always been like this: causes and conditions—interdependent. We practice the Way together. We enter the Way together.
4. Tell me, what is it that Xuansha sees that makes him speak this way?

156 ⌒

Changqing's Clarification of Understanding

MAIN CASE

Huileng of Changqing studied with Lingyun[1] and asked him, "What is the essential meaning of Buddhadharma?"[2]

Lingyun said, "When the donkey matter has not yet left, the horse matter arrives."[3]

Then Changqing came and went between Xuefeng and Xuansha for twenty years but did not clarify the matter,[4] until one day he had great realization while he was rolling up a [bamboo] screen.[5] He wrote a verse to express it:

How extraordinary!
Having rolled up a screen, I see the world.
If someone asks me what essence I understand,
I will hit him in the mouth with my fly whisk.[6]

Xuefeng asked Xuansha, "Has this person seen through?"[7]

Xuansha said, "This could be just an intellectual understanding.[8] He needs further examination."[9]

At night when the assembly met to greet Xuefeng, he said to Changqing, "Xuansha has not yet approved you,[10] but if you do have correct realization, let the assembly know your understanding."[11]

Changqing said in a verse:[12]

The single body revealed among myriad forms.
When affirmed, only then is there intimacy.
In the past I mistakenly searched for the Way.
Now I see it's like ice in fire.[13]

Xuefeng turned to Xuansha and said, "This can't be called intellectual understanding."[14]

COMMENTARY

Only when you have entered the gate of great liberation can you be an exponent of the essential vehicle. Having passed through the forest of brambles, an adept is like a snowflake in a volcano. Lingyun points out the seamlessness of ceaseless practice; Xuefeng and Xuansha help Changqing go beyond the intellectual and bring it into accord with reality.

Still, the question of intimacy remains. Since there is only the single body, what is it that remains to be intimate with? If you can see into it here and give a turning word, you are the master of your life regardless of the circumstances you may encounter. If you have not seen into it yet, work with it singlemindedly until you can truly make it your own.

CAPPING VERSE

When reason is exhausted and words and ideas forgotten,
    what is it that remains for comparison?
When the fruit is truly ripe,
    it leaves the tree of its own accord.

NOTES

1. Unavoidably, it will be hard to stay. His boots are worn, his mind is jumping.
2. It's a worn-out question. Still, he has to check it out for himself.
3. He asked for a light and Lingyun set him on fire. There are no gaps in ceaseless practice.
4. He hopes his diligence will make up for his dullness.
5. Like finding a light in the darkness. But say, what did he see?
6. Among the dead, here's a live one, or half-live. Still, he needs further checking.
7. He wants the whole family to agree.
8. When a dragon roars, you should be able to see the fire.
9. He is still learning how to discern dragons from snakes.
10. Siblings seem to be more intolerant than parents.
11. Why drag everyone into it? Still, it's necessary to be discriminating. This type of kindness is difficult to repay.
12. His first error wasn't enough. How many times will it be compounded?
13. When you look, you go blind.
14. He settles things according to the imperative. It's been like this for eighty-six generations.

157 ∾

Guishan Laughs Twice

MAIN CASE

Shushan went to see Guishan and said, "Master, I heard that you had said,[1] 'Words are like wisteria vines coiled around a tree.' When the tree falls down and the wisteria dies, where do the words go?"[2]

Guishan burst into laughter.[3]

Shushan said, "I came four thousand li, peddling cloths to get here.[4] How can you fool around with me?"[5]

Guishan called the attendant monastic and said to him, "Bring some money and reimburse this elder monastic."[6]

Later Guishan said, "In the future a one-eyed dragon will reveal the point for you."[7]

Shushan went to see Mingzhao Deqian and told this story.[8]

Mingzhao said, "Guishan should have said, 'Head is right, tail is right.'[9] You did not meet someone who understood you."[10]

Shushan said, "When the tree falls down and the wisteria dies, where do the words go?"[11]

Mingzhao said, "Guishan laughs again."[12]

Upon hearing this, Shushan had realization.[13] Then he said, "Guishan hid a sword in his laughter."[14]

COMMENTARY

In saying "it is," we should understand that there is nothing that "is" can affirm. In saying "it is not," we should see clearly that there is nothing that "it is not" can negate.

When "is" and "is not" are transcended, and gain and loss forgotten, everything is free, clear, naked, and exposed. Don't you know that in twenty-five hundred years, even the thousand sages and the golden-faced one before them have not transmitted a single phrase?

CAPPING VERSE

Before the mouth is opened or a phrase uttered,
    it is revealed.
Fields, mountains, and the great earth,
    all taken by a great laugh.
Nothing remains.

NOTES

1. Too bad—he carries it around with him. Still, he wants to discern the truth.
2. What will you do with another's view?

3. Cut. Why is he tormenting this monastic?
4. Although he claims poverty, he still carries a full load.
5. This one doesn't understand intimacy. He should be hit.
6. Pay him off and let him go.
7. There's an echo in these words.
8. He still carries it around with him.
9. A thief always recognizes another thief.
10. Intimacy is like that. There's no place to take hold.
11. He uses diligence to make up for being stupid and fatheaded.
12. Guishan drinks and Mingzhao gets drunk. Very intimate, very intimate indeed.
13. He finds a lamp in the darkness. Still, this adds error to error. The first cut only annoyed him, the second cut went deep. But say, what is it that he realized?
14. The sword that kills is the sword that gives life. There is such a thing, you know.

158 ❧

Yunmen's "Each and Every Particle Samādhi"

MAIN CASE

Once Yunmen was asked by a monastic, "What is each-and-every-particle samādhi?"[1]
Yunmen said, "Rice in the bowl. Water in the bucket."[2]

COMMENTARY

If you come to this saying of Yunmen's looking for rationalizations, you are missing the wonder of the day's dawning. The sun rises over the mountains, but it is still dark. If you go to Yunmen's words to understand it, you have surely missed its subtle mystery.

Cut off the myriad streams of thought, set down the backpack, and see it directly in phenomena itself. Then you will be leaping with life in the bright light of day, and for the first time you will have arrived at the sacred place where there are originally no seams, no flaws, no gaps.

CAPPING VERSE

The rain falls and the earth gets wet,
    clouds part and the sun appears.
The valley of the everlasting spring
    is not a place of this and that.

NOTES

1. To encounter one dharma is to practice one dharma—moment to moment, nonstop flow.
2. Then why are there so many still dying of hunger and thirst?

159 ❧

Nanyang's Ten Bodies

MAIN CASE

Once Nanyang was asked by Emperor Suzong, "What is someone whose ten bodies are complete?"[1]
    Nanyang stood up and said, "Do you understand it?"[2]
    The emperor said, "No, I don't."[3]
    Nanyang said, "Your Majesty, please pass me the water jar."[4]

COMMENTARY

In the *Flower Garland Sūtra* it is said, "The ten bodies are the ten kinds of others' experience of the body of the Buddha." Emperor Suzong, having heard of this, asks the National Teacher for clarification. Although Nanyang compassionately reveals it all, he skillfully withholds the details. The emperor says he doesn't understand it. Understand what—the ten bodies or Nanyang's standing up?

One body transforms into ten bodies, ten bodies transform into a hundred bodies, and so on up to millions and billions of bodies. Yet in their totality they are but a single body revealed. I ask you, what is the single body revealed? The National Teacher tries to dislodge what was stuck and open a route, so he sends the emperor to fetch the water jar. But say, if you think the truth of this kōan is about Nanyang standing up or the National Teacher asking the Emperor to fetch the water jar, then you have missed it by a thousand miles.

CAPPING VERSE

Unifying the myriad reflections,
    one's own light is quiescently radiant.
Opened up, the ground of being
    is always meeting itself.

NOTES

1. Although an imperial crown graces his head, his sandals are still unworn.
2. What more can he do? He has given over his whole body and mind.
3. Wear out a meditation cushion or two, then maybe we can talk about it.
4. He is being extremely indulgent. Covered with mud, he makes a valiant effort to bring the emperor to life. Did he pass the water jar?

160 ∿

Prince Nalakuvara's Original Body

MAIN CASE

Once Touzi Datong was asked by a monastic, "Prince Nalakuvara cut out his bones to return them to his father and sliced his flesh to return to his mother. What is his original body?"[1]
    Touzi threw down the staff he was holding.[2]

COMMENTARY

Since Prince Nalakuvara returned his flesh and bones to his parents, his original body must be more than flesh and bones. The monastic wants to know what this original body is. The original body of all beings is the body you had before your parents were born. It is the body beyond space and time, being and nonbeing, and therefore it exists thus.

Aside from this matter, tell me, what is the meaning of old master Touzi's throwing down his staff? Is he simply dismissing the monastic, or is he saying something? If he is saying something, what is it? More important, what is your original body?

CAPPING VERSE

The original body is always in accord with the myriad things,
    yet it is unborn and unextinguished.
The ignorant wear out their cushions seeking it,
    polishing a tile trying to make a mirror.

NOTES

1. When the five skandhas are forgotten, what is it that remains?
2. Giving play to his spirit, he loses his life.

161 ∾
The Mill Worker's Staff

MAIN CASE

Worker Shishi saw a monastic coming. He held up a staff and said, "Buddhas in the past are just this. Buddhas of the present are just this. Buddhas of the future are just this."[1]

COMMENTARY

Worker Shishi was a student of Master Mazu's. Shishi, during the persecution of Buddhism, took up work in a mill. He clearly understood the Zen workings of the staff, and whenever a Zen monastic showed up, he would hold up his staff and say, "The buddhas of the three times are just this!" Do you understand? In a single gesture he envelops heaven and earth—thus! The buddhas of all time and space come home in a single instant. But do you understand that instant?

It is not a matter of arriving at the moment or entering the moment. It's more like spring meeting spring, the teacher meeting the teacher, the student meeting herself, buddha meeting buddha. It does not concern understanding or believing, yet it is not devoid of understanding or believing. It's not mindfulness or mindlessness, nor is it a question of delusion or enlightenment. It's just this.

Just this does not ignore past and future but rather is a realization of the moment. When the moment is realized with the whole body and mind, the ten thousand kalpas have at once been realized as well. If you still cannot see it, then look. See the ten thousand blossoms opening with the spring breeze. Listen to the sounds of the valley streams, and then enter there.

CAPPING VERSE

If you want to understand the past,
　　look at the present.
If you want to understand the future,
　　look at the present.

NOTES

　1. What is he making such a fuss about? Does he have something to impart or not?

162 ∾

Yunmen's "One Hundred Grasses"

MAIN CASE

Yunmen said to his assembly, "Say a word that covers the tips of the one hundred grasses."[1]
　No one in the assembly responded.[2]
　Yunmen said on behalf of his silent assembly, "Inseparable."[3]

COMMENTARY

Master Yunmen challenges his assembly to leap beyond the holy and the profane and "say a word" that at once includes the heavens and encompasses the earth. His assembly is speechless, so Yunmen, as is his style, answers on their behalf. He says, "Inseparable." But tell me, what is his meaning? Some say that he is pointing to the absolute basis of reality or differentiation within unity. Understanding such as this is far from the truth of Yunmen's teaching. The whole great treasury of the true dharma eye just comes down to a single word. How do you understand it? See into it here and Yunmen's nostrils are in your hands.

CAPPING VERSE

Among the myriad things there is one;
    in the one there are the myriad things.
Can this be called one thing,
    or is it to be called many things?

NOTES

1. This is not an unreasonable question. Anyone who is even half awake should be able to respond.
2. Jaws hanging, mouths agape, they all just stare into space. Sad, sad.
3. Seamless, not a gap to be found.

163 ৵

Xuansha Builds a Seamless Monument

MAIN CASE

Once Xuansha accompanied Xuefeng for a mountain walk.[1] Xuefeng said, "I want to make this place my eternal home."[2]

Xuansha said, "Indeed,[3] this place is well suited for a seamless monument."[4]

Xuefeng immediately made a gesture of measuring.[5]

Xuansha said, "That's all right,[6] but I don't see it that way."[7]

Xuefeng said, "How do you see it?"[8]

Xuansha said, "It's built!"[9]

Xuefeng said, "Good, good."[10]

COMMENTARY

Since they are both from the same household, it's only natural that they indulge each other the way they do. But tell me, is there anything to what they say, or is this just two old monastics playing with mud balls?

If you wish to see into this dialogue, you must first understand that within a single speck of dust, the whole earth is contained. When a single blossom opens, the entire universe arises. But before the particle of dust appears, before the blossom opens, how will you see it?

Cut away all complications and bring out your own treasure, and you will see that there are originally no seams or gaps, not a single flaw or scar, and that each and every thing is perfect and complete, above and below, in front and behind.

CAPPING VERSE

The field of longevity fills all of space,
    the seamless monument towers beyond the eye's reach.
Breaking a jewel, each fragment is precious;
    cutting sandalwood, each piece is equally fragrant.

NOTES

1. In going, they follow the summer breeze. In coming, they pursue the fragrant grasses.
2. Please create one without edges.
3. Dirt from the same hole is the same.
4. Where do you start? What does it look like?
5. He doesn't hesitate. Parent and child both seem to know it exists.
6. The older one lies and the younger one swears to it.
7. Without a seam or all seam—is there a difference?
8. Without blinking an eye, they exchange faces.
9. Vast and boundless, reaching everywhere.
10. If the ancestor doesn't finish it, the descendants must.

164 ॰ঌ

Linji's "Host and Guest"

MAIN CASE

In the assembly of Linji, two monastics were debating. The junior monastic said, "Please speak a phrase for me that is free from medium or low capacity."[1]

The senior monastic said, "You missed it as soon as you asked."[2]

The junior monastic said, "If so, let me bow to you."[3]

The senior monastic said, "You thief."[4]

Hearing about it, Linji said to the assembly, "If you want to understand my phrases about host and guest, talk to the two monastics in this hall."[5]

COMMENTARY

Dharma encounter at Linji's monastery on the Hutou River is a common occurrence among the monastics training there. The junior monastic wants to see if the senior can express the truth of Zen directly, rather than in an explanatory or intellectual way. The senior doesn't bring anything out but, rather, immediately snatches up the question and throws it away.

At this point, any ordinary monastic would have been defeated, but this one says, "If so, let me bow to you." Can you see the light he seems to have about him? The senior does and calls him a thief. Can you see what it was that he stole? If you can see into it here, then there is no need to talk to the two monastics of the hall to understand Master Linji's phrases about host and guest.

CAPPING VERSE

Study carefully the exchanging
    of the points of action.
Thrusting and parrying,
    guest and host are holding a single staff.

NOTES

1. *Burp*! Ask me a question that is free from medium or low capacity.
2. I ask you, is he evading the issue or answering the question?

3. Is he treading on the ground of reality or is he mired in mud?

4. An adept would naturally have such an ability, but is he an adept?

5. From start to finish, host and guest are clearly distinguished.

165 ∾

The World-Honored One Did Not Speak a Word

MAIN CASE

When the World-Honored One was about to enter parinirvāṇa, Mañjuśrī asked him to give a sermon once more.[1]

The World-Honored One scolded him, saying, "I have not spoken even a word for forty-seven years.[2] You are asking me to speak once more. Have I ever said a word?"[3]

Mañjuśrī was silent.

COMMENTARY

For forty-seven years the World-Honored One addressed hundreds of assemblies, yet he says, "I have not spoken even a word for forty-seven years." What is his meaning? The transmission to Mahākāśyapa was indeed wordless, as was the teaching given to the outsider. But what about the countless sūtras that are said to have come directly from the mouth of the Buddha? Are these not words? We should understand that the sūtras are the entire universe itself. There is no space and no time that is not the sūtras.

We should investigate thoroughly the fact that although the Buddha did not speak a single word, it cannot be said that he remained silent either. Wordless is not the same as expressionless. All phenomena of the universe, audible and inaudible, tangible and intangible, sentient and insentient, are the clear and ceaseless expression of the buddha nature. These teachings are like thunder resounding through space and time down to this moment itself. Can you hear them? They transcend affirmation and negation, being and nonbeing. They are a reality that is neither dualistic nor monistic. Can you see it? Words and ideas are a description of reality, silence is a negation of reality. What is the reality itself?

CAPPING VERSE

Without falling into speech or silence,
    he completely brings up the true imperative.
The clear solstice moon
    settles its frosty disk among distant pines.

NOTES

1. Even in his last moments, the iron yoke presses on his shoulders.
2. It seems that he has offended the old teacher with his request.
3. It simply cannot be grasped.

166 ∾

Yunmen's "Where Are They?"

MAIN CASE

Once Yunmen was asked by a monastic, "When birth and death come, how do we avoid them?"[1]
    Yunmen said, "Where are they?"[2]

COMMENTARY

With the simple question "Where are they?" Yunmen snatches away all the props and devices and points to the knowledge that has no teacher.

When this single phrase is seen into clearly, the myriad streams of thought abruptly cease and the self that is seeing into is seen.

CAPPING VERSE

In arriving, there is no abode;
    in departing, there is no destination.
Ultimately, how is it?
    Here I have been all the time!

NOTES

1. Dreaming a dream within a dream. Who is it who avoids what?
2. Look! Can you see? It's like a phantom in a dream.

167 ∿
Linji's "Blind Ass"

MAIN CASE

When Linji was about to pass away, he entrusted Sansheng, saying, "After I pass away, do not allow my treasury of the true dharma eye to perish."[1]

Sansheng said, "Master, how could I have your treasury of the true dharma eye perish?"[2]

Linji said, "Later, when someone asks about my teaching, how will you answer them?"[3]

Sansheng shouted.[4]

Linji said, "Who would think that my treasury of the true dharma eye would perish with this blind ass?"[5]

COMMENTARY

Seeing his death appearing, Linji wants to confirm his senior disciple Sansheng as his successor. He says, "After I pass away, do not allow my treasury of the true dharma eye to perish." Since this is a matter that has never advanced nor declined in countless aeons, even before and after the appearance of the buddhas and ancestors, why does he make such a request?

Sansheng understands his teacher and shows his own provisions. Still, not satisfied that the matter has been settled, the master presses further. Linji says, "Later, when someone asks about my teaching, how will you answer them?" Sansheng shouts. Linji has no choice but to respond to the imperative. He says, "Who would think that my treasury of the true dharma eye would perish with this blind ass?" But say, what is Linji's intent in saying this? Did his treasury of the true dharma eye perish or not?

CAPPING VERSE

Eyeball to eyeball,
    each confirms the other.
Passing from mouth to ear, it perishes;
    passing from ear to mouth, it is born anew.

NOTES

1. It's too late to worry about it now.
2. He knows but dares to offend.
3. If you really know, then show me.
4. This is totally devoid of any meaning whatsoever.
5. They both demonstrate that communication is in no way possible.

168 ॐ

Yangshan's "Inconceivable, Clear, Bright Mind"

MAIN CASE

Guishan asked Yangshan, "How do you understand inconceivable, clear, bright mind?"[1]
    Yangshan said, "Mountains, rivers, the great earth, the sun, the moon, and the stars."[2]
    Guishan said, "You only understand things."[3]
    Yangshan said, "Master, what did you just ask me?"[4]
    Guishan said, "How do you understand inconceivable, clear, bright mind?"[5]
    Yangshan said, "Can you call that 'things'?"[6]
    Guishan said, "That's it; that's it!"[7]

COMMENTARY

Mountains, rivers, the great earth, the sun, the moon, and the stars are not things. The inconceivable, clear, bright mind is not a thing. When we clearly understand the identity of seer and seen, we then realize that mountains, rivers, the great earth, the sun, the moon, and the stars are mind itself. However, this does not mean that they are inside the mind, nor can it be said that they are outside the mind. Then where can they be found?

Furthermore, since the three worlds are mind, where can the mind be found? If you realize the origin, you will attain mind and you will see Buddha. Mind is Buddha; Buddha is mind. If you wish to see this truth for yourself, then look into what it is that you call your mind.

CAPPING VERSE

When the heavens collapse
    and the earth disintegrates,
       the inconceivable, clear, bright mind
       is not destroyed.

NOTES

1. The strength of the Guiyang school arose directly from this kind of activity.
2. This may seem OK, but it is still not good enough.
3. He needs to be sure, so he knocks him down to see if he knows how to get up.
4. Yangshan knows how to come out hopping and dancing.
5. The old man goes along with it.
6. Vast foaming waves cover the heavens and encompass the earth.
7. Careful here; too much praise may impair his virtue.

169 ℘

Mahākāśyapa and the Flagpole

MAIN CASE

The Second Ancestor, Ānanda, asked Mahākāśyapa, "Senior brother, besides the golden brocade robe you have received, have you received anything else?"[1]

Mahākāśyapa called out, "Ānanda!"[2]

Ānanda responded, "Yes, Master?"[3]

Mahākāśyapa said, "Take down the flagpole in front of the monastery gate."[4]

Ānanda had a great realization.

COMMENTARY

Although Ānanda is a wellspring of the Buddha's teachings, he has not attained the adamantine wisdom. When his ripeness finally manifests, he wants to know if anything else besides the brocade robe was transmitted on Mount Gridhrakūta.

Mahākāśyapa, seeing that the critical stage has been reached, calls, "Ānanda!" However, we should understand that although he calls out like this, he is not calling Ānanda, nor is the response an answer to his call. All of this notwithstanding, although the message is sent, it does not reach home. Seeing this, Mahākāśyapa pushes against the edges and ultimately walks into Ānanda's belly, saying, "Take down the flagpole at the front gate." At that moment the Buddha's robe enters Ānanda's skull. Not only is the flagpole taken down, but so is Mahākāśyapa, as well as the mountains, rivers, and the great earth itself.

CAPPING VERSE

Dragon sons and daughters are always born of dragon parents—
    but how can it be explained?
The rains have passed,
    and the autumn river runs deep and fast.

NOTES

1. When doubt is born, can truth be far behind?
2. Direct and penetrating—thank you for your teaching. But if a single thought arises, all is lost in intellection.
3. Direct and penetrating, the valley does not know its echo.
4. The whole universe has been taken down. What a pity.

170 ∾

An Outsider Questions the Buddha

MAIN CASE

An outsider asked the World-Honored One, "I am not asking you about the spoken. I am not asking you about the unspoken."[1]

The World-Honored One remained sitting.[2]

The outsider said in admiration, "The greatly compassionate World-Honored One has cleared the cloud of doubt and let me enter the Way." He bowed and left.[3]

Ānanda said to the Buddha, "What point did he realize that he admired you?"[4]

The World-Honored One said, "He was like a fine horse that starts running upon seeing the shadow of the whip."[5]

COMMENTARY

The non-Buddhist comes asking for the ineffable truth of Buddhism, and without making any effort whatsoever, the Buddha is able to awaken him to it. The question is, how? If you think that the truth realized by the non-Buddhist is Buddha's remaining silent or seated, or that his response is silently answering the question, you have missed it.

The non-Buddhist realized a truth that is beyond affirmation and negation, a truth that can neither be given nor received. It has no relationship to either speech or silence. Speech is about the words and ideas that describe a reality—not the reality itself. Silence is simply blank consciousness.

This being the case, what is this truth that was realized? Even Ānanda, the Buddha's attendant, is left with his mouth gaping in awe at the encounter. Furthermore, since nothing is given or received, why is it that the non-Buddhist says the "World-Honored One has cleared the cloud of doubt and let me enter the Way"? Ānanda then asks, "What point did he realize?" Buddha says that he was like a fine horse that moved at the shadow of the whip. Well, what point did the non-Buddhist realize? What is the shadow of the whip? Where is it? Don't tell me about it. Show me!

CAPPING VERSE

The whole universe is the gate of liberation—
    don't you see?
There is no place
    to put this gigantic body.

NOTES

1. Say, what is his question?
2. His thundering voice reaches the heavens and shakes the earth.
3. When the clouds part, the sun appears. Before the clouds part, the sun is there.
4. Too bad he has missed it. It will take him another twenty years to see it.
5. When the fruit is mature, it falls from the tree by itself.

171 ౿
Fayan's "Not Knowing"

MAIN CASE

Fayan of Qingliang Monastery had a profound experience and gave up worldly affairs.[1] He assembled a group of people and traveled away from the lake region. On their way, they were caught by a rainstorm, and the valley stream swelled up,[2] so they temporarily stayed at Dizang Monastery. While there, Fayan asked Abbot Dizang Guichen for instruction.[3]

Dizang said, "Where are you going, Reverend?"[4]

Fayan said, "I am wandering on a pilgrimage."[5]

Dizang said, "What is the purpose of your pilgrimage?"[6]

Fayan said, "I don't know."[7]

Dizang said, "Ah! Not knowing is most intimate."[8]

Straightaway, Fayan had great realization.[9]

COMMENTARY

Fayan's journey starts off innocently enough. However, upon meeting Dizang, things get complicated. Although not knowing is most intimate, ultimately, of what use is it? What will you do with it? On the other hand, it is clear that knowing is illusory. Going to the words and ideas, we inevitably end up entangled in a forest of brambles. Haven't you heard old master Nanquan's saying "The Way is not to be found in knowing or not knowing. Knowing is false consciousness, not knowing is indifference"? This being the case, how are we to proceed?

When illumination and function are simultaneous, knowing becomes a gateway to endless wonders. Just avoid settling down in wonder. When principle and phenomena have merged, not knowing encompasses heaven and earth. There is no place that it does not reach. Just avoid attaching to not knowing.

CAPPING VERSE

The dragon howling in a dead tree
    clearly sees the Way.
In one, there are many things;
    in two, there is no duality.

NOTES

1. Can it be said that this is really possible?
2. This sounds pretty worldly to me.
3. Sometimes it's difficult to fathom how things turn out as they do.
4. He is not trying to pin him down. He just wants to see what he is made of.
5. Just following his feet, he goes where they take him.
6. Having come this far, it's difficult to let him go.
7. This can't be called mindful. But can it be called mindless?
8. He doused him with muddy water. Too bad.
9. When you know that not knowing is intimate, it is no longer intimate. So, what was his realization?

172 ॰๛

Dongshan's "Three Pounds of Flax"

MAIN CASE

Zen master Shouchu of Dongshan [Zonghui] was asked by a monastic, "What is buddha?"[1]

Dongshan said, "Three pounds of flax."[2]

The monastic had realization and bowed.[3]

COMMENTARY

This is an old case that has been echoing in the halls of Zen monasteries for centuries, and yet there have been only a handful who have been able to penetrate Dongshan's meaning. People immediately rush to the words to understand, not realizing that words and speech are just vessels to convey the truth—not yet the truth itself.

If you take Dongshan's "Three pounds of flax" to mean that this, in and of itself, is buddha, then you have missed his intent by a hundred thousand miles. We should understand at the outset that "Three pounds of flax" is not just a reply to the question about buddha, and it cannot be understood in terms of buddha. This being the case, then you tell me, what is buddha?

CAPPING VERSE

Seeing a gap opening up in the monastic's question,
    the old master moved quickly to stuff it with flax.
Those who accept words are lost;
    those who linger in phrases are deluded.

NOTES

1. From amid the forest of brambles, a voice calls out.
2. Like a bell when struck, the sound immediately appears.
3. I wonder about this.

173 ∽

The Emperor and the Buddha's Relics

MAIN CASE

Emperor Xian brought the Buddha's relics to the palace and made an offering to the relics,[1] which glowed in the night.[2] Early the following morning, the court celebrated this as being the result of imperial virtue,[3] but Lord Hanyu Wengong alone did not celebrate it.[4]

The emperor said to Wen, "All the other courtiers are celebrating this. Why do you alone not celebrate it?"[5]

Wen said, "When I read a sūtra in the past, it said, "The buddha light is not blue, yellow, red, white, and so on.[6] Therefore, the light must be the light of a dragon deity guarding the relics."[7]

The emperor said, "What does the buddha light look like?"[8]

Wen remained silent.[9] Because of that he was forced to resign.[10]

COMMENTARY

The devout Tang emperor Xian is overjoyed that the Buddha's relics glow in the darkness. Lord Wen, however, seems unmoved by the whole event. When pressed by the emperor, he invokes the sūtras by saying, "The buddha light is not blue, yellow, red, white." What does this mean? When the emperor asks, "What does the buddha light look like?" the question goes outside the written word, and having no provisions of his own, Wen's tongue sticks to the roof of his mouth.

Haven't you heard old master Changsha's saying "The whole universe in the ten directions is the light of the self"? We should understand for ourselves that completely clear, undimmed light is the ten thousand things themselves. To see and hear this light of the self is to have intimately encountered Buddha. But say! How do you hear the light?

CAPPING VERSE

The light shines throughout the whole universe,
    existing right here now.

When you truly see it,
   you will go blind.

NOTES

1. Why does he carry coals to Newcastle?
2. Skin, flesh, bones, and marrow are all brightness itself.
3. Don't they know that there is no merit whatsoever to be gained?
4. Perhaps he knows something the others do not know.
5. The emperor wants to know what it is.
6. *Ring a-ling a-ling a-ling!*
7. What kind of light is that? Is it different from the buddha light?
8. When you look at it, you don't see it. Everything seems dark and dim.
9. The sūtras didn't tell him about this question.
10. Although he was one of the eight great scholars of the Tang and Song dynasties, he had not as yet heard of practice and verification.

174 ∾
Buddha's Begging Bowl

MAIN CASE

One day the World-Honored One said to Ānanda, "It is getting close to mealtime. You should go to town with the begging bowl."[1]

Ānanda accepted his request.

The World-Honored One said, "When you go begging with the bowl, you follow the manner of the Past Seven Buddhas."[2]

Ānanda said, "What is the manner of the Past Seven Buddhas?"[3]

The Buddha said, "Ānanda!"[4]

Ānanda responded, "Yes, Master."[5]

The Buddha said, "Go begging."[6]

COMMENTARY

Ānanda's confinement between the two iron mountains of a buddha view and a dharma view obscures all the possibilities for liberation. His cage is so comfortable that even the yellow-faced old Gautama couldn't do anything about it.

Discerning the problem, the Buddha tries to stir things up, but Ānanda just wants to add this to his collection of views. Buddha moves to smash the golden chains by entering directly into principle, and although Ānanda can hear him knocking, he cannot let him in. All in all, it will take Ānanda another thirty years to get it.

CAPPING VERSE

When the mist dissolves,
    the moon appears.
But the truth is and always has been
    perfect and clear.
Some see it, others do not.

NOTES

1. Since time immemorial, all mendicant monastics have practiced the dharma in this way.
2. He diminishes the man with his meddling. Doting parents sometimes do this.
3. He has been diminished.
4. This is a wake-up call.
5. I hear you knocking, but you can't come in.
6. After all, there is still this.

175 ∾
Jianyuan's "Matter before the Seven Buddhas"

MAIN CASE

One day Jianyuan was sitting behind a paper curtain. A monastic came and opened up the curtain, saying, "How are you?"[1]

Jianyuan just looked at the monastic. After a while he said, "Do you understand it?"[2]

The monastic said, "No, I don't."[3]

Jianyuan said, "How come you don't understand the matter before the Seven Buddhas?"[4]

COMMENTARY

Even if you can see through clearly, trust completely, and are without a hair of blinding obstruction, if you still have not fundamentally understood the matter that predates the Seven Buddhas, you are not yet free in all circumstances. Jianyuan's monastic opens up the curtain, saying, "How are you?" Jianyuan just looks at the monastic. I ask you, is he saying something, or is it silence? Do you understand it?

Some people hearing this lower their heads deep in thought, trying to intellectualize it without realizing that all they are accomplishing is manifesting countless ghosts in their skulls. This is not a matter of past, present, or future times.

If you wish to understand Jianyuan's deep meaning, you must first realize that there exists a person who is not realized through others, who does not receive teachings from others, and who does not fall into patterns or stages. If you wish to meet such a person, you must be such a person. To be such a person is the conclusion of the practice and realization of an entire lifetime.

CAPPING VERSE

Outside the window, rain in the pine trees;
　　on the riverbank, the willow dances with the wind.
The timeless message has always been present,
　　but how many are there who have actually heard it?

NOTES

1. This fellow is looking for trouble. He should just shut his mouth.
2. A steep and precipitous mountain—who can scale it?
3. An honest person is hard to find.
4. What will he say? Even if he had realized it, it simply can't be explained.

176 ∾

Xuefeng's "Thirst and Starvation"

MAIN CASE

Xuefeng said,[1] "There are many people who sit beside a rice bucket dying from starvation.[2] There are also many who sit beside a great body of water dying of thirst."[3]

Xuansha said, "There are many who sink their heads inside a rice bucket[4] and still starve to death.[5] There are also many who stick their heads into the water and yet die of thirst."[6]

Yunmen later said, "Throughout the entire body is rice.[7] Throughout the entire body is water."[8]

COMMENTARY

If you can see it clearly, then you know how to use it on the road freely, like a bird in flight or a fish in the water. If you have not yet seen it, the road prevails and you're like a bird in a cage, a fish in a bucket.

At times, a single phrase is like a lion stalking its prey. At another time, it's like a surfer riding the waves. And sometimes a single phrase is like a diamond sword that cuts off the tongues of everyone on earth. When adepts meet, they can see what is appropriate, are able to distinguish right from wrong, and together witness each other's clarity.

CAPPING VERSE

Born in the same way,
    they know the household's pantry well.
Dying in different ways,
    each travels in a separate direction.
Where will you find them? Look! Look!

NOTES

1. Unavoidably, he's bound to create complications. It's a dirty job, but someone has to do it.

2. He said it. It's not like it's ten thousand miles away.
3. As before, he said it. Monasteries of Zen are filled with thirsty people.
4. This is not yet intimacy.
5. If you don't swallow it, you can't digest it.
6. Some even drown before death by thirst.
7. Fine, but are they still dying of starvation?
8. Still, this is only half.

177 ∾
Fayan's "Single Body Revealed"

MAIN CASE

Head Monastic Zhizhao went to see Fayan and asked, "Master, who is your teaching handed down from?"[1]

Fayan said, "Dizang."[2]

Zhizhao said, "Aren't you turning your back on our late honorable teacher, Changqing?"[3]

Fayan said, "I don't understand one of Changqing's sayings."[4]

Zhizhao said, "Why don't you ask me about it?"[5]

Fayan then asked, "Among the ten thousand things, a single body is revealed. What does this mean?"[6]

Zhizhao straightened his fly whisk.[7]

Fayan said, "This is the point you learned with Changqing. In your head monastic's position, what can you do?"[8]

Zhizhao couldn't respond.[9]

Fayan said, "Just as a single body is revealed among the ten thousand things, does this obliterate or not obliterate the ten thousand things?"[10]

Zhizhao said, "It does not obliterate the ten thousand things."[11]

Fayan said, "Two."[12]

The attendants and students on both sides said, "It obliterates the ten thousand things."[13] Then Fayan said, "Among the ten thousand things, only a single body is revealed.[14] *Nii*!"[15]

COMMENTARY

Setting up the teachings and establishing monasteries is the function of genuine masters of our school. Distinguishing dragons from snakes, adepts from imitators, is what an accomplished teacher must do in order to act in accord with the imperative. Having freed himself from birth and death, he sets the teachings in motion with ease. Without blinking an eye, he kills or gives life. After all, if all the waves of Caoxi were the same, the teaching would have long ago lost its ability to heal and to nourish.

CAPPING VERSE

Although he may look like a mountain lion,
      it turns out he has no fangs or claws.
Obliterating, not obliterating—
      dim-witted indeed.

NOTES

1. He wants to test this old adept.
2. A truthful man is hard to find.
3. Danger. Playing with a lion, you're apt to be bitten.
4. The hook is baited and lowered into the stream.
5. He climbs onto the hook and impales himself. How cooperative.
6. The earth rumbles, mountains shake, the sky darkens. Something ominous is about to occur.
7. *Baaah!* I see a snake hidden behind that dragon mask.
8. Without batting an eye, he runs him through.
9. That's the nature of the diseased. They can't respond.
10. He can't let him go like this so he digs a pit.
11. *Plop!* Into the pit he goes.
12. *Yaaah!* He walks up and pierces him right through.
13. They all jumped into the pit after him.
14. How fresh. How new.
15. Out, out, damned spot! A wooden stake for the vampire, a silver bullet for the werewolf, *Nii!* for Zen apparitions.

178 ❧

Linji Sees Huangbo Reading a Sūtra

MAIN CASE

Linji joined a summer practice at the monastery of Huangbo after it had already begun.[1] He went to greet Huangbo and saw him reading a sūtra.[2] Linji said, "I thought you were a true person,[3] but I see that you are just an old master who is counting black beans, after all."[4] Linji stayed for a few more days and then went to take his leave of Huangbo.[5]

Huangbo said, "You were late coming into the summer training period and now you are leaving early."[6]

Linji said, "I just came here to bow to you."[7]

Huangbo hit him and drove him out.[8]

After walking a few miles, he began to have doubts about the matter.[9] He then returned and completed the training period.[10]

COMMENTARY

Linji arrives late to Huangbo's training period sporting a major attitude. When he sees the old teacher reading a sūtra, and blinded by his own arrogance, he summarily dismisses him, saying, "I thought you were a true person, but I see that you are just an old master who is counting black beans, after all." Huangbo lets it pass. A few days later, when Linji goes to take leave of the old master, Huangbo says, "You were late coming into the summer training period, and now you are leaving early." Linji says, "I just came here to bow to you." What is he calling bowing? After four demonstrations of the shallowness of his practice and training, Huangbo has no choice but to drive him out.

In the long run, Linji's spiritual drive outweighs his arrogance. The great doubt appears and he returns to the training period.

CAPPING VERSE

When the light has not yet penetrated fully,
    distant objects may appear close,
    close objects may appear distant.

Yet how many are there
    who are able to regain their way?

NOTES

1. Drawing water, he is limited by the size of his bucket.
2. Painted cakes do satisfy hunger.
3. What is an untrue person?
4. Exposed! He has a lot of Zen, but what good is it?
5. This is a practice for long-distance runners, not sprinters.
6. Why waste time even discussing it? Drive him out!
7. Having already spat on him, why does he now want to bow?
8. What took you so long?
9. A poor person worries about an old debt.
10. When one realizes one's fault, one should reform, but how many people can?

179 ∾
Shishuang's "When All the Doors Are Closed"

MAIN CASE

Zhiyuan of Mount Yungai was studying at the assembly of Shishuang Qingzhu when a monastic asked Shishuang, "When all the doors are closed, what then?"[1]

Shishuang said, "How do you understand what happens inside?"[2]

After half a year the monastic finally understood and said, "No one can teach me."[3]

Shishuang said, "Your words are roughly right, but it's only eighty or ninety percent."[4]

Yungai heard about it and asked Shishuang to comment.[5]

Shishuang said nothing.[6]

Yungai grasped Shishuang and said, "Master, if you don't speak, I will hit you."[7]

Shishuang said, "All right."[8]

Yungai began making deep bows.[9]
Shishuang said, "No one knows you."[10]
With these words, Yungai attained realization.[11]

COMMENTARY

Examining the causes, understanding the effects, settling the beginning, completing the end. Face-to-face there is nothing hidden, yet fundamentally there is nothing that can be explained. When all the doors are closed, nothing can enter and nothing can exit. Wisdom is not a matter of covering our ears and eyes and retreating into a shell. We must emerge from the dark cave, penetrate the forest of brambles, and manifest ourselves naked, open, and free as an ordinary person. Breathing in is always followed by breathing out.

The monastic who questions Shishuang finally understands something, but it is still only eighty percent. Yungai wants to see all of it, so he presses the old master. Shishuang skillfully holds back until he is sure of the tapping from inside the shell. Yungai is able to reveal his face. Do you understand?

CAPPING VERSE

Boundless wind and moon, the eye within eyes—
    inexhaustible heaven and earth, the light beyond light.
The willow dark, the flower bright,
    ten thousand houses, knock at any door—
    there is one who will respond.

NOTES

1. Like a clam in its shell, he acts like no one is around him.
2. The old master is concerned about the clam.
3. Although it took a long time to get there, he is beginning to see something.
4. The old man squeezes his head; there is more to be seen.
5. When the teachings are in the air, sooner or later they will find their rightful vessel.
6. Holding back, he primes the pump and delivers the teaching.
7. This is not an expression of casual interest.

8. Letting go, clusters of blossoms and flowers herald spring.
9. All the doors are wide open.
10. Lightning flashes, thunder rolls through the valley.
11. This case is not completed until you too have seen it.

180 ○

Yantou's "Original Permanence"

MAIN CASE

Ruiyan Shiyan asked his teacher Yantou,[1] "What is the original permanence?"[2]
Yantou said, "Movement."[3]
Ruiyan said, "What happens when movement takes place?"[4]
Yantou said, "You don't see the original permanence."[5]
Ruiyan silently reflected on the matter.[6]
Yantou said,[7] "If you agree with this, you are bound by subject and object.[8]
If you disagree with this, you fall into an endless cycle of birth and death."[9]

COMMENTARY

When whole body and mind activity fills the universe, there are no edges.
When things have no edges, they are free to roll in every direction. It's like
navigating a canoe in fast-flowing rapids. There is no intention in moment-to-moment samādhi.

Seeing that Ruiyan is about to fall into the pit of this and that, Yantou
deepens the pit with agreement and disagreement. Haven't you heard old
Baizhang Huaihai's saying "When you agree or disagree you are not free
from senses and matter. Take away both agreement and disagreement and
the six consciousnesses naturally return to the ocean of awareness"?

Free yourself of delusive attachments, ideas, and positions. Clear away the
entanglements and realize that the truth itself is right where you stand, filling
each and every activity. Peaceful dwelling is not a matter of gain and loss.

CAPPING VERSE

Each and every thing
    is in a constant state of becoming.

It is because change reaches everywhere
    that permanence is originally present.

NOTES

1. He's going to try out this old fellow. The mountain's peace is sure to be disrupted.
2. This monastic must be a family member. All of Yantou's successors seem to have the same sickness.
3. He doesn't make a fuss. He just sees the target and releases an arrow.
4. Not satisfied with pulling the tiger's tail, he climbs into its mouth.
5. After all, he really can't say. Yet Yantou always extends his head willingly.
6. *Duh!* He'll inevitably end up in the forest of brambles.
7. What will he say? It can't be explained.
8. Seeing a fire, he builds a fire.
9. Medicine and sickness always heal each other.

181 ℃

Nanquan Kills a Cat

MAIN CASE

Once Nanquan saw the monastics of the eastern and western halls arguing over a cat.[1] He held up the cat and said to the monastics, "If you can say a turning word, I will not kill it."[2]

No one in the assembly could answer.[3] So Nanquan cut the cat in two.[4]

Later he told the story to Zhaozhou. Zhaozhou took off his straw sandals, put them on his head, and walked away.[5]

COMMENTARY

In the resolution of conflict, one can turn to council, the law, or the dharma. Council and law are dependent upon the power of others, the dharma is based on one's own natural powers of equanimity. Nanquan does not turn to forgiveness, encouragement, reprimand, or chastisement. He simply holds up the whole community at the edge of his diamond sword.

This kōan is not about killing or not killing but, rather, about transformation. An ancient sage said, "When you find yourself at an impasse, change; when you change, then you will easily pass through." No one in the assembly can see past the thickness of their own skin. Nanquan follows through the imperative and cuts the cat in two.

Later Zhaozhou is able to settle the case. He listens to the story told by Nanquan, takes off his straw sandals, puts them on his head, and walks away. Nanquan approves. The active edges of teacher and disciple conform seamlessly. But what is Zhaozhou's meaning? How do you say a turning word that would save the cat? The turning points of these two adepts are subtle and profound. Leap free of the words if you really want to see into them.

CAPPING VERSE

Entering into the monastics' entanglements
    the old master tried to cut open a trail for them.
Only Zhaozhou knew the path well—
    sandals on his head, a pure spring breeze followed him out.

NOTES

1. This kind of haggling continues right up to the present day.
2. A drawn sword immediately creates an acute imperative for action.
3. Poor cat. Its life is in the hands of a bunch of phony Zen practitioners.
4. The sword of wisdom directly cuts, no-cut.
5. When struck, he reverberates immediately; when pushed over, he knows how to roll and come out upright.

182 ❧

Baizhang's Wild Geese

MAIN CASE

Baizhang Huaihai accompanied Mazu on a walk. They saw a group of wild geese flying by. Mazu said, "What is that?"[1]
    Baizhang said, "They are wild geese."[2]

Mazu said, "Where are they going?"[3]
Baizhang said, "They flew away."[4]
Mazu then grabbed Baizhang's nose and twisted it.[5]
Baizhang screamed in pain and said, "Ouch, ouch!"[6]
Mazu said, "Do you still say that they flew away?"[7]
Baizhang broke out into a sweat. Then he had realization.[8]
Next day Baizhang went to hear Mazu's lecture. Before Mazu started talking, Baizhang went forward and rolled up Mazu's bowing mat.[9]
Mazu got down from the teaching seat and returned to the abbot's room. Later he asked Baizhang, "When I went up to the seat, why did you roll up my bowing mat before I spoke?"[10]
Baizhang said, "My nose was hurt when you grabbed it yesterday."[11]
Mazu said, "Where in your mind do you keep yesterday's matter?"[12]
Baizhang said, "My nose does not hurt today."[13]
Mazu said, "You understand today's matter very well."[14] Baizhang made a bow and left.

COMMENTARY

See into this case clearly and you will have at once seen into the ten thousand things and will be able to manifest the truth in any circumstances you may encounter. If you are unable to see it, consider that if Mazu had not manifested the Bodhisattva of Great Compassion, Baizhang would have missed the great matter of right now. But say, what is the great matter of right now? Furthermore, when Baizhang later rolls up the master's bowing mat, what is his meaning?

CAPPING VERSE

Mountains and rivers
    should not be seen in a mirror.
The voices of the wild geese still resound—
    do you hear them?

NOTES

1. Why does he ask? He should know what they are.
2. An honest person is hard to find. Nevertheless, wrong!

3. He is such an old grandmother; he doesn't mind spoon-feeding his students.
4. Wrong!
5. What's this?
6. It's nice to know that he is alive, but did he get it? Do you?
7. He's so kind. I would have just walked away.
8. What did he realize?
9. Is he being a pest, or is he saying something?
10. Even the old master wants to know.
11. Yesterday already happened.
12. It doesn't exist unless we create it.
13. Right now fills the universe. There is no place it does not reach.
14. *Bah!* Doting old grandma. He spoils the whole thing.

183 ⌁

Xuefeng Checks Out the Hermit

MAIN CASE

At the foot of Xuefeng [Elephant Bone] Mountain,[1] a monastic of deep insight[2] built a hermitage in which he lived by himself.[3] For many years he didn't even cut his hair, and lived simply, making a wooden ladle with which he drank water from the stream.[4]

Once, as he was dipping water from the stream, a monastic came by and asked him, "What is the meaning of the Ancestor's [Bodhidharma's] coming from India?"[5]

The old hermit replied, "Where the valley is deep, the dipper handle must be long."[6]

The monastic returned and related this conversation to Xuefeng.[7]

Xuefeng said, "Really strange.[8] Although it's just like that,[9] it still needs to be checked out."[10]

One day, Xuefeng took a razor with him and left with his attendant to visit the hermitage.[11] As soon as they met the hermit, Xuefeng pulled out the razor[12] and said, "If you can say a word of Zen,[13] I won't cut your hair."[14]

The hermit monastic washed his hair in the stream.[15] Then Xuefeng shaved his head.[16]

COMMENTARY

Competent adepts of our school have all mastered cutting through nails and climbing the mountain of swords. If you avoid the sword and run away from the barrier, when will you ever experience today?

Holding fast and letting go totally rest in yourself. If you want to be free of hindrances and cut through entanglements, you must go beyond sound and form, and avoid all traces of mental activity. It is here that the reality of all things is manifested, perfect, complete, and lacking nothing.

But say, what is the meaning of the hermit's saying "Where the valley is deep, the dipper handle must be long"?

CAPPING VERSE

The wind blows, the grasses bend—
    the more you direct yourself to it,
    the further away you move.
There's nothing that can be done about spring—
    when it arrives, it's truly here.

NOTES

1. There's no bottom to Elephant Bone; nor is there a top.
2. Don't slander the poor man.
3. Like each and every thing, alone.
4. This is as it should be.
5. Everything is so beautiful just as it is. Why is he complicating it? This is an old kōan, and everybody knows it. Still, it seems this monastic wants to know.
6. Long handle for a deep stream, short handle for a shallow stream. Anything else?
7. After all, he misunderstands. This monastic is not very clever.
8. When you see something strange as not strange, the strangeness vanishes of itself.
9. So it is, covering this monastic head and toe, inside and out.
10. He drags the monastic along by the nostrils. But say, where's the trap?

11. Poor hermit. He should move deeper into the mountains.

12. *Aiiee!* What will he do? He can't have his head.

13. Even a thousand sages can't leap clear of this.

14. It's all dirt from the same hole.

15. The inexhaustible lion's roar. Thank you for your answer.

16. Thank you for your teaching. But after all, what's the point? Did the monastic get it?

184 ೞ
Yunyan's Lion

MAIN CASE

Guishan asked Yunyan, "I hear that you played with a lion when you were at Yaoshan's. Is it true?"[1]

Yunyan said, "Yes, it is."[2]

Guishan said, "Did you always play with it, or did you sometimes stop?"[3]

Yunyan said, "I played when I wanted to. I stopped when I wanted to."[4]

Guishan said, "Where was the lion when you stopped?"[5]

Yunyan said, "Stop! Stop!"[6]

COMMENTARY

Many teachers of old lived isolated in caves high in the mountains and were known to have shared their quarters with tigers and lions. Yunyan and his teacher before him were said to be such persons. The term "lion," however, was also used in ancient times as a metaphor for an enlightened one, a buddha. What lion are they discussing here? Is it the old buddha Yaoshan, or the wild lion of the mountain? If you can see past this, I will grant that you are halfway there.

Guishan and Yunyan had both studied with Baizhang Huaihai. Guishan succeeded him and went on to live on Mount Gui. Yunyan stayed for twenty years but did not meet the source. After Baizhang's death he continued his studies with Yaoshan and succeeded him. Later, while on a pilgrimage, Guishan and Yunyan met on Mount Gui.

Although their conversation seems casual and friendly, there is no small talk. Guishan immediately enters the realm of function and essence, action and nonaction, asking, "Did you always play with it, or did you sometimes stop?" Yunyan responds by walking right into his belly without hesitation: "I played when I wanted to. I stopped when I wanted to." Guishan persists, and Yunyan—alive and hopping—manifests the inexhaustible lion's roar that bursts the brain of a jackal. Can you hear it?

Have you heard the *Diamond Sūtra*, saying, "Enliven the mind without dwelling on anything"? Not dwelling on anything means not dwelling on form, sound, enlightenment, delusion, function, or essence. Enlivening the mind means manifesting the mind in all places. If you enliven the mind dwelling on good, goodness appears. If you enliven the mind dwelling on evil, fear, or pain, then evil, fear, or pain appears, and the original mind becomes obscured. If the mind doesn't dwell on anything, anywhere, then the whole world is but one mind. The Great Way is none other than this mind—it has no abiding place. The essence of this nonabiding mind is the spiritual light of the life of each one of us. Have you seen it yet?

CAPPING VERSE

The white clouds are rootless,
    the summer breeze has no color.
Filling the canopy of sky, limitless, and trackless,
    supporting the burden of the earth, powerful.

NOTES

1. Such events have happened, you know.
2. A truthful person is hard to find.
3. The conversation has turned from casual to serious. What kind of probe is this?
4. Yunyan is on to it and goes along easily.
5. Careful here! There is a pitfall for a lion in the tall grasses.
6. An adept knows how to cut away all complications.

185 ❧

Nanquan's "Storehouse of the Mani Jewel"

MAIN CASE

Luzu Baoyun said to Nanquan [Wang], "Nobody recognizes the mani jewel,[1] but there is one in the storehouse of the Tathāgata [Śākyamuni Buddha].[2] What is this storehouse?"[3]

Nanquan replied, "Teacher Wang and yourself,[4] coming and going,[5] is nothing other than that."[6]

Luzu asked, "What about those who don't come and go?"[7]

Nanquan replied, "They are the storehouse too."[8]

Luzu asked, "Then what is the jewel?"[9]

Nanquan called, "Master Zu!"[10]

Luzu answered, "Yes?"[11]

Nanquan said, "Go away. You don't understand what I mean."[12]

At that moment, Master Luzu had an insight.[13]

COMMENTARY

It includes heaven and encompasses the earth. It is beyond the sacred and the secular. On the tips of a hundred thousand weeds, it reveals the wondrous mind of nirvāṇa and the exquisite teachings of formless form.

From deep within the forest of brambles, the light of the mani jewel is released. This is the adamantine eye of the adept.

CAPPING VERSE

It illuminates itself,
    the solitary light of the mani jewel.
No! It illuminates the ten thousand things—
    see, there are no shadows.
Seeing, not seeing—*bah!*
Riding backward on the ox,
    distant mountains endlessly unfold.

NOTES

1. When you look at it, you're blinded.
2. Where did he get the news?
3. If you don't know what it is, why do you think there is one?
4. Not two. Yet when the fish swims, the water gets muddy.
5. Not two. When the bird flies, feathers fall.
6. Good news. But say, what is it good for?
7. There are many who still have doubts about this.
8. He keeps making piles of bones on level ground. Just don't talk about it.
9. Hit him. Let him have the jewel. It won't do to let him go.
10. The whole universe calls out.
11. The ten thousand dharmas answer.
12. Don't explain it for him. Let him go wrong for the rest of his life.
13. Confined in prison, he increases in wisdom. Still, he will never attain it.

186 ∽
Heshan Beats the Drum

MAIN CASE

Zen master Wuyan of Heshan [Chengyuan] said in his instruction, "Cultivating study is called learning.[1] Going beyond study is called closeness.[2] To pass beyond these two is called true passing."[3]

A monastic came forward and said, "What is true passing?"[4]

Heshan said, "Heshan knows how to beat the drum."[5]

The monastic said, "What is the true principle?"[6]

Heshan said, "Heshan knows how to beat the drum."[7]

The monastic asked further, "I am not asking you about mind is buddha. What is no mind, no buddha?"[8]

Heshan said, "Heshan knows how to beat the drum."[9]

The monastic said, "What is going beyond buddha?"[10]

Heshan said, "Heshan knows how to beat the drum."[11]

COMMENTARY

Heshan compassionately points out to his assembly that when learning has been exhausted and there is nothing to study, this is called "cutting off study." It is the realm of nondoing, which is free in every direction. But still, there is something beyond this that is neither study nor cutting off study. This is called true passing.

The monastic presses the old master, and Heshan says, "Heshan knows how to beat the drum." If you want to see into this case, you must first understand that from the beginning, there is nothing about it that can be discussed. The only way into it is directly. When the black lacquer bucket's bottom is broken, nothing remains.

Without falling into Heshan's rut of four phrases on "knowing how to beat the drum," how do you respond to the monastic's questions? Say a word on "What is true passing?" "What is the true principle?" "What is no mind, no buddha?" and "What is going beyond buddha?" If you can avoid following after others and show something new and fresh, I will grant that you have passed through and are free and at ease in everything you do.

CAPPING VERSE

If you are unable to leap free of old habits,
　　how will you be able to get out of what binds you?
The morning mist that fills the valley
　　makes many people miss the river.

NOTES

1. It sounds like he is going to use his power to mystify people.
2. Ultimately, when you get to it, there is no place to stand.
3. You should know that there is such a place.
4. This monastic is alive and quick.
5. Many people are at a loss when they hear this.
6. The real and the apparent are not two. Have a cup of tea.
7. A forest of brambles, difficult to pass through.
8. This monastic is using diligence to make up for incompetence.
9. A pile of dry bones. Just don't try to speak about it.

10. Don't slander our golden-faced old master.

11. What will you say when asked a fifth or sixth time?

187 ∾

Jinfeng's Rice Cake

MAIN CASE

One day Zen master Congzhi of Jinfeng [Xuanming] was in the monastics' hall, where sesame rice cakes were being served. He took up one of them and from the teacher's end of the platform he rolled it into the assembly.[1]

The assembly of monastics joined their hands palm to palm.[2]

Jinfeng said, "Even if you pick it up, you have only half of it."[3]

When Jinfeng gave instructions in the evening, a monastic said, "When you had a rice cake, seeing the monastics joining their hands, you said, 'Even if you pick it up, you have only half of it.' Master, please say it all for me."[4]

Jinfeng gestured, holding up a rice cake, and said, "Do you understand it?"[5]

The monastic said, "No, I don't."[6]

Jinfeng said, "I have expressed only half of it."[7]

COMMENTARY

Zen ancestors have always understood that explaining the teachings inevitably results in a mire of words in which the truth sinks away. Jinfeng thus takes up a rice cake and rolls it into the assembly. The monastics, not knowing how to take it, respond like a herd of trained seals. The master, trying to press the matter further, says, "Even if you pick it up, you have only half of it." Half of what?

Later, when asked by a monastic to "please say it all," Jinfeng holds up a rice cake, but the monastic does not understand. Again he says, "I have expressed only half of it." Why doesn't he express it all as the monastic asked? If you say it cannot be expressed, then why did he bring it up in the first place? If you say that it can be expressed, then show it now. After all, if there is one half here, there must be another half somewhere.

CAPPING VERSE

If you wish to understand it all,
    then look at September, look at October.
The golden wind, heavy with autumn's fragrance,
    enters the mouth of the valley.

NOTES

1. He wants to feed the whole congregation at once.
2. What is wrong with them? I'm afraid they have all fallen into the same pit.
3. Hoping for a sign of life, he stirs the pot again.
4. A live one has appeared. All is not lost after all.
5. The entire teaching of countless generations is right in his face.
6. Too bad. After all, the teacher can't do it alone.
7. Although you bump into it everywhere, it's still hard to talk about it.

188 ❧
Guizong Holds Up a Fist

MAIN CASE

Once Guizong Zhichang was asked by Governor Libo, "I am not asking about the Three Vehicles and the Twelve Divisions of Sūtras. But what is the meaning of the Ancestor's [Bodhidharma's] coming from India?"[1]

Guizong held up his fist and said, "Do you understand?"[2]

Libo said, "No, I don't."[3]

Guizong said, "You have studied extensively, yet you don't know what a fist is!"[4]

Libo said, "Truly, I don't understand it."[5]

Guizong said, "If you meet a true person, you are fulfilled in the Way.[6] If you do not meet a true person, you spread worldly truth."[7]

COMMENTARY

Governor Libo is a scholar and student who wants some insight into the reality that is Zen, rather than the words and ideas that describe it. Guizong holds up his fist. With a single action he cuts off all calculations and rationalizations. If you can see into it here, then I will grant that you are free and clear in every way. If you don't see it, then it's important to avoid falling into the pit of intellectualizations. The governor does not understand. Clearly his studies are of little value here. But say, is this an expression of his ignorance or is it an expression of intimacy?

If you think that the truth of this kōan is in the fist, then you are a hundred thousand miles from the truth. But if it's not in the fist, then where can it be found? The old master is compassionate and sacrifices his eyebrows, saying, "If you meet a true person, you are fulfilled in the Way. If you do not meet a true person, you spread worldly truth."

We should understand that encountering a true person is not the same as casually meeting someone along the way. Encountering a true person means seeing with the whole eyeball. Encountering a true person means attaining penetration. It means seeing into the skin of one's own face and knowing how thick it is. Aside from this, there is nothing further.

CAPPING VERSE

Holding up a fist, he swallows all of space and time—
    this is the spring that is neither yin nor yang.
Buddhas and ancestors vanish like a dream—
    not a single trace of their passing remains.

NOTES

1. Each time it comes up it's fresh and new.
2. He should have hit him with it instead of just holding it up.
3. See? If he had hit him with it, further complications would have been avoided.
4. Too much study dulls the mind.
5. An honest person is hard to find these days.
6. The eyes are horizontal, the nose is vertical.
7. Mud six feet deep, brambles six feet high.

189 ⌒

Qingxi's "When a Thief Breaks In"

MAIN CASE

Once Zen master Qingxi Hongjin was asked by a monastic, "What happens when you are poor and a thief breaks in?"[1]

Qingxi said, "The thief cannot take away everything."[2]

The monastic said, "Why can't the thief take everything away?"[3]

Qingxi said, "Because the thief is in the family."[4]

The monastic said, "If the thief is in the family, how can it be that he turns out to be a thief?"[5]

Qingxi said, "If there is no help from the inside, an outsider couldn't do a thing."[6]

The monastic said, "If the thief is caught, who will get the reward?"

Qingxi said, "There has never been such a thing as a reward."[7]

The monastic said, "Then hard work will result in no accomplishment?"[8]

Qingxi said, "It's not that there is no accomplishment. It's just that it does not last."[9]

The monastic said, "Why does the accomplishment not last?"[10]

Qingxi said, "Don't you see what I mean? Gaining a peaceful society is accomplished by a general, but it cannot be maintained by a general."[11]

COMMENTARY

This monastic's question makes it sound as if he is bragging, but on closer examination it's clear that he has a hidden cache. Qingxi takes it at face value and responds to the imperative. Each time Qingxi opens up a path for the monastic, he meets with still another question. Why Qingxi keeps explaining and doesn't just drive the monastic out is still a mystery.

Although this old master does not avoid imparting the teachings according to potentialities, this monastic clearly presents a challenge. Rewards and accomplishments, *bah*! What is he talking about? He doesn't know that it is necessary to be clean and naked right where he stands if he is to see where the ancients met.

Haven't you heard the ancient saying "Where there is buddha, do not stay. If you do, your head will sprout horns. Where there is no buddha, quickly run past. If you don't, weeds will grow ten feet high"?

CAPPING VERSE

Distinguishing enlightenment, dismantling delusion—
    the bandit leads the sheriff's brigade.
Accomplishment, before it is exhausted,
    is just an extra thumb.

NOTES

1. If it is really a destitute family, then there is nothing to take away.
2. Some things must just be thrown away.
3. You are really the only one who knows where things are hidden.
4. Parental commitment knows no limits.
5. Of necessity, it must be an inside job.
6. A stranger wouldn't know his way around the house.
7. Don't you see? There is no payoff. There is just the road ahead.
8. It must be said that this monastic makes up for his thick head by persevering.
9. It's just another dead end.
10. Let it go and get on with your life.
11. If the general is still around, how can it be called a peaceful society?

190 ∾

Mazu's "Meaning of the Ancestor's Coming"

MAIN CASE

Mazu was asked by a monastic, "What is the meaning of the Ancestor's [Bodhidharma's] coming from India?"[1]
    Mazu said, "Come closer and I will tell you."[2]
    The monastic went closer.[3]

Mazu grabbed the monastic's ear and hit him, saying, "You shouldn't discuss this with the six ears."[4]

COMMENTARY

This question about the meaning of the Ancestor's coming from India has been widely discussed in Zen circles since time immemorial. Countless masters have responded to it, each in a unique way. Why have there been so many different answers to the same question? Is it that they only appear to be different, but are really the same answer? Is it that the real answer to the question has simply never been expressed? Or indeed, is it that the answer to this question is fundamentally inexpressible?

Haven't you heard? Master Xuefeng went to test the understanding of a hermit. As soon as Xuefeng greeted the hermit, he said, "If you can express the Way, I will not shave your head." The hermit monastic brought some water and washed his head. Xuefeng then shaved his head. I ask you, did the hermit come before Xuefeng as an expression of the Way, or did he come before him because he was unable to express the Way?

Mazu said, "Come closer and I will tell you." The monastic went closer. How could he not have known that Mazu was going to hit him? Mazu grabbed the monastic's ear and hit him, saying, "You shouldn't discuss this with the six ears." Tell me, did Mazu answer the monastic's question?

CAPPING VERSE

In speaking the dharma, there is neither speaking or teaching;
    in hearing the dharma, there is neither hearing nor attainment.
Since there is no speaking or teaching, hearing or attainment,
    why are there so many complicated kōans and teachings?

NOTES

1. Centuries of Zen practitioners have leaped into this same pit.
2. Tread carefully here.
3. Is there more to it than this?
4. He exposes or transforms in accord with the imperative.

191 ∾

Shitou's "Not Attaining, Not Knowing"

MAIN CASE

Shitou was asked by Tianhuang, "What is the fundamental meaning of the Buddhadharma?"[1]
    Shitou said, "Not to attain; not to know."[2]
    Tianhuang said, "Is there some turning point in going beyond, or not?"[3]
    Shitou said, "The vast sky does not hinder white clouds from flying."[4]

COMMENTARY

Tianhuang is from Shitou's household, so Shitou knows precisely the medicine that is called for. We should understand that his answer, "Not to attain; not to know" does not mean that there is no aspiration, training, practice, or enlightenment—it is just beyond attaining, beyond knowing. Shitou is pointing to reality. Since there is nothing lacking to begin with, what is it that can be attained? Since knowing is an illusion, a conceptual shadow of reality, how can that which is real be known?

Tianhuang is an adept. He wants to know whether there is something further to be seen or actualized. Shitou says, "The vast sky does not hinder white clouds from flying." His meaning is that the sky does not hinder the sky, clouds do not hinder the clouds, the self does not hinder itself or others. Each and every thing possesses boundless freedom. We should study these words carefully and meet our own self and the self of others. In so doing, we meet the Buddha, and the Buddha meets the Buddha.

CAPPING VERSE

Each and every thing, all real,
    each and every one, all complete.
Where attainment and knowing cannot reach,
    there it stands, alone, perfect, and complete.

NOTES

1. There have been many different ways of asking this question, yet the answer always comes down to the same thing.
2. It's like finding a lamp in a dark cave.
3. He is not finished with the matter yet. It deserves to be pressed further.
4. This old teacher knows well how to move in all directions at once.

192 ∾

Changqing's "Seeing Form, Seeing Mind"

MAIN CASE

Changqing asked Baofu Congzhan, "Seeing form is no other than seeing mind.[1] Do you see a boat?"[2]

Baofu said, "Yes, I do."[3]

Changqing said, "Putting the boat aside, what is mind?"[4]

Baofu pointed at the boat.[5]

COMMENTARY

Although the three worlds are nothing but mind, when you search for it, it cannot be found. Haven't you heard the Buddha's saying "Subhūti, it is impossible to retain past mind, impossible to hold on to present mind, and impossible to grasp future mind"? As much as he tried, Huike could not bring his mind to Bodhidharma.

Be that as it may, is it Baofu who sees the boat, or is it the boat that sees Baofu? Does the form enter the eye, or does the eye go to the form? Step beyond form and formlessness and say a word on "what is mind?"

CAPPING VERSE

Better to master the mind than to master the body—
    when the mind is at peace, the body is no longer troubled.
When body and mind have both fallen away,
    the ten thousand things have come home to the self.

NOTES

1. Where did he get the news?
2. He seems in a hurry to lower the hook.
3. He doesn't seem to be greedy, just willing.
4. A yank of the fishing line.
5. The hook comes up empty. Since they are from the same household, it's not so surprising.

193 ⌒

Shishuang's "Transcendent Wisdom That Meets the Eye"

MAIN CASE

Shishuang Qingzhu went to study with Daowu and asked, "What is the transcendent wisdom that meets the eye?"[1]

Daowu called out, "Novice!"

A novice monastic responded.

Daowu said to the novice, "Add some water to the jar."[2] Then he said to Shishuang, "What did you ask?"[3]

Shishuang repeated the question.[4]

Daowu stood up and walked away.[5]

At this point Shishuang had realization.[6]

COMMENTARY

If your potential is frozen in a fixed position, you will end up falling into the sea of delusion. Cut off the myriad streams of thought and the eyes abruptly open wide. Before meeting Daowu, Shishuang studied with Daowu's teacher Yaoshan and with Guishan. Here he is primed and ready for a spark to open up the reality that meets the eye.

When Shishuang poses the question, Daowu wants to see how he understands "meeting the eye," and so sets out a snare. Shishuang misses it, and Daowu walks away. A spark, and Shishuang realizes it. But say, realizes what? If you think this is about calling out and responding, or filling the water jar, you are still thousands of miles from the truth of this encounter.

If you want to understand what is realized, first study the phrase "The entire world is not concealed," and then you can begin to understand "the transcendent wisdom that meets the eye."

CAPPING VERSE

Wisdom has no teacher;
>   meeting the eye is direct.
It is not like reflections in a mirror—
>   when one side is realized, the other side is dark.

NOTES

1. It's easy to open your mouth, difficult to open your eyes.
2. He is using the novice to bait his trap.
3. It's hard to believe that he has already forgotten the conversation.
4. Oops!
5. Thank you for your teaching.
6. His diligence has made up for his dull-wittedness.

194 ∽
Caoshan's "Myriad Things"

MAIN CASE

A monastic asked Caoshan, "It is said in the scriptures that the ocean does not harbor a corpse. What is the ocean?"[1]
    Caoshan said, "It contains myriad things."[2]
    The monastic said, "Then why does it not harbor a corpse?"[3]
    Caoshan said, "Those who have stopped breathing cannot stay."[4]
    The monastic said, "If the ocean contains myriad things, why can't those who have stopped breathing stay?"[5]
    Caoshan said, "Myriad things do not stop breathing."[6]

COMMENTARY

This monastic, having encountered this phrase in the *Flower Garland Sūtra*, goes to Caoshan for clarification. He wants to know why, if the "sea of samādhi" contains the myriad things, it does not include extinction (a corpse). Caoshan's "sea of samādhi" does not admit subject-object dualities, therefore he says, "Myriad things do not stop breathing." This is the samādhi of the hands and eyes of great compassion. This is Yunmen's "Rice in the bowl, water in the bucket."

Master Dōgen taught that the "sea of samādhi" is the practice and vow to awaken self and other. All things eventually return to this great "sea of samādhi." It is the original source of Zen practice and enlightenment and the basis of the Buddhist way of life. We should investigate these words and the words of Caoshan carefully. We should understand for ourselves that the virtue of moving over the surface of the "sea of samādhi" is at once movement along the bottom of its fathomless depths.

CAPPING VERSE

This body is composed of only real dharmas.
When dharmas appear there are just dharmas—
    no self.
When dharmas disappear there is just disappearance—
    no self.
Buddha said to take it this way.

NOTES

1. What is it that it is not?
2. It's right in your face, on your head, under your feet. Where are you?
3. This seems like a reasonable question that deserves a reasonable answer.
4. He seems to be serving pictures of cakes. This won't satisfy the monastic's hunger.
5. Indeed.
6. He should be careful of his eyebrows. This is not a matter that can be settled through discussion.

195 ᰫ
Zhaozhou's "Dao"

MAIN CASE

Nanquan said to the assembly,[1] "The Dao is not an outside thing."[2]

Zhaozhou stepped forward[3] and said, "What is the Dao of outside things?"[4]

Nanquan hit him.

Zhaozhou said, "Your Reverence, don't beat me. You may be hitting someone in error."[5]

Nanquan said, "It's easy to distinguish a dragon from a snake,[6] but it's hard to deceive you."[7]

COMMENTARY

When you have realized the ability to smash space, level mountains, astonish the heavens, and shake the earth, then for the first time you have arrived at the place where there are originally no seams, no gaps, no flaws, or scars, and communication is impossible. But tell me, why does Nanquan hit Zhaozhou? Is Zhaozhou in error, or is Nanquan in error?

Are there any who attain alike, realize alike, live alike, and die alike?

CAPPING VERSE

Old Zhaozhou is truly extraordinary.
He knows how to turn around
    and come out hopping and jumping.
He wraps up everything
    and presses the old Buddha.
In their words and actions,
    they reveal their freedom and clarity.
Nanquan, heedless of the mud,
    knowingly offends.
Zhaozhou, eager to serve the master,
    hits him with a mud ball.

NOTES

1. One blind man leading a crowd of the blind. He doesn't mind his offensive stench.
2. The old master is using his power to deceive the people. Trailing mud, dripping water, he creates a mess.
3. Danger! Zhaozhou is an extraordinary thief who steals in broad daylight. He sees an opportunity and he acts.
4. He comes on directly. He wants everybody to know.
5. He sticks his head into the lion's mouth to count the teeth.
6. He knows, yet he deliberately offends. Only an adept can do this.
7. If they weren't sleeping in the same bed, how would they know the blanket has holes in it?

196 ॐ
Longya's "Thief in an Empty Room"

MAIN CASE

A monastic asked Zen master Judun of Longya [Zhangkong], "When do the teachers of old get stuck?"[1]

Longya said, "When the thief slips into an empty room."[2]

COMMENTARY

If you can penetrate Longya's phrase thoroughly and trust yourself completely, you will find that from the beginningless beginning you have always been free and untethered. Let go, and even river rocks radiate light; hold on, and even the mani jewel loses its brilliance.

In an empty room there is nothing to steal, nothing to protect, hold on to, lose, or change. It is filled with potential. However, as for me, I would have pulled out the nails, kicked out the wedges, and collapsed the whole structure. After all, the room is just more baggage. Having come this far, you must still be able to discern the phrase outside of patterns. Then, when one is raised, you will understand three.

CAPPING VERSE

When the mind is empty,
    the eyes are finally clear.
Shining through detachment and subtlety—
    the root of creation.

NOTES

1. This dull-witted monastic speaks up.
2. When it is warm, the whole universe is warm. When it is cold, the whole universe is cold.

197 ✧

Master Deng's "Voice like Thunder"

MAIN CASE

Deng Yinfeng visited Guishan and unwrapped his bowls and robes at the senior monastic's seat on the meditation platform.[1]

Hearing that his dharma uncle had come, Guishan got formally dressed and went into the monastics' hall.[2]

As soon as Deng saw Guishan coming, he lay down and pretended to be asleep,[3] so Guishan went back to the abbot's room.[4]

Deng departed.

After a while Guishan asked his attendant monastic, "Is my dharma uncle still here?"

The attendant monastic said, "He has already left."

Guishan said, "What did he say before he left?"[5]

The attendant monastic said, "He said nothing."[6]

Guishan said, "Don't say he said nothing. His voice is like thunder."[7]

COMMENTARY

Guishan's dharma uncle Deng is an adept from the lineage of Mazu. He arrives at Guishan's monastery carrying a probing pole. Guishan too, has trained for a long time and has a sharp active edge about him. Can you see how, when one gathers in, they both gather in? When the other lets go, they both let go? If you want to understand them thoroughly, you must be an intimate acquaintance. In the Zen school, this is known as the "merging of perspectives."

Tell me, when Master Deng lies down upon seeing Guishan, what is his meaning? If you take this as unconcern, you have missed it. If you can see beyond the surface of this encounter, you will understand that Deng and Guishan are having an extraordinary dharma conversation that is unhindered by words. Both are endowed with the seven items of a teacher and know how to use them well. If only the monastic had been aware, he could have been released from his cage of brambles. Guishan says, "His voice is like thunder." I ask, can you hear it?

CAPPING VERSE

When meeting a person of the Way,
    do not greet him with words or with silence.
Words cannot convey the truth, silence is only half—
    how will you greet him?

NOTES

1. Apparently his intention is to move in.
2. This is an occasion to show some family courtesy.
3. How kind of him.
4. The arrow was not shot without purpose.
5. Were there any further kindnesses that he imparted?
6. The attendant monastic was listening at a different frequency.
7. These teachings are still reverberating at Mount Gui.

198 ꙮ

Dongshan and Shenshan Cross the River

MAIN CASE

Zen master Sengmi of Shenshan crossed a river with his dharma brother Dongshan.[1] Dongshan said, "Don't make a mistake with your steps and slip into the current."[2]

Shenshan said, "If I make a mistake with my steps, then I won't live to cross the river."[3]

Dongshan said, "What is the state without mistakes?"[4]

Shenshan said, "Crossing the river with the elder."[5]

COMMENTARY

Face-to-face, there is nothing hidden, yet fundamentally, there is no way of explaining it all. No self and no other, then how can we speak of right and wrong? Dongshan and Shenshan are from the same household. Both know well the contents of the kitchen pantry.

We should understand that, in reality, mistakes are called learning, and the state of no mistake is called nowness. In nowness there is no before or after, no goals, agendas, or fixed direction. Like the meandering river, it twists and turns in accord with circumstances but always knows how to find its way to the great ocean. If you wish to travel like this, you must go alone, not carry any baggage, and trust yourself implicitly.

CAPPING VERSE

A hazy autumn moon, solitary and full,
　　falls as it may on the winding river ahead.
There are those who seek perfect clarity,
　　yet, sweep as they may, they cannot empty the mind.

NOTES

1. These two traveling together always manage to create complications.
2. In crossing to the other side, sure-footedness is definitely a virtue.

3. The river treats all things equally.
4. Though few may know it, there is such a thing.
5. Arriving as it departs, simultaneously, the moment is always fresh.

199 ❧
Dongshan's Essential Path

MAIN CASE

When Zen master Xiujing of Huayan Monastery [Baozhi] was studying with Dongshan, he said, "I still cannot see the essential path; I still can't become free of discriminating consciousness."[1]

Dongshan said, "Do you think there is such a path?"[2]

Huayan said, "No, I do not think there is such a path."[3]

Dongshan said, "Where did you acquire your discriminating thinking?"[4]

Huayan said, "I am asking in all seriousness."[5]

Dongshan said, "Go to a place where there is no grass for a myriad li."[6]

Huayan said, "How can I go to a place where there is no grass for a myriad li?"[7]

Dongshan said, "Go directly, right now."[8]

COMMENTARY

The essential path is wild, unregulated, self-maintaining, intelligent, sacred, and free. Its temple is the wilderness; its liturgy is the gāthā of rock and water, the voice of the coyote, a wind song. Its teachings are infinite wonder. Yet, if you direct yourself toward it, you are surely moving away from it. This monastic wants to be free and to accord with the nature of things. Dongshan is trying to let him see that in his very effort he is creating complications. Haven't you heard that in order to live in accord with natural principles and the fundamental nature of things, all intentional efforts must first vanish? The essential path abides in nonaction, and yet nothing is left undone.

But say, if there is no grass for a myriad li, how can you go? Where can you go? Who would go? If you linger at the source, you will miss its radiance; if you chase after shadows, you will become entangled in brambles. What will you do?

CAPPING VERSE

Wet with the morning dew,
    the tips of ten thousand grasses
    all contain the light of day.

NOTES

1. Set down the backpack, take off the blinders, and look! Where are you?
2. He sets out a bowl of both honey and poison.
3. Either way, he loses the path.
4. Why do you make one into two?
5. I am afraid he just doesn't get it.
6. Look! There is grass growing between his toes.
7. Up, no limit. Down, no bottom. Sides, no edges. What is it?
8. What is he talking about? There is grass all over the place.

200 ॐ

Ruiyan's "What Kind of Moment Is Now?"

MAIN CASE

Zen master Shiyan of Mount Ruiyan said to Jiashan, "Thus is easy. Not-thus is difficult.[1] Thus and thus are clear. Not-thus and not-thus abide in the realm of emptiness.[2] Master, please explain this for me quickly."[3]

Jiashan said, "This old priest may deceive you."[4]

Ruiyan yelled and said, "Old priest, what kind of moment is now?" Then he walked away.[5]

Later a monastic told Ruiyan's teacher, Yantou, this story.

Yantou said, "How painful. Thus floats away my branch of the Buddha-dharma."[6]

COMMENTARY

Ruiyan arrives seeking an explanation, but he is given clarification instead. Although the message is sent, Ruiyan does not receive it. He is looking for something to grasp. Thus cannot be grasped, not-thus cannot be grasped. If you wish to see into thusness, you must see into nongrasping. If you want to see into nongrasping, you must see into thusness.

Since all of this is a matter beyond explanations, Jiashan does not deceive Ruiyan. Do you understand? Ruiyan doesn't. He yells and says, "Old priest, what kind of moment is now?" He has mistaken the moment for thusness. Thusness is neither existent nor nonexistent. Therefore, thusness cannot be grasped, and thusness cannot not be grasped.

Yantou, hearing of this encounter, says, "How painful. Thus floats away my branch of the Buddhadharma." Tell me, what does he mean? Where does it go?

CAPPING VERSE

You and I are the same thing,
    yet I am not you and you are not me.
No coming, no going, no arising, no abiding—
    as each dharma appears, each dharma is practiced.

NOTES

1. If you say so.
2. He tries to make up for his dullness with a loud voice and an attitude.
3. If he had his way, he would drag everyone into this pit with him.
4. His kindness is outstanding. Why not just drive him out?
5. He thinks he has seen something, but he has only an idea.
6. What is admired by adepts is having no edges.

201 ∾

Bodhidharma's "Skin, Flesh, Bones, and Marrow"

MAIN CASE

Venerable Bodhidharma was about to go back to India. He said to his students, "The time has come. Can you express your understanding?"[1]

One of the students, Daofu, said, "My present view is that we should neither be attached to letters nor be apart from letters, and allow the Way to function freely."[2]

Bodhidharma said, "You have attained my skin."[3]

Nun Zongchi said, "My view is that it is like the joy of seeing Akṣobhya Buddha's land just once and not again."[4]

Bodhidharma said, "You have attained my flesh."[5]

Daoyu said, "The four great elements are originally empty and the five skandhas do not exist. Therefore I see nothing to be attained."[6]

Bodhidharma said, "You have attained my bones."[7]

Finally Zen master Dazu Huike [Zhengzong Pujue] came forward, made a full bow, stood up, and returned to where he was.[8]

Bodhidharma said, "You have attained my marrow."[9] Thus he transmitted the dharma and robe to Huike.[10]

COMMENTARY

If you take these different responses as being superior or inferior to each other, you have missed Bodhidharma's intent. We should realize that although each disciple's expression of the dharma is different from the others, nonetheless, each in his or her own way contains the teacher's whole being.

Given that Bodhidharma is not approving depth of understanding by the use of the terms skin, flesh, bones, and marrow, who did he transmit the dharma to? If you say all four received the dharma, then why is it said, "Thus he transmitted the dharma and robe to Huike"? If you are able to see into it here, you will understand Bodhidharma's heart.

CAPPING VERSE

Before a step is taken,
    you have already arrived.
Before a word is spoken,
    the truth has been expressed.

NOTES

1. Finding one general among the four will be a difficult task indeed.
2. Avoiding the curbsides, he navigates right down the middle of the road.
3. He doesn't avoid grandmotherly kindness.
4. Only an adept can speak like this; after all, she's a lion cub.
5. Although there are many who travel the way, those who know the tune are rare.
6. Deaf, dumb, and blind, he stumbles along.
7. A spirit recognizes a spirit, a thief acknowledging a thief.
8. Proceeding by Bodhidharma's own road, he walks right into the old man's belly.
9. Clearly a case of an overindulgent parent.
10. One blind man leading a crowd of blind people. What will all of this come down to?

202 ∾

"No Zen Masters"

MAIN CASE

Huangbo said to the assembly,[1] "All of you are eaters of dregs.[2] If you continue to travel about like this,[3] where will you settle today's matter?[4] Don't you know there is not a single Zen master in all of the great Tang country?"[5]

Then a monastic came forward and said, "How about those who train students and administer monasteries?"[6]

Huangbo said, "I am not saying there is no Zen. It's just that there are no Zen masters."[7]

COMMENTARY

Even in the most eloquent of Zen teaching, nothing has ever been imparted. Before a word of dharma is spoken, "it" is already present. In his forty-seven years of addressing thousands of assemblies, the Buddha never uttered a single word.

Because the truth exists outside patterns and devices, ultimately no communication whatsoever is possible. This is the light that does not belong to yin or yang.

CAPPING VERSE

There's no abode that can contain this gigantic body;
    there is no place to conceal the wondrous mind of nirvāṇa.
The subtleties cannot be passed on—
    ultimately, we can only nod to ourselves.

NOTES

    1. His responsibility is to stir up the assembly.
    2. Don't confuse the vintage wine with the "*lie de vin.*"
    3. Like summer butterflies flitting from flower to flower.
    4. Where do you find yourself?
    5. The whole idea is to let down a hook and fish out people's questions.
    6. Strike!
    7. I wonder, if there were Zen masters, what would they be like?

203 ∾

Xuansha's "Person of Three Disabilities"

MAIN CASE

Xuansha said to the assembly, "Elders in various places all talk about interacting with and benefiting all beings.[1] If you encounter a person with three disabilities, how will you guide that person?[2] Even if you take up a mallet or raise a whisk, the blind do not see you.[3] Even if you speak eloquently, the deaf do not hear you.[4] Even if you ask them to speak, the mute cannot speak.[5] How will you guide them?[6] If you cannot guide them, the Buddha-dharma has no marvel."[7]

At that time, Dizang was in the assembly. He came forward and said, "I have eyes and ears. Master, how do you guide me?"[8]

Xuansha said, "I am ashamed." Then he returned to the abbot's room.[9]

COMMENTARY

Blind, deaf, mute—where will you enter? Xuansha has compassionately cut away all the teaching devices so that no communication whatsoever is possible. Now, what will you do? We should understand that there are five kinds of blindness, deafness, and muteness. What is the kind that Xuansha is speaking of? Does it matter?

If you truly want to see into this kōan, then you must enter the marvel of the Buddhadharma or see into Xuansha's shame and not look to blindness, deafness, and muteness for your insight.

CAPPING VERSE

Before the question is even asked,
    there is only one piece.
After the question is asked,
    ten thousand pieces, all illuminated.

NOTES

1. Responding to the imperative and gouging healthy flesh.
2. Hopeless.
3. It is not necessary to be blind to not see.
4. It is not necessary to be deaf to not hear.
5. It is not necessary to be mute to not speak.
6. He has covered the tracks of the ancients and erected a hidden barrier.
7. See it here! See it here!
8. Deaf, dumb, and blind. Go away.
9. It is this shame that has been transmitted down to the present. What is it?

204 ⚬

Qinglin's "Dead Snake on the Path"

MAIN CASE

Zen master Dongshan Shiqian [Qinglin] was once asked by a monastic, "What happens if I take a shortcut on the path?"[1]

Qinglin said, "A dead snake lies in the great road. I warn you, don't step on its head."[2]

The monastic said, "What happens if I step on its head?"[3]

Qinglin said, "You will lose your life."[4]

The monastic said, "What happens if I don't step on it?"[5]

Qinglin said, "There is no way to go around it."[6]

The monastic said, "What happens at such a time?"[7]

Qinglin said, "You miss it."[8]

The monastic said, "Where shall I go?"[9]

Qinglin said, "The grass is deep. There is no place to look for it."[10]

The monastic said, "Master, you too should be careful."[11]

Qinglin clapped his hands and said, "This is all poisonous."[12]

COMMENTARY

This monastic has an agenda that he seems to be seeking to confirm; he even thinks he has a shortcut. What he has not yet understood is that his shortcut is already the long way around. Qinglin wants to help him and immediately manifests the dead snake. This monastic is fearless and presses on, saying, "What happens if I step on its head?" Can you see how the poison already has a hold of him? Qinglin blocks him, saying, "You will lose your life."

Although this monastic is a bit reckless, he is not dull. He starts looking for a way out: "What happens if I don't step on it?" The old man snatches this away too, with "There is no way to go around it." At this point, finding himself squeezed between two iron mountains, the monastic asks for guidance. Qinglin says, "The grass is deep. There is no place to look for it."

Actually, it's so deep that even the sky above is blocked out, and both teacher and disciple are bogged down in it. The monastic comes alive and says, "Master, you too should be careful." Qinglin uses a dead snake to awaken this monastic, and in the end, its coils are wrapped around both master and disciple. Seeing the poison permeate heaven and earth, Qinglin claps his hands and says, "This is all poisonous." Tell me, where is the poison?

CAPPING VERSE

Riding the winding river deep into the night,
  both banks dissolve in darkness.
Being found by the wonder of the flow,
  my way opens of its own.

NOTES

1. Even a single step is the long way.
2. He brings out poison.
3. Some may call this reckless, some may see it as gutsy. Still, he has to know.
4. What do you expect?
5. Already the poison has taken its toll.
6. The old man is closing all the gates on his cage.
7. There must be a way out of this.
8. There is giving and then there is taking away.
9. He is asking the jailer to help him escape.
10. Boundlessly filling the ten directions. Where are the edges?
11. Suddenly, he comes back hopping and jumping.
12. The crook and the thief meet each other.

205 ◌

Longya Passes the Meditation Brace

MAIN CASE

Longya went to study with Cuiwei for the first time and asked him, "What is the meaning of the Ancestor's [Bodhidharma's] coming from India?"[1]

Cuiwei said, "Pass me that meditation brace."[2]

Longya passed the meditation brace to him.[3]

Cuiwei received it and hit Longya with it.[4]

Longya said, "It's all right that you hit me. But the point is that there is no meaning of the Ancestor's coming from India."[5]

Later Longya went to study with Linji and asked the same question.[6]

Linji said, "Let me have that sitting mat."[7]

Longya passed the sitting mat to him.[8]

Linji received it and hit Longya with it.[9]

Longya said, "Your answer is the same as Cuiwei's."[10]

Later, after Longya became abbot, a monastic asked him, "When you saw the two venerable masters, did you understand them?"[11]

Longya said, "I did understand them. The point is that there is no meaning of the Ancestor's coming from India."[12]

COMMENTARY

The ancients had a powerful resolve to clarify the great matter. They would travel about mountains and rivers calling on adepts to test them, and to sharpen their own understanding. An old master said that this was true at that time, but do practitioners these days still have blood under their skin?

Longya is not dull-witted. How can he not know that Cuiwei will hit him with the meditation brace when he hands it over? Why doesn't he just throw it down in front of Cuiwei? Do you understand? Something else is going on here. Again he travels the same road with Linji. Tell me, these two masters are not of the same household. Why is their functioning the same?

The masters hold fast, Longya holds fast; there are thorns in the soft mud. Do you see them? It can't be said that the old masters are wrong, nor can it be said that Longya is missing their point. They are not both right, nor are they both wrong. When you reach this place, you must know that there is something further that is extraordinary. What is it?

CAPPING VERSE

The dharma wheel turns in both directions—
     if it doesn't go east, then it goes west.
If the waves of Caoxi were the same,
     people would drown on dry land.

NOTES

1. Everybody seems to want to know about this.
2. At this point, if he was at all alert, he would have known something was happening.
3. He knows how to follow instructions, but is he awake?
4. Alas, what else could he do?
5. He closes the barn door after the horse has escaped.
6. Why is he still carrying the same burden?
7. This seems familiar. Doesn't he see that?
8. Again he goes along with it. Is he making a point?
9. Having taken it this far, he had to follow through.
10. It's nice that he noticed, so it can't be said that he is dull-witted.
11. Yes, everyone would like to know.
12. Too bad. It seems that whenever he is pressed he goes blind in one eye.

206 ∾

The Essential Matter

MAIN CASE

Shiti asked his attendant monastic, "Where have you been?"[1]

The monastic said, "I went to the monastics' hall and had a meal."[2]

Shiti said, "Do you think I don't know that you went to the monastics' hall and had a meal?"[3]

The monastic said, "What else could I have said?"[4]

Shiti said, "I was asking you about the essential matter."[5]

The monastic said, "If you ask me about the essential matter, I say I went to the monastics' hall and had a meal."[6]

Shiti said, "You didn't miss it. That's why you are my attendant."[7]

COMMENTARY

Hearing this master's comment to his monastic has caused many a Zen practitioner to conclude that the essential matter of Zen is taking a meal or chopping wood and carrying water. This kind of understanding is nothing more than the self-styled notion of "everything I do is Zen." Nothing could be further from the truth of the rightly transmitted dharma of the buddhas and ancestors.

The essential matter of Zen is not just about feeding the mouth and filling the belly. It's about feeding the mouth and filling the belly of all beings, sentient and insentient alike. How do you feed the mouth and fill the belly of all beings? Take the backward step and study the self thoroughly. When we study the self thoroughly, we understand others thoroughly as well. As a result, self and other merge in a single thusness. The essential matter of Zen is the complete merging of all dualistic opposites. Sacred and mundane, self and other, taking a meal and giving a meal, saving the self and saving all sentient beings, are a single reality.

The sacred activity of nondoing is the hallmark of the Zen school; it is not the same as ordinary consciousness. When it rains, you open an umbrella. If you don't have an umbrella, you get wet. When sleep comes, you close your eyes; when someone hurts, you feel the hurt; if they fall, you pick them up; when you take off your shoes, you feel your feet. If you still miss what's being said here, then you must take up the search deep in the night. How else will you ever attain unity?

CAPPING VERSE

Those who think that in the mundane
    nothing is sacred
    have not yet understood
    that in sacredness nothing is mundane.

NOTES

1. This is not a question about geography.
2. The answer is not about geography either.
3. The old man needs to shake this out to see where it comes down.
4. There is an echo in his words. He is not just asking for instruction.
5. What essential matter are you speaking of, dull-witted teacher?
6. There is a bit of fragrant air about this monastic.
7. In the end it's all dirt from the same hole.

207 ⌘

Linji's "Not Studying Sūtras, Not Studying Zen"

MAIN CASE

One day the emperor's attendant Wang Jingchu went to the monastics' hall with Linji and asked him, "Do monastics in this hall study sūtras?"

Linji said, "No, they don't study sūtras."[1]

Wang said, "Do they study Zen?"

Linji said, "No, they don't study Zen."[2]

Wang said, "Not studying sūtras and not studying Zen, what *do* they do?"[3]

Linji said, "All we do is make them become buddhas and ancestors."[4]

Wang said, "Even precious gold dust, if it gets into your eyes, will cause blindness. Don't you think so?"[5]

Linji said, "I always thought you were just a worldly person."[6]

COMMENTARY

If you wish to understand the dharma of Linji, you must first realize that sūtras, buddhas and ordinary beings, enlightenment and delusion, as well as all phenomena of this world and other worlds, are devoid of intrinsic nature. To seek after or attempt to avoid any of these is like chasing after phantoms and illusions and will only lead to pain and suffering.

Understand, therefore, that the true buddha is without form, the true dharma is without characteristics. Why trouble yourself trying to grasp them? Stop all contrivances and realize that each and every being, just as it is, never fails to cover the ground upon which it stands.

Wang Jingchu is a successor of Master Guishan and understands Linji's intent clearly. Therefore he says, "Even precious gold dust, if it gets into your eyes, will cause blindness. Don't you think so?" But tell me, what is his meaning? What is the gold dust he speaks of, and what kind of blindness is he referring to? Moreover, does Linji approve him or not?

CAPPING VERSE

If you attach to the sacred and avert the secular,
    you are bobbing around in the sea of birth and death.

All desires exist because of mind—
 when there is no mind, how can anything bind you?

NOTES

1. These are the words and ideas that describe reality. Tell me, what is
   the reality?
2. This would be like trying to put a head on top of the one you already
   have.
3. Is he really looking for information, or is he testing the old master?
4. Be careful not to deceive people, old man. It's not about becoming.
5. It seems that he understands what's going on.
6. It's rare indeed for old master Linji to be so kind.

208 ∽

Yunmen's "End of the Ninety-Day Training Period"

MAIN CASE

Yunmen was once asked by a monastic, "If, at the beginning of autumn,
after the summer training period is over, someone asks me about the fu-
ture, what shall I say?"[1]
 Yunmen said, "The assembly adjourns."[2]
 The monastic said, "What will happen after that?"[3]
 Yunmen said, "Pay me for the ninety days of meals."[4]

COMMENTARY

This encounter must have been very disappointing for Yunmen. After having spent ninety days rigorously training his monastics, it turns out that
this one is completely lost in the illusion of some distant time. The future
doesn't exist—it hasn't happened yet. The past doesn't exist—it's already
happened. What is right here now? This is where life takes place. I would
have driven this monastic out before the words were out of his mouth.

Yunmen is being unusually kind when he says, "The assembly adjourns." When the wind blows from India, the leaves gather in the east. In the midst of today, the monastic persists with what happens next, saying, "What will happen after that?" Nothing happens next. This is it!

Do you understand why Yunmen demands payment for the ninety days of meals? If the monastic is using the monastery as a hotel, he should pay hotel rates.

CAPPING VERSE

If you want to understand the past,
    look at the present.
If you want to understand the future,
    look at the present.
Buddha said to take it this way.

NOTES

1. Just tell them that you're not a prophet.
2. Old Yunmen knows what's underfoot.
3. I can't seem to find "after that." There only seems to be just this.
4. This poor old monastic is trying to collect some kind of rebate on his failure.

209 ∾

Guishan's Water Buffalo

MAIN CASE

Guishan said to the assembly, "One hundred years from now I will be reborn as a water buffalo at the foot of this mountain.[1] On the left side of the buffalo's chest the characters, 'I am a monastic of Guishan' will be written.[2] If you call it the monastic of Guishan, it will be a water buffalo.[3] If you call it a water buffalo, it will be the monastic of Guishan.[4] Tell me, what will you call it?"[5]

Yangshan came forward from the assembly, bowed, and walked away.[6]

COMMENTARY

These brambles Guishan has set out are not about water buffalos, the front gate, the foot of the mountain, or the characters "I am a monastic of Guishan." Although Yangshan understands Guishan, don't look to his bow or his walking away to see into Guishan's teaching. Where do you see the heart of the Ancestor [Bodhidharma]?

If you want to understand the effect, look at the cause. If you want to understand the cause, look at the effect. Then understand that the truth is not to be found in either, nor in both. Cause and effect are one. Cause does not precede effect, effect does not follow cause. Do you understand? If so, then tell me, what is the one?

CAPPING VERSE

The summit of Heavenly Light Mountain [Tenkozan] is difficult to reach.
Those who've seen it had to grope their way
     through boulders and clouds.
Night falls. Phoenicia to the north is dark,
     Ashokan to the south is shrouded in mist.
And yet, and yet—
     the Great Way is not hidden from you.

NOTES

1. There is such a thing, you know.
2. We should be able to see where he is going with this.
3. This is only half of it.
4. This is the other half, but it is still incomplete.
5. He wants us to see the trap that we fall into every day.
6. Yangshan has an eye on his forehead, but what is his meaning?

210 ❧

The National Teacher's "Original Body of Vairocana"

MAIN CASE

Nanyang was once asked by a monastic, "What is the original body of Vairocana?"[1]

Nanyang said, "Bring me the water jar."[2]

The monastic came back with a water jar.[3]

Nanyang said, "Put it back where it was."[4]

The monastic asked the same question again.[5]

Nanyang said, "The old buddha has been gone for a long time."[6]

COMMENTARY

In speaking of Vairocana, there can be neither explanation nor teaching. In listening to the dharma, there can be neither hearing nor attainment. What can be done to clarify the Way, then?

This monastic arrives at the National Teacher's place filled with ideas and notions about Vairocana Buddha. He seems to understand that Vairocana is characterized by completion and perfection—out of which all sentient and insentient forms as well as the moral order arise. But these are only the words and ideas that describe Vairocana Buddha. They are not yet the reality.

The National Teacher is extremely indulgent and asks him to fetch the water jar. Do you understand? If you think the point he is making has to do with bringing the water jar, returning the water jar, the water, or the jar, then you too, like the monastic, will be asking the same question for the rest of your life.

If you wish to see into the National Teacher's dharma, then you must cut away all traces of thought at this very moment, wash away all words and ideas, and bring out your own treasure.

CAPPING VERSE

Raising your eyebrows to look, you won't see—
   it has already passed by.

Stop looking under another's feet;
    look under your own.

NOTES

1. At this point, all further complications could be avoided by a simple knock on the head.
2. Thank you for your answer.
3. Hello! Anybody home?
4. Only old grandmothers and indulgent teachers are like this.
5. Today we have encountered a monastic fast asleep.
6. How sad. All of this effort and searching without finding.

211 ✑

Caoshan's "Love between Parent and Child"

MAIN CASE

Caoshan was once asked by a monastic, "A child went back to her parent. Why didn't the parent pay attention to her?"[1]
    Caoshan said, "It is quite natural just like that."[2]
    The monastic said, "Then where is the love between parent and child?"[3]
    Caoshan said, "The love between parent and child."[4]
    The monastic said, "What is the love between parent and child?"[5]
    Caoshan said, "It cannot be split apart, even when hit with an ax."[6]

COMMENTARY

At the time of birth, parent and child become each other. This means that in the middle of the night, before the moon has appeared, do not be surprised that people meet without knowing each other. At this point, the empty sky has vanished and the iron mountain has crumbled. There is not an inch of ground to stand on. Be that as it may, mountains are high and valleys are low. Thus Caoshan says the love between parent and child neither arises nor vanishes. Then how can it be divided into fragments and segments?
    All of this notwithstanding, how is it that parent and child can meet and yet not know each other?

CAPPING VERSE

Why must yin and yang be placed in an arrangement?
    If you do, you will never have today.
When the wind blows, the grasses bend;
    when the rains come, the river fills.

NOTES

1. They meet but don't recognize each other.
2. Although this is true, why does he call it "natural"?
3. This monastic thinks love is about differentiation.
4. Beginningless and endless, intimacy is a continuum.
5. He is still sitting by the river, dying of thirst.
6. It is simply not two.

212 ॐ

Dizang Plants the Fields

MAIN CASE

Dizang once asked a monastic, "Where are you from?"[1]
    The monastic said, "From the south."[2]
    Dizang said, "How is Buddhadharma in the south?"[3]
    The monastic said, "It's being discussed all over."[4]
    Dizang said, "How can it compare to my planting rice, growing food, and eating?"[5]
    The monastic said, "What about the three worlds?"[6]
    Dizang said, "What is it that you call the three worlds?"[7]
    The monastic had realization.[8]

COMMENTARY

This monastic had already encountered Dizang during a previous visit, and although he was in the midst of pure light at that time, his eyes were closed and he did not see it. On his second visit, still bogged down in the mundane, he blindly walks past Dizang's compassionate teachings. However, the old master persists until the monastic has some insight.

If you think Dizang's "planting rice, growing food, and eating" are about agriculture or dining, you too are bogged down in the mundane. If you want to understand Dizang's words, you must first realize that in the mundane nothing is sacred. Then you must realize that in sacredness nothing is mundane.

CAPPING VERSE

Passing from mouth to ear,
  the teaching inevitably disintegrates.
When words and ideas are finally obliterated,
  the light spontaneously appears.

NOTES

1. This is not a question about geography.
2. He misunderstands and answers geographically.
3. The old man lets it pass, then walks into the monastic's belly.
4. He conveniently impales himself on the teacher's hook.
5. He proclaims it in a loud voice so that everyone will know it. Still, it's a little excessive.
6. What?
7. Indeed!
8. Say a word on what it was that this monastic finally realized.

213 ∾

The Bodhisattva of No Miraculous Power

MAIN CASE

Daowu was once asked by a monastic, "Why is it so difficult to find traces of a bodhisattva of no miraculous power?"[1]
  Daowu said, "Those who travel together know it."[2]
  The monastic said, "Master, do you know it?"[3]
  Daowu said, "No, I don't."[4]

The monastic said, "How come you don't know it?"[5]
Daowu said, "Go away. You don't understand what I mean."[6]

COMMENTARY

Having heard of the bodhisattva of no miraculous power, this monastic wants to know why it is not possible to find traces of such a being. Daowu's "Those who travel together know it" means that it's like one bright pearl whose radiance cannot be contained. "Cannot be contained" means reaching everywhere, traceless. The monastic's "Do you know it?" clearly shows he still doesn't get it.

Haven't you heard old master Baizhang's saying: "When the moment is not hindered by being and nonbeing, or reliance on knowing and not knowing, this is called miraculous power. Not being attached to this miraculous power is called being without miraculous power. Bodhisattvas without miraculous power thus leave no traces. This is the mark of continuous development beyond buddha."

In the end, this encounter just turns out to be playing in the mud with no redeemable virtue whatsoever. That is, unless you can say a word on behalf of the monastic and manifest the bodhisattva of no miraculous power right here now.

CAPPING VERSE

Present without thinking,
    its presence is inherently intimate.
Completed without interacting,
    its completion is inherently verified.

NOTES

1. Not difficult really, except for those who are searching for it.
2. Though they may know it, they are still unable to speak of it.
3. Hello, hello! Have you been listening to this old monastic?
4. He just offers the actual facts, but I'm afraid this monastic still won't get it.
5. He still doesn't get it.
6. You should have sent him away right from the beginning, then all of this could have been avoided.

214 ⌒

Fengxue's "Particle of Dust"

MAIN CASE

Fengxue Yanzhao taught the assembly, "If you raise a particle of dust, the nation will flourish and the people will frown.[1] If you do not raise a particle of dust, the nation will perish and the people will be at ease.[2] If you realize clarity from this, then this old monastic is an ācārya.[3] If this is not clarified for you, then I am just an old monastic.[4] The old monastic and the ācārya can enlighten others and delude others.[5] Do you want to understand this old monastic?" Fengxue clapped his hands once on his left side and said, "Just this.[6] Do you want to understand the ācārya?" He clapped his hands once on his right side and said, "Just this."[7]

COMMENTARY

If we can realize a single particle of dust, we can realize the entire universe. If we understand one dharma, we understand all dharmas. When the nation flourishes, mountains, rivers, and the great earth fill the ten directions, myriad forms of good and bad are in great profusion. This is a cause of great concern.

If a particle of dust is not raised, the nation perishes, a chill wind blows, and the people rejoice. There is no affirmation or negation, no good, no bad, no buddhas or sentient beings, no life and no death. But tell me, is it best to raise a particle of dust, or is it best not to raise a particle of dust? If you wish to see into this, you must first manifest your own great function.

Since there are many who would make a nest here, Fengxue kindly brings the arrowheads point to point. Left side is "just this," right side is "just this." What is he saying? Are these the same or are they different? We should understand that in the samādhi of self-fulfilling activity, dualities are not obliterated or even blurred, they are not even transcended but are, rather, realized. Absolute freedom is realized in duality, not apart from it. In the school of Dongshan Liangjie this is called the fifth rank. This being the case, how do you express the truth of Fengxue's two arrowheads meeting point to point?

CAPPING VERSE

When illumination arrives, the darkness vanishes,
    when wisdom arises, confusion dies out.
Magnificent, outstanding, clear and at ease—
    all of these are things on the road.

NOTES

1. When this is encountered, you realize it is originally existent.
2. When this is encountered, you realize it is originally nonexistent.
3. The light shines throughout the whole universe.
4. Although the light still shines, it is nevertheless dark and dim.
5. Heads and tails are two sides of the same coin.
6. If there is one side there must be another side.
7. If there is one side there must be another side.

215 ॐ

Tiantong's Precise Instruction

MAIN CASE

Xianqi of Tiantong was once asked by a monastic, "I have come with an extraordinary understanding of the dharma.[1] Master, please give me precise instruction."[2]

Tiantong said, "By shitting once, all is done. What kind of extraordinary and precise thing should I talk about?"[3]

The monastic said, "Since you have answered in this way, it would be good if I buy a pair of sandals and go on traveling."[4]

Tiantong said, "Come closer."[5]

The monastic went close.[6]

Tiantong said, "What's wrong with my answer?"[7]

The monastic did not respond.[8]

Tiantong hit him.[9]

COMMENTARY

Half-green and half-yellow, stuck in his skin and clinging to his bones, this monastic dares to yank on the lion's whiskers. Those who have truly attained it have first passed through the forest of brambles. Those who have not passed through inevitably get bogged down in the subtleties and are unable to extricate themselves.

Haven't you heard the ancient saying "In clear illumination there is no such thing as awakening"? The concept of awakening turns around and deludes people. When you stretch out both feet and sleep, there is no false and there is no true—there is just thus. No before or after. Have you seen it?

But tell me, what is Tiantong's meaning? Is there indeed an extraordinary and precise truth? Did Tiantong express it? How do you say it?

CAPPING VERSE

Zen practitioners the world over
   are always rushing about, asking about transcendental matters.
Words flow and the gap opens—see how transparent it is?
   Even a knock on the head with a staff didn't settle it.

NOTES

1. How sad! You have my deepest sympathy.
2. This monastic arrives wearing chains and wants to enter a cage.
3. Kind of vulgar, but nonetheless it reaches heaven and covers the earth.
4. Let him go. It will take another ten to twenty years to pierce his fatheadedness.
5. The old master must have seen a spark for him to act like this.
6. After all, he really wants to know.
7. He is boring into the monastic's skull. It's not hard to see where he is coming from.
8. This monastic's tongue has dropped to the ground. He doesn't know where to turn.
9. This final kindness was the only thing left to give him. Thank you for your teaching.

216 ☙

Linji's "Have You Sold It All?"

MAIN CASE

Linji asked the monastery director, "Where did you come from?"

The director said, "I was selling rice all over the region."

Linji said, "Did you sell it all?"

The director said, "Yes, I did."[1]

Linji drew a line with a staff and said, "Have you sold this?"[2]

The director shouted.

Linji hit him.[3]

Then the head cook of the monastery came to see Linji, who told him the story.

The head cook said, "The director did not understand you."

Linji said, "What about you?"

The head cook bowed.[4]

Linji hit him also.

COMMENTARY

Drawing a line with the staff is an action that contains the whole catastrophe; thus! Did you sell it all? Did you sell trimming the shrub, planting a tree, cooking the soup, editing a text? Is there any sacred activity that remains, or is it all gone? The director walks into Linji's trap and answers with a shout. He leans and falls over. Linji responds to the imperative and hits him. How would you have answered Linji?

The head cook sees that the director misses the point and presents his understanding with a bow. Linji hits him too. Tell me, are these two hits the same or different? To say the same misses it, to say different is off the mark, to say both or neither is a thousand miles from the truth. If you want to see into the point of Linji's actions, you must first understand being-as-it-is, which is the nature of things in objective reality, without the distortion of ideas and concepts.

CAPPING VERSE

Eloquent mouth and clever tongue diminish virtue;
    cutting off the ten directions gets a failing grade.
Opening up and kneading together,
    spring is met at every turn.

NOTES

1. Although this seems like a casual conversation, it is not.
2. The barb is revealed.
3. He should be hit. But can you see why?
4. Does he understand or not?

217 ꙮ
Linji's "One Blow"

MAIN CASE

Zhixian of Guanxi went to study with Linji. Seeing Guanxi, Linji grabbed him.[1]
    Guanxi said, "I understand."[2]
    Linji let go of him[3] and said, "I give you one blow."[4]
    After becoming abbot of a monastery,[5] Guanxi taught the assembly,[6] saying, "When I saw Linji, I had no words.[7] Until now, I have been satisfied and never been hungry."[8]

COMMENTARY

Although Guanxi succeeded in Linji's dharma, he leaves him with only a half-full ladle. He says, "I understand," and later, "I had no words." Is this realization or is he just dull-witted? Later he prostrates himself before the nun Moshan and asks for the teachings. He then receives another half-full ladle. Still, it's only half a ladle.

    When the truth does not fill our body and mind, we think that we have enough. When the truth fills our body and mind, we realize that something is missing. If Guanxi had persevered further and fully awakened to the truth, perhaps he would have clarified the matter and his line would not have died out.

CAPPING VERSE

If you don't leave the nest of ideas and clichés,
    how will you free yourself from the cage?
You meet it everywhere—
    it is just you yourself, yet you are not it.

NOTES

1. Speak, speak! Say a word of Zen.
2. What? Back into your hole, mouse.
3. Let him go on fooling himself forever.
4. Even sixty blows would not be enough.
5. Now he is fooling not only himself but a whole congregation as well.
6. Before teaching, it's important to have something to teach.
7. Beware of the one-eyed monastic.
8. Not hungry, but dying of starvation.

218 ❧

"Turtle Mountain Attains the Way"

MAIN CASE

Xuefeng, Yantou, and Qinshan Wensui formed a group and visited masters of different monasteries.[1] They went to Feng Region, where Qinshan became abbot of a monastery.

Xuefeng and Yantou continued traveling and because of a snowstorm stayed in a monastery at Turtle Mountain. Yantou slept every day.[2] Xuefeng was always fully engaged in zazen.[3]

One day Xuefeng called Yantou, saying, "Senior brother, get up."[4]

Yantou said, "What's the matter?"

Xuefeng said, "Things are not going well with me.[5] We traveled with Qinshan, but got separated from him. Then I have been traveling with you, and you do nothing but sleep."[6]

Yantou yelled at him, saying, "You should sleep too. Sitting on the platform every day is just like being in a remote village.[7] Someday you may end up deceiving people."[8]

Xuefeng pointed to his chest and said, "In here, I have something unsettled. I am deceiving myself."[9]

Yantou said, "I think you will someday get to the top of a solitary peak, build a hut, and raise a great teaching. Yet you are still talking like this."[10]

Xuefeng said, "Truly I am not at peace."[11]

Yantou said, "If that's so, tell me all according to your way of seeing it. If it's correct, I'll approve it for you. If it's not, I'll point that out for you too."[12]

Xuefeng said, "I first went to study with Yanguan, saw him lecture on the meaning of form and emptiness, and got the entering point."[13]

Yantou said, "Even thirty years from now you should avoid talking about it."[14]

Xuefeng said, "When I read Dongshan Liangjie's poem on crossing the river, it said, 'Don't follow others in your search, or you will be far apart from yourself.' "[15]

Yantou said, "If you are like that, you will not be able to save even yourself."[16]

Xuefeng said, "Later, I went to study with Deshan Xuanjian and asked, 'Do I have some understanding on the essential matter of the school?'[17] He gave me a blow with a stick and said, 'What are you saying?' It was just like the bottom of a wooden bucket falling out."[18]

Yantou yelled, "Don't you see what he said? Something that enters the gate is not a treasure of the house.[19] If you want to raise a great teaching, everything has to flow out from your own heart. It completely covers the heavens and the great earth."[20]

Hearing these words, Xuefeng had great realization. He made a full bow,[21] got up, and yelled out: "Senior brother, just today Turtle Mountain has attained the Way! Just today Turtle Mountain has attained the Way!"[22]

COMMENTARY

Setting up monasteries and centers, expounding the great matter of life and death, is gilding the lily. If we simply take off the blinders and set down the backpack, we will see clearly that this is the season of great peace. The sky cannot cover it, the earth cannot support it, empty space itself cannot contain it, the sun and moon cannot illuminate it. Why? There are no gaps. All of time and space fill this single moment. To realize this for oneself is to realize the great shining illumination and to be naked and free in the midst of phenomena. Wherever you go, whatever you see, there is nothing that is not it. But tell me, what is it that Xuefeng realized that is so extraordinary?

CAPPING VERSE

Spontaneously illuminated,
    the myriad sounds and forms.
When the route has opened,
    flowers fall and the tree casts no shadow.
When looking, who doesn't see?
Seeing or not seeing,
    Turtle Mountain walks on water,
    the stone woman gives birth to a child in the night.

NOTES

1. Complications are sure to arise. This is no casual journey.
2. If tired, sleep. When hungry, eat.
3. When in doubt, sit!
4. He wants to drag his companion into the pit with him.
5. Clearly he is not happy.
6. He's tired.
7. It's like polishing a brick to get a mirror.
8. The lantern will inevitably be passed from the closed-eyed to the blind.
9. Indeed. You should know that it shows.
10. Yantou's spine is usually as hard as iron. Why doesn't he immediately drive Xuefeng out into the snow?
11. This is half-asking. Still, it amounts to something.
12. The hook is set.
13. *Bah!* Cover your mouth. Don't let anyone hear you.
14. It's embarrassing. Even the buddhas are red faced.
15. What is he saying? Where are his own provisions?

16. Why explain? He has confused the picture with the reality.

17. Even his question shows how far afield he is from the truth.

18. Not enough of a beating. The stick is not yet broken.

19. What gate? Where is it? Now Yantou is nostril deep in it.

20. Can't everyone see it? Still, it must be embarrassing to have to say it.

21. What did he see that made him bow?

22. But tell me, what does all of this really mean? I say wrong! It's not Turtle Mountain that has attained the Way, but rather the Way that has attained Turtle Mountain.

219 ∽
Guishan Brings a Mirror

MAIN CASE

When Yangshan was abbot of a monastery at Donping, Guishan sent a letter and a mirror to him.[1]

During his talk in the dharma hall, Yangshan received the letter, held up the mirror, and said to the assembly, "Guishan has sent a mirror. Tell me, is this Guishan's mirror or Yangshan's mirror?[2] If you say it's Yangshan's mirror, I say Guishan sent it.[3] If you say it's Guishan's mirror, I say it's in Yangshan's hand.[4] If you can say a word, I will keep it. If you can't say a word, I will destroy it."[5]

Yangshan said this three times.[6] No one in the assembly responded,[7] and Yangshan struck the mirror.[8]

COMMENTARY

Master and disciple conspire to drive Yangshan's monastics to the abyss of dualistic contradictions. They want to see if there is a golden carp among the minnows. In order to be really free in living our everyday life, we need to be able to transcend the dualities of affirmation and negation and emerge with a new and fresh point of view.

Without falling into speech or silence, how do you respond to Yangshan's question and clear away the brambles of self and other? If a single thought enters here, you will spend the rest of your life transmigrating the six realms. If, however, you can stop all contriving and see into this directly, you are a teacher of humans and gods.

CAPPING VERSE

Where committing and negating merge
    there is no abiding place to be found.
How is it ultimately?
Everything under the sun bows at once.

NOTES

1. He personally delivers a fishing pole and hook to his successor.
2. Yangshan wants to have the whole assembly climb onto the hook for him.
3. When the fish swims, the water is muddied.
4. When a bird flies, feathers fall.
5. Someone should have slapped him across his head.
6. Shut that dog's mouth.
7. He gathers it up. Although the frogs jump, they can't get out of the basket.
8. He has acted in accordance with the imperative. Still, it's sad.

220 ⌒

Dongshan's Great Matter

MAIN CASE

Priest Mingzhe of Beiyan was once visited by Dongshan and his dharma uncle Mi [Shenshan].[1]
    Beiyan asked them, "Where are you two students from?"
    Dongshan said, "From Hunan."
    Beiyan said, "What is the family name of the imperial inspector there?"
    Dongshan said, "I don't know his family name."
    Beiyan said, "What is his given name?"
    Dongshan said, "I don't know his given name."[2]

Beiyan said, "Do you understand the great matter?"[3]
Dongshan said, "There is a curtain in the hallway."[4]
Beiyan said, "Do you go in and out of it?"[5]
Dongshan said, "No, I don't."
Beiyan said, "You certainly don't."[6]
Dongshan flapped his sleeves and walked away.[7]

The following day before daybreak, Beiyan entered the monastics' hall. He asked the two senior monastics to come close and said, "The conversation I had with both of you yesterday did not satisfy me. I was not at ease over the night. Please say another turning word. If it satisfies me, let's have the morning meal and have a summer training period together."

Dongshan said, "Master, please ask me."
Beiyan said, "Do you go in and out?"
Dongshan said, "Awesome!"[8]

Beiyan had the morning meal and spent the summer training period with them.[9]

COMMENTARY

These two troublemakers traveled around China visiting family members to stir things up and see how they would fall. Beiyan is a dharma uncle of these two dharma brothers. The elder teacher's examination is disarming, to say the least. The questions seem irrelevant until the great matter is brought up.

Beiyan probes and says, "Do you understand the great matter?" Dongshan says, "There is a curtain in the hallway." How would you have answered him? Beiyan keeps pressing the edges and says, "Do you go in and out of it?" The mud starts to get sticky. Dongshan stumbles and says, "No, I don't." Do you see how he stumbles? Beiyan's "You certainly don't" diminishes the man. Dongshan flaps his sleeves and walks away.

The old teacher could have just let the whole matter rest where it was. However, this is a family matter and is not to be taken lightly. So he invites Dongshan to present another turning word. When Dongshan says "Awesome!" Beiyan is delighted, and they spend the summer training period together. Be that as it may, do you see the difference between Dongshan's saying "No, I don't" and his saying "Awesome!"? If not, then you should enter here and find out.

CAPPING VERSE

Although the nature of adamantine wisdom
     is devoid of even a single speck of dust,
how can it compare to sitting alone beneath an empty window,
     watching autumn leaves fall, each in its own time.

NOTES

1. When there is a gathering of adepts, there is sure to be something unimaginable to follow.
2. He just doesn't seem to be in touch with matters of state. But say, is there more to be seen?
3. Suddenly, the old lion is in a crouching position.
4. Very skillful. The cub is quick and nimble.
5. The old monastic gave another swipe of an unsheathed claw.
6. He doesn't seem to be impressed.
7. Only the young can be this confident and haughty.
8. Delightful!
9. Since they finished the beginning and finished the end, no one on earth has been able to find any of them.

221 ꙮ

Jiufeng's "One Who Transmits Words"

MAIN CASE

Zen master Jiufeng Daoqian [Dajue] was once asked by a monastic, "I heard that you said that one who transmits words is outstanding among the sages. Is it true?"[1]

Jiufeng said, "That's right."[2]

The monastic said, "Śākyamuni emerged in this world, pointed to heaven and earth, and said, 'Above earth and under the heaven, I alone am venerable.' How can you call him one who transmits words?"[3]

Jiufeng said, "I call him one who transmits words because he pointed to heaven and earth."[4]

COMMENTARY

The great master Bodhidharma said, "Zen is a special transmission outside the scriptures with no reliance on words and letters." Master Jiufeng said, "One who transmits words is outstanding among the sages." The visiting monastic is seeking clarification on this matter; he does not yet understand that language and activity are one reality. Sūtras, kōans, words, silence, the cooing of an infant, images, gestures, right action, the sounds of the river valley, and the form of the mountain are all the expression of the buddha nature and absolute emptiness.

Jiufeng says, "I call him one who transmits words because he pointed to heaven and earth." I say that even the insentient transmit words. These mountains and rivers themselves are continually manifesting the words of the buddhas and ancestors. Indeed, if we examine this teaching carefully, we see that all the phenomena of this great universe: audible and inaudible, tangible and intangible, conscious and unconscious, are constantly expressing the truth of the universe, the buddha nature. Do you hear it? Can you see it? If not, then heed the instructions of the great master Dongshan and "see with the ear, listen with the eye." Only then will you understand the ineffable reality of the word.

CAPPING VERSE

Summer pond, silent and wordless,
    naturally opens a path.
Even Śākyamuni didn't understand it—
    how can anyone transmit it?

NOTES

1. He thinks there must be an error here.
2. The old man confirms his heresy.
3. These words have resounded for eighty-four generations. Still, he believes it's wordless.
4. For this old teacher, throughout the whole universe, everything is food.

222

Longshan's Clay Oxen

MAIN CASE

Longshan met Dongshan and Shenshan when they were traveling together.

Seeing a vegetable leaf floating down a valley stream, Dongshan said, "There must be a Zen practitioner deep in this mountain."[1]

They followed the stream up the mountain and met a hermit.

The hermit Longshan said, "There is no path in this mountain. How did you two Zen practitioners get here?"[2]

Dongshan said, "Let's put aside the matter of no path. Reverend, from where did you enter?"[3]

Longshan said, "I did not come following clouds or water."[4]

Dongshan said, "How long have you lived in this mountain?"[5]

Longshan said, "I am not concerned about the passing of spring or autumn."[6]

Dongshan said, "Did you live here first or did the mountain live here first?"[7]

Longshan said, "I don't know."[8]

Dongshan said, "How come you don't know?"[9]

Longshan said, "I did not come here for humans or devas."[10]

Dongshan asked further, "Why have you been living in this mountain?"[11]

Longshan said, "I saw two clay oxen struggling with each other until they fell into the ocean. Ever since then, all fluctuations have ceased."[12]

COMMENTARY

Dongshan's entering the mountain is his entering another reality. Although he persistently probes the old monastic for some concrete rationale, in the end it is clear that the old hermit does not have even the slightest notion of reason or judgment, nor even a place to abide. Thus he says, "I saw two clay oxen struggling with each other until they fell into the ocean. Ever since then, all fluctuations have ceased."

If you, too, wish to understand the old hermit's teaching, you must cut the endless stream of thoughts, let go of conscious knowledge, and trust the inherent wisdom of mountains, rivers, earth, plants, people, and animals. Only when you reach this realm will the unsurpassed wonder of it all reveal itself to you. Don't you see? The ten directions are without edges.

CAPPING VERSE

These mountains and rivers are free of dust—
    who can say that their eye is not truly open?
Following birdsongs deep into the forest,
    propelled by rivers, the ancient flow.
To be in the wilderness
    is a flower that opens in the world.

NOTES

1. Albeit a sloppy one.
2. Perhaps it's time to move deeper into the mountains.
3. Seeing the old hermit's snare, Dongshan creates one of his own.
4. The old man, too, knows how to avoid pitfalls.
5. Seeing that there is something here, Dongshan probes further.
6. The old hermit has no idea what he is doing.
7. Now he's trying to get tricky; he's still young and wants to learn.
8. Very intimate, very intimate indeed.
9. Very clumsy. Still, he had to ask.
10. This old monastic is very patient and understanding.
11. At this point the hermit should have used his staff to drive him off the mountain.
12. Now I can see "that which is creating, that which is destroying."

223 ॐ

Nanyue Examines Mazu

MAIN CASE

Nanyue, upon hearing that Mazu had begun to teach in Jiangxi, asked the assembly, "Has Mazu spoken dharma to the assembly?"[1]

    The assembly of monastics said, "He has."

Nanyue sent a monastic to Mazu, instructing him to wait until Mazu taught in the dharma hall and then ask him, "How is it?" and bring back Mazu's response.[2]

The monastic did just as he was instructed. He reported to Nanyue, "Master Ma said 'For thirty years following confusion, there has never been a lack of salt and soy sauce.'"[3]

Nanyue approved Mazu.[4]

COMMENTARY

After his enlightenment under Nanyue, Mazu continues his studies with the master for ten more years. He then begins a pilgrimage through the length and breadth of China to perfect his understanding. When Nanyue hears that his main disciple has settled and is teaching, he wants to know how deep the well is. He sends a monastic to ask Mazu how he understands it. The monastic reports Mazu's words: "For thirty years following confusion, there has never been a lack of salt and soy sauce." This is called "promoting the good that has already occurred." Master Dōgen says, "It is the Buddha having seen for himself the bright star, going on to make others see the bright star."

This has been the great matter and the sole reason for the eighty-six ancestors' having ceaselessly entered the room. Before it has been seen, it all seems like a mile-high mountain, like an iron wall. When you are finally able to pass through, it becomes clear that from the very beginning, it was you yourself who was the mile-high mountain, the iron wall. If you want to attain such a state, you must trust yourself and be intimate with the whole of reality. At such a time, one obtains realization right there.

CAPPING VERSE

Years of struggle and anguish
    lost in the forest of brambles.
Now in the dawn of the first day,
    startled by the sound of the mourning dove.

NOTES

1. Just another doting parent wanting his offspring to succeed.
2. This is not for his benefit. He wants the whole assembly to know.

3. The colt has trampled everyone on earth to death.

4. He sees the sixteen-foot golden body of the Buddha in a heap of dust.

224 ∾

The National Teacher's Dharma Realms

MAIN CASE

The National Teacher Yanguan asked a lecturer, "What kind of sūtras and commentaries do you read?"[1]

The lecturer replied, "*The Flower Garland Sūtra.*"[2]

The National Teacher then asked, "How many kinds of dharma realms are there in the sūtra?"[3]

The lecturer said, "Briefly, there are four kinds,[4] but from a wider perspective, they're really overlapping and infinite."[5]

The master straightened his fly whisk and asked, "In which dharma realm is this contained?"[6]

The lecturer faltered, and remained silent for a long time.[7]

The master said, "Thinking about it, you'll know it.[8] Contemplating it, you'll understand it.[9] All of that, however, is just making a living in a ghost cave.[10] In broad daylight the lamp has certainly lost its brightness.[11] Get out of here."[12]

COMMENTARY

When the mind moves, images appear, and heaven and earth are separated. Yet if the mind does not move, this is blank consciousness—a dead person living in a fox cave.

However, if you can penetrate the truth of this kōan and thoroughly trust yourself, you will find that there is no hindrance. It's like an eagle soaring on the wind, the mountain lion crouched on a cliff. Let go, and the river rocks emit light. Hold on, and even pure gold becomes dull and colorless. At this point, how do you understand the National Teacher's fly whisk?

CAPPING VERSE

Holding up the fly whisk,
    he freely kills and gives life.

Where absolute and relative interfuse,
    even the buddhas and ancestors beg for their lives.

NOTES

1. A probing pole. Still, it's necessary to pose the question.
2. A dumb fish climbs onto the hook.
3. Seeing a cage, he builds a cage.
4. Wrong. A caged bird can't do much flying.
5. Like a person in quicksand, each move gets him in deeper.
6. How will he take hold of this? Among thousands, tens of thousands, maybe one or two can see into this.
7. He kills the man without blinking an eye.
8. What is he saying? It can't be explained.
9. What is he saying? He's just confusing the man all the more.
10. He's trying to be kind, but why so many complications?
11. *Bah*! This old man talks too much.
12. Good! If you're going to kill him, then see the blood. If you're going to give life, then do the utmost for him.

225 ∾

Dongshan's "Cold and Heat"

MAIN CASE

Dongshan was once asked by a monastic, "When cold or heat comes, how can we avoid it?"[1]
    Dongshan said, "Why don't you go to the place where there is no cold or heat?"[2]
    The monastic said, "What is the place where there is no cold or heat?"[3]
    Dongshan said, "When it is cold, let the cold kill you. When it is hot, let the heat kill you."[4]

COMMENTARY

Dongshan's "go to the place where there is no cold or heat" is like flowers blooming on a withered tree in the midst of the frozen tundra. His "let the cold kill you . . . let the heat kill you" is a roaring furnace that consumes every phrase, idea, and thing in the universe. Even the buddhas and sages cannot survive it—nothing remains.

However, we should understand clearly that this "let the cold kill you" is not about cooling off. Cold is just cold, through and through. "Let the heat kill you" is not about facing the fire. Heat is just heat, through and through. Furthermore, there is no relationship whatsoever between Dongshan's heat and cold. Heat does not become cold; cold does not become heat. The question really is, where do you find yourself?

CAPPING VERSE

Is it the bowl that rolls around the pearl,
    or is it the pearl that rolls around the bowl?
Is it the weather that is cold,
    or is it the person who is cold?
Think neither cold nor heat—
    at that moment, where is the self to be found?

NOTES

1. Consider for a moment not trying to avoid it. What is that?
2. Dongshan freely enters the weeds with the monastic. No cold or heat is not a place.
3. Seeing a hook, the monastic freely impales himself on it.
4. Beyond description, utterly beyond description.

226 ৵

Zaoshu's Dharma Path

MAIN CASE

Zaoshu, being bidden farewell by a monastic, said, "If people in different monasteries ask you about my dharma path, what will you say?"[1]
    The monastic said, "I will wait till they ask, then I will answer."
    Zaoshu said, "Where can you find a buddha without a mouth?"

The monastic said, "That would be difficult."[2]
Zaoshu held up his whisk and said, "Do you see this?"[3]
The monastic said, "Where is a buddha without an eye?"[4]
Zaoshu said, "That would be difficult."[5]
The monastic walked around the sitting platform once and was about to leave.
Zaoshu said, "You have responded well."[6]
The monastic shouted.[7]
Zaoshu said, "I don't know you."[8]
The monastic said, "What's the use of knowing me?"[9]
Zaoshu hit the platform three times.[10]

COMMENTARY

In traveling about visiting teachers and monasteries, we should realize that questions and answers provide a mirror for distinguishing dragons and snakes and are a divining rod for locating places of true practice. Zaoshu wants to test his monastic before he begins his pilgrimage.

A buddha without a mouth or an eye is indeed difficult to find. Do you understand why this is so? The eyeballs, hands, feet, and face of a buddha fill the ten directions and yet there is no place that they can be found. Having established this much, the monastic then circles the master's sitting platform. What is his meaning? The master approves and the monastic shouts. Can you see how well the monastic knows how to hold his ground and not fall into Zaoshu's trap?

Zaoshu then says, "I don't know you." Why does he not know the monastic and what is the meaning of his hitting the platform three times in answer to the monastic's question, "What's the use of knowing me"? If you can see into this dialogue clearly, then you too are a master of distinguishing the real from the imitation and know how to live your life freely and without hindrance.

CAPPING VERSE

Shining through arising and vanishing,
     the root of reality.
Setting the eyes before the body,
     you can see the gate.

NOTES

1. He seems to be concerned about his reputation.
2. Indeed, in all my years I have yet to meet one.
3. Only a blind person can see it.
4. Can't be found.
5. Indeed, in all my years I have yet to meet one.
6. Don't be prematurely indulgent.
7. He knows how to receive the compliment.
8. It's impossible for anyone to find him.
9. Oops! Got him.
10. He snatches it all away.

227 ∾

Priest Xixian's "I Am Watching"

MAIN CASE

Xixian Faan of Lushan was asked by a government officer, "When I took the city of Jinling with an army troop, I killed countless people.[1] Am I at fault?"[2]

Xixian said, "I am watching closely."[3]

COMMENTARY

Priest Xixian's response, "I am watching closely," is at once fatheaded and misguided. He has missed an opportunity to cause an evil that has already arisen to be extinguished, and to cause good that has not arisen to arise. Both he and the general deserve thirty blows of my stick.

Governments and rulers are traditionally driven by power, politics, and money, and are usually not inclined toward clear moral commitments. However, for a Zen priest to avoid taking moral responsibility when asked is inexcusable.

Enlightenment without morality is not yet enlightenment. Morality without enlightenment is not yet morality. Enlightenment and morality are nondual in the Way. One does not exist without the other. The truth is not beyond good and evil as is commonly believed. It is, rather, a way of living one's life with a definite moral commitment that is practiced, realized, and verified within the realm of good and evil itself, yet remains undefiled by them.

Setting aside impostor priests and phony followers, you tell me, how do you transform watching into doing, the three poisons into the three virtues? More important, what is it that you call yourself?

CAPPING VERSE

Utterly devoid of abilities, the guide can't lead;
     lost in self-deception, the evil one can't find his way.
Take off the blinders, set down the pack, and see
     beyond god masks and devil masks, there is a Way.

NOTES

1. To kill and destroy is easy. To affirm life and nourish is difficult.
2. Cause and effect are one. How can you not know?
3. Stop watching and close the gap. Then there won't be anything to protect.

228 ～
Yunyan's "This Is It"

MAIN CASE

Dongshan Liangjie asked Yunyan, "Years after you have passed away, when someone asks me if I have received your portrait, how should I respond?"[1]

Yunyan said, "Just tell the person, 'This is it.'"[2]

Dongshan paused for a while.[3]

Yunyan said, "Reverend Liangjie, if you want to get this matter right, you should examine it in detail."[4]

Dongshan remained silent.[5]

Yunyan hit him.[6]

Later when Dongshan held a memorial service in the presence of

Yunyan's portrait, a monastic asked him, "The late master said, 'This is it.' What does it mean?"[7]

Dongshan said, "At the time when I heard it, I did not understand his meaning."[8]

The monastic said, "I wonder if the late master knew it."[9]

Dongshan said, "If he didn't know it, how could he have said these words?[10] If he did know it, how could he have said these words?"[11]

COMMENTARY

"This is it" is not a matter of intellect. The more you linger in thought over it, the further you stray from the truth. A lightning bolt arrives as it departs, in a single instant. Any reflection on the matter is an abstraction of its reality. Now tell me, without falling into intellectual interpretations and without standing in dumb silence, how do you see it?

As for ancestor Dongshan's answer to the monastic, "If he didn't know it, how could he have said these words?" it is as clear as the bright dawning sun of the first morning. As for "If he did know it, how could he have said these words?" it is as present as the valley stream hidden in the morning mist.

CAPPING VERSE

Deep in these mountains
    is an ancient pond.
Shallow or deep,
    its bottom has never been seen.

NOTES

1. The old man should have hit him before he even finished talking.
2. Guilty. But say, what is the "this" that is it?
3. Clearly he has doubts on the matter.
4. Just see it directly; stop thinking and reflecting.
5. He seems to be indulging in stupidity.
6. Why did he wait so long?
7. What is he saying? It has no meaning whatsoever.
8. Yes, but do you understand it now?

9. Too much knowing impairs one's virtue.
10. Even explanations require a modicum of understanding.
11. His tongue would have dropped to the ground.

229 ∿

Dizang's Broom

MAIN CASE

Dizang saw a monastic coming and held up a whisk.[1]
  The monastic bowed.[2]
  Dizang said, "What did you see that made you bow?"[3]
  The monastic said, "I thanked you for your instruction."[4]
  Dizang hit the monastic[5] and said, "You saw me hold up the whisk and thanked me. Why don't you thank me when you see me sweep the ground every day?"[6]

COMMENTARY

When the sacred has not yet been clarified, there is only the mundane. When sacredness fills the body and mind, nothing is mundane. Be that as it may, if you take the holding up of the fly whisk as having any meaning whatsoever, you are ten thousand miles from the truth. This being the case, what is the point of holding it up at all?

CAPPING VERSE

If you can understand the whisk,
    you will know the broom.
Then realize that the truth of the universe
    is not found in the broom, nor the whisk.

NOTES

  1. It covers the heavens and supports the earth.
  2. Monastics are prone to doing this. But what does it mean?
  3. Dizang wants to see where this monastic's edges are.

4. But what did you see?

5. He deserves to be hit. Do you understand why?

6. It covers the heavens and supports the earth.

230 ∾

Hearing the Sound of the Wooden Fish

MAIN CASE

Guishan was sitting in the dharma hall one day. The head of the kitchen hit the wooden fish announcing the noon meal. The fire attendant threw a piece of wood he was holding into the fire, clapped his hands, and burst into laughter.[1]

Guishan said, "Someone in the assembly should get him here and ask him what's going on."[2]

The fire attendant said, "I did not have the morning meal, so I was hungry. That's why I was happy to hear the sound of the wooden fish."[3]

Guishan nodded.[4]

COMMENTARY

For the person who practices the Buddha Way, to gain one dharma is to illuminate one dharma; to encounter one activity is to practice one activity. People these days spend much time and effort either missing dharmas and dodging encounters or being deluded by dharmas and overwhelmed by activities.

Gaining one dharma and illuminating one dharma, encountering one activity and practicing one activity is called one-practice samādhi. When food arrives, you open your mouth; when tired, you close your eyes. In washing the face, you discover your nose; when you take off your socks, you feel your feet. Each and every one of us, wherever we are, do not fail to cover the ground upon which we stand.

At Guishan's monastery, even the junior monastics have a bit of this light about them. See how the fire attendant, without introducing even the slightest hair of reason or judgment, says, "I was hungry. That's why I was happy to hear the sound of the wooden fish."

CAPPING VERSE

Needlessly creating toil,
    watching over the ox.
Beyond, there is a mysterious subtlety—
    eyes are horizontal, nose is vertical.

NOTES

1. His mind was struck by the sound.
2. There could be a number of reasons for the laugh. The teacher
   wanted to know.
3. When it itches, scratch it.
4. He seems to understand.

231 ❧

Yunmen's Entryway

MAIN CASE

Yunmen said to the assembly, "If you have not as yet gained entry,[1] know
that all the buddhas in the past, present, and future are at the tips of your
feet,[2] and the storehouse of the sūtras of Śākyamuni's entire lifetime is on
the tips of your tongues.[3] You should understand this, facing the place of
entangled vines."[4]

COMMENTARY

If you can see it immediately, then it's clear that you are walking in Buddha's shoes, eating Buddha's food, speaking Buddha's words, and living
Buddha's life. However, we should clearly understand that walking, standing, sitting, and reclining are not what the Buddhist teachings are about.

Be that as it may, if someone came to me who understands this truth, I
would chase the person away with my stick. Why? Don't you know? If you
are to experience pure gold, you must see it in the midst of the roaring
furnace.

CAPPING VERSE

When the moon is cold and the wind is high,
    I sit closer to the fireplace.
When the rains come,
    I open my umbrella.
If there is no fire, it's cold;
    when there is no umbrella, I get wet.

NOTES

1. He makes it sound as if there were an inside and an outside.
2. His paternal kindness is admirable, but what good is an explanation?
3. If you speak it, you will choke to death.
4. Rocks shatter, mountains crumble.

232 ☙

The Truth of Words and Actions

MAIN CASE

Shitou told the assembly, "Words and actions have nothing to do with the truth."[1]
    Yaoshan said, "Going beyond words and actions also has nothing to do with the truth."[2]
    Shitou said, "In this place, even a needle cannot enter."[3]
    Yaoshan said, "In this place, it's just like planting flowers on a rock."[4]

COMMENTARY

Keeping silent and refraining from discussing the Way is a truly extraordinary practice. This is hearing what is impossible to hear, encountering what is impossible to encounter. Yet, even if all contrivances are cut off, there is still the pit of liberation called "dharma attachment." Even if we try to establish classes or stages, we should understand that fundamentally there are no boundaries or edges to be found.
    Yaoshan understands that the ineffable truth that Shitou is pointing to

is not to be discerned by conscious cognition of sound and form, nor is it to be found by going beyond sound and form. This being the case, you tell me, where is it to be found?

If you wish to understand these great adepts, you must first see into the place where "even a needle cannot enter" and then realize the place that's "just like planting flowers on a rock." Without relying on seeing and hearing, and without trying to know objects, we should observe and realize that which is underneath it all.

CAPPING VERSE

Cease from following after sound and form,
    refrain from going beyond sound and form.
The spring breeze unknowingly rousts out the hibernating tree frogs—
    cherry blossoms, wordlessly, open a path.

NOTES

1. He is shaking the tree to see if the fruit is ripe.
2. It's all right here.
3. No gaps.
4. No gaps.

233 ❧
Zhaozhou's Cup of Tea

MAIN CASE

Zhaozhou asked a newly arrived monastic, "Have you been here before?"[1]
    The monastic said, "Yes, I have been here."[2]
    Zhaozhou said, "Have a cup of tea."[3]
    Later he asked another monastic, "Have you been here before?"[4]
    The monastic said, "No, I haven't been here."[5]
    Zhaozhou said, "Have a cup of tea."[6]
    The monastery director then asked Zhaozhou, "Aside from the one who has been here, why did you say 'Have a cup of tea' to the one who had not been here?"[7]

Zhaozhou said, "Director."[8]
The director responded, "Yes?"[9]
Zhaozhou said, "Have a cup of tea."[10]

COMMENTARY

In the real truth, there is no other thing that is present. In worldly truth, the ten thousand things are always present. We should clearly understand that real truth and worldly truth are nondual and that this, in and of itself, is the highest meaning of the holy truths.

The monastery director was lost in the differences between the two monastics, so Zhaozhou moved in all directions at once to help him see it. If you go to the words to understand this, you will miss it. If, however, you see into it directly, it will be like the bottom falling out of a bucket. Nothing remains. How do you see into it directly? Have a cup of tea.

CAPPING VERSE

In the ordinary,
　　nothing is sacred.
In sacredness,
　　nothing is ordinary.

NOTES

1. He first needs to get the monastic's attention.
2. A truthful person is hard to find.
3. The ten directions cannot contain it.
4. The old master won't stop until he has stirred up the whole community.
5. The monastic climbs onto the hook and waits to be reeled in.
6. The light shines again.
7. I am afraid he has missed the whole thing.
8. How kind, but does he really get it?
9. Although there were three cups of tea already served, the director has yet to wet his lips.
10. This is a kindness that is hard to requite.

234 ∾
Changsha Remains Silent

MAIN CASE

Changsha once had Sansheng in his assembly. Sansheng requested Senior Monastic Shen to ask Changsha, "After Nanquan passed away, where did he go?"[1]

Changsha said, "When Shitou was a novice, he studied with the Sixth Ancestor [Dajian Huineng]."[2]

Shen said, "Master, I am not asking you about Shitou studying with the Sixth Ancestor. I am asking, after Nanquan passed away, where did he go?"[3]

Changsha said, "I want Sansheng to contemplate this."[4]

Shen said, "Master, even if you have a one-thousand-foot-tall cold pine, you don't have a stone sprout coming out of the rock."[5]

Changsha remained silent.[6]

Shen said, "Thank you for your instruction."[7]

Changsha was still silent.[8]

Shen told Sansheng what Changsha said.

Sansheng said, "If this is true, he excels Linji by seven steps.[9] However, wait till I test him tomorrow." The next day he went up to the abbot's room and said, "Master, your response yesterday was unprecedented."[10]

Changsha did not answer.[11]

Sansheng said, "I have doubts about this fellow."

COMMENTARY

After receiving Linji's dharma and after the death of his teacher, Sansheng traveled about encountering various masters to polish his understanding. While visiting Changsha he asks, "After Nanquan passed away, where did he go?" Changsha says, "When Shitou was a novice, he studied with the Sixth Ancestor." It should be understood at the outset that the old master is not ignoring the question or changing the subject. He is directly pointing. This is why he says, "I want Sansheng to contemplate this." But, I ask you, pointing to what? Monastic Shen does not understand and tries to press it further, but Changsha just remains silent.

When Sansheng hears of this, he seems impressed but wants to test it further. The next day Sansheng goes to see him. After Sansheng extols the master's virtues, Changsha still remains silent. Tell me, what is Changsha's meaning? When Sansheng says, "I have doubts about this fellow," is he approving or disapproving the old master?

Master Doushuai Congyue said, "If you are free from life and death, you know where you will go. When the four elements decompose, where do you go?" I ask you, where do you go?

CAPPING VERSE

In a single consciousness, the whole of eternity;
    the whole of eternity, this very moment.
To see into this very moment is to realize
    no coming, no going, no abiding.

NOTES

1. There are many people who have doubts about this matter.
2. Now, here is a hard cold fact that almost anyone can bite into.
3. Even the yellow-faced old Buddha, in forty-seven years of teaching, did not answer this question.
4. Everyone should contemplate this matter.
5. I'm afraid that he has misunderstood the old teacher.
6. Don't say that this is not communicating something. What is he saying?
7. When at a loss, just bow and withdraw.
8. Since the monastic doesn't get it, there is nothing more to say.
9. Actually, it doesn't come down on either side.
10. *Bah!*
11. Why doesn't he just bring his stick down across the monastic's back?

235 ⚘
Thirteenth Daughter's Dharma

MAIN CASE

The thirteenth daughter of the Zheng family, at age twelve, went to study with Guishan, accompanied by her senior dharma sister.[1] The senior made a full bow to Guishan and stood up.

Guishan said to the senior dharma sister, "Where do you live?"[2]

She said, "I live near Nantai River."[3]

Guishan yelled and told her to leave.[4] Then he said to Zheng, "Where does that woman behind you live?"[5]

Zheng relaxed her body, walked close to Guishan, and stood still with her hands joined.[6]

Guishan repeated the question.[7]

Zheng said, "Master, I have already told you."[8]

Guishan said, "Go away."[9]

Zheng quietly left and went up to the dharma hall.

The senior dharma sister said, "You keep saying that you understand Zen. That was an immature statement. Today you were questioned by a great master and uttered no words."[10]

Zheng said, "My goodness, how can you talk like that? And you still say that you're on a pilgrimage. Take off your patched robe and give it to me."[11]

Later Zheng said to Luoshan,[12] "When I saw Guishan, I responded to him in this way. Did I attain equanimity?"[13]

Luoshan said, "You were not faultless."[14]

Zheng said, "What's my fault?"[15]

Luoshan scolded her.[16]

Zheng said, "It's like spreading flowers on brocade."[17]

COMMENTARY

These two dharma sisters are visiting their dharma uncle Guishan to test their understanding. Guishan loses no time in dispatching the senior monastic. But where is her fault? The younger traveler fearlessly steps right up and into the old man's belly. Guishan pushes and Zheng rolls like a floating gourd and pops right back up. Can you see her strength? Do you see her weakness? Like Achilles, she is free in every way, except for one stumbling point. But say, where does she stumble?

Although the senior dharma sister is right there, she seems to have missed the point. Zheng wants to settle the matter, so she takes it to Luoshan. Again she is pushed, and again she rolls and pops back up. Luoshan scolds, and again the lion's snarl echoes through the mountains. It just shows that even a nimble lass can sometimes lose her footing on a slippery floor. But say, what is her fault? If you say there is none, you miss it. If you say there is, you're ten thousand miles from the truth. If you try to say that there's neither fault nor no fault, I'll run you out of here with my stick. What do you say?

Stop talking and contriving, and the stone woman will give birth to a child in the night.

CAPPING VERSE

Fangs bared, claws unsheathed,
   the lion cub hasn't learned fear.
It's not a matter for hesitating over—
   the mother lode is always right here.

NOTES

1. They plan to gang up on the old man. Why gather a crowd?
2. Everyone in the world is the same. Still, he must ask. He has a vow to make trouble. She will inevitably understand it in the ordinary way.
3. She may be misguided, but I will say she's truthful.
4. This is as it should be. Let her go on wearing out her sandals.
5. Let's see if they both fit on the same skewer.
6. This child walks right up and into the tiger's mouth. Check!
7. Better check it out. Even tiny ponds are sometimes as deep as the ocean.
8. *Ahh!* Too much, too soon, too fast, too bad. Still, it amounts to something.
9. Indeed. Inevitably Guishan diminishes people's worth.
10. Suddenly the little one doesn't seem so small.
11. Indeed, get her. No, don't get her. Let her go on deceiving herself.

12. If you've lost your way, check the map and compass.
13. Wrong. But I wonder, does this question have a barb in it?
14. A good hunter doesn't leave tracks.
15. She has misunderstood. Cubs are trained through play.
16. A nip on the rump is not quickly forgotten.
17. Still she shows her fangs, but the old thief has already left with everything.

236 ❧

Shaozhou's Reality

MAIN CASE

Shaozhou Zhangjing said to the assembly, "If you take one step forward, you will be at odds with reality.[1] If you take one step backward, you will lose touch with phenomena.[2] If you remain immovable, you will be like an insentient being."[3]

A monastic asked, "How can we not be like an insentient being?"[4]

Shaozhou said, "Keep moving in your daily activities."[5]

The monastic said, "How can we not be at odds with reality and not lose touch with phenomena?"[6]

Shaozhou said, "One step forward, one step backward."[7]

The monastic made a bow.[8]

Shaozhou said, "In going beyond, one may understand it in this way. But I will not approve it."[9]

The monastic said, "Master, please point directly for me."[10]

Shaozhou hit him and drove him out.[11]

COMMENTARY

Some people lower their heads and linger in thought like Rodin's *Thinker*, trying to figure it out with their intellect. They don't realize that they are chasing ghosts inside their skulls. Haven't you heard? If you encounter buddha, do not stay; if you stay, your head will sprout horns. If you reach the place where there is no buddha, quickly, keep moving; if you don't, weeds will grow ten feet high.

Pure and naked, free and unbound, eyeballs clear and ears perked up, if the mind doesn't grasp at it, the whole catastrophe will simply take you out dancing in the light of the full moon.

CAPPING VERSE

If you still don't understand,
    look at September, look at October.
Leaves of red and gold
    cover the mountain and fill the valley.

NOTES

1. The deluded activity of heaven and hell.
2. Two eyes staring out of a coffin.
3. The practice of a dead person breathing.
4. How do you understand insentient being?
5. Each step follows the other.
6. Shut up and sit!
7. What is he saying? The monastic should have turned over his meditation seat.
8. Hit him!
9. Why is he being so kind? Let him go on entertaining himself forever.
10. What? What? Go away. You don't understand the old man.
11. This is as it should be. If the hit didn't reach him, then send him away.

237 ∾
Qingyuan's Sacred Truths

MAIN CASE

Qingyuan asked the great master Dajian Huineng, "What is the work that does not fall into stages?"[1]
    Huineng said, "What have you done?"[2]
    Qingyuan said, "I haven't even practiced the sacred truths."[3]
    Huineng said, "Why isn't that falling into stages?"[4]

Qingyuan said, "I have not even done anything about the sacred truths. How can that be called falling into stages?"[5]

Huineng said, "Just so, just so. You should maintain it well."[6]

COMMENTARY

Qingyuan, upon hearing that the Sixth Ancestor was teaching at Caoxi, travels there to study with him. He asks the master, "What is the work that does not fall into stages?" Master Huineng recognizes him as a dharma vessel, so he cuts right to the quick and says, "What have you done?" Anyone but an adept would be hard-pressed to respond. Qingyuan says, "I haven't even practiced the sacred truths." Can you really hear what he is saying? Many Zen practitioners who reach this point end up stagnating in the deep pit of liberation.

Qingyuan has not only realized the fundamental nature of reality but passed beyond the barrier of religious attachment. Huineng tests this by saying, "Why isn't that falling into stages?" Qingyuan understands that the Buddha Way is beyond being and nonbeing, therefore he says, "I have not even done anything about the sacred truths. How can that be called falling into stages?" Huineng approves.

This being the case, why is it that Zen teachings the world over establish stages? Why is it that Buddha said that even bodhisattvas who have passed through the ten stages are still unable to see buddha nature clearly? You tell me, what does it mean to see buddha nature clearly? If you can leap past all rhetoric and go beyond seeing and hearing, you will discover that which has always been there—a clear and lucid wisdom that has no teacher.

CAPPING VERSE

Even if you try to set up stages,
    where would you rest the steps?
The clear luminous body of the mystic way
    has always been present.

NOTES

1. You should know that there is such a practice.
2. First he must probe to see if there are any soft spots.

3. This could be one of Yunmen's sicknesses; it should be tested.

4. He tests it. Do you understand?

5. If you try to interpret this literally, you will find yourself living in a ghost cave for the rest of your life.

6. You should understand that what is being approved here is quite ordinary.

238 ❧
Zhimen's Strength

MAIN CASE

Zhimen spent some time journeying on a distant mountain and returned to the monastery.[1]

The head monastic came out with the assembly and greeted him. He said to Zhimen, "Master, you went to the mountain. I suppose the climb was steep and difficult."[2]

Zhimen held up his staff and said, "I have gained this much strength."[3]

The head monastic came forward, grabbed his staff, and threw it down with all his might.[4]

Zhimen fell to the ground, and the assembly of monastics rushed to help him up.[5] Zhimen held up the staff again and drove everyone away.[6] He turned back to his attendant monastic and said, "I have gained this much strength."[7]

COMMENTARY

Having returned from his long journey on the distant mountain, Zhimen takes this as an opportunity to teach his assembly. When the head monastic greets him and says, "I suppose the climb was steep and difficult," he immediately employs the three essential seals to test them all: sealing mud, sealing water, and sealing space. But say, what is the meaning of his holding up the staff and saying, "I have gained this much strength"? How much is "this much strength"? Where does it come from? What is the meaning of his holding up the staff?

When the head monastic grabs the staff and throws it down, why does Zhimen fall down? Why does he then drive the monastics away? Again he holds up the staff and says, "I have gained this much strength." We should understand that this single action contains both the provisional and real, both illumination and function. If you can see into it here, then you too are studying with old master Zhimen.

CAPPING VERSE

Carpet of wildflowers among the tall pines;
　　flowing streams, vast and endless.
If you wish to understand the ancients' teaching,
　　you simply must go into the distant mountains.

NOTES

1. On an occasion such as this there is always a reception committee.
2. He wants to try this old fellow. Not easy, not difficult. Go away.
3. He is like an old turtle emerging from the swamp dripping water and mud.
4. A thrust. The head monastic shows some provisions of his own.
5. Since they were at a loss to take appropriate action, they were inappropriate.
6. He doesn't avoid grandmotherly kindness. But then, who among them can appreciate it?
7. He should have hit him with the staff. You are colliding with it; you are bumping into it. Can't you see it?

239 ∽
Zhaozhou's Raft

MAIN CASE

Zhaozhou said to the assembly, "Practitioners, to someone who comes from the south, let them unload the raft.[1] To someone who comes from the north, let them load the raft.[2] If you go to the one unloading and ask about the Way, you lose the Way.[3] If you go to the one loading and ask about the Way, you get the Way.[4]

"Practitioners, if the right person expounds the wrong dharma, even the wrong dharma becomes correct.[5] If a wrong person expounds the right dharma, even the right dharma becomes wrong.[6] At other places, it's difficult to understand but easy to attain.[7] At this place, it is easy to understand but difficult to attain."

Zhaozhou also said to the assembly, "The essential matter is like a bright pearl in the palm of your hand. When a northerner comes, a northerner appears; when a southerner comes, a southerner appears. This old monastic takes a blade of grass and turns it into the sixteen-foot golden body of the Buddha.[8] He takes the sixteen-foot golden body of the Buddha and turns it into a blade of grass."[9]

COMMENTARY

The practice of going upriver is very intimate, very intimate indeed. When the headwaters are reached, night descends and no communication whatsoever is possible. Descending the river, we meet the ten thousand things leaping with life in the bright light of day.

When you can take action on the road, you are like a cougar in the mountains, free in every direction. When you get stuck in worldly interpretations, you are like an eagle caught in a net, born with the gift of freedom and flight, yet unable to fly.

As for Zhaozhou's bright pearl in the palm of your hand, each and every one of us is born with it. Once you realize it is there, turning a blade of grass into the sixteen-foot golden body of the Buddha becomes an everyday matter.

The truth is easy to explain but difficult to accomplish. Though it fills the eyes, we don't see it. Though it fills the ears, we can't hear it. Take off the blinders, unplug the ears, set down the pack, and see for yourself that right where you stand is the valley of the endless spring.

CAPPING VERSE

The sky is clear and the sun appears,
　　rain falls and the earth is moistened.

Without extensive discussion, everything is clear as it is,
     yet how few are really able to see it.

NOTES

   1. You can only reach the headwaters when you have an empty pack.
   2. Take a step off the hundred-foot pole.
   3. No one in the world has ever found it.
   4. Have a cup of tea.
   5. The dharma is not found in the words and ideas that describe it.
   6. The dharma is not found in the words and ideas that describe it.
   7. Pictured cakes have never satisfied hunger.
   8. If you cling to existence, he speaks of nonexistence.
   9. If you attach to nonexistence, he speaks of existence.

240 ∾

Jinfeng's "The Way of Going Beyond"

MAIN CASE

Jinfeng was once greeted by a monastic. Jinfeng grabbed the monastic and
said, "The way of going beyond is not easy to attain."[1]
     The monastic gestured to listen. Jinfeng then slapped him.[2]
     The monastic said, "Why did you slap me?"
     Jinfeng said, "I want to have this kōan practiced."[3]

COMMENTARY

"The way of going beyond" is the continuous practice that takes place after
having personally realized the truth. It is a practice that endlessly unfolds
beyond realization and transmission. There is no resting place for the clear-
eyed. At times they are on the great mystic peak, among the weeds and
brambles. At other times they are in the middle of the busy marketplace,
free and at peace with everything. Sometimes revealing an angry devil face,
he cuts away the extra and kills the ego. At other times, manifesting the ten

thousand hands and eyes of the Bodhisattva of Compassion, she heals and gives life.

The ineffable truth that Jinfeng is pointing to cannot be discerned by conscious cognition of sound and form—nor is to be found by going beyond sound and form. This being the case, you tell me, where is it to be found?

"The way of going beyond" is not about doing special practices. It's just that the way is not the familiar way that we have become accustomed to practicing. Therefore, it is said that buddhas do not know about devices for going beyond, and the ancestors don't understand how to accept what is right here. Only people who have entered the way of going beyond can use a broken key to open a lock with no keyhole.

CAPPING VERSE

Although the highest peak of the sacred mountain
    has been ascended,
There is still a mysterious subtlety beyond—
    eyes are horizontal, nose is vertical.

NOTES

1. It's just not what you think it is.
2. Got him! His kindness is overwhelming.
3. Jinfeng would like him to use diligence to compensate for his incompetence.

241 ∿

Xuansha Hears the Sound of a Swallow

MAIN CASE

Xuansha was informally addressing his monastics[1] when he heard a swallow singing.[2] He said to the assembly, "This is the profound dharma of real form.[3] It skillfully conveys the essence of the true teaching."[4] He then descended from the teaching seat.[5]

A monastic asking for an explanation said, "I don't understand."[6]

Xuansha said, "Go away. No one will believe you."[7]

COMMENTARY

If you wish to understand the truth of this kōan, you must first understand that Xuansha's "This is" is not referring to the swallow that is teaching the profound dharma of real form, nor is it referring to Xuansha, who teaches the profound dharma of real form. Then what is it pointing to? Real form is all dharmas as they are. "As they are" is neither sentient nor insentient, form nor emptiness, being nor nonbeing. They are the inexpressible moment, thus!

Be that as it may, what is the meaning of Xuansha's descending from the teaching seat, the monastic's "I don't understand," and the master's "Go away. No one will believe you"? Keep in mind that even if this monastic said, "I understand," Xuansha would still have had to say, "Go away. No one will believe you." Why is this so?

CAPPING VERSE

A jewel, shining bright—
    there are absolutely no flaws.
Sacred and mundane, just as they are,
    intermingle freely.

NOTES

1. It is within the mundane that the pure light is at its brightest.
2. Song of the mystical subtlety.
3. Pervading the universe, vast and without edges.
4. When has the buddha principle ever been a principle?
5. When the fish is in the net, the fisherman can go home.
6. But of course, that's one of the characteristics of the ineffable.
7. Obviously. The correct imperative must be carried out.

242 ॐ

Daoist Wu's Painting

MAIN CASE

Zen master Jingxuan of Mount Dayang [Mingan] once asked Liangshan, "What is the formless seat of enlightenment?"[1]

Liangshan pointed to a painting of Avalokiteśvara[2] and said, "That is a painting by Daoist practitioner Wu."

Dayang was about to speak.[3]

Liangshan suddenly grabbed him and said, "This has form. What is it that has no form?"[4]

At that moment Dayang had realization. He just stood there.[5]

Liangshan said, "Why don't you speak a phrase?"[6]

Dayang said, "It's not that I am unwilling to say something. I just fear that it will end up as brush marks on paper."[7]

Liangshan then approved him.[8]

COMMENTARY

The essential matter of Zen practice and realization is this formless seat of enlightenment. This is a place that is not bound by name or form; it cannot be reached by words or ideas, and yet it clearly exists.

Liangshan holds up a mirror for Dayang to see, and as he is about to fall into the pit of babble, the master snatches him up and asks, "This has form—what is it that has no form?" By employing that which has no function, he helps Dayang to realize his original face, the face he had before his parents were born.

Be that as it may, tell me, what is it that has no form and yet clearly exists? Furthermore, what is it that has no function? And most important, what is your original face? Don't explain it, reveal it!

CAPPING VERSE

Unifying the myriad reflections,
    one's own light is without hindrance.

Opened up, the ground of being
    ceaselessly meets itself.
If you take it conceptually,
    you will miss it by ten thousand miles.
If you take it as blank consciousness,
    you're just a dead person breathing.

NOTES

1. Ten thousand studies is not as good as one seeing. He wants to see it.
2. Thank you for your answer.
3. What is it that could possibly be said? Shut up and see!
4. The crashing of thunder, howling winds. He is about to be charred by a fire-breathing dragon.
5. Eyes wide open, mouth agape, he has finally lost his tongue.
6. Is this just stupidity or has he seen something?
7. The rains come and the parched earth blooms.
8. Although this is true, the question remains, what did he see? If you can see into it here, then Dayang, Liangshan, and you yourself will be run through with the same skewer.

243 ❧
Xiangyan's Person up a Tree

MAIN CASE

Xiangyan said to the assembly, "What if you are hanging by your teeth from a tree on a one-thousand-foot cliff, with no place for your hands to hold or your feet to step on?[1] All of a sudden someone asks you the meaning of the Ancestor's [Bodhidharma's] coming from India.[2] If you respond, you will lose your life.[3] If you don't respond, you do not do justice to the question.[4] At just such a moment, what would you do?"[5]

Then Senior Monastic Hutou came out and said, "Master, let's not talk about being in a tree.[6] But tell me, what happens before climbing the tree?"[7]

Xiangyan burst into laughter.[8]

COMMENTARY

Old master Xiangyan's words are clearly lethal. The only path through this dualistic dilemma is to die the great death and realize real freedom. How is this accomplished? We should appreciate the fact that the questioner, in asking about the Ancestor's coming from India, is also "hanging from a tree on a one-thousand-foot cliff." If you can answer Xiangyan, you will free not only yourself but the questioner as well.

Master Dōgen says, "If we look at this kōan with a 'nonthinking mind,' we can attain the same real, free samādhi as Xiangyan and grasp its meaning even before he has opened his mouth." What is this "nonthinking mind"? Setting aside Xiangyan, the tree, and the cliff, you tell me, what is the meaning of the Ancestor's coming from India? If you open your mouth to answer, you have missed it. If you don't open your mouth, you are a thousand miles from the truth. Senior Monastic Hutou makes it clear. In the tree, below the tree, before the tree, after the tree—it's all dirt from the same hole.

CAPPING VERSE

Where affirmation and negation merge,
    there it is, alone and revealed.
On the solitary mystic peak,
    the blue mountains have not a speck of dust.

NOTES

1. The ancestors all had a way of creating complications where there are none.
2. This may be an old question, but it still needs to be addressed by each generation.
3. Xiangyan makes sure this is indeed a question of life and death.
4. You and the questioner hang from the same tree.
5. If you truly wish to understand the teachings of the Zen school, you need to see into it here.
6. He wants to change the subject.

7. No. He is not changing the subject, just the hand that holds the sword.

8. This amounts to something. He can let go, he can gather in.

244 ॰

Mayu's True Eye

MAIN CASE

Mayu asked Linji, "Among the one thousand hands and eyes of the Great Compassionate One [Avalokiteśvara], which is the true eye?"[1]

Linji said, "Among the one thousand hands and eyes of the Great Compassionate One, which is the true eye? Say it now. Say it now!"[2]

Mayu yanked Linji off the meditation platform and went back to his seat.[3]

Linji got up, went over to him, and said, "How are you?"[4]

Mayu was about to say something.[5]

Linji pulled Mayu off the meditation platform and went back to his seat.[6]

Mayu shouted and walked away.[7]

COMMENTARY

The true eye is the eye of wisdom. When it is open, it sweeps away all discriminating thoughts and allows us to see the absolute unity of all things.

The reality of this true eye is that it is not in opposition to Avalokiteśvara's ten thousand hands and eyes. Indeed, it is because of the true eye that the hands and eyes of great compassion are able to function in absolute freedom. It can be said that her whole body is nothing other than hands and eyes.

The great compassionate heart of Avalokiteśvara cannot be attached to any particular view, because it is not like something. Linji and Mayu clumsily try to reveal this truth, but in the end, it turns out to be just another mud fight. Setting all of this aside, you tell me, among the ten thousand hands and eyes, and the twelve faces of Avalokiteśvara Bodhisattva, where is the true eye to be found? Indeed, what is the true eye?

CAPPING VERSE

The river runs through it,
    never having wet it.
The spring breeze passes through it,
    never having entered.
There is no place to put
    the great heart of compassion.

NOTES

1. Right on your head, right in your face. Where are you?

2. What is he saying? Did he answer the monastic?

3. Good show. After all, he asked for it.

4. What is he saying? He is trying to wash off the mud in a mud bath.

5. Oops! He falters. He will be sorry.

6. After this has gone on from dawn to sunset, then what?

7. Sooo! Which is the true eye of great compassion?

245 ⌒

Juzhi Holds Up One Finger

MAIN CASE

Jinhua Juzhi, whenever he was asked a question, held up one finger.[1]

A young acolyte in his assembly was asked by someone, "What kind of essential dharma does your master teach?"

The acolyte held up one of his fingers.[2]

When Juzhi heard about it, he cut off the young acolyte's finger with a knife.[3]

The acolyte cried out in pain and began to run away.[4]

Juzhi called the acolyte.[5]

As the acolyte turned his head, Juzhi held up a finger.[6]

At this moment the acolyte had realization.[7]

When Juzhi was about to pass away, he said to the assembly, "I inherited Hangzhou Tianlong's one-finger Zen and have not exhausted it throughout my entire lifetime.[8] Do you want to understand it?" He then held up a finger and died.[9]

COMMENTARY

Although Juzhi is free and boundless, nevertheless, his understanding is not really refined. The acolyte, imitating his master, not only misses the truth of the teaching but falls into a pit of brambles as well. Juzhi, however, is quick to rescue him. Wielding a sharp knife, he cuts away the complications.

Although the boy lost a finger, he gained his nostrils. Don't you see? The truth of Juzhi's teachings is not to be found in the finger. This being the case, you tell me, if the truth is not in the finger, then where is it?

CAPPING VERSE

If you are not intimate with it,
    when it's revealed, you think it's something.
When words and ideas are finally eradicated,
    the light first appears.
Finger or no finger, wet with the morning dew—
    the tips of ten thousand grasses.

NOTES

1. A blind man making his way with a finger.
2. A facsimile is always a facsimile, not the original.
3. If you understand it, then the finger is extra.
4. He should have run away before he lost his finger.
5. What will he say?
6. Encompassing the heavens, covering the earth.
7. Aside from the missing finger, what else did he realize?
8. Pretty dull-witted if you ask me. Don't you have any other provisions?
9. *Bah!* If I had been there, I would have looked away before he could raise a finger and then asked him to say it so that it could be heard.

246 ∿

Yangshan Chanting the Sūtras

MAIN CASE

One day when Yangshan was a novice, he was reciting a sūtra.
    Shaozhou Ruyuan said, "Huiji, your chanting sounds like weeping."[1]
    Yangshan said, "This is how I do it, Master. I wonder how you would do it."[2]
    Shaozhou just looked around.
    Yangshan said, "If you chant like that, how is it different from weeping?"[3]
    Shaozhou was silenced and walked away.

COMMENTARY

Although Yangshan is feisty and slippery, he is still a willing student. But alas, Shaozhou, in trying to respond, slips and falls. Nonetheless, Yangshan should understand that if chanting lacks spiritual power, although it may pass from mouth to ear, it inevitably will fail to pierce the heart. How does one manifest spiritual power that can pierce the heart?

The attainment of spiritual power simply depends on penetrating the principle and fully engaging the ten thousand dharmas. Master Zhaozhou said, "People, just sit and penetrate the principle." All practices, such as eating, working, prostrating, and chanting the sūtras are to be done in the spirit of zazen. If you wish to understand this kind of spiritual power, you must first understand the dharma of chanting. An ancient once said, "If it's not present in your mind, your mouth chants empty words." Chanting, like invoking, means to call to mind. Chanting and invoking have to do with thought and not with language.

Be that as it may, say a word of Zen for Shaozhou in answer to Yangshan's question, "I wonder how you would do it?"

CAPPING VERSE

The talkative teacher can't open his mouth,
    the tricky student misses the point.

Spiritual powers and their wondrous functioning—
    hauling water and carrying firewood.

NOTES

  1. He diminishes the man.
  2. When you press down on a floating gourd, it rolls over and pops
     back up.
  3. He diminishes the man.

247 ∾
Ruiyan Calls "Master!"

MAIN CASE

Ruiyan was in the abbot's room when he called to himself, "Master!"[1]
    He himself responded, saying, "Yes, Master."[2]
    Then he said, "Clear all the way. Never be deceived by others."[3]
    Then he answered himself, "Yes, yes."[4]

COMMENTARY

Although Ruiyan talks to himself, we should not mistake this as simple-mindedness. If you can see into his teaching, then, when it is warm, all the way to heaven it is warm; when it is cool, all the way to heaven it is cool. If, however, you go to the words to see this, then complications are sure to arise.

    But say, this soliloquy of self-approval is easy to do, but what does it have to do with reality? Without imitating Ruiyan and without falling into words and ideas, how do you understand the truth of the master that transcends time and space, self and other, and indeed, life and death itself?

CAPPING VERSE

Since there is neither self nor other,
    how can there be calling or answering?

The nature of adamantine wisdom
　　is free of even a particle of dust.
Yet the great blue heron knows how to go its own way—
　　it comes and goes, leaving no traces.

NOTES

　1. What is he saying? Who is he talking to?
　2. It's easy to approve oneself, but what does it mean?
　3. Although this is good advice, of what value is it? It just misleads
　　people.
　4. *Bah!* He should hit himself on the side of the head.

248 ∾
Shigong's Emptiness

MAIN CASE

Master Shigong Huizang asked Zhigong, a former abbot, "Do you know
how to grasp emptiness?"[1]
　Zhigong said, "Yes, I know how to grasp emptiness."[2]
　Shigong said, "How do you grasp it?"[3]
　Zhigong grasped at the air with his hand.[4]
　Shigong said, "You don't know how to grasp emptiness."[5]
　Zhigong responded, "How do you grasp it, elder brother?"[6]
　Shigong poked his finger in Zhigong's nostril and yanked his nose.[7]
　Zhigong grunted in pain and said, "It hurts! You are pulling off my
nose."[8]
　Shigong said, "This is how to grasp it."[9]

COMMENTARY

Zhigong's potential is stuck in a fixed position, so Master Shigong is compelled to shake him loose. If you want to free what is stuck and loosen what
is bound, you must simply cut away all traces of thought, let go of all words
and ideas, and experience it directly. This whole great earth is contained in

a single speck of dust. When a single flower blooms, the ten thousand things come into being.

Although in yanking Zhigong's nose, Shigong was able to hide in his nostrils, we should understand that the truth of this kōan is not to be found in the nose or the finger. What is the truth of this kōan? Indeed, what does it mean that Shigong was able to hide in Zhigong's nostrils?

CAPPING VERSE

From within the single body,
    myriad forms arise.
In one, there are many kinds;
    in many kinds, there is no duality.

NOTES

1. Shaking the tree, he wants to see what falls out.
2. The tree leaned and fell over.
3. It wouldn't do to let him go on like this.
4. Oops! Them bones, them bones, them dry bones.
5. He can only call it as he sees it.
6. After all, at this point he must ask.
7. Very intimate, very intimate indeed.
8. It fills the universe. There is no place it does not reach.
9. His eyebrows have fallen off. Too bad.

249 ∾

Nanquan's "Dharma That Has Never Been Spoken"

MAIN CASE

Priest Nirvāṇa of Baizhang [Weizheng] asked Nanquan, "Is there any dharma that has not been spoken by the sages in the past?"[1]
    Nanquan said, "It's not mind, it's not Buddha, it's not a thing."[2]
    Nirvāṇa said, "Have you finished speaking?"[3]
    Nanquan said, "I am like this. What about you?"[4]

Nirvāṇa said, "I am not a teacher. How should I know if there is a dharma that has or has not been spoken?"[5]

Nanquan said, "I don't understand."[6]

Nirvāṇa said, "I have said enough for you."[7]

COMMENTARY

In the world of Zen adepts, with a single phrase or word, with a single encounter or a single response, you should be able to see whether one is deep or shallow. These two adepts, meeting like this, are clearly extraordinary. Nirvāṇa's question is indeed difficult to respond to, but Nanquan, still fresh from Mazu's monastery, didn't hesitate in responding: "It's not mind, it's not Buddha, it's not a thing." But say, did he speak the dharma that had not been spoken by the sages of the past?

Nirvāṇa wanted to know if that was all he had to say about the matter, and Nanquan used this as an opportunity to turn the spear around. Nirvāṇa, too, was skillful, and though he seems dead, he is not. His answer was extraordinary: "I am not a teacher. How should I know if there is a dharma that has or has not been spoken?" The spear was again turned around.

Nanquan then said, "I don't understand." Do you think he really didn't understand? Nirvāṇa's response to this was that he had already said enough. But what did he say that was enough? Is there a truth that has not been spoken to the people? If so, what is it? If not, why not? If your eyes are open, you should be able to clearly see through this encounter. How will you judge them?

CAPPING VERSE

Buddhas have not appeared in the world,
    nor is there a truth that can be given to the people.
There is only the yellow-voiced, cold cricket
    singing in a pile of autumn leaves.

NOTES

1. If there is such a thing, a master should know it.
2. Since it is not these things, then what is it?

3. Does he know something that makes him look for more?

4. He knows how to let go and turn it around in a single action.

5. Rolling out and rolling in. Where is all of this going?

6. This seems like a bit of bragging. But it's not really.

7. This seems like a bit of brashness. But it's not really.

250 ೧৩

Caoshan's Eyebrows and Eyes

MAIN CASE

Caoshan was once asked by a monastic, "Do the eyebrows and eyes know each other?"[1]

Caoshan said, "No, they don't."[2]

The monastic said, "How come they don't know each other?"[3]

Caoshan said, "Because they are together in the same place."[4]

The monastic said, "If so, don't they share something in common?"

Caoshan said, "Eyebrows are not eyes."[5]

The monastic said, "What are eyes?"

Caoshan said, "Go straight ahead."[6]

The monastic said, "What are eyebrows?"

Caoshan said, "I also wonder about them."[7]

The monastic said, "Master, why do you wonder about them?"

Caoshan said, "If I didn't wonder about them, I would be going straight ahead."[8]

COMMENTARY

If you approach this encounter thinking that this is a discussion limited to eyebrows and eyes, you will never see into the heart of Master Caoshan. The family style of the house of Caodong has a way of working with dualities. It is because these two apparently different things are in the same place that they cannot know each other. However, eyebrows are eyebrows and eyes are eyes. They should not be confused with each other.

The monastic needs clarification, so he asks, "What are eyes?" Like a flash of lightning Caoshan says, "Go straight ahead." I ask you, what is his meaning? Further, why would Caoshan be going straight ahead if he were clear about eyebrows?

In order to appreciate Caoshan's teaching, we must first realize that light and dark, though different, do not hinder one another. The mountain is high, the river deep, and in the midst of contradictions, clarity of understanding always eases the way.

CAPPING VERSE

See how the Great Bodhisattva
    enters the marketplace with empty hands.
Understand that although this is so,
    she has never abandoned the household.

NOTES

1. What is he saying? Where did he get this question?
2. But of course! How could they?
3. I must say that it was reasonable on the monastic's part to ask.
4. This too is reasonable.
5. Even little children know this much.
6. On the road, yet not having left the mountain.
7. Having left the mountain, but not yet on the road.
8. If it's not one, it must be the other.

251 ∾

Daowu's Place of No Birth and No Death

MAIN CASE

Daowu said to Yunyan, who was sick, "Apart from this leaky shell, where do we meet?"[1]

Yunyan said, "We meet at the place of no birth and no death."[2]

Daowu said, "Why don't you say that we will not meet in the place that is not of no birth and no death?"[3]

COMMENTARY

To inquire into the question of life and death and realize one's true nature is the central theme of Zen practice. Daowu wants to see if his dharma brother—who is ill—has settled the question. Although it cannot be said that Yunyan is asleep, it is clear that he is not yet awake. Daowu presses it further, saying, "Why don't you say that we will not meet in the place that is not of no birth and no death?" Tell me, what is the point that Daowu is making? We should examine carefully what is meant by meeting and not meeting, and examine even further what is the place that is not of no birth and no death.

In unity there is no meeting, no communication, no duality. In the place of no birth and no death, there is birth and death. Birth is a period of itself, death is a period of itself. One does not become the other. This being the case, say a word for Yunyan in answer to Daowu's "Apart from this leaky shell, where do we meet?"

CAPPING VERSE

In arriving there is no abode;
in departing there is no destination.
Ultimately how is it?
Here you are, where you have always been.

NOTES

1. There is an echo in these words. He is trying to discern deep from shallow.
2. He is defeated before he even opens his mouth.
3. Daowu is boring into his skull; it's not difficult to see where he is coming from.

252 ∾

Fayan's "You Are Huichao"

MAIN CASE

Guizong Cejin [family name Huichao] asked Fayan, "What is buddha?"[1]
Fayan said, "You are Huichao [literally, 'Going Beyond Wisdom']."[2]

COMMENTARY

From ancient times down to the present, upon hearing this kōan Zen practitioners the world over have rushed to the words and come up with intellectual interpretations. Some say Fayan answered as he did because Huichao is himself buddha. Others say it's like the fire god looking for fire, or that just asking the question is it. None of this has anything to do with the reality revealed by Fayan and realized by Huichao.

If you wish to see into this teaching, you must first pass beyond sound and form and then understand the device of simultaneously breaking in and breaking out. This is the place where there are no seams, not a single gap for a thought to slip in. If you can't hear it, you have missed it. If you try to figure it out, you will never realize it.

CAPPING VERSE

In breaking in and breaking out,
  chick and hen do not know each other.
Not knowing each other,
  they naturally know how to work together.

NOTES

1. Although this is an old question, it's worth bringing it up again.
2. This kind of answer is sure to be misunderstood and provide a nest for future generations.

253 ∿
Śākyamuni's Flower

MAIN CASE

One day the World-Honored One held up a flower in front of the assembly of myriads of beings, and twirled it.[1]
 Mahākāśyapa alone smiled.[2]
 The World-Honored One said, "I entrust the treasury of the true dharma eye of all buddhas to Mahākāśyapa."[3]

COMMENTARY

The treasury of the true dharma eye has never been given to others and has never been received by another. Because of this, the World-Honored One held up the flower and revealed the truth; Mahākāśyapa did not conceal it and smiled. The lifeblood of Śākyamuni intermingled with that of Mahākāśyapa and flowed into past, present, and future. Do you see it?

But say, since no one has ever transmitted nor received the treasury of the true dharma eye, why was Mahākāśyapa singled out from among the thousands gathered? What is the meaning of holding up the flower and Mahākāśyapa's smile? What if everyone had smiled or if no one had smiled— what would have happened to the dharma?

If you think the truth of this kōan lies in holding up a flower, twirling, or smiling, then you have missed the treasury of the true dharma eye of the buddhas and ancestors by a hundred thousand miles. The meeting on Mount Gridhrakūta is definitely present right here. Root and branches are fleeting moments of the one reality. We should not miss seeing it.

CAPPING VERSE

Appearing without form,
    responding in accord with the imperative.
The fragrance of the flower held up
    fills the universe existing right here now.

NOTES

1. The golden-faced old master is about to deceive the whole assembly.
2. It takes a swindler to recognize a swindler.
3. You tell me, what did he give him?

254 ⌒

Fayan's "Nonabiding Origin"

MAIN CASE

Fayan was once asked by a monastic, "I learned in sūtras that all dharmas are based on the nonabiding origin.[1] What is the nonabiding origin?"[2]

Fayan said, "Form is born from formlessness and name comes from the unnameable."[3]

COMMENTARY

This monastic seems to have been studying the *Vimalakīrti Sūtra*, where the householder Vimalakīrti clarified the matter of the nonabiding origin for Mañjuśrī by saying, "Mañjuśrī, all things are created from a nonabiding basis." The monastic wants to understand the nature of this nonabiding origin. To understand it is to understand the fundamental nature of existence.

The first moving thought is the nonabiding origin, and because of this, conceptions arise. Because of conceptions, there is discrimination; because of discrimination, there is desire; because of desire, there is the body. When the body exists, good and evil are born—thus the ten thousand things arise.

However, we should understand that nonabiding itself has no origin. If nothingness is the origin, then existence is born based on nothingness; nothing is not based on nothing, so there is no further origin. This subtle truth has no location, because there is no place that it does not reach.

Fayan said, "Form is born from formlessness and name comes from the unnameable." I ask you, what is the formless, what is the nameless?

CAPPING VERSE

When you look at it, it has no form—
    it fills heaven and earth.
Yet, in one there are many kinds;
    in two there is no duality.

NOTES

1. Rushing to the words to find understanding was his first mistake.
2. Throughout the universe, is there any trace of where it comes from?
3. Once forms and names appear, floating mists disturb the clarity.

255 ∾
Linji Holds Up His Fly Whisk

MAIN CASE

Linji saw a monastic coming and held up a whisk.[1]
    The monastic made a full bow.[2]
    Linji hit him.[3]

COMMENTARY

Countless generations of Zen ancestors have held up the fly whisk to convey the teachings. Sometimes it functions as a probing pole, at other times it helps to expound the truth. In the hands of some masters, it transforms into Mañjuśrī's sword and cuts away delusions. At times it functions as a crouching lion. It is also said that those who hold up the fly whisk are numerous, but those who hold up the fly whisk are not many. Do you understand? Can you see how Linji is using it?

The monastic makes a full prostration. Master Dōgen once said that in encountering a true teacher, one should make a full prostration and obtain the marrow. Does this monastic obtain the marrow? What does Linji see that causes him to hit the monastic? Indeed, what is the meaning of his striking the monastic after he prostrates himself? Say a word for the monastic.

CAPPING VERSE

He comes head-on—
    do you see how Linji helps people?
Where the reward is great,
    the person must be valiant.

NOTES

1. They must be of like heart and mind for this to make sense.
2. What is he doing? Is this alert or dull-witted?
3. The imperative must always be addressed.

256 ᴥ

Changsha's "Original Person"

MAIN CASE

Changsha was once asked by a monastic, "Does the original person become a buddha?"[1]

Changsha said, "Tell me, does the emperor of China weed and harvest rice?"[2]

The monastic said, "After becoming a buddha, what will the person be?"

Changsha said, "That will be your becoming a buddha. Do you or don't you know it?"[3]

COMMENTARY

If you wish to understand Changsha's teachings, you first need to understand the monastic's question. This original person that he speaks of existed before the appearance of the world. If the world were to end, this original person would not end. From the moment you realize true self, there is only this, the master. So what is there to be sought outside? Indeed, what are you calling outside?

The monastic still doesn't get it and asks, "After becoming a buddha, what will the person be?" Haven't you heard the words of the Sixth Ancestor "If you understand that you yourself have buddha nature, this is the pivotal cause for becoming a buddha"?

Changsha, in his rush to help this monastic, drowns him with kindness, saying, "That will be your becoming a buddha. Do you or don't you know it?" In the end, the monastic doesn't get it. Do you?

CAPPING VERSE

In arriving, there is no abode;
    in departing, there is no destination.
Ultimately, where does it all come down?
    Right here, where you have always been.

NOTES

1. It's right in your face, under your feet, on top of your head. Where
   are you?
2. It's not worth bringing it up. Examine this for yourself.
3. Too much talking. He should be careful of his eyebrows.

257 ❧

Yunmen's "Hearing Sounds and Realizing Enlightenment"

MAIN CASE

Yunmen said to the assembly, "Hear sound and be enlightened.[1] See form
and clarify the mind.[2] What is hearing sound and being enlightened? What
is seeing form and clarifying the mind?"[3]

Then he raised his hand and said, "Avalokiteśvara has brought some
money to buy a sesame rice cake."[4] Lowering his hand, he said, "I see! After
all, it's originally just a bean cake."[5]

COMMENTARY

The crack of a pebble striking bamboo and Xiangyan entered the dharma
gate of the unborn. A simple glimpse of peach blossoms and Lingyun
awoke in the valley of the endless spring. Hearing sounds and realizing the
essence, seeing form and clarifying the mind, are the wondrous functioning
of mystical powers. We should understand that this mystical power is present in the state where box and lid fit together.

The ten thousand hands and eyes manage the diamond net, penetrating and transforming with ease. Entering the mystery in a male form, she
emerges as a female form, holding up heaven and supporting the earth. But
do you see? Where differences merge, there is nothing that is lacking.

Yunmen wants everyone to know what it is like when every organ of
perception and every object of perception is extended throughout the universe. Do you understand? I thought it was a bean cake; after all, it's a
sesame rice cake.

CAPPING VERSE

Seeing sounds, the valley streams
    expound the dharma.
Hearing forms, the mountain's body
    covers heaven and earth.

NOTES

1. Reaching everywhere, it's not like something.
2. If you really see it, you will go blind.
3. He is using his powers to mystify us.
4. Stop making your living in a ghost cave. This tune is getting too lofty.
5. After all it turns out that dog shit still smells like dog shit.

258 ॐ

Nanquan Banishes the Bodhisattvas

MAIN CASE

Nanquan Wang said to the assembly, "Last night Mañjuśrī and Samanta-bhadra aroused a buddha view and a dharma view, and both were given twenty blows of the stick. Then they were banished to the two iron mountains Cakravada and Cakravala."[1]

Zhaozhou came out and said, "Master, who will strike you with the stick?"[2]

Nanquan said, "What's the problem? Has teacher Wang committed an error?"[3]

Zhaozhou bowed.[4]

Nanquan got down from his teaching seat and returned to the abbot's room.[5]

COMMENTARY

Nanquan sets out a pot of glue. He tells his assembly that because Mañjuśrī and Samantabhadra gave rise to a buddha view and a dharma view, they were given twenty blows of the stick and were banished to the two iron mountains where demons reside. Haven't you heard Master Wumen's warning "To have a buddha view and a dharma view is to be confined between two iron mountains"?

Zhaozhou comes out and says, "Master, who will strike you with the stick?" What is Zhaozhou's point in speaking in this way? Some say Zhaozhou disagreed with his teacher, others say he misunderstood the teaching. What do you say? Indeed, what is Nanquan teaching?

Nanquan says, "Has teacher Wang committed an error?" Zhaozhou bows. Why? What does he see that makes him bow? If you run to the words to understand this case, you will never see it. Nanquan gathers it up and concludes it. Getting down from his teaching seat, he returns to the abbot's room.

From antiquity to the present, these ancient kōans have provided a route through the forest of brambles. If you can find your way through, you will find that it is addressing your own life right now, and that you have always been free in all directions.

CAPPING VERSE

A profound conversation beyond any one or two;
   demons and bodhisattvas speaking through the same mouth.
What is the reality that exists beyond dualities?
Aside from the dust, where is wisdom and compassion to be found?

NOTES

1. A spirit recognizes a spirit. Can you discern the adamantine cage?
2. Indeed, anyone would have doubts about this.
3. Well, has he?
4. As it turns out, he has had his nostrils pierced by the old man.
5. It's not worth further discussion. See for yourself.

259 ∿
Bajiao's Question and Answer

MAIN CASE

Master Bajiao Huiqing of Ying Region was once asked by a monastic, "Master, please show me a way not to fall into conditions."[1]

Bajiao said, "When there is a question, there is an answer."[2]

COMMENTARY

The visiting monastic wants to know if there is a way to meet situations without getting stuck. When Bajiao says, "When there is a question, there is an answer," he completes the case. Do you understand? Bajiao knows how to give what you have and take away what you don't have. If you want to know how to avoid falling into conditions, you first need to know that playing with a deadly snake is a matter for an adept.

If you are grabbing at reflections, trying to reach the form, you haven't yet recognized that the form is the source of the reflections. If you are raising your voice trying to stop an echo, you have not yet understood that the voice is the cause of the echo. In order to free that which is stuck and loosen that which is bound, it is necessary to cut away all traces of thought and all remnants of the sound of words. This is called discerning the phrase outside of patterns.

CAPPING VERSE

Responsible for humanity, you can't defer.
    Much talk. Who knows that it leaks one's potential?
Transcending patterns, leaving the clamor,
    spiritual work goes into action.

NOTES

1. It's too late. You are already nostril deep in it.
2. Unless there is a question, there can never be an answer.

260 ∾

Suffering Cannot Reach It

MAIN CASE

A monastic asked Caoshan, "It is scorching hot now. Where do we go to avoid the heat?"[1]

Caoshan said, "Into a pot of boiling water or the burning charcoal of a furnace [hell]."[2]

The monastic said, "How can you avoid heat there?"[3]

Caoshan said, "No suffering can reach there."[4]

The monastic was silent.[5]

COMMENTARY

Before it has been seen into, it all seems like an impenetrable forest of brambles, like a hundred-foot-high wall. When the myriad streams of thought cease and the gap is closed, it becomes clear that from the very beginning, the forest of brambles and the hundred-foot-high wall are nothing but the self.

Peaceful dwelling does not require the solitude of mountains and rivers. When you have extinguished the mind fire, wherever you may find yourself, you are standing in the midst of a buddha field.

CAPPING VERSE

When you truly see it, all things are one reality;
    if you do not, they are separate and different.
When you don't see it, all things are one reality;
    if you do, they are separate and different.

NOTES

1. This is not a question about seasons.
2. No one in the world can ever find this place.
3. This is not a place of yin and yang.

4. Rather than give the body relief, give relief to the mind.

5. *Duh!* Eyes wide open, mouth agape, he wants to figure it out.

261 ✇

Yunmen Composes a Verse

MAIN CASE

Yunmen was once asked by a monastic, "How do we not waste time throughout the day?"[1]

Yunmen said, "How do you focus on that question?"[2]

The monastic said, "I don't know, Master. Please instruct me."[3]

Yunmen composed a verse and gave it to the monastic:

If you don't pay attention,
you will miss it.[4]
If you think about it,
in what aeon will you realize it?[5]

COMMENTARY

This monastic goes to Yunmen seeking crumbs and is instead served a six-course meal. Lowering your head and lingering in thought, trying to figure it out with your intellect, simply moves you further from the truth. Yet if you don't pay attention, you will surely miss it.

Now tell me, without falling into intellect, without being caught up in affirmation and negation, how do you understand paying attention without thinking? Haven't you heard master Yaoshan's teaching "Think not-thinking?" How do you think not-thinking? Nonthinking.

We should understand clearly that nonthinking is not just to transcend thinking and not-thinking but to realize both as this very life itself. Nonthinking is objectless, subjectless, formless, goalless, and purposeless, but it is not a vacuum devoid of vitality and life. It is rather the self-fulfilling samādhi of joyous activity, the life of the buddhas and ancestors, your life and my life. To miss it is to miss life itself.

CAPPING VERSE

Ten thousand kinds of clever talk—
      how can they be compared to the great reality?
From within the myriad forms,
      the single body is revealed.

NOTES

1. At all costs, try to avoid silly questions.
2. Listen carefully to what you are saying.
3. This monastic is dull but persistent.
4. It's too late. He has already missed it.
5. At a time such as this, what will you do?

262 ∾

Caoshan's Bell Sound

MAIN CASE

Hearing the sound of a bell, Caoshan said, "*Aya! Aya!*"[1]
      A monastic said, "Master, what is it?"[2]
      Caoshan said, "It struck my mind."[3]

COMMENTARY

When Caoshan is suddenly struck by the bell sound, there is just this. Out of compassion for the monastic's dullness, however, he comes forth dripping with mud and dragging his tongue, all to no avail. Still, how can anyone explain it?
      When the ear is transcended, the whole universe is nothing but ear. When the eye is transcended, the whole universe is nothing but eye.

CAPPING VERSE

Sitting in absolute silence,
      mind like still water.

The sound of the bell
    and the six gates enter.

NOTES

1. After all, there is just this.
2. Although they both occupied the same space, the bell sound only reached one of them. I wonder why?
3. It's too late. The cows are scattered all over the mountain.

263 ∾

Layman Wang Holds Up His Brush

MAIN CASE

The emperor's attendant Wang was tending affairs in his office when Jingzhao came. Wang took up his writing brush and showed it to him.[1]

Jingzhao said, "Can you distinguish empty space?"[2]

Wang threw down the brush, went into his house, and did not invite Jingzhao to come in.[3]

Jingzhao wondered about it. The next day he had Huayan talk to Wang at a tea gathering. Huayan said, "What statement of Master Jingzhao's made you stop seeing him?"

Wang said, "A lion bites humans and a hound of the ancient kingdom of Han chases a lump of mud."[4]

Overhearing these words, Jingzhao laughed. "I understand it. I understand it."[5]

Wang said, "You may understand it, but try to say it."[6]

Jingzhao said, "Officer, ask me a question."

Wang held up a chopstick.[7]

Jingzhao said, "You fox spirit."[8]

Wang said, "This fellow has gone through."[9]

COMMENTARY

When dragons and snakes intermingle, it's hard to tell them apart. Both Wang and Jingzhao are senior students of Master Guishan. Wang is a lay practitioner and secretary to the emperor. Jingzhao is a priest from the capital city. If you want to understand the truth that encompasses heaven and earth, then study Wang's actions. If you want to move where it's impossible to move, turn around where it is impossible to turn around, then look to Jingzhao's words. If you want to be free of the two iron mountains of buddha and dharma, then look to yourself and find your own provisions.

CAPPING VERSE

When the illusion of objects is dissolved,
    the light first appears.
When the self and things are both forgotten,
    the way is clear and unhindered.

NOTES

1. At that moment, I would have shouted and left. Why indulge him?
2. After all, it just comes down to being trite.
3. He just acts according to the imperative and doesn't bother to test further.
4. Fundamentally, he was disappointed.
5. He proceeds to pull the arrow out of the back of his head.
6. The layman doesn't quite buy it.
7. If he was alert, at that point he should have just turned and walked away.
8. They are a pair of wild fox spirits.
9. He should not be let go of so easily. Why is Wang being so kind-hearted?

264 ∿
Baoying's Barrier

MAIN CASE

Baoying was once asked by a monastic, "A one-thousand-foot-tall barrier is on top of this lump of red flesh. Isn't this your phrase, master?"[1]

The master said, "Yes."[2]
The monastic turned over the meditation seat.[3]
Baoying said, "Look at how this blind man is acting."[4]
The monastic was about to say something, but Baoying hit him and chased him out of the monastery.[5]

COMMENTARY

Before you have passed through it, the thousand-foot-tall barrier seems like an impenetrable granite mountain. When you have been able to pass through it, you see that from the beginning the barrier is nothing other than yourself. The monastic thinks he has a way through the barrier and turns over the meditation seat. Baoying calls him blind. But say, what kind of blindness is he speaking of? If you can see into it here, you have seen into this kōan. If not, then enter here to find out.

The monastic is about to enter the realm of words and ideas. Baoying cuts off his tongue with a blow and drives him out. When lightning flashes and the sound of thunder fills the sky, it's too late to cover your ears. Do you understand? The sting of Linji's hit can still be felt in the third generation.

CAPPING VERSE

Everywhere, confined in the thousand-foot barrier;
      everyone, vainly discussing it.
Dawn has arrived but it is still dark.
Though the pure spring breeze blows,
      deep in the pit, it can't be felt.

NOTES

1. A lump of red flesh with a barrier on top spontaneously appears.
2. It's nice that he doesn't try to hide it.
3. He has already fallen.
4. Baoying calls it as he sees it.
5. If you want to realize the truth, avoid being caught up in thinking.

265 ∿
Shuilao's Enlightenment

MAIN CASE

Shuilao asked Mazu, "What is the exact meaning of the Ancestor's [Bodhidharma's] coming from India?"[1]

Mazu pushed him so hard that he knocked him over.[2]

Shuilao had immediate realization. He got up, clapped his hands, and said in laughter, "Marvelous, marvelous. Hundreds and thousands of samādhis, the boundless and wonderful meanings are all on the tip of a single hair.[3] I have understood the fundamental source all at once."[4] Then he made a bow and left.

COMMENTARY

Mazu has a way of getting right to the point of the matter. After all, Shuilao wants to know the *exact* meaning of the Ancestor's coming from India.

Clearly, this is not a matter for intellection or explanation. But, be that as it may, we should ask ourselves, what are hundreds and thousands of samādhis and the boundless and wonderful meanings found on the tip of a single hair?

CAPPING VERSE

Trampled to death by a horse,
    an heir has come to life.
A single glimpse of reality,
    and the whole universe comes alive.

NOTES

1. It's an old worn-out question, known everywhere. But still, he wants to put it to the test.
2. He goes right up and takes him out. Why is he being so kind to this monastic?

3. It engulfs the myriad forms. Between heaven and earth, what more is there?

4. Among the dead, a live one. He's treading on the ground of reality. What is the fundamental source that he saw?

266 ～

Guishan's "Why Have You Come Here?"

MAIN CASE

One day Guishan called the monastery director. The director came, and Guishan said to him, "I called for the monastery director. Why have you come here?"[1]

The monastery director did not give a response.[2]

Guishan asked the attendant monastic to get the head monastic. The head monastic came, and Guishan said to him, "I called for the head monastic. Why have you come here?"[3]

The head monastic did not give a response.[4]

COMMENTARY

Master Guishan wants to see if the chief administrators of his monastery know who they really are. When he calls the director and the director appears, he says, "I called for the monastery director. Why have you come here?" The monastery director does not give a response. Say a word for the monastery director. He then asks his attendant to get the head monastic. When the head monastic appears he again says, "I called for the head monastic. Why have you come here?" The head monastic also did not give a response. Where is the complication?

What is the intent of Guishan's calling his administrator monastics and then asking why they have come? Is there any contradiction here? Have you heard the *Diamond Sūtra*'s saying "Subhūti, the Tathāgata declares that all these molecules [that make up the world] are not really such; they are called 'molecules.' [Furthermore] the Tathāgata declares that a world is not really a world; it is called 'a world'"? I ask you, what is the difference between the name and the reality of the thing itself?

We should consider the words of the Chinese monastic Mengcan, who said, "Think about your own name. Then ask yourself, 'Is this me? Who is it? Since this is who I am, I may as well say it's me.' This is what is meant by practice. What else can you use to practice?" We should reflect on this matter. Is there a reality beyond the names and designations that we identify ourselves with? Who are you really? See into it here and detach from all forms. Say a word of Zen and merge with all things.

CAPPING VERSE

When forms and names appear,
  floating mists obscure the clarity.
When you truly look, it has no form, it covers heaven and earth;
  when you really listen, it has no sound, it fills the universe.

NOTES

1. I know you didn't call. That's why I'm here.
2. Was he dumbfounded or just silent?
3. If the attendant had called, I might not have come.
4. Is this bewilderment or clarity?

267 ∾

Baizhang's "No Means of Livelihood"

MAIN CASE

Baizhang Huaihai was asked by Yunyan, "Master, you work on details all day.[1] Who are you doing it for?"[2]

Baizhang said, "There may be someone who requires it."[3]

Yunyan said, "Why don't you let that person take care of it?"[4]

Baizhang said, "Because that person may not have the means of making a livelihood."[5]

COMMENTARY

Writers work with the pen, farmers with the hoe. Zen practitioners work on details all day long. Only those who have investigated this matter fully truly know the everyday affairs that encompass the heavens and cover the earth.

Old Baizhang certainly knows how to wholeheartedly engage the Way and avoid stumbling over words and phrases. Haven't you heard that aside from the details, there is nothing more to be found?

CAPPING VERSE

When you find the mountain dragon's mani jewel,
    it will be clear that it is numberless.
Seeing this in that and that in this,
    there is no doubt that it is all of one flavor.

NOTES

1. Although I have searched, I have not found anything other than this.
2. Look around you. Who else is there?
3. Someday, sometime; you can never tell.
4. To get this, it is first necessary to pass beyond the forest of brambles.
5. Be kind and hit him with the hoe, hit him with the hoe!

268 ∾

Baizhang's "Fundamental Principles of the Great Matter"

MAIN CASE

One day the old monastic Baizhang Huaihai, addressing his assembly, said,[1] "Plow the rice field for me,[2] and I'll instruct you[3] in the fundamental principles[4] of the great matter."[5]

After the monastics had plowed the rice field for the master,[6] they said,[7] "Now Master, please instruct us in the fundamental principles of the great matter."[8]

The master spread open his arms.[9]

COMMENTARY

There is no place in the entire universe to hide it. All of its activities are openly revealed. It functions freely in all directions, without hindrance. It has no form, yet it appears, filling the ten directions, responding spontaneously and immediately in accord with circumstances.

It's not just a matter of understanding three when one is raised, or judging grains or ounces at a single glance, but rather a function of the knowledge that has no teacher, the action of nonaction.

Tell me, what is this marvelous function? If you take it as activity, then surely farmers, generals, beggars, and thieves must also have it. That being the case, what is the purpose of practice and training? If you say it does not include all activity, then what activity is this marvelous functioning?

CAPPING VERSE

Laughing aloud from within the cloud-covered peaks,
    he holds it up with both hands.
No one has ever seen it.
If there were a single adept among them,
    the deception would have been exposed from the outset.

NOTES

1. He exposes or transforms according to the occasion.
2. Is it because he is old and feeble that he must rely on others to do his work?
3. What is he saying? Can it be imparted or not? What will he instruct them about?
4. The bottom line and the top line are the same line.
5. He knows, yet he is deliberately offensive.
6. Extraordinary! The true body of reality—though some may realize it, some may not.
7. Still in the forest of brambles, they have not yet finished with it.
8. Clutching the loot and pleading innocence, they still want to know why they have been confined to prison.
9. Old Baizhang is a competent master of our school. Why is he so shameless?

269 ∾

Shoushan's Stick

MAIN CASE

Shoushan Xingnian held up a bamboo stick[1] and said to the assembly, "If you call it a stick, you defile it.[2] If you don't call it a stick, you miss it.[3] What do you call it?"[4]

Shexian Guixing, who heard him, had great realization.[5] He went close to Shoushan, snatched away the stick, and broke it in two. He threw the pieces down on the ground and said, "What is this?"[6]

Shoushan said, "You blind fool!"[7]

Shexian bowed.[8]

COMMENTARY

If you call it a stick, you are caught up in the words and ideas that describe it, and that misses it. If you say it is not a stick, you deny its existence, and that, too, misses it. To say it is both a stick and not a stick is a thousand miles from the truth. To say it is neither a stick nor not a stick is like living in a ghost cave.

Putting aside Shoushan's question, how do you understand Shexian's actions? Moreover, what is his blindness? If you can say a word of Zen and clarify this matter without opening your mouth to explain, I'll grant that you have a bit of understanding.

CAPPING VERSE

In the middle of the night, there is light;
    within light, there is night.
The truth of this matter is not to be seen
    within the realm of yin and yang.

NOTES

1. Throughout heaven and earth, there is just this.
2. Why create limitations?

3. It would be difficult to deny its existence.
4. *Gaa!* He's asking them to speak of the unspeakable.
5. I wonder, what did he realize?
6. Without a moment's hesitation, he comes right back. But does he really see it?
7. Indeed! But what kind of blindness is it?
8. Teacher and student are both bathing in the same foul water.

270 ෴
Changsha's Liturgy

MAIN CASE

A monastic asked Changsha, "What is a dhāranī?"[1] Changsha pointed to the left of his meditation seat[2] and said,[3] "This monastic is reciting the dhāranī."[4]

The monastic asked, "Is there anybody else who can recite it?"[5]

Changsha pointed to the right of his meditation seat[6] and said,[7] "That monastic is reciting it, too."[8]

The monastic asked, "Then why can't I hear it?"[9]

Changsha said,[10] "Haven't you heard that real chanting makes no sound,[11] and in real listening there is no hearing?"[12]

The monastic asked,[13] "Doesn't sound enter into the nature of the dharma realms?"[14]

Changsha said, "Leaving form to observe form isn't a correct view. Leaving sound to seek listening is impaired hearing."[15]

COMMENTARY

In ceremony, there are forms and there are sounds; there's understanding and there's believing. In liturgy, there's only intimacy. Haven't you heard the ancient master's teaching "Seeing forms with the whole body and mind, hearing sounds with the whole body and mind, one understands them intimately"?

Intimate understanding is not like ordinary understanding. Ordinary understanding is seeing with the eye and hearing with the ear. Intimacy is seeing with the ear and hearing with the eye. How do you see with the ear and hear with the eye? Let go of the eye, and the whole body and mind is nothing but the eye. Let go of the ear, and the whole universe is nothing but the ear.

CAPPING VERSE

Though it fills the eyes,
    he doesn't see form.
Though it fills the ears,
    she doesn't hear sound.
Mañjuśrī is always
    covering his eyes,
Avalokiteśvara is always
    covering her ears.

NOTES

1. The question and the answer are both water from the same spring.
2. Thank you for your answer.
3. His eyebrows have dropped to the ground.
4. His kindness smothers the monastic to death.
5. He still doesn't see it, so he presses on.
6. Thank you for your answer.
7. His tongue is six fathoms long. He should shut up.
8. Both his monastics suffer from the same sickness.
9. The monastic stumbles along without realizing that "seeing" is not about the eyes, "hearing" is not about the ears.
10. When the wolf howls, everything in the valley is aware.
11. Utterly beyond sound.
12. Utterly beyond hearing.
13. Carrying three arrows in the back of his head, he requests still another.
14. What are you calling dharma realms?
15. Changsha is a competent master of our school. Why does he talk so much?

271 ⌒

Huangbo's Sacred Labor

MAIN CASE

Huangbo was at the assembly of Baizhang Huaihai, who said, "Ācārya Huangbo, it is not easy to plow a rice field."[1]

Huangbo said, "I just follow the assembly and work."[2]

Baizhang said, "You just labor in the Way."[3]

Huangbo said, "I don't mind the labor."[4]

Baizhang said, "How much rice field have you plowed?"[5]

Huangbo hit the ground three times with his hoe.[6]

Baizhang shouted.[7]

Huangbo ran away, covering his ears with his hands.[8]

COMMENTARY

The old master is not starting up a casual conversation by saying, "It is not easy to plow a rice field." He is probing for a way in. Huangbo, however, shows little concern. He says, "I just follow the assembly and work." The master probes deeper, and again Huangbo holds his ground. As long as the questions are dealing with realities, Huangbo can be easy. However, when the master tried to drag him into a pit, Huangbo got real and hit the ground three times with his hoe. You tell me, is there a Buddhist teaching to be seen in this? Why did Baizhang shout? Did he approve or disapprove, or does his shout have nothing to do with it all?

Although plowing the rice fields and working alongside the saṃgha is just an ordinary everyday affair, when you investigate it thoroughly, you will see that it manifests in a myriad of circumstances. The plowing of a rice field, when it is free and undefiled by dualism, is nothing other than an act of giving. So, too, building a bridge and earning a living become acts of giving when it is clear that giver and receiver are nondual. It is in this way that the purposeless and noninstrumental activity of the Bodhisattva is actualized.

If you wish to discover wonder in the flow of events, you must first be able to hear the silent discourse that is before words. You must experience for yourself the hidden activity that is spontaneously revealed. For Huangbo, this is all familiar ground. This is why he had to run away covering his ears with his hands when Baizhang shouted.

CAPPING VERSE

In going, pushed along by the winter wind;
     in returning, following after falling snowflakes.
With mystical power and wondrous activity,
     each step follows the other.

NOTES

1. Not easy, not difficult.
2. He is just doing what he is doing while he is doing it.
3. The old master is searching for a gap.
4. No gaps, no seams, no edges. I think he is just enjoying himself.
5. He wants to see whether a crack will appear if he hits hard enough.
6. No gaps, no seams, no edges.
7. This is just a bad habit that he picked up from his teacher.
8. It's just more than he can bear.

272

Jinfeng's "Frost on Top of Snow"

MAIN CASE

Jinfeng said to a monastic who stood beside him, "I will give you a kōan.[1] First of all, you should not be confused by it."[2]
     The monastic said, "Master, please give it to me."[3]
     Jinfeng held up his whisk.[4]
     The monastic was silent for a while.[5]
     Jinfeng said, "I know that you are confused."[6]
     The monastic looked toward the east, then the west.[7]
     Jinfeng said, "You have added frost on top of snow."[8]

COMMENTARY

Twenty-five hundred years ago the World-Honored One held up a flower on Mount Gridhrakūta. Since that time, countless masters of our school have employed this teaching device of "holding up." But say, what does it mean to hold something up? Guizong Zhichang held up a spade and another time his fist, the priest of Mount Wutai held up a spear, Yunyan held up a broom, Chuanzi an oar, Deshan Xuanjian a torch, Juzhi one finger, the emperor's attendant Wang a chopstick, Shoushan a stick; Jinfeng held up a pillow, Yunmen held up his fan, Xiaotang held up the corner of his vestment, the hermit of Lotus Flower Peak held up his staff, Nanquan held up a cat, and here Jinfeng holds up his whisk.

Is it that all these old masters have created a nest in the Buddha's holding up of a flower, or is there a fresh teaching to be seen each time? It would seem that each master employed what was at hand: a stick, a whisk, a flower, and when there was nothing within reach, a fist.

Now I ask you, is there a single truth that is revealed here? If so, what is it? The monastic is silent and the master calls it confusion. Say a word for the monastic. The monastic tries again and the master dismisses him with "You have added frost on top of snow." How has the monastic failed?

CAPPING VERSE

Holding up has a meaning so subtle and profound
    that it has never been communicated.
Aimlessly, the spring breeze, of itself,
    knows how to enter the scars of the burning.

NOTES

1. An unexpected gift.
2. If you don't think about it, there will be no confusion.
3. He is willing to walk the edge of the sword.
4. Thunder fills the valley.
5. Is this being profound or just dull-witted?
6. Why is he being so kind?
7. Is this an act of desperation, or does he see something?
8. He has lost his body and life and doesn't even know it.

273 ⌘
Yantou's Two Disapprovals

MAIN CASE

Luoshan accompanied Yantou and visited a mountain. He said, "Master."

Yantou said, "What is it?"

Luoshan went close to him, bowed, and said, "Master, is it true that you did not approve Dongshan when you were at his assembly thirty years ago?"[1]

Yantou said, "That is true."[2]

Luoshan said, "Is it true that you inherited dharma from Deshan Xuanjian and did not approve him?"[3]

Yantou said, "That is true."[4]

Luoshan said, "I am not asking you why you did not approve Deshan. Just let me ask you, what was lacking in Dongshan?"[5]

Yantou paused for a while and said, "Dongshan was a good buddha. He just didn't shine."[6]

Luoshan bowed.

COMMENTARY

Yantou traveled widely and studied with many masters. He was difficult to please. Haven't you heard that once, when Dongshan said, "If it wasn't for Yantou, then the meaning couldn't be grasped," and at that time Yantou said, "Old Dongshan doesn't know right from wrong. He's made a big error. At that time I lifted up with one hand and pushed down with one hand"? At another time Yantou said of his teacher, "Old Deshan doesn't know the last word of Zen."

See how he has a naturally sharp and demanding edge to his personality. There is no one who can really handle him. If you want to get to the real meaning of Yantou's two disapprovals, you must examine the two encounters. What does he mean when he says that old Dongshan doesn't know right from wrong, that at the time he was lifting up with one hand and pushing down with the other? What does it mean not to shine?

It seems obvious that Yantou would know that Deshan was a truly accomplished master; he succeeded him. Why did he then say, "Old Deshan doesn't know the last word of Zen?" What is the last word of Zen? If you can see into this, you will know why Luoshan didn't even bother to ask about it.

CAPPING VERSE

If the student's understanding equals the teacher's,
    the teaching is diminished by half.
Only when the student has surpassed the teacher,
    has the teaching been truly transmitted.

NOTES

1. He wants to separate the rumor from the truth.
2. An honest person is hard to find.
3. His reputation for disapproval is widespread.
4. At this point it would be hard to deny it.
5. Haven't you heard? He's deaf, dumb, and blind.
6. He did not shine, nor was he dull. Do you understand?

274 ❧

Jinfeng Holds Up a Pillow

MAIN CASE

One day Jinfeng held up a pillow and said, "People call this a pillow. I say it is not a pillow."[1]
    A monastic said, "Master, what do you call it?"
    Jinfeng held up the pillow.
    The monastic said, "If so, I will practice accordingly."[2]
    Jinfeng said, "What do you call it?"
    The monastic said, "A pillow."[3]
    Jinfeng said, "You have fallen into my pit."

COMMENTARY

To call it a pillow is to be caught up in a name. To say it's not a pillow is to negate the fact. Jinfeng willingly goes nostril deep into the mud with his statement. The monastic inadvertently gives him an escape route by asking a question. Do you understand how this is so?

The monastic seems to grasp his teaching and says, "I will practice accordingly." Fortunately for the monastic, Jinfeng pursues the matter and tests him further. When Jinfeng asks, "What do you call it?" the monastic has no notion that this is a question that can never be answered. Although the monastic ends up in Jinfeng's pit, you can avoid the same fate by saying a turning word. Leap clear of the contradictions of pillow and not a pillow and show a clear and definite way out. Tell me, what do you call it?

CAPPING VERSE

Holding up a pillow, setting up a pitfall,
    he is prepared to kill or give life.
Where affirmation and negation have merged,
    even sages are at a loss for words.

NOTES

  1. *Behhhh*! Wrong.
  2. He is acting as if he attained something.
  3. Back into your hole, frog.

275 ∾

Guishan's "You Have to Find Out for Yourself"

MAIN CASE

Guishan was once asked by Commander Lu in the monastics' hall, "Among these advanced monastics, who are meal servers and who are meditators?"[1]
    Guishan said, "There are no meal servers and no meditators."[2]
    Lu said, "Then what are they doing here?"[3]
    Guishan said, "Officer, you will have to find that out for yourself."[4]

COMMENTARY

Commander Lu was a frequent visitor to Mount Gui and often engaged in dialogues with Guishan and his successor Yangshan. Here he asks which of the monastics are servers and which are the meditators. Guishan can see that the real question is still hidden and tries to bring it out, saying that there are no servers or meditators. The real question appears, "Then what are they doing here?"

Haven't you heard the saying "If you want to attain intimacy, don't approach it with questions"? Guishan says, "You will have to find that out for yourself." How touching. In a single phrase the old master opens up a path for him to follow. From ancient times to the present, buddhas and ancestors have never spoken a word for the people. This practice of not helping people should be investigated thoroughly. Even an answer that is sweet as honey, when clearly understood, turns out to be just another poison. You just have to find out for yourself.

CAPPING VERSE

Buddhas and ancestors have not appeared in the world,
    nor is there any truth to be given to the people.
They were just able to observe the hearts of beings
    and dispense medicine according to their ills.

NOTES

1. What is he talking about? What kind of a question is this?
2. He peels back the shell for him to reveal the nut.
3. How can it be explained?
4. Ultimately, it always comes down to this.

276 ∿

Dongshan's "Deep or Shallow"

MAIN CASE

Crossing a river with Yunju, Dongshan asked, "Is the water deep or shallow?"[1]
    Yunju said, "It's not wet."[2]
    Dongshan said, "That's coarse."[3]
    Yunju said, "Tell me, Master, how would you say it?"
    Dongshan said, "It's not dry."[4]

COMMENTARY

Transmitting the teachings, they must be imparted night or day, at work or at rest. In testing the waters, the probing pole is always employed when it is least expected. If you really understand the great function well, you will know how to make use of it on the road. Dongshan lets down a hook to test this, saying, "Is the water deep or shallow?" Although Yunju manages to avoid being impaled, he nonetheless stumbles and falls. Dongshan says, "That's coarse." Tell me, why is it coarse? How would you say it? Dongshan says, "It's not dry." See how Dongshan knows how to break up discrimination and intellectual ideas. In the Caodong family, this is called the point of transformation that is beyond doctrines. Here, there are no buddhas or sentient beings, no high or low, gain or loss. But tell me, what power can get one to be this way?

CAPPING VERSE

Picking and choosing,
    the seam opens into a gap.
Cutting off both sides—
    no seams, no gaps.

NOTES

1. It's not that this question is so lofty, it's just that you must know for yourself.
2. Striking and resounding. Good words. Nevertheless, not good enough.
3. The polishing of the pearl is not over until the coarseness is smoothed away.
4. The one bright pearl reflects the ten directions equally.

277 ◐

Zhaozhou's "Carry It with You"

MAIN CASE

Yanyang Shanxin asked Zhaozhou, "How is it when nothing comes up?"[1]
    Zhaozhou said, "Cast it off."[2]
    Yanyang said, "When nothing comes up, how can you cast it off?"[3]
    Zhaozhou said, "Then carry it with you."[4]

COMMENTARY

Yanyang arrives at Zhaozhou's place in dire poverty, looking for a helping
hand. Zhaozhou's penetrating eye immediately sees the enormous burden
that he is carrying and suggests that he let it go. Since he has nothing to let
go of—no eye, ear, nose, tongue, body, mind—the monastic cannot understand Zhaozhou's instructions. Not having yet penetrated Yunmen's sicknesses, he persists in his ignorance.

    In the end, Zhaozhou acquiesces and lets him carry the whole thing off.
At this point the old master, bringing it out like this, ends up pulling the rug
out from under Yanyang. If he realized the weight of the load he was bearing, in an instant he would be free of it.

CAPPING VERSE

A bodyless person suffering a grave illness
    sweeps away tracks, leaving a trail.
Only those who have thoroughly explored it
    can know the wonder of the ceaseless flow.

NOTES

1. He should not go around bragging about it. What a pity, here's another cloud-dwelling saint.
2. I ask you, what else could be said?
3. What kind of thing is no thing?
4. Zhaozhou's haggling is just about dragging this monastic out into
   the sunshine.

278 ∾

Mazu's "Mind Is Buddha"

MAIN CASE

Damei Fachang asked Mazu, "What is buddha?"[1]
Mazu said, "Mind is buddha."[2]

COMMENTARY

The buddha mind is the basis of truth, and gateless is the dharma gate. If you seek after the dharma, you will move away from it. Outside of mind there is no buddha; outside buddha there is no mind.

Although Mazu is able to enlighten Damei with his "Mind is buddha," in the end he only succeeds in creating a nest for generations of practitioners that persists to this day.

Putting aside the words and ideas of "Mind is buddha," right now, show me the reality.

CAPPING VERSE

The truth fills the universe—
    nothing is hidden.
Yet if you are not intimate with it, when it's revealed,
    you'll think about it for the rest of your life.

NOTES

1. This is an old question that has been batted around monasteries for centuries; still, it deserves an answer.
2. Although it is true, it is a pity to have said so.

279 ❦

Guishan's "Great Capacity, Great Function"

MAIN CASE

Guishan said to the assembly, "People nowadays have great capacity but do not have great function."[1]
  Yangshan related this to a temple priest.[2]
  The temple priest kicked over a stool.[3]
  Hearing about it, Guishan burst into laughter.[4]

COMMENTARY

Each and every one is born with the great capacity of a spiritual being, but if this potential does not leave its fixed position, it cannot impart strength on the road. In the Zen school, in a single word or action, with one entry or exit, one encounter, one response, it becomes clear whether someone is deep or shallow.

  Guishan wants everyone in his assembly to know this, so he lifts up with one hand and presses down with the other. The great function is not found within fixed patterns. If we wish to free what is stuck and loosen what is bound, we must first cut away all traces of thought, take off the blinders, and set down the pack. It is here that the season of great peace becomes freely functional in the midst of chaos and confusion.

  The temple priest, hearing of Guishan's teaching, kicks over a stool, and Guishan bursts into laughter. What is the meaning of the temple priest's action and Guishan's laughter? If you want to understand this encounter, you should first understand that a true person of great function cannot even lift a leg.

CAPPING VERSE

Everywhere, suffering and pain;
    everyone, vainly discussing the self.
Though they are buddha,
    it's all buried beneath years of conditioning.

NOTES

1. He brings out medicine and sickness at the same time.
2. He is not just a blabbermouth; he wants to see if it is understood.
3. This old fellow is acting strange. The tip of his foot has a mind of its own.
4. Guishan takes notice. But say, what realm is this?

280 ∾

Yunmen's Sixty Blows

MAIN CASE

Dongshan Shouchu went to see Yunmen, who said, "Where are you from?"[1]
Dongshan said, "From Jiangxi, Master."[2]
Yunmen said, "Where did you spend the summer practice period?"[3]
Dongshan said, "At Baoci Monastery in Hunan."[4]
Yunmen said, "When did you leave there?"[5]
Dongshan said, "On the twenty-fifth day of the eighth month."[6]
Yunmen said, "I will give you sixty blows of my stick."[7]
The next day Dongshan went to the abbot's room[8] and said, "Master, you gave me sixty blows yesterday. I don't understand what my fault was."[9]
Yunmen cried out, "You rice bag! Have you been prowling about like this from Jiangxi to Hunan?"[10]
Hearing these words, Dongshan had great realization.[11]

COMMENTARY

It has no form, yet it is constantly present. Vast and boundless, it reaches everywhere, responding spontaneously and working freely in accord with the imperative. Yet, Zen practitioners everywhere vainly search for it over the four corners of the earth. Coming and going, asking and telling, poking and examining, they ask, "Where's the gold?"

In Zen training, one's understanding and clarity is seen in one's attitudes and actions, words and phrases, one's asking and responding. Ultimately its concern is, where do you find yourself? We should investigate this matter thoroughly.

Those who search for the Way do not see the truth. They only know discriminating consciousness. This is the cause of pain and suffering. Before we have taken a single step, we have already arrived. Buddha said to take it this way.

CAPPING VERSE

Deep or shallow—whatever it may be—
    it's all in your hands.
Throughout the country,
    only a handful can appreciate this.
The universe is itself the Great Way,
    and the philosopher's stone
      is your life itself.

NOTES

1. The windup and the pitch. After all, he must test the monastic.
2. Strike one!
3. Again the pitch.
4. Strike two!
5. A searing fastball.
6. Strike three. You're out!
7. His kindness is only exceeded by his generosity. He gives him everything.
8. He makes up for his dullness with persistence.
9. This is not a casual question; it comes from the heart of his spiritual struggle.
10. This is even more brutal than the sixty blows.
11. Careful here. Gold dust in the eyes is not an aid to perception.

281 ❧
Zhaozhou Sees Through Two Hermits

MAIN CASE

Zhaozhou called on a hermit and said, "Are you there? Are you there?"[1]
The hermit held up his fist.[2]
Zhaozhou said, "The water is too shallow here. It's not a place to anchor a vessel."[3] Then he went away.
Later Zhaozhou called on another hermit and said, "Are you there? Are you there?"[4]
The hermit held up his fist.[5]
Zhaozhou said, "You have the power to give and take away, to kill and to give life."[6] He bowed and went away.

COMMENTARY

In visiting these two hermits, it would appear on the surface that Zhaozhou approves the understanding of one and disapproves the understanding of the other, but do not be misled by appearances. We should thoroughly investigate this fist. After all, a fist is a fist. Can it be said that there is a distinction of superior or inferior between two fists being held up?

How then can Zhaozhou see the true nature of these two hermits who both hold up their fists in the same manner? If you can truly see into the fist, then you will see not only into the hermits but into you yourself and Zhaozhou as well.

If you say that one hermit is superior to the other, then you have missed it. If, on the other hand, you say that there is no difference between the two hermits, this too is a hundred miles from the truth of this kōan. Leap clear of sameness or difference and you will enter directly into Zhaozhou's heart.

CAPPING VERSE

The fist contains the myriad things;
    the myriad things contain the fist.
When words and ideas fade,
    the light is evident.

NOTES

1. Anybody home? He wants to know if the hermit is alive or dead.
2. Outstanding! But say, what does it mean?
3. There are echoes in these words that still reverberate to this day.
4. Again, are you alive or are you dead?
5. Outstanding! But what does it mean?
6. Tread carefully here, there are thorns in the mud.

282 ॐ

Xuansha Draws a Circle

MAIN CASE

Xuansha saw Gushan Shanyan coming and drew a circle on the ground.[1]
Gushan said, "People cannot get out of this place."[2]
Xuansha said, "I guess you do things in a donkey's womb and horse's belly."[3]
Gushan said, "Master, what about yourself?"[4]
Xuansha said, "People cannot get out of this place."[5]
Gushan said, "You said so and I said so. So what's wrong with me?"[6]
Xuansha said, "I have got it but you haven't."[7]

COMMENTARY

Can you discern the depth of teaching of old master Xuansha? Do you see the adamantine cage he freely manifests? Why is it that people cannot get out of this place, and what kind of place is it? The younger dharma brother Gushan is clearly an adept, yet Xuansha says, "I guess you do things in a donkey's womb and horse's belly." What is his meaning? If you are a person that's alive and hopping, you will naturally not rush to words and phrases and create interpretations.

When Gushan asks, "Master, what about yourself?" Xuansha also says, "People cannot get out of this place." Why is Xuansha correct and Gushan wrong? You should understand that a competent teacher of our school will always try to dissolve away the sticking points and remove the bonds. Can you see Gushan's sticking points?

Gushan says, "You said so and I said so. So what's wrong with me?" Xuansha responds, "I have got it but you haven't." What is the *it* that he has and how does he know that Gushan does not have it?

CAPPING VERSE

Vertically, extending through the three times;
    horizontally, encompassing the ten directions.
There are no gaps, no obstructions,
    no way in, no way out.
What kind of place is this?

NOTES

1. This circle has been rolling around Zen monasteries for centuries and has never been exhausted.
2. There seems to be a bit of fragrant air about this one.
3. He diminishes the man. What does he see?
4. On level ground he manages to find a pit to stumble into.
5. At this point, he is just carrying out the correct imperative.
6. The further he probes, the deeper the pit becomes.
7. Although this is true, how does he know?

283 ∾

Xuefeng's "Ancient Valley Stream"

MAIN CASE

A monastic asked Xuefeng, "What about the time when the spring freezes in the ancient ravine?"[1]

Xuefeng replied, "You gaze attentively into it, but still cannot see the bottom."[2]

The monastic then asked, "What happens to the person who drinks from that stream?"[3]

Xuefeng said, "That person drinks without water even entering the mouth."[4]

Later the monastic told Zhaozhou the story. Zhaozhou said, "It cannot enter through the nostrils."[5]

Then the monastic asked, "What about the time when the spring freezes in the ancient ravine?"[6]

Zhaozhou replied, "Suffering."[7]

The monastic asked, "What happens to the person who drinks it?"[8]

Zhaozhou said, "The person dies."[9]

Xuefeng heard this and said, "Zhaozhou is an ancient buddha."[10]

After that the monastic stopped discussing the matter.[11]

COMMENTARY

Infinitely brilliant, the original buddha mind. What can surpass the virtue of this brilliance? Radiantly pure, its light covers the universe, and yet no one has ever seen it. Unbounded by ideas of vast or small, round or square, birth or death, this truth reaches everywhere. Xuefeng says, "You . . . cannot see the bottom." Zhaozhou replies, "Suffering." Are these the same or different?

Everything everywhere: blooming flowers, snow-covered landscapes, mountains, rivers, and all the creatures of this great earth are the body, mind, and spirit of the original buddha mind. Xuefeng says, "That person drinks without water even entering the mouth." Zhaozhou says, "It cannot enter through the nostrils." We should understand that if it enters through the gate, it is not the original buddha mind. When you finally see it, you go deaf, dumb, and blind. This is the skin, flesh, bones, and marrow of all the ancient buddhas.

CAPPING VERSE

The sun rises, but it's still dark;
    the mist has dissolved, but the valley is dim.
Though Xuefeng and Zhaozhou are radiant,
    it has all been lost in vain discussions.
Yet even in the cave of demons, the pearl shines.
Some may realize it, some may not.

NOTES

1. Many monastics have made their nests here. He should find out for himself.

2. If you go to the road to understand this, you will spend the rest of your life searching.

3. Still, he presses the old monastic.

4. It fills the heavens and covers the earth.

5. Nor the eye, the ear, the tongue, the body, or the mind. How will it enter then?

6. In the long run, this monastic will end up a believer. It seems that's what he's trying to accomplish.

7. Bitter through and through. Among ten thousand, a hundred thousand, only one or two may get it.

8. Confined to prison, all he can do is rattle the cage and run off at the mouth.

9. When you die once, you can never die again. An iron flute with no holes.

10. Zhaozhou drinks and Xuefeng gets drunk. It's all dirt from the same hole.

11. He closes the gate after the horses have strayed.

284 ❧

Tianping's Three Wrongs

MAIN CASE

Congyi of Tianping, during his traveling, visited Siming Monastery. He often said, "Don't say that in the present time you can encounter the Buddhadharma. When we look for someone who can, it is impossible to find one."[1]

One day Tianping came out of the dharma hall. Abbot Xiyuan Siming called out to him, "Tianping!"[2]

Tianping looked up.[3]

Xiyuan said, "Wrong."[4]

Tianping took a few steps.

Again Xiyuan said, "Wrong."[5]

Tianping went close to him. Xiyuan said, "Are these two wrongs my wrongs or your wrongs?"[6]

Tianping said, "My wrongs, Master."[7]

Xiyuan said, "Wrong."[8]

Tianping gave up.[9] Xiyuan said, "Senior monastic, stay here for a while, and let us examine these wrongs."[10]

Tianping walked away.[11] Later he became abbot of Tianping Monastery and said, "A long time ago, when I was traveling, I was blown by karmic winds to Elder Xiyuan's assembly. He pointed out my two wrongs. He asked me to stay over the summer and examine these wrongs. I did not realize them as wrong at that time. But when I headed south, I knew right away why he had said 'Wrong.'"[12]

COMMENTARY

The masters of old could not avoid imparting the teachings in accord with the imperative that they encountered. The Great Compassionate Vows are relentless. They are not a matter of success or failure. Sometimes they reach home, and sometimes no one is home.

Tianping stuffs himself with dead words and goes south on his pilgrimage. The heat in the furnace of Xiyuan's two wrongs confuses him, and although he has a bellyful of Zen, he does not know how to use it on the road.

But say, why is Tianping wrong, and how can he turn the spear around and send the old master running? If you can say a turning word on this matter, I'll grant you have a bit of life in you. If, on the other hand, you can't say a word, then it's time to just shut up and sit. We should finally understand that these three wrongs notwithstanding, from the beginning, nothing whatsoever is lacking.

CAPPING VERSE

The way to the top of Heavenly Light Mountain
    is steep and difficult.
The path is strewn with boulders
    and the peak is covered in mist.
And yet, each step on the way to the summit
    is the summit itself.

NOTES

1. Although this is true, it somehow has the musty smell of books about it.
2. Old Xiyuan wants to see if he can hook him.
3. Without any hesitancy, he climbs onto the hook.
4. The old man pulls the rug out from under him.
5. He can get on his feet, but he doesn't know how to stay there.
6. Xiyuan wants to take away everything that's cherished by the man.
7. What a pity. Sometimes the armor is so thick even a skilled craftsman can't find a way in.
8. There are three kinds of live horses, and then there is the dead horse.
9. Some are made of iron and some are made of shit, yet both are buddhas.
10. This old teacher's compassion is boundless. Why doesn't he just drive him out?
11. He may look like a practitioner and act like a practitioner, but he is really an impostor.
12. Wrong! Years later he is still wearing the dragon mask. Phony Zen practitioners are a dime a dozen.

285 ∾
Shushan's "Nature of the Dharma Body"

MAIN CASE

Shushan said to the assembly, "I understood things about the margin of Dharmakāya before the Xiantong era and going beyond Dharmakāya after the Xiantong era."[1]

Yunmen came out from the assembly and said, "What is the margin of dharma body?"[2] Shushan said, "A dead camellia."[3]

Yunmen said, "What is going beyond dharma body?"[4]

Shushan said, "Not a dead camellia."[5]

Yunmen said, "Would you allow your student to speak about it?"[6]

Shushan said, "Yes, I would."

Yunmen said, "Does a dead camellia clarify the margin of dharma body?"[7]

Shushan said, "Yes, it does."[8]

Yunmen said, "Does something that is not a dead camellia clarify going beyond dharma body?"[9]

Shushan said, "No, it doesn't."[10]

Yunmen said, "The dharma body encompasses all things, doesn't it?"[11]

Shushan said, "Dharma body is all-prevailing. How can it not encompass all things?"[12]

Yunmen pointed to a water jar and said, "Is the dharma body in there?"[13]

Shushan said, "Don't just understand what is at the margin of the water jar!"[14]

Yunmen bowed.[15]

COMMENTARY

Yunmen, though only a traveling monastic, is still an adept. He does not hesitate in distinguishing dragons from snakes, wherever he encounters them. Whether they are monastics or heads of temples, all receive the same relentless probing.

Haven't you heard of Yunmen's sickness regarding the dharma body? It is the sickness that even having reached the dharma body, because of a persisting self-view, one abides at the margins, and attachments to it still persist. Thus, having heard Shushan's statement about the margin and going beyond the dharma body, Yunmen was compelled to probe, and although Shushan was able to roll over and recover like a gourd in water, still, the whole affair was embarrassing.

But say, since the dharma body is all-prevailing, why is the dead camellia the margin of the dharma body? Furthermore, what is at the margin of the water jar? See into it here and I will concede that you and Yunmen walk hand in hand.

CAPPING VERSE

When it is necessary to even the uneven,
       even great adepts seem inept.
Even the buddhas and ancestors cannot hone it;
       every branch of coral supports the moon.

NOTES

1. Why even bring it up in the first place?
2. He seems to have some doubts about this.
3. Why are these two talking about margins?
4. Now, this seems like a reasonable question.
5. This seems like a reasonable answer.
6. Yunmen seems to be going somewhere with this.
7. Why clarify it? What will you do with a clarified margin?
8. But tell me, what does this really mean?
9. By now they are both nostril deep in cow dung, and the whole assembly is in danger of drowning in it.
10. We have already passed by this point. Why beat a dead horse?
11. We have now entered the realm of Buddhism 101.
12. Wonderful! You may now proceed to Buddhism 102.
13. At last! Yunmen is an adept. Why did it take so long to get here?
14. The clouds part and the sun appears.
15. By now the whole assembly is covered in mud. Still, it's something.

286 ೞ

Jingqing's "Sound of Rain"

MAIN CASE

Jingqing asked a monastic, "What is that sound outside the gate?"[1]
The monastic said, "It's the sound of raindrops."[2]
Jingqing said, "People these days are confused and out of touch with themselves.[3] They only go about chasing after things."[4]
The monastic said, "How about yourself, Master?"[5]
Jingqing said, "I hardly ever lose track of what I am."[6]
The monastic said, "What do you mean?"[7]
Jingqing said, "To bring out the body is easy.[8] To be free from the body is difficult."[9]

COMMENTARY

Zen practitioners the world over work day and night at untying what is bound and releasing what is stuck. But if we are confused and out of touch with what we really are, it all becomes a matter of running around chasing after things. At such a time, how will you have today? Sensing the monastic's uneasiness, Jingqing gently lowers a hook, asking, "What is that sound?" The monastic responds, and although the answer misses it, concern is born and possibility emerges. Because he has the skill to help people, Jingqing does not spare his eyebrows in explaining. The monastic cannot hear it. Pressed by the monastic, Jingqing says, "I hardly ever lose track of what I am."

If you go to Jingqing's words to understand this, you too will miss his point. To understand "I hardly ever lose track of what I am," you must first examine the question: what are you? Again, the monastic is off pursuing things and asks for a meaning. Asking "What do you mean?" is chasing after things. The truth is not out there. In intimacy there is no meaning whatsoever. The old master's kindness is excessive. Without hesitation he rolls it out and walks on top of sound and form for his student. But say, how does he walk on top of sound and form? What does it mean "to be free from the body"?

CAPPING VERSE

If you call it the sound of rain,
    you have missed it.
If you don't call it the sound of rain,
    then what will you call it?
When clouds gather in the Rocky Mountains,
    rains fill the Catskill valley streams.

NOTES

1. It is important to know just what it is that he is asking.
2. Why would the master not know that it was the sound of raindrops?
3. If you wish to understand the universe, you must begin with yourself.
4. What things is he speaking about? What things do you chase after?
5. The monastic seems alive; he comes out hopping and jumping.
6. Jingqing's feet are treading the ground of reality.

7. As it turns out, this monastic is dull-witted. He wants to beat this statement to death.
8. We do it all the time.
9. It almost never happens.

287 ∾

The Fire Dharma of Xuefeng and Xuansha

MAIN CASE

Xuefeng said to the assembly, "All buddhas in the three worlds turn the dharma wheel in the fire."[1]

Xuansha said, "When the fire expounds dharma to all buddhas in the three worlds, they stand and listen."[2]

COMMENTARY

Teacher and student know each other intimately. Xuefeng says that all buddhas turn the dharma wheel in the fire; Xuansha says that the fire preaches to all buddhas. Xuefeng speaks of the donkey looking into the well; Xuansha speaks of the well looking at the donkey. However, if we wish to clarify this even further, we should understand that it's not just a matter of the donkey seeing the well but also the donkey seeing the donkey, the well seeing the well, beings seeing beings, mountains seeing mountains. When the great dharma wheel turns, it always goes in both directions.

Further, there is the teacher meeting the student, and there is the student meeting the teacher. For the student to meet the teacher, she must be the teacher. For the teacher to meet the student, he must be the student. Isn't this the teacher meeting himself, the student meeting herself? In this kind of encounter, no relationship whatsoever is possible. From time immemorial this has been the way of practice and verification of our school.

CAPPING VERSE

They have said it all for us,
    light and dark walking hand in hand.

In the depths of the night,
  let us together see mountains and valleys,
  all taken by the snow.

NOTES

1. Although what he says is correct, unfortunately he has said only eighty percent of it.
2. It's all dirt from the same hole. One lifts up, the other presses down.

288 ∾

Zhaozhou's "Indestructible Nature"

MAIN CASE

Zhaozhou was once asked by a monastic, "Before the world existed, there was already the original nature.[1] When the world is destroyed, true nature is not destroyed.[2] What is this indestructible nature?"[3]
  Zhaozhou said, "Four great elements and five skandhas."[4]
  The monastic said, "They are destroyed. What is this indestructible nature?"[5]
  Zhaozhou said, "Four great elements and five skandhas."[6]

COMMENTARY

Caught in the double barrier of permanence and impermanence, this monastic comes to Zhaozhou looking for answers. In a flash of lightning, the old master snatches up everything at once, leaving the monastic with nothing to hold on to. Because, from the beginning, this monastic does not understand his own true nature, he persists with his question. Zhaozhou, seeing that the monastic is still lingering in duality, compassionately repeats himself.
  Don't you see? When a single flower blooms, the earth arises; when a single speck of dust appears, the universe is born. But before the speck of dust arises, before the flower opens, what is it? Where do you find yourself?

CAPPING VERSE

Beyond being and nonbeing, the root of creation;
        outside of space and time, the gate appears.
Knowing the ineffable—blue mountains fill the eyes.
What question could there be?

NOTES

1. True enough, but how do you understand original nature?

2. Where did he get the news? It's clear he didn't find out for himself.

3. Look, it's not hidden. It's right in front of your eyes.

4. Vast, billowing waves reach the heavens and cover the earth.

5. People all over whirl around in the stream of words. I'm afraid that he misunderstands, after all.

6. Vast, billowing waves reach the heavens and cover the earth.

289 ⟆
Daowu's "Alive or Dead"

MAIN CASE

Daowu visited a family with Jianyuan for a condolence call.[1] Jianyuan tapped the coffin three times and said, "Alive or dead?"[2]
    Daowu said, "I won't say alive. I won't say dead."[3]
    Jianyuan said, "Why won't you say?"[4]
    Daowu said, "I won't say. I won't say."[5]
    Jianyuan could not understand at the time.[6] Later he heard the Avalokiteśvara chapter of the *Lotus Sūtra* being chanted. It said, "For one who has attained the monastic body, Avalokiteśvara appears in the monastic's body and expounds the dharma." Hearing this, Jianyuan came to realization.[7]

COMMENTARY

Even in his not saying, Daowu has said it all, but Jianyuan does not know that it is right in his face. Later, hearing a workman chanting the Avalokiteśvara chapter of the *Lotus Sūtra*, Jianyuan suddenly realizes Daowu's compassionate teaching, and says, "At the time I was wrongly suspicious of my late teacher. How was I to know that this was not a matter of words and phrases?"

If you call it alive, you will have negated the fact. If you say dead, you have missed the truth of the matter by one hundred thousand miles. To say it is neither alive nor dead, or both alive and dead, compounds the absurdity. At such a time, what will you call it?

CAPPING VERSE

In birth, not an atom is added;
    in death, not a particle is lost.
Therefore, life is called the unborn;
    death is called the unextinguished.

NOTES

1. If you wish to understand the question of life and death, you must enter the arena of life and death.
2. Seeing the opportunity, he poses the question.
3. Hearing the question, he compassionately responds. But say, what does it mean?
4. This poor fellow makes up for his dullness by persistence.
5. Even the Buddha in his forty-seven years of teaching wouldn't say.
6. If you go to the words and phrases to understand this, you will never get it.
7. Within death he has found life. But tell me, what did he realize?

290 ⌒

Xuefeng's Meeting

MAIN CASE

Xuefeng said to the assembly, "I have met you at Wide View Pavilion.[1] I have met you on Crow Rock Peak.*[2] I have met you in front of the monastics' hall."[3]

Baofu Congzhan said to his fellow student Dayi of Mount Ehu [Huijue], "Aside from the monastics' hall, what about meeting at Wide View Pavilion and on Crow Rock Peak?"[4]

Ehu ran to the abbot's quarters.[5] Baofu lowered his head and entered the monastics' hall.[6]

COMMENTARY

Xuefeng, in addressing his assembly, wants everyone to know that each and every one of them contains the whole universe. In Xuefeng's expression, his whole body and mind is the true dharma eye, where at once Xuefeng meets Xuefeng, the monastics' hall meets the monastics' hall. There are no edges.

Baofu wants to see if his dharma brother Ehu understands the truth of the state of meeting each other, and the monastics' hall's having met itself. When asked, Ehu runs to the abbot's quarters. I ask you, does he understand? Baofu then lowers his head and enters the monastics' hall. What is his meaning? If you can say a turning word, I will grant that Wide View Hut, Crow Rock Peak, and Mount Xuefeng are, at this moment, underfoot.

CAPPING VERSE

For someone to meet the teacher,
    he must be the teacher.
The teacher teaching someone
    is the teacher meeting herself.

---

* Wide View Hut is on Crow Rock Peak at Mount Xuefeng.

NOTES

1. The view is vast and boundless.
2. There is nothing outside the great vastness.
3. In every respect it covers heaven and earth.
4. He wants to judge others on the basis of himself.
5. He knows how to give play to his spirit, but does he understand?
6. Those who know how to meet it are few and far between.

291 ∽

Zhaozhou's "Eye That Grasps the Universe"

MAIN CASE

Zhaozhou said, "The eye that grasps the universe[1] is so perceptive that it does not miss even a single thin thread.[2] I want you to see into this.[3] How do you understand it?"[4]

COMMENTARY

We should carefully examine Master Zhaozhou's "eye that grasps the universe" and see that it is untainted, free of attachment, beyond being and nonbeing, and not dependent upon intellectual comprehension. This is the true eye of all beings. It creates a clarity, which allows us to see that nothing in this universe is hidden.

When the true eye functions, it goes beyond looking and enters the realm of "seeing." Looking is superficial perception; it's about labeling, identification, accepting, and rejecting. It speaks to what things are. Seeing reveals what else things are. It's a direct encounter that involves the whole body and mind. The barrier of subject and object dissolves, and one understands it intimately.

If you wish to understand the wondrous functioning of such spiritual powers, you must avoid describing and discussing at all costs, or else you will see ghosts in front of your skull. If you seek it in thought, you are sitting beneath the black mountain. Look! the bright shining sun lights up the sky. Listen! the pure whispering wind circles this great earth. Enter here.

CAPPING VERSE

In the depths of stillness, all words melt away—
  clouds disperse and it vividly appears before you.
When seen, it is filled with wonder—
  vast and without edges, nothing concealed.

NOTES

  1. The ten directions cannot contain it.
  2. Deaf, dumb, and blind, you know it intimately.
  3. This type of kindness is difficult to requite.
  4. To think about it is totally beside the point.

292 ∾

Jiashan's "There Is Nothing in Front of You"

MAIN CASE

Jiashan told the assembly, "There is nothing in front of you.[1] There is just mind in front of you.[2] Other things are not in front of you, nor anywhere your ear or eye can reach."[3]

COMMENTARY

The *Flower Garland Sutra* says, "If a person wishes to know the three worlds and all the buddhas, he or she must realize that everything in the dharma world is created in the mind." Master Jiashan tells his assembly, "There is just mind in front of you." He wants his assembly to understand that appearances are illusions and that manifold gates to reality originate in the mind. When we can see through the appearances of the mind, the truth of thusness is revealed.

In the *Diamond Sutra*, the World-Honored One spoke a gāthā to Subhūti, saying:

  Who looks for me in form,
  who seeks me in a voice,

indulges in wasted effort.
Such people see me not.

Do you understand? The dharma body is not found in the realm of cognition. This dharma body is not just the real body of the Tathāgata but the pure, uncreated, and formless real body of all beings—a reality beyond sight or sound. Thus, Master Baofu says to his assembly, "I cover your eyes to let you see what is not seen. I cover your ears to let you hear what is not heard. I restrain your mind to let you give up thinking."

Although Jiashan's kindness is boundless and he willingly exhausts all of his resources in teaching his assembly, ultimately this is a matter that will never be communicated.

CAPPING VERSE

To look for a form or search for a sound
    is to stumble down the wrong path.
Here the wisdom that cannot be taught
    alone reveals that which is enduring and real.

NOTES

1. Vast and boundless, like a cloudless sky.
2. In what place shall we seek for the mind?
3. If you want to really see and hear, then cover your eyes and ears.

293 ❧

Nanquan's "Badgers and White Oxen"

MAIN CASE

Nanquan said to the assembly, "I don't know about the existence of all buddhas in the three worlds,[1] but I do know the existence of badgers and white oxen."[2]

COMMENTARY

Nanquan is an unparalleled teacher of our school. He acts unasked, and in a single phrase knows how to kill and give life. In one action, he is able to roll it out and roll it in.

If you wish to understand the body of reality, don't look to ideas and descriptions. Don't look to buddhas of the past, present, or future for the truth. You must see for yourself. What's here now? Don't you see? Each particle of food in the bowl is tasty; each drop of water in the spring is wet.

CAPPING VERSE

I don't know much about history,
    don't know much about philosophy.
I only know the cool breeze
    rising in my sleeves.

NOTES

1. Not knowing is always most intimate.
2. I see that which is creating; I see that which is destroying.

294 ∾
Xuefeng's "Mirror-Backed Monkeys"

MAIN CASE

Xuefeng, while traveling with Sansheng, saw a herd of monkeys and said, "Each of these monkeys carries an ancient mirror [on its back]."[1]

Sansheng said, "The vast kalpa has no name. How come you bring out ancient mirrors?"[2]

Xuefeng said, "It has a scratch now."[3]

Sansheng said, "Fifteen hundred teachers would not understand your talk."[4]

Xuefeng said, "This old monastic is busy with abbot's work."[5]

COMMENTARY

After Linji's passing, Sansheng traveled about testing his understanding. Xuefeng, too, wants to test him, saying, "Each of these monkeys carries an ancient mirror." Sansheng's "The vast kalpa has no name. How come you bring out ancient mirrors?" misses having today, so Xuefeng calls it a scratch. We should understand that the cause of the scratch, and the scratch itself, are both the ancient mirror.

Sansheng does not approve, and holds fast. Xuefeng lets it go; he knows clearly that this old monastic's practice is just "this old monastic." But say, how about you? How do you see these venerable old teachers? Where will you find the ancient mirror? After all, there is no living thing that lacks it.

CAPPING VERSE

Wonderful! Marvelous! The ancient mirror
    transmitted from buddha to buddha.
Seer and the seen, reflector and the reflected,
    are one reality, actualized in all things.

NOTES

1. He probes with a sword.
2. Ancient mirror! Ancient mirror!
3. Even so, it's still the ancient mirror.
4. Indeed, maybe one or two at best.
5. I'm like this. You can go away now.

295 ᴏᴡ
Yunmen's Treasure

MAIN CASE

Yunmen said to the assembly, "In the universe, there is a treasure that is hidden in this heap of flesh.[1] It holds up the lantern and goes inside the buddha hall.[2] It brings the monastery gate to the top of the lantern."[3]

COMMENTARY

Although you may understand Yunmen's "It holds up the lantern and goes inside the buddha hall," the question is, how do you understand "It brings the monastery gate to the top of the lantern"? It just cannot be discussed. It is here that Yunmen demonstrates his skill at shattering intellection and dualities. He pulls out the nails, kicks out the wedges, and lets the whole construct collapse. Only then does the wonder of the mystery remain. We should enter here.

An old master once said, "The spiritual light shines alone, far transcending the senses." Yunmen has snatched the senses away for you. Are you willing to trust and enter the mystery? Real teachers of our school don't just present Buddhist principles and doctrines; they cut away the complications. Don't you see? Self-nature is buddha nature. The true nature of ignorance is at once Buddhahood; the illusion of the pure body is in itself the Dharmakāya. The question remains, where do you find yourself?

CAPPING VERSE

A frosty autumn moon
    floats golden on the pond.
Quiet night, the fish are cold,
    hook and bait, useless.

NOTES

1. The heap of red flesh is itself the treasure.
2. Easy to do, difficult to understand.
3. Easy to understand, difficult to do.

296 ౿

Fayan's "Sound and Form"

MAIN CASE

Fayan was once asked by a monastic, "How can we pass beyond sound and form?"[1]

Fayan said to the assembly, "If all of you can understand the meaning of this monastic's question, it will not be difficult for you to pass beyond sound and form."[2]

COMMENTARY

This monastic's question is not a casual one. Having heard of Xiangyan's enlightenment on hearing the sound of a pebble striking bamboo, and Lingyun's on seeing a peach blossom, he is asking how we can pass beyond the objective reality that is perceived by the sense organs and enter the realm of intimacy with sound and form.

Fayan, in pointing to the monastic's question, is saying that seeing form with the whole body and mind, hearing sounds with the whole body and mind, and understanding them intimately is nothing other than just see-ing, just hearing, just standing, and sitting—the moment-to-moment di-rect experience of our lives. Do you understand? If so, then tell me, does the sound come to the ear, or does the ear go to the sound? Does the form come to the eye, or does the eye go to the form? If you can see into it here, then I will concur that you have heard the sound of the stringless lute.

CAPPING VERSE

Going beyond sound and form
    is not a matter of this and that.
Mountains and rivers are not seen in a mirror—
    where one side is illuminated and the other is dark.

NOTES

1. The sound of rain is wet through and through. Blue mountains are blue through and through.
2. He lights a lamp in the darkness for them. Still, so many people are at a loss when they get here.

297 ᴄⱱ

Longya's Stone Tortoise

MAIN CASE

Longya was once asked by a monastic, "What is the meaning of the Ancestor's [Bodhidharma's] coming from India?"[1]

Longya said, "I will tell you when the stone tortoise speaks."[2]

COMMENTARY

In answer to this same question, Dongshan said, "Wait until the Dong Creek flows backward—then I'll tell you." Yantou said, "If you move Mount Lu, I'll tell you." Cuiwei said, "Wait until nobody is here, and I will tell you." Shitou said, "Ask the pillar." We should examine carefully these responses. Are they all avoiding the question, or has it indeed been answered each time?

When Longya was a student, he carried the same question to three different masters. He was hit by two of them in response to this and said, "Since you hit me, I let you hit me. In essence, though, there is no meaning of the Ancestor's coming from India." Later when he was told by Dongshan, "Wait until the Dong Creek flows backward—then I'll tell you," it is said that Longya for the first time realized its meaning. Is this what he is saying when he says, "I will tell you when the stone tortoise speaks"?

We should investigate Longya's words. Since the speaking of a stone tortoise is inconceivable, can it be said that the meaning of the Ancestor's coming is also inconceivable? Or is he saying that when you can hear the voice of the stone tortoise, you will know the meaning of the Ancestor's coming?

But say, how do you hear the voice of the stone tortoise?

CAPPING VERSE

East Mountain moves over water;
    the stone woman gives birth to a child in the night.
Outstanding, awesome—
    the teachings of the insentient.

If you listen with the ear, you will never get it;
when you hear with the eye, everything is clear and undisguised.

NOTES

1. It's too bad that this question still needs asking.
2. It's too bad that this question still needs answering.

298 ❧

Baofu's "The Tathāgata's Expression"

MAIN CASE

Changqing once said, "I would rather say that arhats have three types of poison than say that the Tathāgata [Śākyamuni Buddha] has two kinds of expression.[1] It's not that the Tathāgata has no expression.[2] It is just that he does not have two kinds of expression."[3]

Baofu Congzhan asked, "What is the Tathāgata's expression?"[4]
Changqing asked, "How can a deaf person hear it?"[5]
Baofu said, "I knew you were speaking on a secondary level."[6]
Changqing said, "Then what is the Tathāgata's expression?"[7]
Baofu said, "Have a cup of tea."[8]

COMMENTARY

The saṃgha of Xuefeng is like this, always probing and testing each other to refine their understanding. Changqing drags out the arhats to make the point that the World-Honored One, in more than three hundred assemblies, dispensed medicine thousands of different ways in a single voice. Baofu suspects some sticking taking place, so he wants to loosen it up. He asks, "What is the Tathāgata's expression?" When Changqing answers, "How can a deaf person hear it?" it is clear that this is a voice from the ghost cave. Baofu calls it, saying, "I knew you were speaking on a secondary level." Although Changqing slips and falls, he still knows how to ask, "What is the Tathāgata's expression?" Baofu says, "Have a cup of tea." If at this point you think that this has settled the case, or that Changqing is wrong and

Baofu is right, then you are a million miles from the truth. To avoid making a living in stagnant water, you should first understand that this matter, in its entirety, is not only a matter of the donkey looking at the well and the well looking at the donkey but also of the well looking at the well and the donkey looking at the donkey. If you want to understand the Tathāgata's expression, then see into it here.

CAPPING VERSE

The moon and the pointing finger
    are a single reality.
Aside from painted cakes,
    there is no other way to satisfy hunger.

NOTES

1. He does not yet know it at this point, but he is digging his own pitfall.
2. Where did he hear about this? This is the first indication that something is amiss here.
3. He seems to be walking in circles.
4. It's difficult to avoid taking a shot at him.
5. He makes it sound as if there are two things. Can you see it?
6. He makes it sound as if there are two things. Can you see it?
7. He doesn't just pontificate; he also knows how to inquire.
8. Got it! Did you get it?

299 ଓ
Wuxie Turns His Head

MAIN CASE

Wuxie Lingmo went to study with Shitou and said, "If one phrase is merged, I will stay. If not, I will go away."[1]

Shitou did not pay attention.[2]

Wuxie flapped his sleeves and walked away.[3]
When he got to the monastery gate, Shitou called out, "Ācārya!"[4]
Wuxie turned his head.[5]
Shitou said, "From birth till death, just this.[6] How come you turned your head?"[7]
Wuxie was merged with realization.[8]

COMMENTARY

Wuxie arrives at the great master Shitou's place with an attitude—his student's mind is not yet open. Shitou compassionately ignores him, but alas, Wuxie cannot let the teaching in. Flapping his sleeves, he turns and leaves in disdain. Shitou lets him get as far as the monastery gate and then calls out, "Ācārya!" Having been called, Wuxie has to turn his head, and Shitou's "From birth till death, just this" closes the gap.

Although Wuxie has seen something, he is not yet fully illuminated. Shitou does not wait for him to ask for more instruction but strikes while he is still reeling from his insight. The single question "How come you turned your head?" settles the uncertainty.

I ask you, what is Shitou's intent in ignoring Wuxie? What is the significance of Wuxie's turning when called, and what is "From birth until death, just this"? If you can say a turning word, I will grant that you, too, have merged with realization.

CAPPING VERSE

Among the myriad forms, a single reality.
    Only when one sees it for oneself is it real.
Silence, rather than clamor, is the way of the Zen school—
    endless kinds of clever talk only describe it.

NOTES

1. He arrives carrying a huge burden. What do you want with so many views?
2. A thunderclap.
3. Wrong! He missed it because it did not fit his expectations.

4. Why call him? Let him go on like this for the rest of his life.
5. Wrong! But then, he must know something is missing.
6. Vast billowing waves cover heaven and earth.
7. At first he just toyed with this monastic, now he has clutched him by the throat.
8. No gaps.

300 ∾
Linji's "Ordinary or Sacred"

MAIN CASE

Linji visited an army camp for a meal. Seeing a staff officer at the gate, he pointed to a pillar and said, "Is this ordinary or sacred?"[1]

The staff officer was silent.[2]

Linji hit the pillar and said, "Even if you could say something, this is just a piece of sandalwood."[3] Then he went in.

COMMENTARY

When people encounter the double barrier of ordinary and sacred, many falter and get mired in complications. Staff Officer Yuanliao is a student of Linji's. Yuanliao knows enough to see where he is going with his question, and is stopped dead in his tracks. Do you see where Linji is going?

The ancients have used pillars to prop up the teachings since time immemorial, and Zen practitioners through the years have made them a nesting place. Linji wants to shake the tree and loosen the nest, so he points to a pillar and asks, "Is this ordinary or sacred?" If you can understand it the instant it is uttered, you are free and unhindered. But if you hesitate, you have fallen into the pit of brambles. Yuanliao hesitates. He is enough of an adept to see Linji's pitfall but not enough of an adept to leap free of it. Say a word for Yuanliao.

Linji hits the pillar and says, "Even if you could say something, this is just a piece of sandalwood." Too bad Linji is so talkative. In the end, they both fall in the same pit. Do you understand?

CAPPING VERSE

When affirmation and negation have merged,
　　there is no way to speak of it.
The truth of ordinary and sacred, wherever it is encountered,
　　is, after all, in your hands alone.

NOTES

1. Many people are at a loss when they get here.
2. Was he silent or dumbfounded? Either way, he still missed it.
3. Alas! His tongue fell to the ground and he tripped over it.

Appendix A
Cross-References to Kana Shōbōgenzō *and Other Dōgen Texts*

The purpose of this appendix is twofold: first, it shows the kōans that appeared in the classical kōan collections of Song China and were thereafter collected by Dōgen as part of his three hundred kōans. Second, it demonstrates where Dōgen used the three hundred kōans in his other writings—most notably in the *Kana Shōbōgenzō* (ninety-five-fascicle version) and *Eihei Kōroku* (nine volumes). The kōans, listed by number in column one, are cross-referenced in three sections, as described below.

Column 2: The three traditional kōan collections from Song China; the abbreviation of a Song source title is followed by the kōan number in that particular collection—for example, case 6 appears in the *Book of Serenity* as case 100, so it is listed here as BOS 100. Text abbreviations are given in the section "Song Kōan Collections" below.

Column 3: Kana Shōbōgenzō fascicles; the numbering follows Gudo Nishijima and Chodo Cross's four-volume translation—for example, case 1 is mentioned in fascicle 24, "Bukkyo"; it is listed here as 24. Names of individual fascicles are listed in "*Kana Shōbōgenzō* Fascicle Titles" below; the English translations are by Andrew Hōbai Pekarik.

Column 4: Eihei Kōroku and *Shōbōgenzō Zuimonki;* listed by volume number and the section (in parentheses) in which the kōan appears—for example, *Eihei Kōroku* volume 9, section 44 is listed as EK 9 (44); *Shōbōgenzō Zuimonki,* volume 2 section 24 is SZ 2 (24). For items that appear in volume 8 of the *Eihei Kōroku,* the reference also indicates whether the type of talk was *hōgo* (dharma words) or *shōsan* (dharma encounter). Text abbreviations are listed in the section "Other Dōgen Texts" below.

References that appear in bold indicate that a case is quoted in its entirety. All others indicate a brief or indirect mention of the kōan. A line indicates that the kōan is not mentioned at all. For example, case 23, "Yang-shan's 'High and Low,'" does not appear in the Song kōan collections; is mentioned in fascicles 34 and 61 of the *Kana Shōbōgenzō*; is mentioned in volume 4, section 273 of the *Eihei Kōroku*; is quoted in its entirety in *Eihei Kōroku*, volume 9, section 66; and is mentioned in the *Chiji Shingi* and *Tenzokyōkun*.

The sources used as references are as follows:

> *The Blue Cliff Record*, translated by Thomas Cleary and J. C. Cleary.
> *Book of Serenity*, translated by Thomas Cleary.
> *The Gateless Gate*, translated by Zenkei Shibayama.
> *Shōbōgenzō* (Four Volumes), translated by Gudo Nishijima and
>   Chodo Cross.
> *Eihei Kōroku* and *Eihei Shingi*, translated by Dan Taigen Leighton and
>   Shohaku Okumura.
> *Shōbōgenzō Zuimonki*, translated by Rev. Shōhaku Okumura.

Abbreviations for Cross-Referenced Texts:

Song Kōan Collections

BCR   *Blue Cliff Record*
BOS   *Book of Serenity*
GG   *Gateless Gate*

Other Dōgen Texts

EK   *Eihei Kōroku (The Extensive Record of Eihei Dōgen)*
FK   *Fukanzazengi (Universal Recommendations for Zazen)*
SZ   *Shōbōgenzō Zuimonki (Sayings of Eihei Dōgen Zenji)*

From the *Eihei Shingi* (Dōgen's Pure Standards for the Zen Community)

BH   *Bendōhō (The Model for Engaging the Way)*
CS   *Chiji Shingi (Pure Standards for the Temple Administrators)*
TK   *Tenzokyōkun (Instructions to the Cook)*

Kana Shōbōgenzō *Fascicle Titles*

1. *Bendōwa*—A Talk on Practicing the Way
2. *Maka hannya haramita*—The Practice of Great Wisdom
3. *Genjōkōan*—Realizing the Teaching
4. *Ikka myōju*—One Bright Pearl
5. *Jū'undoshiki*—Rules for the Hall of Additional Monks
6. *Sokushin zebutsu*—Mind Itself Is Buddha
7. *Senjō*—Washing and Purifying
8. *Raihai tokuzui*—Prostrating and Receiving the Marrow
9. *Keisei sanshoku*—Sounds of the Valley Streams, Forms of the Mountains
10. *Shoaku makusa*—Not Creating Evil
11. *Uji*—Existence and Time
12. *Kesa kudoku*—The Merit of the Robe
13. *Den'e*—Transmitting the Robe
14. *Sansuikyō* Mountains and Rivers Sūtra
15. *Busso*—Buddhas and Ancestors
16. *Shisho*—Document of Transmission
17. *Hokke tenhokke*—The Dharma-Flower Engages the Dharma-Flower
18. *Shinfukatoku*—Mind Cannot Be Grasped (The Former)
19. *Shinfukatoku*—Mind Cannot Be Grasped (The Latter)
20. *Kokyo*—The Ancient Mirror
21. *Kankin*—Reading Sūtras
22. *Busshō*—Buddha Nature
23. *Gyōbutsu igi*—The Way of Life of Practicing Buddhas
24. *Bukkyō*—Teachings of the Buddha
25. *Jinzū*—Mystical Power
26. *Daigo*—Great Enlightenment
27. *Zazenshin*—The Needle of Zazen
28. *Butsu kōjōji*—Transcending Buddhahood
29. *Inmo*—Suchness
30. *Gyōji 1*—Ceaseless Practice
    Gyōji 2—Ceaseless Practice
31. *Kaiin zammai*—Ocean-Sealed Samādhi
32. *Juki*—The Promise of Buddhahood

Cross-References

KŌAN	SŌNG SOURCES	KANA SHŌBŌGENZŌ FASCICLES	OTHER DŌGEN TEXTS
1.	—	24	EK 3 (212), 9 (18)
2.	—	—	EK 2 (131), 6 (423), 9 (44)
3.	—	—	EK 2 (175)
4.	—	73, 77	—
5.	—	—	—
6.	BOS 100	9, 36	EK 9 (46)
7.	BOS 62	26	EK 9 (47)
8.	—	20, 27, 44, 73	EK 4 (270), (281), (345), 6 (453), 7 (499), 9 (38), SZ 2 (22)
9.	—	30(1)	EK 8 (14-hōgo), 9 (48)
10.	—	—	EK 9 (49)
11.	—	—	EK 9 (43)
12.	—	28	EK 9 (50)
13.	—	25, 42	EK 3 (189), 9 (17)
14.	—	91	EK 9 (40)
15.	—	4, 20, 23, 60	EK 1 (107), 9 (41)
16.	—	9	EK 9 (42)
17.	—	20, 30(1), 68, 75	EK 6 (441), (457), 8 (2-hōgo), 9 (62); SZ 2 (26), 4 (5)
18.	—	30(1)	EK 4 (267), 9 (63)
19.	GG 19	22, 25, A1	EK 4 (292); SZ 2 (14)
20.	—	22	EK 4 (328), 9 (65)
21.	—	—	EK 9 (67)
22.	—	20, 27, 31	—
23.	—	34, 61	EK 4 (273), 9 (66), CS, TK
24.	BCR 29, BOS 30	73	EK 9 (83)
25.	—	—	—

(continued)

KŌAN	SŌNG SOURCES	KANA SHŌBŌGENZŌ FASCICLES	OTHER DŌGEN TEXTS
26.	BCR 99	38, 62	—
27.	BOS 86	49, 52	EK 2 (160), 7 (493), 8 (hōgo: 2, 11), 9 (51)
28.	—	65	—
29.	—	—	EK 2 (161), CS
30.	—	—	—
31.	—	25	—
32.	—	—	—
33.	—	29, 43	—
34.	—	51	—
35.	—	—	EK 9 (54)
36.	—	—	—
37.	GG 48, BOS 61	60	—
38.	—	4, 33, 73	EK 3 (228)
39.	—	22	EK 1 (32)
40.	—	—	—
41.	—	22, 37	EK 5 (356)
42.	—	—	—
43.	—	—	—
44.	—	—	—
45.	—	24, 52, 68	EK 4 (291)
46.	BCR 9	47	EK 9 (21)
47.	—	—	—
48.	—	—	—
49.	—	—	—
50.	—	—	—

(continued)

KŌAN	SŌNG SOURCES	*KANA SHŌBŌGENZŌ* FASCICLES	OTHER DŌGEN TEXTS
51.	—	—	EK 4 (313)
52.	BCR 49, BOS 33	20	—
53.	—	—	—
54.	—	—	EK 1 (50), 8 (11-hōgo), 9 (82)
55.	BOS 98	25, 40, 62	—
56.	—	—	—
57.	—	A1	EK 9 (61)
58.	—	22, 23, 27, 32	—
59.	—	23, 32, 38, 61	EK 3 (212), 8 (3-hōgo)
60.	—	32, 37, 60, 69	—
61.	—	25, 52, 55, 73	EK 1 (17), 5 (394)
62.	—	48	—
63.	—	—	—
64.	—	55, 81	—
65.	—	—	TK
66.	—	—	—
67.	GG 7, BOS 39	—	EK 3 (210), 6 (436)
68.	BOS 15	—	—
69.	—	—	—
70.	—	30(2), 54, 60, 64, 75	—
71.	—	40, 60	EK 9 (36)
72.	—	28	—
73.	—	—	—
74.	—	21	—
75.	—	31	—
76.	—	—	—

(continued)

KŌAN	SŌNG SOURCES	*KANA SHŌBŌGENZŌ* FASCICLES	OTHER DŌGEN TEXTS
77.	—	30(1), 73	EK 1 (10), 7 (498)
78.	—	—	—
79.	BOS 7	21	EK 7 (492), 8 (15-shōsan)
80.	—	—	SZ 5 (20)
81.	BCR 86	23, 36, 43	EK 1 (97)
82.	BOS 89	23, 79	EK 2 (130), 4 (274), 8 (6-shōsan)
83.	BOS 21	42, 63, 73	EK 4 (277), (344), 7 (521), 9 (12)
84.	—	—	—
85.	—	—	—
86.	—	—	—
87.	BOS 23	—	EK 9 (79)
88.	—	22, 32, 36, 38, A1	EK 1 (9), 4 (296), (329), 9 (9), CS
89.	—	—	—
90.	—	14, 38	EK 4 (277), 8 (8-hōgo), 9 (10, 22, 28)
91.	—	—	EK 1 (12)
92.	—	—	—
93.	—	—	—
94.	—	—	—
95.	BCR 14 and 15	—	—
96.	—	22, 25, 56, 64, 69, 73, 77	—
97.	—	—	—
98.	BOS 94	—	—

(continued)

KŌAN	SŌNG SOURCES	*KANA SHŌBŌGENZŌ* FASCICLES	OTHER DŌGEN TEXTS
99.	—	—	—
100.	—	—	—
101.	—	1, 7, 14, 20, 22, 23, 24, 25, 29, 30(1), 30(2), 32, 35, 36, 37, 40, 51, 52, 54, **62**, 69, 75, 77, 91, A1	EK 1 (3), 4 (301), 5 (374), 7 (490), (497), (523), 8 (shōsan: 13, 17), 9 (59)
102.	GG 2, BOS 8	8, 23, 34, 73, **76, 89**	EK 1 (62), (80), (94), 3 (205), (212), 5 (402), 7 (482), (510), 9 (77); SZ 1 (6)
103.	—	—	—
104.	GG 28	18	EK 9 (24)
105.	BCR 89, BOS 54	31, **33**, 38, 41, 42, 50, 53, 60, 73, 76, 91	EK 3 (200)
106.	—	—	EK 9 (55)
107.	BOS 11	—	—
108.	BCR 73, BOS 6	—	EK 2 (135), 3 (206), 7 (497), 9 (78)
109.	—	20	7 (528)
110.	—	—	—
111.	—	20	—
112.	—	23, 37, 44, 47	EK 6 (415), 9 (2)
113.	—	—	—
114.	GG 1, BOS 18	22, 73	EK 3 (226), 4 (330), 6 (429), 9 (73)
115.	—	22	EK 9 (39)
116.	—	20	EK 5 (411)
117.	—	20	—

(continued)

KŌAN	SŌNG SOURCES	*KANA SHŌBŌGENZŌ* FASCICLES	OTHER DŌGEN TEXTS
118.	—	—	—
119.	GG 37, BOS 47	35, 37	EK 1 (64), 6 (433), 7 (488), (520), 8 (9-shōsan), 9 (45)
120.	BOS 70	—	EK 1 (101)
121.	—	—	SZ 6 (7)
122.	—	1	EK 1 (15), 4 (299), 6 (462), CS
123.	—	3	—
124.	—	—	EK 9 (70)
125.	BOS 52	10, 33, 42, 73, A1	EK 4 (345), 5 (403)
126.	—	—	—
127.	BCR 35	22, 42, 43, 5/, /6	—
128.	—	33	—
129.	—	27, 37, 58, 67, 73, 79	BH, EK 4 (270), 5 (373), (389), 7 (524), FK
130.	BOS 37	73	EK 4 (306)
131.	—	37, 43, 46, 47, 50, 62, 73, 91	EK 9 (37)
132.	—	—	—
133.	GG 31, BOS 10	—	—
134.	—	—	—
135.	—	27, 37, 73	—
136.	BCR 41, BOS 63	—	—
137.	—	—	EK 1 (84), 5 (408)
138.	—	—	—
139.	—	61	—
140.	—	—	—

(continued)

KŌAN	SŌNG SOURCES	*KANA SHŌBŌGENZŌ* FASCICLES	OTHER DŌGEN TEXTS
141.	BCR 92, BOS 1	—	EK 3 (254)
142.	—	—	—
143.	—	64	EK 9 (57)
144.	—	—	—
145.	—	18	—
146.	GG 29	8, 29	EK 6 (430), 9 (8)
147.	BOS 38	43, 48	EK 4 (317)
148.	—	9, 53	EK 6 (452), 9 (52)
149.	—	—	—
150.	—	11	—
151.	—	—	—
152.	—	—	—
153.	—	—	—
154.	—	14	EK 8 (3-hōgo), 9 (81)
155.	—	9, 38, 68, 74, 75	EK 4 (308), (317), 6 (421), (441), 6 (457), 9 (72); SZ 2 (26), 4 (5)
156.	—	10, 11, 17, 73	EK 5 (390), (399), 9 (29)
157.	BOS 87	22, 23	—
158.	BCR 50, BOS 99	—	EK 5 (401), 6 (416)
159.	BCR 99	—	—
160.	—	—	—
161.	—	—	—
162.	—	—	—
163.	—	—	—
164.	—	—	—
165.	—	—	—

(continued)

KŌAN	SŌNG SOURCES	*KANA SHŌBŌGENZŌ* FASCICLES	OTHER DŌGEN TEXTS
166.	—	—	—
167.	BOS 13	49	—
168.	—	6, 37	SZ 1 (6)
169.	GG 22	46	EK 1 (11), 3 (252), 8 (4-hōgo)
170.	GG 32, BCR 65	85	—
171.	BOS 20	—	EK 1 (59), 9 (16)
172.	GG 18, BCR 12	—	EK 9 (68), TK, SZ 4 (5)
173.	—	36	—
174.	—	—	—
175.	—	—	—
176.	—	—	—
177.	BOS 64	—	—
178.	—	—	—
179.	—	—	—
180.	BOS 75	—	—
181.	GG 14, BCR 63 & 64, BOS 9	—	EK 9 (76), SZ 1 (6)
182.	BCR 53	—	—
183.	—	39, 73	EK 9 (71)
184.	—	—	—
185.	BOS 93	—	—
186.	BCR 44	—	—
187.	—	—	—
188.	—	—	—
189.	—	—	—
190.	—	—	—

(continued)

KŌAN	SŌNG SOURCES	*KANA SHŌBŌGENZŌ* FASCICLES	OTHER DŌGEN TEXTS
191.	—	28	EK 1 (22)
192.	—	A1	—
193.	—	—	—
194.	—	31	—
195.	—	—	—
196.	—	—	—
197.	—	—	—
198.	—	—	—
199.	—	—	—
200.	—	—	—
201.	—	8, 9, 12, 13, 14, 16, 19, 21, 22, 23, 26, 27, 31, 32, 34, 36, 37, 38, 39, 44, **46**, 47, 48, 49, 50, 52, 53, 57, 59, 60, 61, 62, 68, 69, 75, 77, 79, 80, 81	EK 1 (**46**), (80), 4 (304), (317), 5 (349), (395), 6 (445), 7 (486), 8 (hōgo: 11, 14)
202.	BCR 11, BOS 53	—	EK 1 (125), 4 (301)
203.	BCR 88	—	EK 9 (34)
204.	BOS 59	21	—
205.	BCR 20, BOS 80	—	—
206.	—	—	—
207.	—	—	—
208.	—	79	EK 4 (292), 8 (6-shōsan)
209.	—	—	EK 3 (234), 4 (274), **9 (69)**, TK
210.	BOS 42	—	—

(continued)

KŌAN	SŌNG SOURCES	*KANA SHŌBŌGENZŌ* FASCICLES	OTHER DŌGEN TEXTS
211.	—	—	—
212.	BOS 12	—	EK 6 (425)
213.	—	—	—
214.	BCR 61, BOS 34	10	—
215.	—	—	—
216.	BOS 95	—	—
217.	—	8, 42	—
218.	—	—	EK 9 (15)
219.	—	—	—
220.	—	—	—
221.	—	50	—
222.	—	—	EK 4 (345)
223.	—	73	EK 1 (11), 8 (5-hōgo)
224.	—	—	—
225.	BCR 43	66	EK 9 (74)
226.	—	—	—
227.	—	—	—
228.	BOS 49	—	EK 7 (494)
229.	—	—	—
230.	—	—	—
231.	—	—	—
232.	—	—	—
233.	—	64	EK 5 (380), 6 (428), (455), 7 (499), (522), 8 (7-shōsan)
234.	—	—	—
235.	—	—	—

(continued)

KŌAN	SŌNG SOURCES	*KANA SHŌBŌGENZŌ* FASCICLES	OTHER DŌGEN TEXTS
236.	—	—	—
237.	—	—	EK 4 (301), 9 (19)
238.	—	—	—
239.	—	19, 62, 69	EK 4 (339)
240.	—	—	—
241.	—	50	—
242.	—	—	—
243.	GG 5	67	EK 9 (87)
244.	—	33	—
245.	GG 3, BCR 19, BOS 84	62	EK 3 (211), 8 (hōgo: 5, 11, 14), SZ 4 (4)
246.	—	—	—
247.	GG 12	35	—
248.	—	68, 73, 74, 77	EK 4 (258), 9 (53)
249.	GG 27, BCR 28	—	EK 4 (292)
250.	—	—	—
251.	—	—	—
252.	BCR 7	—	EK 9 (84)
253.	GG 6	9, 11, 18, 22, 32, 37, 38, 43, 46, 47, 48, 49, 50, 51, 52, 53, 57, 59, 61, 64, 67, 68, 73, 75, 81	EK 1 (80), (89), 3 (257), 4 (317), (334), 5 (349), (395), 6 (428), (441), (445), (458), 7 (486), (488)
254.	BOS 74	—	—
255.	—	—	—
256.	—	—	—
257.	BOS 82	33	EK 1 (123)

(continued)

KŌAN	SŌNG SOURCES	KANA SHŌBŌGENZŌ FASCICLES	OTHER DŌGEN TEXTS
258.	—	—	—
259.	—	—	—
260.	—	—	EK 9 (56)
261.	—	—	—
262.	—	—	—
263.	—	—	—
264.	—	—	—
265.	—	—	—
266.	—	—	CS
267.	—	—	—
268.	—	—	—
269.	GG 43	24	—
270.	—	—	—
271.	—	—	—
272.	—	—	—
273.	—	—	—
274.	—	—	—
275.	—	—	—
276.	—	—	—
277.	BOS 57	—	—
278.	GG 30	30(1), 50, 81	EK 1(8), 4 (319), (323), 5 (354), (365), 8 (9-hōgo), 9 (75), SZ 1 (6)
279.	—	—	—
280.	GG 15	—	—
281.	GG 11	22	—

(continued)

KŌAN	SŌNG SOURCES	*KANA SHŌBŌGENZŌ* FASCICLES	OTHER DŌGEN TEXTS
282.	—	73	EK 1 (114)
283.	—	35, 44, 46	—
284.	BCR 98	—	—
285.	—	—	—
286.	BCR 46	—	EK 1 (39)
287.	—	23, 63	—
288.	—	—	EK 2 (140), 4 (331)
289.	BCR 55	—	CS
290.	—	36, 73	EK 6 (454)
291.	—	—	—
292.	—	—	EK 9 (35)
293.	BOS 69	23, 73	EK 2 (161), 4 (309)
294.	—	20	—
295.	BCR 62, BOS 92	37	—
296.	—	—	EK 1 (52)
297.	—	—	—
298.	BCR 95	—	EK 9 (64)
299.	—	73	EK 9 (31)
300.	—	37	—

Appendix B
Lineage Charts

Bodhidharma and the Early Chinese Zen Ancestors

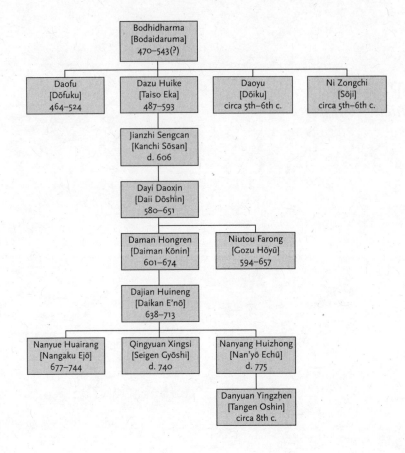

Guiyang (Igyō) School

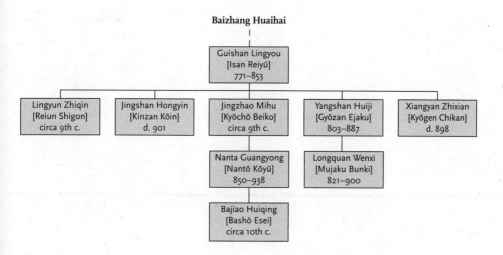

Hunan (Konan) School and Its Descendants

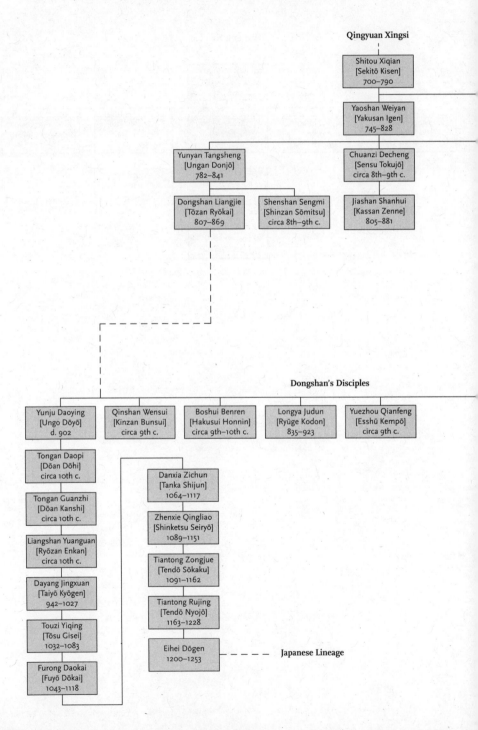

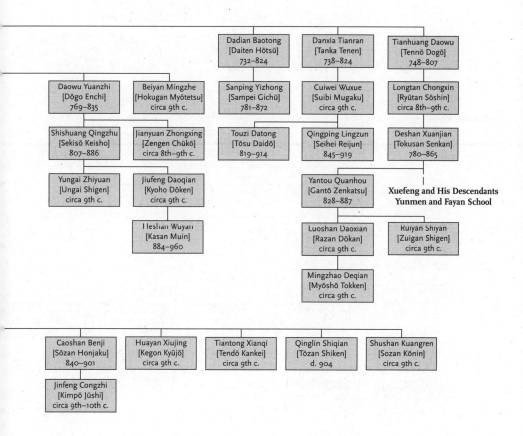

Caodong [Sōtō] School

Hongzhou (Kōshū) School and Its Descendants

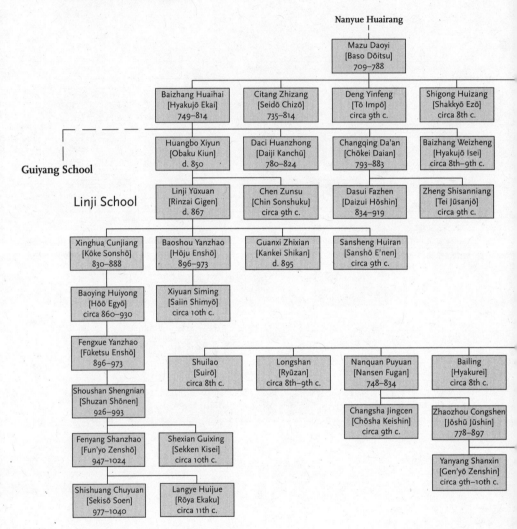

Mazu's Disciples

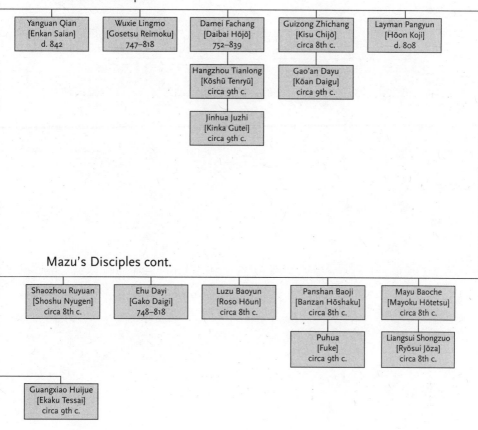

Yanguan Qian
[Enkan Saian]
d. 842

Wuxie Lingmo
[Gosetsu Reimoku]
747–818

Damei Fachang
[Daibai Hōjō]
752–839

Guizong Zhichang
[Kisu Chijō]
circa 8th c.

Layman Pangyun
[Hōon Koji]
d. 808

Hangzhou Tianlong
[Kōshū Tenryū]
circa 9th c.

Gao'an Dayu
[Kōan Daigu]
circa 9th c.

Jinhua Juzhi
[Kinka Gutei]
circa 9th c.

Mazu's Disciples cont.

Shaozhou Ruyuan
[Shoshu Nyugen]
circa 8th c.

Ehu Dayi
[Gako Daigi]
748–818

Luzu Baoyun
[Roso Hōun]
circa 8th c.

Panshan Baoji
[Banzan Hōshaku]
circa 8th c.

Mayu Baoche
[Mayoku Hōtetsu]
circa 8th c.

Puhua
[Fuke]
circa 9th c.

Liangsui Shongzuo
[Ryōsui Jōza]
circa 8th c.

Guangxiao Huijue
[Ekaku Tessai]
circa 9th c.

Xuefeng (Seppō) and His Descendants
Yunmen School and Fayan School

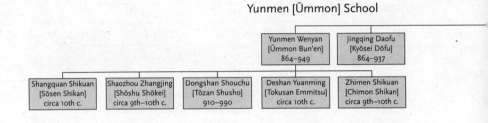

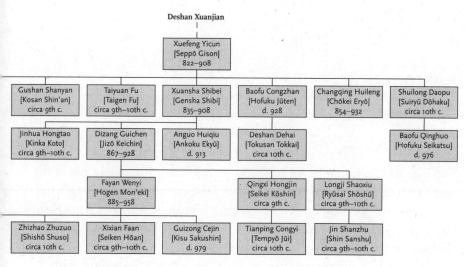

Fayan [Hogen] School

Biographical Notes

This list includes the names of Buddhist masters (mostly Chinese and Japanese) and deities such as Avalokiteśvara Bodhisattva (Kannon), and the cases in which they appear. Names appear first in Sanskrit (if available), then Pinyin, with the Wade-Giles and Japanese spellings in parentheses. Chinese provinces are also in parentheses.

Masters commonly took the name of the monastery, town, or mountain where they taught. Therefore, Cunjiang of Xinhua Monastery would be listed as Xinhua Cunjang. In rare cases where the master's posthumous name is well known, this name is used in the main case as well.

Ānanda (A-nan-t'o; Ānanda). He was the Buddha's cousin and one of his most important disciples. He was known for his extraordinary memory, by virtue of which he retained all the Buddha's discourses. Cases 169, 170, 174.

Anguo Huiqiu (An-kuo Hui-ch'iu; Ankoku Ekyū; d. 913; also called Wolong [Lying Dragon]). Dharma heir of Xuansha Shibei. Taught at Anguo Monastery, Mount Wolong, Fu Region (Fujian). Case 131.

Avalokiteśvara (Kuanyin; K'uan-yin; Kannon). Bodhisattva of compassion, sometimes described as having one thousand hands and eyes. Her name means "One who hears the sounds [of the sufferings of the world]." Cases 105, 128, 242, 244, 257.

Bailing (Pai-ling; Hyakurei; ca. eighth century). Dharma heir of Mazu Daoyi. Case 153.

Baizhang Huaihai (Pai-chang Huai-hai; Hyakujō Ekai; 749–814). Dharma heir of Mazu Daoyi. Founder of Dazhi Shousheng Monastery, Mount

Baizhang, Hong Region (Jiangxi). He was the initiator of monastic regulations for Chinese Zen. Cases 2, 54, 102, 108, 110, 118, 128, 182, 267, 268, 271.

Baizhang Weizheng (Pai-chang Wei-cheng; Hyakujō Isei; ca. eighth to ninth century). Dharma heir of Baizhang Huaihai. He was called Priest Nirvāṇa, as he was always chanting the *Nirvāṇa Sūtra*. Case 249.

Bajiao Huiqing (Pa-chiao Hui-ch'ing; Bashō Esei; ca. tenth century). Dharma heir of Nanta Guanyong. Taught at Mount Bajiao, Ying Region (Hubei). Case 259.

Baoen Xuanze (Pao-en Hsüan-tse; Hoon Gensoku; ca. ninth to tenth century). Dharma heir of Fayan Wenyi. Taught at Baoen Monastery, Jinling (Jiangsu). Cases 25, 122.

Baofu Congzhan (Pao-fu Ts'ung-chang; Hofuku Jūten; d. 928). Dharma heir of Xuefeng Yicun. Founded Baofu Monastery, Zhang Region (Fujian). Cases 113, 192, 290, 298.

Baofu Qinghuo (Pao-fu Ch'ing-huo; Hofuku Seikatsu; d. 976). Dharma heir of Shuilong Daopu. Taught at Baofu Monastery, Zhang Region (Fujian). Case 63.

Baoshou Yanzhao (Pao-shou Yen-chao; Hōju Enshō; 896–973). Dharma heir of Linji Yixuan. Taught at Baoshou Monastery, Zhen Region (Hebei). Case 40.

Baoying Huiyong (Pao-ying Hui-yung; Hōō Egyō; ca. 860–930). Dharma heir of Xinghua Cunjiang. Taught at Baoying Monastery, Ru Region (Henan). Case 264.

Beiyan Mingzhe (Pei-yen Ming-che; Hokugan Myōtetsu; ca. ninth century). Dharma heir of Yaoshan Weiyan. Taught at Beiyan, E Region (Hebei). Case 220.

Bodhidharma (P'u-t'i-ta-mo; Bodaidaruma; 470–543[?]). Dharma heir of Prajñadhāra (Hannyatara) and the First Ancestor of Chinese Zen. Taught at Shaolin Temple, Mount Song, Luo Region (Henan). Regarded as the founder of Zen, which he brought to China from the West (India). Cases 10, 41, 45, 56, 108, 119, 183, 188, 190, 201, 205, 243, 265, 297.

Boshui Benren (Po-shui Pen-jen; Hakusui Honnin; ca. ninth to tenth century). Dharma heir of Dongshan Liangjie. Founded and taught at Boshui Monastery, Gaoan Prefecture (Sichuan). Case 132.

Caoshan Benji (Ts'ao-shan Pen-chi; Sōzan Honjaku; 840–901). Dharma heir of Dongshan Liangjie. Taught at Mount Cao, Fu Region (Jiangxi). Dongshan and Caoshan are considered the cofounders of the Caodong (J. Sōtō) school, one of the five schools of Chinese Zen. His posthumous name is Great Master Yuanzheng. Cases 28, 30, 33, 55, 70, 125, 194, 211, 250, 260, 262.

Changqing Da'an (also known as Guishan Da'an) (Ch'ang-ch'ing [Kuei-shan] Ta-an; Chōkei [Isan] Daian; 793–883). Dharma heir of Baizhang Huaihai. Taught at a temple established by his dharma brother Guishan Lingyou on Mount Gui, Tan Region (Hunan).

Changqing Huileng (Ch'ang-ch'ing Hui-leng; Chōkei Eryō; 854–932). Dharma heir of Xuefeng Yicun. Taught at Changqing Monastery, Fu Region (Fujian). His posthumous name is Great Master Chaojue. Cases 156, 177, 192, 298.

Changsha Jingcen (Ch'ang-sha Ching-ts'en; Chōsha Keishin; ca. ninth century; also called Tiger Cen). Dharma heir of Nanquan Puyuan. Taught at Luyuan Monastery, Changsha (Hunan). His posthumous name is Great Master Zhaoxian. Cases 16, 20, 234, 256, 270.

Changzi Huang. Shishi Shandao's teacher. Case 161.

Chen, Venerable (Zunsu) (Ch'en Tsun-su; Chin Sonshuku; ca. ninth century). Also known as Daozong (Tao-ming; Dōshō). Chen is his family name. Dharma heir of Huangbo Xiyun. Taught at Longxing Monastery, Mu Region (Zhejiang). Case 69.

Chuanzi Decheng (Ch'uan-tzu Te-ch'eng; Sensu Tokujō; ca. eighth to ninth century). Dharma heir of Yaoshan Weiyan. Taught on Wu River, Huting (Jiangsu). Case 90.

Citang Zhizang (Tz'u-t'ang Chih-chang; Seidō Chizō; 735–814). Dharma heir of Mazu Daoyi. His posthumous name is Great Master Dajue. Case 108.

Cuiwei Wuxue (Ts'ui-wei Wu-hsueh; Suibi Mugaku; ca. ninth century). Dharma heir of Danxia Tianran. Taught at Mount Chumei, Jingzhao (Shanxi). He was given the title Great Master Guangzhao by the emperor. Cases 71, 205.

Daci Huanzhong (Ta-tz'u Huan-chung; Daiji Kanchū; 780–824). Dharma heir of Baizhang Huaihai. Taught at Mount Daci, Hang Region (Zhejiang). His posthumous name is Great Master Xingkong. Case 77.

Dadian Baotong (Ta-tien Pao-t'ung; Daiten Hōtsū; 732–824). Dharma heir of Shitou Xiqian. Taught at Mount Ling, Chao Region (Guangdong). Case 126.

Dajian Huineng (Ta-chien Hui-neng; Daikan E'nō; 638–713). Also known as Caoxi. The Sixth Ancestor of Chinese Zen. Dharma heir of Fifth Ancestor Daman Hongren. Taught at Baolin Monastery, Caoxi, Shao Region (Guangdong). His posthumous name is Great Master Dajian. Cases 1, 53, 59, 101, 146, 234, 237.

Daman Hongren (Ta-man Hung-jen; Daiman Kōnin; 601–674). The Fifth Ancestor of Chinese Zen. Dharma heir of Fourth Ancestor Dayi Daoxin. Taught at Mount Huangmei in China. Case 59.

Damei Fachang (Ta-mei Fa-ch'ang; Daibai Hōjō; 752–839). Dharma heir of Mazu Daoyi. Taught at Mount Damei (Zhejiang). Case 278.

Danxia Tianran (Tan-hsia T'ien-jan; Tanka Tenen; 739–824). Dharma heir of Shitou Xiqian; also studied with Mazu Daoyi. Taught at Mount Danxia in Deng prefecture (Henan). He was given the posthumous name Zhitong by the Emperor.

Danyuan Yingzhen (Tan-yüan Ying-chen; Tangen Oshin; ca. eighth century). Disciple of the National Teacher Nanyang Huizhong. Case 152.

Daofu (Tao-fu; Dōfuku; 464–524; also called Sengfu). Dharma heir of Bodhidharma. Taught at Kaishan Monastery, Jinling (Jiangsu). Case 201.

Daowu Yuanzhi (Tao-wu Yuan-chih; Dōgo Enchi; 769–835; also called Daowu Zongzhi). Dharma heir of Yaoshan Weiyan. Taught at Mount Daowu, Tan Region (Hunan). Cases 29, 57, 83, 89, 90, 105, 191, 193, 213, 251, 289.

Daoyu (Tao-yü; Dōiku; ca. fifth to sixth century). Student of Bodhidharma. Case 201.

Dashu (Ta-shu; Daiju; ca. ninth century). Biography unknown. Case 91.

Dasui Fazhen (Ta-sui Fa-chen; Daizui Hōshin; 834–919). Dharma heir of Changqing Daan. Taught at Mount Dasui, Yi Region (Sichuan). He was given the title Great Master Shenzhao by the emperor. Case 24.

Dayang Jingxuan (Ta-yang Ching-hsüan; Taiyō Kyōgen; 942–1027). Dharma heir of Liangshan Yuanguan. Taught at Mount Dayang, Ying Region (Hubei). His posthumous name is Great Master Mingan. Case 242.

Dayi Daoxin (Ta-yi Tao-hsin; Daii Dōshin; 580–651; also called Shuang-feng). The Fourth Ancestor of Chinese Zen. Dharma heir of Third Ancestor Jianzhi Sengcan. Taught at Huangmei, Qi Region (Hubei). His posthumous name is Great Master Dayi. Case 140.

Dazhang Qiru (Ta-chang Ch'i-ju; Daishō Kainyo; ca. tenth century). Disciple of Xuansha Shibei. After studying with Xuansha, he became a hermit, living in the mountains. Case 63.

Dazu Huike (Ta-tsu Hui-k'o; Taiso Eka; 487–593). The Second Ancestor of Chinese Zen. Dharma heir of Bodhidharma. Taught in the northern capital of Ye (Henan). His posthumous name is Great Master Zhengzong Pujue. Case 201.

De, Senior Monastic (Shongzuo) (Te Shang-tso; Toku Jōza; ca. ninth century). Student of Caoshan Benji. Case 125.

Deng Yinfeng, or *Wutai Yinfeng* (Teng Yin-feng, or Wu-t'ai Yin-feng; Tō Impō, or Godai Impō; ca. ninth century). Deng is his family name. Dharma heir of Mazu Daoyi. Taught at Mount Wutai, Dai Region (Shanxi). Cases 64, 197.

Deshan Dehai (Te-shan Te-hai; Tokusan Tokkai; ca. tenth century). Dharma heir of Baofu Congzhan. Taught at Mount De, Lang Region (Hunan). Case 36.

Deshan Xuanjian (Te-shan Hsüan-chien; Tokusan Senkan; 780–865). Dharma heir of Longtan Chongxin. Taught at Mount De, Lang Region (Hunan). His posthumous name is Great Master Jianxing. Cases 31, 104, 145, 218, 273.

Dizang Guichen (Ti-tsang Kuei-ts'en; Jizō Keichin; 867–928; also called Luohan Guichen). Dharma heir of Xuansha Shibei. Taught at Dizang Monastery, Min (Fujian), and Luohan Monastery, Zhang Region (Fujian). Cases 25, 112, 113, 171, 177, 203, 212, 229.

Dongshan Liangjie (Tung-shan Liang-chieh; Tōzan Ryōkai; 807–869). Dharma heir of Yunyan Tansheng. Taught at Mount Dong, Rui Region (Jiangxi). Author of the "Song of Bright Mirror Samādhi." Dongshan and Caoshan are regarded as the cofounders of the Caodong (J. Sōtō) school, one of the five schools of Chinese Zen. His posthumous name is Great Master Wuben. Cases 12, 30, 49, 55, 62, 72, 77, 78, 82, 84, 93, 98, 148, 198, 199, 218, 220, 222, 225, 228, 273, 276.

Dongshan Shouchu (Tung-shan Shou-ch'u; Tōzan Shusho; 910–990). Yunmen school. Dharma heir of Yunmen Wenyan. Taught at Mount Dong, Rui Region (Jiangxi). His posthumous name is Great Master Zonghui. Cases 172, 280.

Doushuai Congyue (Tou-shuai Ts'ung-yüeh; Tosotsu Jūetsu; 1044–1091). Dharma heir of Baofeng Kewen. Taught at Doushuai Monastery in Longxing (Nanchang City). Case 234.

Du, Emperor's Secretary (Shangshu) (Tu Shang-shu; Jiku Shōsho; ca. ninth century). Case 20.

Ehu Dayi (E-hu Ta-yi; Gako Daigi; 748–818). Dharma heir of Mazu Daoyi. Taught at Mount Ehu, Xin Region (Jiangxi). His posthumous name is Great Master Huijue. Case 290.

Fayan Wenyi (Fa-yen Wen-i; Hōgen Mon'eki; 885–958). Dharma heir of Dizang Guichen. Taught at Baoen Monastery, Jinling (Jiangsu), and Qingliang Monastery, Sheng Region (Jin Ling). Regarded as the founder of the Fayan school, one of the five schools of Chinese Zen. His posthumous name is Great Master Fayan. Cases 72, 111, 122, 135, 171, 177, 252, 254, 296.

Fengxue Yanzhao (Feng-hsüeh Yen-chao; Fūketsu Enshō; 896–973). Dharma heir of Baoying Huiyong. Taught at Mount Fengxui, Ru Region (Henan). Case 214.

Fenyang Shanzhao (Fen-yang Shan-chao; Fun'yō Zenshō; 947–1024). Dharma heir of Shoushan Shengnian. Taught at Taizi Temple in Fenzhou Region (Shanxi). His posthumous name is Great Master Wude.

Furong Daokai (Fu-jung Tao-k'ai; Fuyō Dōkai; 1043–1118; also called Dayang). Dharma heir of Touzi Yiqing, Caodong school. Taught at Mount Dayang, Ying Region (Hubei), and later at Lake Furong (Shandong). Case 143.

Gao'an Dayu (Kao-an Ta-yü; Kōan Daigu; ca. ninth century). Dharma heir of Guizong Zhichang. Taught in Gao'an, Rui Region (Jiangxi). Case 27.

Gautama. See *Śākyamuni Buddha*.

Guangxiao (Iron Beak) Huijue (Kuang-hsiao Hui-chüeh; Ekaku Tessai; ca. ninth century). Dharma heir of Zhaozhou Congshen. Taught at Guangxiao Monastery, Yang Region (Jiangsu). Case 135.

Guanxi Zhixian (Kuan-hsi Chih-hsien; Kankei Shikan; d. 895).   Dharma heir of Linji Yixuan. Taught in Guanxi, Changsha (Hunan). Case 217.

Guishan Lingyou (Kuei-shan Ling-yu; Isan Reiyū; 771–853). Dharma heir of Baizhang Huaihai. Taught at Mount Gui, Tan Region (Hunan). Guishan and his heir Yangshan are regarded as the cofounders of the Guiyang school, one of the five schools of Chinese Zen. He was also called Dagui. His posthumous name is Great Master Dayuan. Cases 14, 17, 23, 44, 47, 56, 61, 68, 76, 103, 110, 115, 118, 130, 134, 142, 155, 157, 168, 184, 197, 209, 219, 230, 235, 266, 275, 279.

Guizong Cejin (Kuei-tsung Ts'e-chin; Kisu Sakushin; d. 979).   Dharma heir of Fayan Wenyi. Taught at Guizong Monastery, Mount Lu (Jiangxi). His family name is Huichao, and his posthumous name is Great Master Fashi. Case 252.

Guizong Zhichang (Kuei-tsung Chih-ch'ang; Kisu Chijō; ca. eighth century).   Dharma heir of Mazu Daoyi. Taught at Guizong Monastery, Mount Lu (Jiangxi). Cases 43, 65, 188.

Gushan Shanyan (Ku-shan Shan-yen; Kosan Shin'an; ca. ninth century). Dharma heir of Xuefeng Yicun. Taught at Mount Gu, Fu Region (Fujian). Cases 32, 282.

Hai, Senior. See *Baizhang Huaihai.*

Hangzhou Tianlong (Hang-chou Tien-lung; Kōshū Tenryū; ca. ninth century).   Dharma heir of Damei Fachang. Case 245.

Hanyu Wengong, Lord (Han-yü Wen-kung; Kan'yu Bunkō; 718–824).   A government officer and renowned essayist. He was associated with Master Dadian Baotong. Cases 126, 173.

Heshan Wuyan (Ho-shan Wu-yen; Kasan Muin; 884–960).   Dharma heir of Jiufeng Daoqian. Taught at Mount Heshan, Ji Region (Jiangxi). He was given the title Great Master Chengyuan by the emperor. Case 186.

Huangbo Xiyun (Huang-po Hsi-yüan; Obaku Kiun; d. 850).   Dharma heir of Baizhang Huaihai. Taught at Mount Huangbo, Ning Region (Jiangxi). His teachings are collected in the *Essential Teaching of Transmission of Mind*. His posthumous name is Great Master Duanji. Cases 2, 9, 27, 54, 91, 102, 178, 202, 271.

Huanglong Huiji (Hui-chi; Hui-ch'ih; Ōryū Kaiki).   A student of Yantou. He lived on Huanglong Mountain in Ezhou Region (Jianxi).

Huayan Xiujing (Hua-yen Hsiu-ching; Kegon Kyūjō; ca. ninth century;
also called Jingzhao). Dharma heir of Dongshan Liangjie. Taught at
Huayan Monastery, Jingzhao (Shanxi). His posthumous name is Great
Master Baozhi. Cases 199, 263.

Huian of Songshan, National Teacher (Hui-an of Tsung-shan; E'an of
Suzan; 582–709). A disciple of the Fifth Ancestor Daman Hongren.
Nanyue Hairang studied with him before meeting the Sixth Ancestor
Huineng. Case 101.

Hutou, Senior Monastic (Shangzuo) (Hu-t'ou Shang-tso; Kozu Jōza; ca.
ninth century). Student of Xiangyan Zhixian. Case 243.

Jianhong, Senior Monastic (Shangzuo) (Chien-hung Shang-tso; Kanko
Jōza; ca. ninth century). Studied with Guishan Lingyu.

Jianyuan Zhongxing (Chien-yüan Chung-hsing; Zengen Chūkō; ca. eighth
to ninth century). Dharma heir of Daowu Yuanzhi. Taught at Mount
Jianyuan, Tan Region (Hunan). Cases 29, 175, 289.

Jianzhi Sengcan (Chien-chih Seng-ts'an; Kanchi Sōsan; d. 606). The
Third Ancestor of Chinese Zen. Dharma heir of Dazu Huike. Taught
at Mount Sikong, Shu Region (Anhui). Author of the "Song of Faith
in Mind." His posthumous name is Great Master Jianzhi. Case 140.

Jiashan Shanhui (Chia-shan Shan-hui; Kassan Zenne; 805–881). First
taught at Zhulin Monastery, Jingkou, Run Region (Jiangsu), then became dharma heir of Chuanzi Decheng and taught at Mount Jia, Feng
Region (Hunan). His posthumous name is Great Master Chuanming.
Cases 90, 200, 292.

Jin, Head Priest (Shanzhu) (Chin Shan-chu; Shin Sanshu; ca. ninth to
tenth century). Student of Longji Shaoxiu. Case 120.

Jinfeng Congzhi (Chin-feng Tsung-chih; Kimpō Jūshi; ca. ninth to tenth
century). Dharma heir of Caoshan Benji. Taught at Mount Jinfeng, Fu
Region (Jiangxi). His posthumous name is Great Master Xuanming.
Cases 187, 240, 272, 274.

Jingqing Daofu (Ching-ch'ing Tao-fu; Kyōsei Dōfu; 864–937). Dharma
heir of Xuefeng Yicun. Taught at Longce Monastery, Hang Region
(Zhejiang). Cases 39, 42, 286.

Jingshan Hongyin (Ching-shan Hung-yin; Kinzan Kōin; d. 901). Dharma
heir of Guishan Lingyou. Taught at Mount Jia (Zhejiang). He was given
the title Great Master Faji by the emperor. Case 85.

Jingzhao Mihu (Ching-chao Mi-hu; Kyōchō Beiko; ca. ninth century). Dharma heir of Guishan Lingyou. Cases 7, 263.

Jinhua Hongtao (Chin-hua Hung-t'ao; Kinka Koto; ca. ninth to tenth century). Dharma heir of Xuansha Shibei. Case 117.

Jinhua Juzhi (Chin-hua Chü-chih; Kinka Gutei; ca. ninth century). Dharma heir of Hangzhou Tianlong. Case 245.

Jiufeng Daoqian (Chiu-feng Tao-ch'ien; Kyūhōō Dōken; ca. ninth century). Dharma heir of Shishuang Qingzhu. Taught at Mount Jiufeng, Yun Region (Jiangxi). His posthumous name is Great Master Dajue. Case 221.

Kāśyapa (K'a-sha-p'a; Kashō). The Buddha of the world age preceding the present one. Case 102.

Langye Huijue (Lang-yeh Hui-chüeh; Rōya Ekaku; ca. eleventh century). Dharma heir of Fenyang Shanzhao. Taught at Mount Langye, Chu Region (Anhui). His posthumous name is Great Master Guangzhao. Cases 6, 91.

Liang, Lecturer (Jiangshi) (Liang Chiang-shih; Ryō Zasu; ca. eighth century). Student of Mazu Daoyi. He secluded himself on Mount Xi, Hong Region (Jiangxi). Case 4.

Liangshan Yuanguan (Liang-shan Yüan-kuan; Ryōzan Enkan; ca. tenth century). Dharma heir of Tongan Guanzhi. Taught at Mount Liang, Ding Region (Hunan). Case 242.

Liangsui, Lecturer (Jiangshi) (Liang-sui Chiang-shih; Ryōsui Jōza; ca. eighth century). Dharma heir of Mayu Baoche. Taught in Shou Region. Case 121.

Liao, Monastery Director (Yuanzhu) (Liao Yüan-chu; Ryō Inju; ca. tenth century). Student of Anguo Huiqiu. Case 131.

Libo, Governor (Cishi) (Li-po Tzü-shih; Ribotsu Shishi; 772–831). Governor of Jiang Region (Jiangxi). Studied with Guizong Zhichang. Case 188.

Lingyun Zhiqin (Ling-yün Chih-ch'in; Reiun Shigon; ca. ninth century). Dharma heir of Guishan Lingyou. Taught at Mount Lingyun, Fu Region (Hunan). Cases 155, 156.

Lingzhao (Ling-chao; Reishō; ca. ninth century). Layman Pangyun's daughter. Case 88.

Linji Yixuan (Lin-chi I-hsüan; Rinzai Gigen; d. 867). Dharma heir of Huangbo Xiyun. Taught at Linji Monastery, Zhen Region (Hebei).

Regarded as the founder of the Linji school, one of the five schools of
Chinese Zen. His posthumous name is Great Master Huizhao. Cases 22,
27, 96, 147, 164, 167, 178, 205, 207, 216, 217, 234, 244, 255, 300.

Longji Shaoxiu (Lung-chi Shao-hsiu; Ryūsai Shōshū; ca. ninth to tenth
century). Dharma heir of Dizang Guichen. Taught at Mount Longji,
Fe Region (Jiangxi). Case 120.

Longquan (Wuzuo) Wenxi (Lung-ch'üan [Wu-tso]; Wen-hsi; Mujaku
Bunki; 821–900). Dharma heir of Yangshan Huiji. Taught in Hang Re-
gion (Zhejiang). His posthumous name is Wuzuo. Said to be the same
Wuzuo who saw Mañjuśrī. Case 127.

Longshan (Lung-shan; Ryūzan; ca. eighth to ninth century). Originally
from Tan Region (Hunan). Dharma heir of Mazu Daoyi. He secluded
himself on Mount Long, Hang Region (Zhejiang). Case 222.

Longtan Chongxin (Lung-t'an Ch'ung-hsin; Ryūtan Sōshin; ca. eighth to
ninth century). Dharma heir of Tianhuang Daowu. Taught at Longtan,
Feng Region (Henan). Cases 104, 106.

Longyu Judun (Lung-ye Chü-tun; Ryūge Kodon; 835–923). Dharma heir
of Dongshan Liangjie. Taught at Mount Longya, Tan Region (Hunan).
His posthumous name is Great Master Zhangkong. Cases 196, 205, 297.

Lu, Commander (Shiyu) (Lu Shih-yü; Riku Rōchū; ca. ninth century).
Student of Yangshan. Cases 139, 275.

Luoshan Daoxian (Lo-shan Tao-hsien; Razan Dōkan; ca. ninth century).
Dharma heir of Yantou Quanhuo. Taught at Mount Luo, Fu Region
(Fujian). Cases 97, 235, 273.

Luzu Baoyun (Lu-ts'u Pao-yün; Roso Hōun; ca. eighth century). Dharma
heir of Mazu Daoyi. Taught at Mount Luzu, Chi Region (Anhui). Cases
87, 185.

Mahākāśyapa (Mo-ho-chia-hsieh; Makakashō). A student of the Buddha
renowned for his ascetic self-discipline and moral strictness. He took
over the leadership of the saṃgha after the Buddha's death. Cases 34,
141, 169, 253.

Mañjuśrī (Wen-shu; Monju). The bodhisattva of wisdom. He is depicted
with two lotus blossoms on his head, on which his attributes—a sword
and a book of the prajñāpāramitā literature—are placed. Cases 127, 153,
165, 258.

Maudgalyāyana (Mo-chia Mu-chien-lien; Maka Mokkenren, or Mokuren).
One of the ten major disciples of Śākyamuni Buddha, he was known
for his outstanding miraculous powers. Case 61.

Mayu Baoche (Ma-yü Pao-ch'e; Mayoku Hōtetsu; ca. eighth century).
Dharma heir of Mazu Daoyi. Taught at Mount Mayu, Pu Region
(Shanxi). Cases 121, 123, 244.

Mazu Daoyi (Ma-tsu Tao-i; Baso Dōitsu; 709–788). Dharma heir of
Nanyue Huairang. Lived in Kaiyuan Monastery, Zhongling (Jiangxi).
His posthumous name is Great Master Daji. Cases 4, 5, 8, 54, 99, 108,
150, 182, 190, 223, 265, 278.

Miaoxin, Nun (Ni) (Ni Miao-hsin; Ni Myoshin; ca. ninth century). Studied with Yangshan Huiji. Her answer to the Sixth Ancestor's
kōan, "Neither the Wind nor the Flag": "It is neither the wind nor the
flag nor the mind that is moving," was said to enlighten a group of sev-
enteen monastics all at once. Case 146.

Mimoyan Changyu (Mi-mo-yen Ch'ang-yü; Himagan Jōgū; 817–888).
Dharma heir of Yongtai Lingtuan. Taught at Mimo Grotto, Mount
Wutai (Shanxi). Case 73.

Ming, Senior Monastic (Shangzuo) (Ming Shang-tso; Myō
Jōza). Biography unknown. Case 124.

Mingzhao Deqian (Ming-chao Te-ch'ien; Myōshō Tokken; ca. ninth century; also called One-Eyed Dragon). Dharma heir of Luoshan Daoxian. Case 157.

Moshan Liaoran (Mo-shan Liao-jan; Massan Ryōnen; ca. ninth century).
Dharma heir of Gao'an Dayu. Taught at Moshan Temple in Ruizhou
Region (Jiangxi). Case 217.

Nanquan Puyuan (Nan-chüan P'u-yüan; Nansen Fugan; 748–834).
Dharma heir of Mazu Daoyi. Lived at Mount Nanquan, Chi Region
(Anhui). He called himself Old Master Wang. Cases 3, 18, 19, 51, 57, 64,
87, 138, 154, 181, 185, 195, 234, 249, 258, 293.

Nanta Guangyong (Nan-t'a Kuang-yung; Nantō Kōyū; 850–938). Dharma
heir of Yangshan Huiji. Taught at Mount Yang in Yuanzhou (Jiangxi).

Nanyang Huizhong (Nan-yang Hui-chung; Nan'yō Echū; d. 775).
Dharma heir of Sixth Ancestor Dajian Huineng. Taught at Nanyang

(Hunan). His posthumous name is National Teacher Dazheng. Cases 17, 26, 152, 159, 210.

Nanyue Huairang (Nan-yüeh Huai-jang; Nangaku Ejō; 677–744). Dharma heir of Sixth Ancestor, Dajian Huineng. Taught at Panre Monastery, Nanyue (Mount Heng), Heng Region (Hunan). His posthumous name is Great Master Dahui. Cases 8, 101, 116, 153, 223.

Niutou Farong (Niu-t'ou Fa-jung; Gozu Hōyū; 594–657). He was said to be the dharma heir of Fourth Ancestor Dayi Daoxin. Taught at Mount Niutou (Jiangsu). Regarded as the founder of the Niutou school. Case 51.

Pangyun, Layman (Xuanze) (Pao-en Hsüan-tse; Hōon Koji; d. 808). A lay student of Mazu Daoyi. He lived in Xiang Region (Hubei) and made his living by making baskets, which his daughter Lingzhao [Reishō] sold. Cases 5, 88, 99, 153.

Panshan Baoji (P'an-shan Pao-chi; Banzan Hōshaku; ca. eighth century). Dharma heir of Mazu Daoyi. Taught at Mount Pan, You Region (Hebei). His posthumous name is Great Master Ningji. Case 21.

Peixiu, Minister (Xiangguo) (P'ei-hsiu Hsiang-kuo; Haikyū Shōkoku; 797–870). An officer of the Tang dynasty government. As a lay student of Huangbo Xiyun, he edited Huangbo's *Essential Teaching of Transmission of Mind*. Case 9.

Puhua (P'u-hua; Fuke; ca. ninth century). Dharma heir of Panshan Baoji. Lived in Zhen Region (Hebei). Cases 22, 96.

Prajñādhāra (J. Hannyatara). Twenty-seventh patriarch in the Indian lineage of Zen. Bodhidharma's teacher.

Qinglin (Dongshan) Shiqian (Ching-lin [Tung-shan] Shih-ch'ien; Seirin [Tōzan] Shiken; d. 904; called the Later Dongshan). Dharma heir of Dongshan Liangjie. Taught at Mount Dong, Rui Region (Jiangxi). Case 204.

Qingping Lingzun (Ch'ing-p'ing Ling-tsun; Seihei Reijun; 845–919). Dharma heir of Cuiwei Wuxue. Taught at Mount Qingping, E Region (Hubei). His posthumous name is Great Master Faxi. Case 71.

Qingxi Hongjin (Ch'ing-hsi Hung-chin; Seikei Kōshin; ca. ninth century). Dharma heir of Dizang Guichen. Taught at Mount Qingxi, Xiang Region (Hubei). Case 189.

Qingyuan Xingsi (Ch'ing-yüan Hsing-ssu; Seigen Gyōshi; d. 740). Dharma heir of Sixth Ancestor Dajian Huineng. Abbot of Jingju

Monastery, Mount Qingyuan, Ji Region (Jiangxi). His posthumous name is Great Master Hongji. Cases 1, 10, 53, 237.

Qinshan Wensui (Ching-shan Wên-sui; Kinzan Bunsui; ca. ninth century). Dharma heir of Dongshan Liangjie. Taught at Qinshan, Feng Region (Hunan). Case 218.

Quanming, Senior Monastic (Shangzuo) (Ch'üan-ming Shang-tso; Zemmyō Jōza; ca. eleventh century). Studied with Shishuang Chuyuan. Case 85.

Ruiyan Shiyan (Jui-yen Shih-yen; Zuigan Shigen; ca. ninth century). Dharma heir of Yantou Quanhuo. Taught at Ruiyan Monastery, Tai Region (Hunan). Cases 180, 200, 247.

Śākyamuni Buddha (the World-Honored One) (Shijiamouni; Shih-chia-mou-ni; Shakamuni; 566 or 563 B.C.E. to 486 or 483 B.C.E.). Siddhārtha Gautama, the founder of Buddhism, who belonged to the Śakya clan of India. Cases 34, 36, 60, 141, 165, 170, 174, 185, 221, 231, 253, 298.

Samantabhadra (Puxian; P'u-hsien; Fugen). Bodhisattva who is venerated as the protector of those who teach the dharma. He is the embodiment of the wisdom of the unity of sameness and difference. Case 258.

Sanping Yizhong (San-p'ing Yi-chung; Sampei Gichū; 781–872). Dharma heir of Dadian Baotong. Taught at Mount Sanping, Zhang Region (Fujian). Case 126.

Sansheng Huiran (San-sheng Hui-jan; Sanshō Enen; ca. ninth century). Dharma heir of Linji Yixuan. Taught at Sansheng Monastery, Zhen Region (Hebei). Cases 40, 52, 92, 167, 234, 294.

Śāriputra (Shelifuduoluo; She-li-fu-to-lo; Sharihotsu, or Sharishi). One of the ten disciples of the Buddha, he came from a Brahman family and, together with Maudgalyāyana, entered the Buddhist order. He became renowned on account of his wisdom. Case 61.

Shaozhou Ruyuan (Shao-chou Ju-yüan; Shoshu Nyugen; ca. eighth century). Dharma heir of Mazu Daoyi. Case 246.

Shaozhou Zhangjing (Shao-chou Chang-ching; Shōshū Shōkei; ca. ninth to tenth century). Dharma heir of Yunmen Wenyan. Taught in Shao Region (Guangdong). Case 236.

Shen, Senior Monastic (Shangzuo) (Shen Shang-tso; Shin Jōza). Biography unknown. Case 124.

Shenshan Sengmi (Shen-shan Seng-mi; Shinzan Sōmitsu; ca. eighth to ninth century). Dharma heir of Yunyan Tansheng. Taught at Mount Shenshan, Tan Region (Hunan). The students of his dharma brother Dongshan called him Dharma Uncle Mi. Cases 62, 93, 198, 220, 222.

Shexian Guixing (She-hsien Kuei-hsing; Sekken Kisei; ca. tenth century). Dharma heir of Shoushan Shengnian. Taught at Guangjiao Monastery, She Prefecture, Ru Region (Henan). Case 269.

Shigong Huizang (Shih-kung Hui-tsang; Shakkyō Ezō; ca. eighth century). Dharma heir of Mazu Daoyi. Taught at Mount Shigong, Fu Region (Jiangxi). Case 248.

Shilou (Shih-lou; Sekirō). Taught in Fen Region (Shanxi). Case 50.

Shishi Shandao (Shih-shih Shan-tao; Sekishitsu Zendō; ca. eighth century). May have been a student of Mazu Daoyi; dharma heir of Changzi Huang. He was also called Worker Shishi, for he labored in a mill. Case 161.

Shishuang Chuyuan (Shih-shuang Ch'u-yüan; Sekisō Soen; 977–1040). Dharma heir of Fenyang Shanzhao. Taught at Mount Shishuang, Tan Region (Hunan). His posthumous name is Great Master Ciming. Cases 28, 82, 85, 89.

Shishuang Qingzhu (Shih-shuang Ch'ing-shu; Sekisō Keishō; 807–886). Dharma heir of Daowu Yuanzhi. Taught at Mount Shishuang, Tan Region (Hunan). His posthumous name is Great Master Puhui. Cases 29, 58, 179, 193.

Shiti (Shih-t'i; Sekitei; ca. ninth century). Dharma heir of Shuyu. Case 206.

Shitou Xiqian (Shih-t'ou Hsi-ch'ien; Sekitō Kisen; 700–790). Ordained by Sixth Ancestor Dajian Huineng and also became the dharma heir of Qingyuan Xingsi. He resided at Nan Monastery, Mount Heng, also called Nanyue (Hunan). He was the author of the poems "Identity of Relative and Absolute" and "Song of the Grass Hut." His posthumous name is Great Master Wuji. Cases 1, 5, 41, 53, 191, 232, 234, 299.

Shoushan Shengnian (Shou-shan Sheng-nien; Shuzan Shōnen; 926–993). Dharma heir of Fengxue Yanzhao. Founded the monastery of Mount Shou, Ru Region (Henan). Case 269.

Shuangquan Shikuan (Shuang-chüan Shih-k'uan; Sōsen Shikan; ca. tenth century). Student of Yunmen Wenyan. He was given the title Great Master Mingjiao by the Emperor. Case 39.

Shuilao (Shui-lao; Suirō; ca. eighth century). Dharma heir of Mazu Daoyi. Case 265.

Shuilong Daopu (Shui-lung Tao-p'u; Suiryū Dōhaku; ca. tenth century). Dharma heir of Xuefeng Yicun. Case 63.

Shun, Emperor (Huangdi) (Shun Huang-ti; Shun Kōtei). He was regarded as the successor of Emperor Yao. Case 143.

Shushan Kuangren (Shu-shan K'uang-jen; Sozan Kōnin; ca. ninth century). Dharma heir of Dongshan Liangjie. Taught at Mount Shu, Fu Region (Jiangxi). Cases 97, 157, 285.

Shuyu (Shu-yü; Soyu; ca. ninth century). Biography unknown.

Subhūti (Xupudi; Hsü-pu-ti; Shubodai). One of the ten great disciples of the Buddha. Because of his profound insight, he usually explained the teaching of emptiness (śūnyatā) in the *Prajñāpāramitā* sūtras.

Sudatta, Elder (Zang) (Su-ta-to Tsang; Sudatta Chōja). A wealthy man who lived in the city of Śravasti, Kausala Kingdom, India. He was moved by one of Śākyamuni Buddha's dharma talks and built and donated a monastery in Jeta Grove with the help of its owner, Prince Jeta. Case 47.

Suzong, Emperor (Huangdi) (Su-tsung Huang-ti; Shukusō Kōtei; ca. eighth to ninth century). Cases 26, 152, 159.

Tai, Head Monastic (Zhuzuo) (T'ai Chu-tso; Tai Shuso; ca. ninth century). Studied with Dongshan Liangjie. Case 78.

Taiyuan Fu (Tai-yüan Fu; Taigen Fu; ca. ninth to tenth century). A student of Xuefeng Yicun. Lived at Baoen Monastery, Taiyuan (Shanxi). Case 32.

Tang, Emperor (Huangdi) (T'ang Huang-ti; Too Kōtei). Founder of the Shang dynasty (ca. 1766 B.C.E. to ca. 1122 B.C.E.). Case 143.

Tianhuang Daowu (T'ien-huang Tao-wu; Tennō Dōgo; 748–807). Dharma heir of Shitou Xiqian. Taught at Tianhuang Monastery, Jing Region (Hubei). Cases 106, 191.

Tianping Congyi (T'ien-p'ing Tsung-yi; Tempyō Jūi; ca. tenth century). Dharma heir of Qingxi Hongjin. Taught at Mount Tianping, Xiang Region (Henan). Case 284.

Tiantong Xianqi (T'ien-t'ung Hsien-ch'i; Tendō Kankei; ca. ninth century). Dharma heir of Dongshan Liangjie. Case 215.

Tongan Guanzhi (T'ung-an Kuan-chih; Dōan Kanshi; ca. tenth century). Dharma heir of Tongan Daopi.

Touzi Datong (T'ou-tzu Ta-t'ung; Tōsu Daidō; 819–914). Dharma heir of Cuiwei Wuxue. Taught at Mount Touzi, Shu Region (Anhui). His posthumous name is Great Master Ciji. Cases 13, 35, 136, 160.

Touzi Yiqing (T'ou-tzu Yi-ch'ing; Tōsu Gisei; 1032–1083). Dharma heir of Dayang Jingxuan. Taught at Mount Touzi, Shu Region (Anhui). Restored the Caodong school. Case 143.

Vairocana Buddha (Piluzhena; P'i-lu-che-na; Birushana). The luminous buddha who embodies the reality of the universe. Cases 26, 210.

Wang Jingchu (Wang Ching-ch'u; O Keishō; ca. ninth century). Lay student of Guishan Lingyou, and the emperor's attendant. Cases 207, 263.

World-Honored One. See *Śākyamuni Buddha.*

Wu (Wu; Go Shoshi). Daoist (Taoist) practitioner. Biography unknown. Case 242.

Wumen Huikai (Wu-men Hui-k'ai; Mumon Ekai; 1183–1260). Dharma heir of Yuelin Shiguan. Author of the *Wumenkuan* or "Gateless Gate." Taught at Huguo Renwang Temple in Hangzhou Region (Zhejiang). He was given the title Great Master Foyan by the Emperor. Case 258.

Wuxie Lingmo (Wu-hsieh Ling-mo; Gosetsu Reimoku; 747–818). Dharma heir of Mazu Daoyi. Taught at Mount Wuxie, Wu Region (Zhejiang). Case 299.

Xian, Emperor (Huangdi) (Hsien Huang-ti; Kensō Kōtei). Biography unknown. Case 173.

Xiangyan Zhixian (Hsiang-yen Chih-hsien; Kyōgen Chikan; d. 898). Dharma heir of Guishan Lingyou. Taught at Xiangyan Monastery, Deng Region (Henan). His posthumous name is Great Master Xideng. Cases 17, 28, 61, 243.

Xiaotang. Biography unknown.

Xinghua Cunjiang (Hsing-hua Ts'un-chiang; Kōke Sonshō; 830–888). Dharma heir of Linji Yixuan. Taught at Xinghua Monastery, Wei Prefecture (Hebei). His posthumous name is Great Master Guangji. Case 92.

Xixian Faan (Hsi-hsien Fa-an; Seiken Hōan; ca. ninth to tenth century). Dharma heir of Fayan Wenyi. Taught at Xixian Monastery, Mount Lu (Jiangxi). Case 227.

Xiyuan Siming (Hsi-yüan Ssu-ming; Saiin Shimyō; ca. tenth century). Dharma heir of Baoshou Yanzhao. Taught at Xiyuan Monastery, Ru Region (Henan). Case 284.

Xuansha Shibei (Hsüan-sha Shih-pei; Gensha Shibi; 835–908; also called Ascetic Bei). Dharma heir of Xuefeng Yicun. Taught at Xuansha Monastery, Fu Region (Fujian). He was given the title Great Master Zongyi by the emperor. Cases 15, 25, 38, 45, 48, 60, 109, 112, 144, 149, 155, 156, 163, 176, 203, 241, 282, 287.

Xuefeng Yicun (Hsüeh-feng I-ts'un; Seppō Gison; 822–908). Dharma heir of Deshan Xuanjian. Taught at Mount Xuefeng, Fu Region (Fujian). His posthumous name is Great Master Zhenjue. Cases 38, 48, 52, 55, 60, 109, 137, 144, 149, 156, 163, 176, 183, 218, 283, 287, 290, 294.

Yangshan Huiji (Yang-shan Hui-chi; Gyōzan Ejaku; 803–887). Dharma heir of Guishan Lingyou. Taught at Mount Yang, Yuan Region (Jiangxi). Guishan and Yangshan are regarded as the cofounders of the Guiyang school, one of the five schools of Chinese Zen. He was given the posthumous name Tongzhi. Cases 7, 14, 23, 47, 56, 61, 68, 103, 110, 115, 118, 130, 134, 139, 142, 168, 209, 219, 246, 279.

Yanguan Qian (Yen-kuan Ch'ien; Enkan Saian; d. 842). Dharma heir of Mazu Daoyi. Taught in Yanguan, Hang Region (Zhejiang). His posthumous name is Great Master Wukong. Cases 115, 218, 224.

Yantou Quanhuo (Yen-t'ou Ch'üan-huo; Gantō Zenkatsu; 828–887). Dharma heir of Deshan Xuanjian. Taught at Mount Yantou, E Region (Hubei). His posthumous name is Great Master Qingyan. Cases 75, 180, 200, 218, 273.

Yanyang Shanxin (Yan-yang Shan-hsin; Gen'yō Zenshin; ca. ninth to tenth century). Dharma heir of Zhaozhou Congshen. Taught at Mount Yanyang (Jiangxi). Case 277.

Yao, Emperor (Yao; Gyō). A legendary, virtuous ruler of ancient China. Case 143.

Yaoshan Weiyan (Yao-shan Wei-yen; Yakusan Igen; 745–828). Dharma heir of Shitou Xiqian. Taught at Mount Yao, Feng Region (Hunan). His posthumous name is Great Master Hongdao. Cases 57, 66, 79, 86, 90, 129, 150, 151, 184, 232.

Yongtai Lingtuan (Yong-tai Ling-t'uan; Eitai Reitan; ca. ninth century).
Taught in Fuzhou Region (Fujian).

Yu, Emperor (Huangdi) (Yu Huang-ti; Uo Kōtei). A successor of Emperor
Shun, known as the founder of the Xia dynasty in prehistoric China.
Case 143.

Yuanliao (Yüan-liao; Inryō; ca. ninth century). Student of Linji Yixuan.
Case 300.

Yuezhou Qianfeng (Yüeh-chou Ch'ien-feng; Esshū Kempō; ca. ninth century). Dharma heir of Dongshan Liangjie. Taught in Yue Region (Zhejiang). Cases 37, 122.

Yungai Zhiyuan (Yün-kai Shou-chih; Ungai Shigen; ca. ninth century).
Dharma heir of Shishuang Qingzhu. Taught at Mount Yungai, Tan Region (Hunan). His posthumous name is Great Master Yuanjing. Case
179.

Yunju Daoying (Yün-chü Tao-ying; Ungo Dōyō; d. 902). Dharma heir of
Dongshan Liangjie. Taught at Mount Yunju, Hong Region (Jiangxi).
His posthumous name is Great Master Hongjue. Cases 34, 94, 137, 276.

Yunmen Wenyan (Yün-men Wen-yen; Ummon Bun'en; 864–949).
Dharma heir of Xuefeng Yicun. He established a monastery at Mount
Yunmen, Shao Region (Guangdong). Regarded as the founder of the
Yunmen school, one of the five schools of Chinese Zen. He was given
the title Great Master Kuangzhen by the emperor. Cases 70, 72, 81, 95,
100, 107, 158, 162, 166, 176, 208, 231, 257, 261, 280, 285, 295.

Yunyan Tansheng (Yün-yen T'an-sheng; Ungan Donjō; 782–841).
Dharma heir of Yaoshan Weiyan. Taught at Mount Yunyan, Tan Region
(Hunan). His posthumous name is Great Master Wuzhu. Cases 57, 83,
84, 90, 105, 148, 184, 228, 251, 267.

Zaoshu (Tsao-shu; Sōju; ca. ninth century). Dharma heir of Huanglong
Huaiji. His name means "date tree." Case 226.

Zhaozhou Congshen (Chao-chou Ts'ung-shen; Jōshū Jūshin; 778–897).
Dharma heir of Nanquan Puyuan. Taught at Guanyin Monastery, Zhao
Region (Hebei). His posthumous name is Great Master Zhenji. Cases 3,
11, 19, 46, 67, 74, 80, 114, 119, 133, 135, 136, 138, 181, 195, 233, 239, 258, 277,
281, 283, 288, 291.

Zheng's Thirteenth Daughter (Cheng's Thirteenth Daughter; Tei Jūsanjō;
ca. ninth century). Dharma heir of Changqing Daan. Case 235.

Zhigong (Chih-kung; Chiyu; ca. eighth century). Biography unknown. Case 248.

Zhimen Shikuan (Chih-men Shi-k'uan; Chimon Shikan; ca. ninth to tenth century). Dharma heir of Yunmen Wenyan. Taught at Shuangquan Monastery, Sui Region (Hebei). His posthumous name is Great Master Mingjiao. Case 238.

Zhizhao, Head Monastic (Zhozuo) (Chih-chao Chu-tso; Shishō Shuso; ca. tenth century). Dharma heir of Fayan Wenyi. Case 177.

Zongchi, Nun (Ni) (Ni Tsung-chih; Ni Sōji; ca. fifth to sixth century). Student of Bodhidharma. Case 201.

Zun, Monastic (Seng) (Tsun Seng; Jun Funō; ca. eighth to ninth century). Student of Yaoshan Weiyan. Case 86.

Glossary of Buddhist Terms

C. = Chinese
J. = Japanese
S. = Sanskrit

absolute and relative. Also light and darkness, day and night; perfectly
 interrelated, mutually arising aspects of reality; absolute is oneness,
 emptiness, the true nature of reality, while the relative is its phenomenal manifestation.
Ācārya (S.). Master of the dharma (as opposed to a teacher of rules and
 discipline).
adamantine. Indestructible, like a diamond; able to cut through any substance without breaking; symbol of transcendent wisdom.
adept. An advanced Zen practitioner.
arhat (S.). "Worthy one" who has attained the highest level of the
 Hīnayāna, that of "no-more-learning"; the ideal of early Buddhism.
 Unlike the bodhisattva of the Mahāyāna, who wishes to free all beings,
 the arhat's main emphasis is on salvation of the self.
awakening. See *enlightenment.*
backward step. Turning inward; studying the self through Zen meditation
 and practice.
barriers. Obstacles that students encounter in Zen practice; also kōans.
before the kalpa of emptiness. Before the formation of the world.
Bhagavān (S.). "Holy one"; one of the ten epithets of the Buddha; also,
 "Holy ones."

457

billion worlds. This universe (this world), which itself contains myriad worlds.

board-carrying monastic. Someone whose view is one-sided, incomplete.

bodhi (S.). "Awakened." Bodhi is wisdom based on insight into the unity of nirvāṇa and saṃsāra, subject and object; the realization of prajñā; awakening to one's own buddha nature; insight into the essential emptiness of the world; and perception of suchness.

bodhisattva (S.). One who practices the Buddha Way and compassionately postpones final enlightenment for the sake of others; the ideal of practice in Mahāyāna Buddhism.

body and mind fallen away. See *samādhi.*

Buddhadharma (S.). Teachings of the Buddha based on his enlightenment experience.

buddha nature. According to Mahāyāna Buddhism, the true, enlightened, and immutable nature of all beings.

buddhas and ancestors. Earlier awakened teachers of the dharma lineage.

Buddha Way. Also the Great Way. The practice of realization taught by Śākyamuni Buddha; the nature of reality.

Buddhist canon (S., Tripitaka). The "Three Baskets": the Vinaya-pitaka, the origins of the Buddhist saṃgha and its rules of discipline; the Sūtra-pitaka, discourses said to have been given by the Buddha or his immediate disciples; and the Abhidharma-pitaka, a compendium of Buddhist psychology and philosophy.

Caodong lineage (C.). One of the five schools of Chinese Zen, founded by Dongshan Liangjie and Caoshan Benji in the ninth century; it was revitalized and brought to Japan by Eihei Dōgen.

Caoxi (C.; J., Sōkei). A stream southeast of Shaochou Kwantung near where the Sixth Ancestor taught. The "waves of Caoxi" also refer to the teaching of the Sixth Ancestor.

clouds and water. Monastics who travel freely in search of realization.

compassion (S., karunā). The outstanding quality of all bodhisattvas and buddhas to aid sentient beings without distinction; based on the enlightened experience of the oneness of all beings.

conversation in the weeds. A deluded conversation.

delusion. State of confusion regarding the nature of absolute truth. See also *saṃsāra.*

devas (S.). Divinities who inhabit the heavenly realm.

dhāraṇi (S.). Short sūtras that contain magical formulas of knowledge made up of syllables with symbolic content, repeated like a mantra (only generally longer) to convey the essence of a teaching or particular state of mind.

dharma (S.). Universal truth or law; the Buddha's teachings; all of phenomena.

dharma body. See *Dharmakāya.*

dharma brothers/sisters. Zen practitioners receiving transmission from the same master.

dharma gate. Entry point into the Buddha's teaching; the gate of truth.

dharma hall. One of the main buildings of a monastery, where formal dharma talks are given.

Dharmakāya (S.). One of the three kāyas, bodies of the Buddha; essential reality.

dharma talk. Also dharma discourse; a formal talk on a kōan or on significant aspects of Zen teachings; not an intellectual presentation or a philosophical explanation but a teacher's direct expression of the spirit of Zen.

Diamond Sūtra. Key text of the *Prajñāpāramitā* literature of Mahāyāna Buddhism; it states that phenomenal appearances are illusory projections of the mind, empty of self.

dragon. A guardian deity; an excellent practitioner of the Way; an enlightened being.

eighty-four thousand hymns. The numerous teachings of the Buddha.

emptiness (S., *śūnyatā*). Void; central principle of Buddhism that recognizes that all things are without self-nature; often equated with the absolute in Mahāyāna, since it is formless and nondual.

endless spring. Realization.

enlightenment. Direct experience of one's true nature.

entanglements. Complications, sometimes created by the teacher to help students see into their true nature; also being caught up in words, and in Dōgen Zenji's usage, being fully immersed in, yet free from, words.

five-flavor Zen. Categories of Zen created by Guifeng Zongmi, the Fifth Ancestor of the Avatamsaka school: non-Buddhist, ordinary people's, Hīnayāna, Mahāyāna, and Supreme Vehicle (Bodhidharma's Zen); Dōgen opposed this classification with the term "one-flavor Zen."

flipping the sleeves. A monastic's expression of disdain.

forest of brambles. See *entanglements.*

Four Continents. Located in the oceans around Mount Sumeru: Jambudipa, which we inhabit, Purvavideha, Aparagodaniya, and Uttarakuru; also refers to all worlds.

frog. Deluded being.

gāthā. Short sūtra that presents the dharma teachings in pithy wording; frequently chanted.

ghost cave. Realm of delusion. See also saṃsāra.

great doubt. One of the three pillars of Zen practice; it provides the edge that keeps practitioners moving forward in their search for clarification of the great matter.

great-grandmotherly compassion. Kindness shown by teachers as they "muddy" themselves with the act of teaching the inexpressible; the teaching may appear to be rough, or even cruel at times.

great kalpa fire. Ultimate destruction of the universe, which will occur after an aeon (an incalculable span of time) has passed.

great matter. Also the essential matter; the great principle; essential question that addresses the true nature of reality and the self as well as the meaning of life and death; practice or awakening.

greed, anger, and ignorance. Three poisons of Buddhism; characteristics of human existence that arise out of a deluded view of the universe.

ground of being. Also buddha nature; the true nature of the self.

han (J.). Wooden board struck by a mallet to signal various happenings in a Zen temple, for instance, to call practitioners to zazen.

hazy moon. Refers to practice after enlightenment; not the bright and clear moon of realization.

Heart Sūtra. Distillation of the vast *Prajñāpāramitā* literature, chanted daily in Zen monasteries.

insentient. Beings ordinarily not called "living," such as mountains, rocks, and tiles, but that nevertheless have the ability to expound the dharma.

kalpa (S.). World cycle, world age; an endlessly long period of time, the basis of Buddhist time reckoning, illustrated by this simile: the length of time it would take to wear away a rock one cubic mile in size by rubbing it once every hundred years with a piece of silk.

kirigami (J.). Literally "cut paper"; a body of unpublished Sōtō literature transmitted one-to-one from teacher to disciple.

kōan (J.). An apparently paradoxical statement or question used in Zen training to induce great doubt, allowing students to cut through conventional descriptions of reality and see directly into their true nature.

li (C.). Chinese unit of measurement equal to approximately one-third of a mile.

Linji lineage (C.; J., Rinzai). One of the five schools of Chinese Zen, derived from Linji Yixuan and based predominantly on kōan introspection.

lion, tiger. See *dragon.*

mani jewel (S.). "Wish-fulfilling jewel," or "jewel beyond price"; it can bring about the cessation of suffering.

marketplace. The world into which enlightened beings must return to manifest their realization.

master's portrait. Also the master's likeness; metaphor for the master's teaching handed down to a successor.

mind-to-mind transmission. Confirmation of the merging of the minds of teacher and disciple; also the recognition of the buddha mind and entrustment of the teaching.

mirror. Fundamental awareness, reflecting reality without conditioning.

mountaintop. Also peak of the mountain; opposite of the marketplace; realm of the absolute, where realization occurs.

Mount Gridhrakūta (S.). Vulture Peak, the site of many of Śākyamuni Buddha's recorded discourses; site of the first transmission from the Buddha, to Mahākāśyapa.

Mount Sumeru (S.). The "world mountain"; according to ancient Indian cosmology, it stands at the center of the universe surrounded by seas and the Four Continents and is the meeting place of the gods.

mud ball. Expression that indicates the student is stuck in the realm of conceptual thinking.

nii! (J.). An old Chinese folk belief held that if a slip of paper with the character *nii* written on it was fastened to the gate of a house, it would charm away all fiends.

Nirmānakāya (S.). One of the three kāyas, bodies of the Buddha; earthly body and manifestation that a buddha assumes to guide all sentient beings to liberation.

nirvāna (S.). Literally, "putting out fire"; union with the absolute; in Zen it is essential to realize that samsāra is nirvāna, form is emptiness, and all beings are innately perfect from the outset.

nondual dharma. Essential principle of all existence; nondiscrimination or the lack of dualistic opposition.

no-self. The anātman doctrine is one of the essential teachings of Buddhism, stating that there is no permanent, enduring substance within any entity; "self" is an idea.

nostril. When used in reference to having someone by the nostrils, it indicates that the student is handing over his or her personal power to the teacher; being led around by others.

oceanic storehouse. Storehouse consciousness; basic consciousness of everything existing; the essence of the world, out of which everything arises.

one bright pearl. Symbol for the whole phenomenal universe; one of Master Xuansha's favorite expressions.

original face. See *buddha nature.*

parinirvāṇa (S.). Total extinction, usually referring to nirvāṇa after death. Can also mean the death of a monk or nun.

plum blossoms. Metaphor for realization.

practice. Also ceaseless practice; according to Master Dōgen, a continuous process of actualizing enlightenment.

precepts. Moral and ethical guidelines that, in Buddhism, are a description of the life of a buddha (one who realizes the nature of existence and acts out of that realization).

raising an ox. Metaphor for the cultivation of the enlightened mind, which means the freedom to act without restraint yet according to and in harmony with circumstances and conditions.

realization. See *enlightenment.*

responding to the imperative. Responding to a situation according to causes and conditions, and in the case of a teacher, to the student's needs.

samādhi (S.). State in which the mind is absorbed in intense concentration, free from distractions and goals; single-pointedness of mind.

Sambhogakāya (S.). One of the three kāyas, bodies of the Buddha; "body of bliss" or reward body, associated with the fruits of practice.

saṃgha (S.). community of practitioners of the Buddha's teaching; also one of the Three Treasures.

saṃsāra (S.). Existence prior to liberation, conditioned by the three attitudes of greed, anger, and ignorance and marked by continuous rebirths.

sentient beings. Living beings, including humans; sometimes indicates those who are not awakened.

shikantaza (J.). "Just sitting." A form of zazen in which one practices pure awareness.

shokei (J.). Kneeling with hands in gasshō. "Walking in shokei" means moving forward on the knees with hands in gasshō.

six realms. Worlds of hell beings, hungry ghosts, animals, humans, demigods, and gods; according to Buddhism, only rebirth in the human realm is conducive to realization.

six senses. Sight, hearing, smell, touch, and taste—plus, in Buddhism, the sixth sense, thought or cognition (as perceived through the mind).

skandha (S.). Term for the five aggregates, which constitute "personality": form, sensation, perception, mental formations, and consciousness.

skillful means. See *upāya.*

snake. A false dragon; deluded being posing as someone who is realized.

Sōkei (J.). See *Caoxi.*

śramaṇa (S.) A wanderer, ascetic, or monastic.

stūpa (S.). Memorial tower often containing sacred relics or texts; symbol of buddha ancestors.

suchness (S., *tathatā*). Also thusness; the absolute, true state of phenomena; it is immovable, immutable, and beyond all concepts and distinctions.

śūnyatā. See *emptiness.*

sūtra (S.). Scripture that contains the Buddha's teaching.

sword of wisdom. Refers to Mañjuśrī Bodhisattva. See *Mañjuśrī* in the glossary of masters.

Tathāgata (S.). One of the titles of the Buddha, the "thus-come-one," referring to one who has attained perfect enlightenment.

ten bodies. The ten bodies of the Buddha: the bodies of the realm of understanding associated with Vairocana Buddha, and the bodies of the realm of practice.

ten directions. North, south, east, west, and their midpoints, plus up and down.

ten thousand dharmas. The numerous teachings of the Buddha.

ten thousand grasses. Phenomena; all things.

ten thousand hands and eyes. Refers to Avalokiteśvara Bodhisattva. See *Avalokiteśvara* in the glossary of masters.

thief. Term of endearment for a Zen teacher who takes away anything that prevents the student from experiencing complete freedom, that is, both attachments and aversions.

three buddha bodies. Dharmakāya, Sambhogakāya, and Nirmānakāya.

Three Peaks, Five Peaks. The groups of mountains where Zen was being practiced in monasteries during the latter part of the Song dynasty in China.

Three Vehicles. According to Mahāyāna Buddhism, the three ways to bring people across the ocean of birth and death to the shore of enlightenment: the Śrāvaka Vehicle, the Pratyeka-buddha Vehicle, and the Great Vehicle; the first two are called the Hīnayāna or Lesser (Small) Vehicles, and the Great Vehicle (Mahāyāna) is also called the Bodhisattva Vehicle.

three worlds. The desire world, which includes the six realms; the form world of those who are free from desire; and the formless world of those who have attained the highest freedom in meditation.

thusness. See *suchness.*

tongue fallen to the ground. Refers to Zen masters' tongues falling out of their mouths when they try to explain the truth of the dharma, for it cannot be spoken of with words.

traveling by night. Dwelling within the realm of the absolute.

turning the dharma wheel. Expounding the teaching of awakening.

turning word. A word or phrase that leads a student to realization.

Twelve Divisions of Sūtras. (1) discourses in prose, (2) discourses in verse, (3) discourses in both prose and verse, (4) stories about the causes of events, (5) stories about the conditions of events, (6) stories about previous worlds, (7) Jātaka tales (previous lives of the Buddha), (8) stories about unprecedented events, (9) parables, (10) teachings offered without request, (11) broadly extended writings, and (12) stories about predictions of enlightenment.

upāya (S.). Skillful means; forms that the teachings take, reflecting their appropriateness to the circumstances in which they appear.

Vulture Peak. See *Mount Gridhrakūta.*

water buffalo. A steady practitioner of the Way.

wato (J.). "Word-head"; the key point of a kōan. It can be a single word or an expression.

World-Honored One. A respectful title for the Buddha.

Yijing (C.; J., *I Ching*). The Chinese *Book of Changes,* an ancient text and system of divination using the principles of yin and yang and their different combinations in sixty-four hexagrams.

yin and yang (C.). A pair of opposites that describes the world in terms of the relationship between the two terms: yin is dark, resting, contracting, and cold; yang is light, active, expanding, and hot.

zazen (J.). Sitting meditation, taught in Zen as the most direct way to enlightenment; practice of the realization of one's own true nature.

Index of Kōan Titles